Honest Bodies

HONEST BODIES

*Revolutionary Modernism in
the Dances of Anna Sokolow*

Hannah Kosstrin

OXFORD
UNIVERSITY PRESS

OXFORD
UNIVERSITY PRESS

Oxford University Press is a department of the University of Oxford. It furthers
the University's objective of excellence in research, scholarship, and education
by publishing worldwide. Oxford is a registered trade mark of Oxford University
Press in the UK and certain other countries.

Published in the United States of America by Oxford University Press
198 Madison Avenue, New York, NY 10016, United States of America.

© Oxford University Press 2017

Library of Congress Cataloging-in-Publication Data
Names: Kosstrin, Hannah, author.
Title: Honest bodies : revolutionary modernism in the dances of Anna Sokolow / Hannah Kosstrin.
Description: Oxford ; New York, NY : Oxford University Press, 2017. |
Includes bibliographical references.
Identifiers: LCCN 2016045543 | ISBN 9780199396924 (hardback) |
ISBN 9780199396931 (paperback)
Subjects: LCSH: Sokolow, Anna. | Choreographers—United States—Biography. |
BISAC: PERFORMING ARTS / Dance / Modern. | MUSIC / Genres & Styles / Dance.
Classification: LCC GV1785.S59.L67 2017 | DDC 792.8/2092 [B]—dc23
LC record available at https://lccn.loc.gov/2016045543

For Bess and Brock
May you too go out and change the world.

CONTENTS

PREFACE

"You can't have honest words from a dishonest body; you can't have honest movement from a dishonest body."[1] Ray Cook, who performed in Anna Sokolow's dance
company during the 1960s and notated many of her dances, told me this aphorism
Sokolow used in rehearsal. Cook connected Sokolow's desire for honesty, or emotional believability in performance, to her work with Moscow Art Theatre director Konstantin Stanislavsky's Method of Physical Action, which teaches actors to
draw on their lived experiences as a kind of personal truth to deepen their performances. Theater and dance practitioners in Europe and the United States, especially those aligned with communist ideals in the early twentieth century, like
Sokolow, employed Stanislavsky's Method because it resonated with the imperatives of socialist realism.[2] Sokolow incorporated these Stanislavskian techniques by
insisting dancers harness raw power through their vulnerability. In rehearsal she
told dancers "I don't believe you" when she felt that they did not fully embody what
she asked them to do.[3] As such, Sokolow trained dancers to be physically and emotionally receptive, available, and earnest. Sokolow's "honest bodies" performed
with sincerity and displayed the influence of their political and aesthetic milieu.
I focus this book around the idea of honest bodies to highlight Sokolow's emphasis on believable, raw vulnerability in performance; her own body as a political,
Jewish, and gendered site of expression; and her complicated movement among

1. Ray Cook, in discussion with the author, October 18, 2009, New York City.
2. Valentina Litvinoff, *The Use of Stanislavsky Within Modern Dance* (New York: American
Dance Guild, 1972), 4, 9, 32, 41; Ellen Graff, *Stepping Left: Dance and Politics in New York
City, 1928-1942* (Durham: Duke University Press, 1997), 70–72; and Larry Warren, *Anna
Sokolow: The Rebellious Spirit* (Princeton, NJ: Princeton Book Company, Publishers, 1991), 116.
3. John Giffin (dancer, choreographer) in discussion with the author, May 30, 2007,
Columbus, OH. Lorry May, a Sokolow dancer, trustee of her work, and Sokolow Dance
Foundation director, calls for a truthful performance when coaching Sokolow's dances. In a
Steps of Silence (1968) rehearsal at The Ohio State University on January 29, 2008, May repeatedly told the dancers she did not believe their performance. She wanted the dancers to draw
on their own experiences to make the work relevant to them, so that the dance would read as
a real, instead of fabricated, experience. May's assistant, Suellen Haag, gave similar directions
in coaching *Rooms* rehearsals at Reed College in October, 2011. See also Graff, *Stepping Left*,
71–73; and Litvinoff, *Stanislavsky*, 13–17.

government agencies. When I articulate the function, implications, or specificity of Sokolow's and her dancers' embodiment in this book, I show how this honest bodies tenet is in play.

I argue that communist ideology is central to understanding how Sokolow's dances functioned within early twentieth- to mid-twentieth-century Jewish and modernist channels of the international Left, and I engage the idea of honest bodies to articulate the meeting of defiant vulnerability, Jewish impetus, formalist aesthetics, Marxist content, and feminist drive in Sokolow's work. Onstage, Sokolow's and her dancers' bodies were barometers for social and aesthetic currents. As a private citizen, Sokolow's communist associations entangled her in government surveillance systems. Sokolow understandably denied her communist allegiances under FBI surveillance and the specter of the Second Red Scare (1947–1957, an early defining moment of the Cold War in the United States). This book activates a discussion of how her 1930s–1940s communist coalitions underwrote her political personhood and changed American modern dance and its place on international stages.

The daughter of a garment worker mother and a fruit peddler father, both Russian Jewish immigrants, Sokolow (1910–2000) filled her seventy-year career fighting for workers' rights and underserved populations through her dances for social change. Born in Connecticut and reared in the working-class immigrant neighborhood of New York City's Lower East Side, Sokolow came of age in a proletarian environment. As a young person she accompanied her mother, a Socialist and organizer for the International Ladies Garment Workers' Union, at rallies for workers' rights.[4] Sokolow danced in settlement houses and became a principal dancer in the field-defining Martha Graham Dance Company from 1930 to 1939. She trained in Graham's movement vocabulary as it became codified, originated roles in Graham's dances including *Primitive Mysteries* (1931), *Celebration* (1933), and *Four Casual Developments* (1933),[5] and was a member of Graham's first company, along with Anita Alvarez, Dorothy Bird, Bonnie Bird, Jane Dudley, Martha Hill, Pearl Lang, Sophie Maslow, May O'Donnell, Evelyn Sabin, Bessie Schönberg, and Gertrude Shurr.[6] Sokolow concurrently founded the Workers (later New) Dance League, an umbrella organization for revolutionary, or workers', dance groups, in 1932 with Miriam Blecher and Nadia Chilkovsky.[7] American communist ideology provided leftist dancers like Sokolow a political platform for their choreography.[8]

4. Warren, *Rebellious Spirit*, 4–7.

5. Dorothy Bird and Joyce Greenberg, *Bird's Eye View: Dancing with Martha Graham and on Broadway* (Pittsburgh, PA: University of Pittsburgh Press, 1997), 96–97.

6. Agnes de Mille, *Martha: The Life and Work of Martha Graham* (1956; reprinted New York: Vintage Books, 1992), 417.

7. Graff, *Stepping Left*, 7–8, 201n7; and Stacey Prickett, "Dance and the Workers' Struggle," *Dance Research: The Journal of the Society for Dance Research* 8, no. 1 (1990): 52–54.

8. Jane Dudley, interview by Richard Wormser, 1981, transcript, 5, Oral History of the American Left, The Tamiment Library and Robert F. Wagner Labor Archives, New York University.

The value systems associated with Sokolow's Jewish working-class cultural environment undergirded her proletarian and anti-fascist choreographic challenges to the
economic status quo, gender roles, and racism.

Sokolow's commitment to communism as a Jew reflected early twentieth- to mid-
twentieth-century communist and Jewish cultural allegiances that circulated among
the United States, Eastern and Western Europe, Mexico, and the socialist Zionist
discourse of the Jewish community in British Mandate Palestine (1917–1948)
and Israel (post-1948).[9] In New York she was active with the International Workers
Order (IWO), a Communist front group that was a fraternal society and insur-
ance organization with a large membership of Jews and other ethnic immigrant
minorities.[10] During New York's 1936 general election Sokolow registered as a
Communist, instead of a Socialist, Democrat, or Republican.[11] Sokolow remained
involved in communist endeavors as the Dies Committee formed in the US House
of Representatives in 1938 to exterminate suspected communist activity from the
US government and its programs. She choreographed for Lenin rallies even after
Josef Stalin's nonaggression alliance with Adolf Hitler in the 1939 Nazi–Soviet Pact
betrayed Communists' ideals by aligning with Fascist leadership; she maintained
her IWO membership through the 1946 reinstallment of the Dies Committee as the
House Un-American Activities Committee (HUAC) at the beginning of the Red
Scare, and she attended a populist American Continental Congress for World Peace
in Mexico City in 1949, which HUAC dubbed the "Communist Peace Offensive."[12]

9. See Daniela Spenser, *The Impossible Triangle: Mexico, Soviet Russia, and the United States in the
1920s* (Durham: Duke University Press, 1999); Friedrich Katz, *The Secret War in Mexico: Europe,
the United States, and the Mexican Revolution* (Chicago: University of Chicago Press, 1981);
Barry Carr, *Marxism and Communism in Twentieth-Century Mexico* (Lincoln: University of
Nebraska Press, 1992); Nina Spiegel, *Embodying Hebrew Culture: Aesthetics, Athletics, and Dance
in the Jewish Community of Mandate Palestine* (Detroit: Wayne State University Press, 2013),
5–18; and Pinhas Ginossar, "From Zionism to Communism and Back: The Case of Moshe
Sneh (1948–1967)," in *Dark Times, Dire Decisions: Jews and Communism*, ed. Jonathan Frankel
(New York: Oxford University Press, 2004), 236–254.

10. FOIPA No. 1138496-000; and Ellen Schrecker, *Many Are the Crimes: McCarthyism in
America* (Princeton, NJ: Princeton University Press, 1998), 38–40.

11. Board of Elections, City of New York, *List of Enrolled Voters: Tenth Assembly District,
Borough of Manhattan* (New York, 1936), 56, SIBL, NYPL. "Communist" was not a registra-
tion option in 1944 and 1948; in these years Sokolow registered with the American Labor
Party (with 1944 choices including American Labor, Democrat, or Republican, and in 1948,
American Labor, Democrat, Liberal, or Republican). Board of Elections, City of New York,
List of Enrolled Voters for the Year 1944–45, Borough of Manhattan—Fifth Assembly District
(New York, 1944), 143, SIBL, NYPL; Board of Elections, City of New York, *List of Enrolled
Voters for the Year 1948–1949, Borough of Manhattan—Fifth Assembly District* (New York,
1948), 128, SIBL, NYPL. No voting record surfaced for 1940. In 1952, Sokolow registered as a
Democrat. Board of Elections, City of New York, *List of Enrolled Voters for the Year 1952–1953,
Borough of Manhattan—Ninth Assembly District* (New York, 1952), 17, SIBL, NYPL. When
Sokolow last registered in 1988, she requested that she not be associated with any party. Author
in phone conversation with Board of Elections, Manhattan Borough Office, June 23, 2010.

12. "Minor at Lenin Rally in Hartford," *Daily Worker*, February 3, 1943, 4, highlights Sokolow's
dances as "a special feature of the evening" by "one of America's finest dance artists." On

Sokolow's retention of communist-affiliated ideals like egalitarianism, workers' rights, and anti-discrimination after cutting her ties to Communist organizations in the 1950s[13] reflected many Eastern European–descended Jews' social practices among the international Left.

A revolutionary spectatorship among audiences who shared proletarian sympathies across this international Left in countries including the USSR, the United States, Germany, Mexico, and Israel enabled the circulation of communist principles through choreography like Sokolow's.[14] By revolutionary spectatorship, I mean the shared empathetic interaction of proletarian-aligned audiences viewing social justice concert dance works in theatrical settings. Sokolow's choreography ignited an activist discourse in the moment of performance, through the honest bodies that charged the space as they danced and their resonances in their audiences' emotions.[15] Like the mid-nineteenth-century Communist "Internationale" that advocated uniting workers across national borders through a common ideological goal,[16] revolutionary spectatorship enlivened disparately geographic audience members to fight injustice locally by gathering them into an imagined revolutionary community.[17] Although the revolutionary movement diminished by the 1960s, transnational

November 8, 1948, Sokolow requested transfer from her IWO lodge in Manhattan to one in Brooklyn, effective January 1, 1949, signifying her continued IWO membership. Memorandum, September 21, 1951, regarding November 8, 1948, Application for Transfer from Lodge No. 478 to Lodge No. 467, FOIPA No. 1138496-000. For the Congress on World Peace, see Committee on Un-American Activities, US House of Representatives, *Report on the Communist "Peace" Offensive: A Campaign to Disarm and Defeat the United States*, 82d Cong., 1st sess., 1951, 23; and Lloyd L. Brown, "What I Saw in Mexico," *Masses and Mainstream* 2, no. 11 (1949): 7–15.

13. Dudley, interview by Wormser, 5.

14. My implementation of spectatorship as a model for understanding dances' meanings in their time is influenced by Susan Manning, *Modern Dance, Negro Dance: Race in Motion* (Minneapolis: University of Minnesota Press, 2004). For Marxist engagements with spectatorship, see Erin Trapp, "Arendt, Preference, and the Revolutionary Spectator," *Cultural Critique* 86 (2014): 31–64; and Jonathan L. Beller, "The Spectatorship of the Proletariat," *boundary 2* 22, no. 3 (1995): 171–228. See also Roland Barthes, "The Death of the Author," in *Image, Music, Text*, trans. Stephen Heath (New York: Hill and Wang, 1977), 142–148; and Janet Lansdale, "A Tapestry of Intertexts: Dance Analysis for the Twenty-First Century," in *The Routledge Dance Studies Reader*, 2nd ed., eds. Alexandra Carter and Janet O'Shea (London: Routledge, 2010), 160–161.

15. Susan Leigh Foster demonstrated that participants' physicality and sense of agency is vital to political demonstrations. Randy Martin identified how this embodiment politically enlivens the space between the performers and the audience. Mark Franko argued that dance and politics are intertwined and are a matter of representation and interpretation within their historical context. See Foster, "Choreographies of Protest," *Theatre Journal* 55, no. 3 (2003): 395–412; Martin, *Critical Moves: Dance Studies in Theory and Politics* (Durham: Duke University Press, 1998), 3, 39–46; and Franko, "Dance and the Political: States of Exception," in *Dance Discourses: Keywords in Dance Research*, eds. Susanne Franco and Marina Nordera (London: Routledge, 2007), 60.

16. https://www.marxists.org/history/ussr/sounds/lyrics/international.htm. Accessed January 31, 2016.

17. See Benedict Anderson, *Imagined Communities: Reflections on the Origin and Spread of Nationalism* (New York: Verso, 1991), 1–7; and Alejandro L. Madrid, "Transnational Musical

revolutionary ideals formed the honest bodies in Sokolow's work throughout her career. This book traces the hybrid meanings of Sokolow's honest bodies, mostly on but also off the concert stage, in the northeastern United States, Mexico City, and Israel, to show how Sokolow's 1930s–1960s choreography was a conduit for communist ideology.

As a result of Sokolow's movement through global channels, her own honest body occupied liminal spaces of conventional/Other, established/rogue, and home/abroad. In Mexico and Israel, presenters reacting to interest in American modern dance sponsored Sokolow, and she attracted substantial attention. Sokolow carved out space for herself in those dance landscapes, working with but overtaking the existing dance scenes in each locale. When she did not stay permanently in either place, subsequent choreographic projects, such as Ana Mérida's Ballet of Mexico City or Bethsabée de Rothschild's Batsheva Dance Company in Tel Aviv, pushed aside popular interest in her work. Working half the year in New York and half in Mexico City during the 1940s, Sokolow was unable to achieve her goal of sustaining her own company in either place. This cycle repeated ten years later in Israel. She felt marginalized because she was not rooted in a group of dancers when the concert dance field valued established companies.[18] Although in one sense Sokolow experienced diasporic unrootedness, more broadly her travel anchored her work within the mobility of international currents. This book shows the implications of this mobility.

Encounters at the U.S.-Mexico Border: An Introduction," in *Transnational Encounters: Music and Performance at the U.S.-Mexico Border*, ed. Madrid (New York: Oxford University Press, 2011), 8.

18. Anna Sokolow to Bessie Schönberg, August 2, 1942, Box 11, Folder 417, Bessie Schönberg Papers, JRDD, NYPL.

ACKNOWLEDGMENTS

The support of many people and institutions made this project possible during the ten years in which it began as a dissertation and developed into a book. I am grateful for the opportunities I was awarded as a graduate student that fostered this project, including the Samuel M. Melton Graduate Fellowship, the Coca-Cola Critical Difference for Women Graduate Studies Grant for Research on Women, Gender, and Gender Equity, and a College of the Arts Student International Travel Grant, all from The Ohio State University, and the P.E.O. Scholar Award from the P.E.O. International Sisterhood. I extend deep thanks to the institutions that have been my corporeal and intellectual homes as a faculty member and have seen this project through to completion. I thank the Reed College Dean of the Faculty Stillman Drake Fund and Summer Scholarship Fund, and The Ohio State University College of Arts and Sciences, Division of Arts and Humanities, and Department of Dance for generous research support.

This project emerged under the expert guidance of my dissertation committee, my advisor Karen Eliot, my minor field advisor Donna Guy, Candace Feck, and Sheila Marion. Their generous patience and expertise in dance analysis, historiographic methods and writing, and Jewish, Latin American, and women's histories shepherded my scholarship in ways that continue to support my work. I also thank Stephanie Smith for her guidance of my research in Mexico. I am grateful to Chrystelle Bond, my undergraduate advisor at Goucher College, who introduced me to embodied scholarship and scholarly organizations, and who shared breakfast with me on that fateful morning in London when dance history chose me.

I had the great fortune of working with an incredible community of scholars during the writing of this book. I extend deep thanks to Angela Ahlgren, Harmony Bench, Kate Bredeson, Rosemary Candelario, Clare Croft, Lynn Kaye, Jeannine Murray-Román, Ila Nagar, and Nina Spiegel for their thoughtful, astute feedback during this process that strengthened my ideas, tightened my writing, and clarified how I articulate my scholarship among the fields I consider my disciplinary homes. I have found great excitement in seeing our field(s) grow through our work together. I also thank Carrie Curtner for her keen eye on the manuscript, and Deb Singer for her administrative support through the endless trail of copyright permissions.

While writing this book I have benefited from the generosity of many scholars. I thank Judith Brin Ingber, Susan Manning, and Janice Ross for their continued mentorship on this project and my scholarship, and am grateful to Jacqueline Dirks, Lynn Garafola, Matt Goldish, Robin Judd, Laura Leibman, Rebecca Rossen, Gail Sherman, and Adena Tanenbaum for providing support and guidance for various ways to approach the material. For help along the way I thank Ann Cooper Albright, Ruth Eshel, Rebekah Kowal, Gay Morris, and Henia Rottenberg. I treasure my Jewish dance exchanges with Hannah Schwadron, Judith, and Rebecca. I am forever grateful to my editor, Norm Hirschy, whose thorough feedback and immeasurable support expertly shepherded me through my first book. I thank my anonymous reviewers on the manuscript, whose careful comments helped me see the intricacies and potentialities of the project.

I was fortunate to interview dancers, choreographers, presenters, and critics who worked with Sokolow. For their generosity in sharing their experiences of Sokolow with me, I extend warm thanks to Helen Alkire, Mary Anthony, Patricia Aulestia de Alba, Lea Avraham, Vickie Blaine, Paul Bloom, Odette Blum, Judith Brin Ingber, Michael Kelly Bruce, Ze'eva Cohen, Ray Cook, Aviva Davidson, Magnolia Flores, Betty Ford, Jan Hart, Samantha Geracht, John Giffin, Louise Guthman, Suellen Haag, Doris Hering, David Jon Krohn, Betty Lindeman Leonard, Pat Leonard, Anadel Lynton Snyder, David K. Manion, Muriel Manings, Sheila Marion, Jim May, Lorry May, Elisa Rodriguez Ostuni, Moshe Romano, Rina Schenfeld, Rebecca Stein, Lucy Venable, Lynne Weber, Bea Weschler, Evan Dawley, Valarie Williams, and Deborah Zall. Thanks also to Ze'eva, Betty, Jim, and Deborah for sharing resources with me.

This project has been nothing if not an ambitious treasure hunt. I am grateful to the librarians of the repositories that I cite throughout the book. For helping with extra aspects of the materials, I extend special thanks to: Libby Smigel and Elizabeth Aldrich at the Library of Congress; Victoria Khudorkovsky at the Dance Collection of the Beit Ariela Library, Tel Aviv; Charles Perrier, Tanisha Jones, and Arlene Yu of the Jerome Robbins Dance Division of The New York Public Library for the Performing Arts; Beatriz Maupomé and Francisco Galindo at Acervo Histórico del Palacio de Bellas Artes, Mexico City; Janet and Nils Morgan at the Barbara Morgan Archives; Anadel Lynton Snyder, Patricia Ruíz, Lourdes Fernández Serratos, and Teresa Nava of Centro Nacional de Investigación, Documentación e Información de la Danza, Mexico City; David K. Manion at Friends of the Dance Library of Israel; Mei-Chen Lu of the Dance Notation Bureau; Jeni Dahmus at the Juilliard School Archives; Margaret Gretchen Atkinson, Nena Couch, Sean Ferguson, Joseph Galron, and Michael Murray at OSU Libraries; Steve Siegel, 92nd Street Y Library; and K. Kevyne Baar, Timothy Johnson, and Sarah Moazeni of the Tamiment Library and Robert F. Wagner Labor Archives at New York University.

I extend deep gratitude to Joyce Greenberg, Lorry May, Suellen Haag, and Anne Warren, who generously hosted me in their homes and allowed me unrestricted access to Dorothy Bird's, Anna Sokolow's, and Larry Warren's collections. I feel so fortunate that these women let me sprawl across their living room floors and dining room tables for days at a time with resources that unquestionably enhanced this book. I reference Sokolow's collection from May as the Sokolow Dance Foundation. Since I first saw Warren's materials, they have been transferred to the Music Division, Library of Congress. I reference them as the Larry Warren Collection on Anna Sokolow and Lester Horton, which is the title the Library of Congress has given this special collection.

During the 2011–2012 academic year, I worked with Victoria Khudorkovsky at Beit Ariela in Tel Aviv, Janice Ross at Stanford University, and Douglas Rosenberg at The University of Wisconsin, Madison, to bring Beit Ariela's Anna Sokolow Centennial Exhibit to our campuses. This experience expanded the way I conceived my Sokolow scholarship, and it brought me deeper into an embodied relationship with her work. I thank my colleagues Carla Mann, Minh Tran, and Stephanie Snyder at Reed College who supported the exhibit and my direction of two solos from Sokolow's *Rooms*, which my students Laura Krause and Gabrielle Quintana set from Labanotation score. I thank Laura and Gabi for their expert staging of these solos, and them and Olivia Jensen, Allison Morgan, Claire Thomforde-Garner, and Adrienne Wise for their deep dedication to this work during the coaching and performing process. These women's questions about and embodiment of this work helped me further unpack this oft-discussed dance. I extend deep gratitude to Janice and Doug, whose support in bringing me to their campuses to lecture in conjunction with the exhibit and accompanying performances came at an important juncture when I was solidifying my voice as a scholar. This book, especially Chapter 4, would not be what it is without their mentoring during that tour. The following summer I attended the first Andrew W. Mellon Foundation Dance Studies in/and the Humanities Summer Seminar. Under the generative mentorship of Susan Manning, Janice Ross, and Rebecca Schneider, and the peer support of my colleagues in that group, this book truly took its shape.

Thanks to Jeremy Cosel, Kristina D'Onofrio, Kathryn Holt, Olivia Jensen, John Luna, Janet Schroeder, Benny Simon, and Roland Wu, my research assistants at Reed College and Ohio State, who tracked down references, transcribed interviews, translated reviews, and handled photographs, bibliographies, and endnotes. I am indebted to musician Mont Chris Hubbard for transcribing archival musical scores through the computer program Finale. I thank Daniela Blei for her meticulous attention copyediting and indexing the book. I thank Galit Golan, Alejandra Jara de Marco, Ali Potvin, Kalman Weiser, and Stav Ziv for their translations.

My utmost thanks goes to my friends, family, and colleagues who generously opened their schedules and pull-out couches for my many research trips: Deborah Friedes Galili and Tal Galili; Keren Yalon and Nitzan Gal; Victoria Phillips; Jen Zoble; my parents; and a special thank you to Sara Lasser Yau and Cyrus Yau for a constantly welcoming revolving door and particularly comfy sofabed since the inception of this project. I am also grateful to Ale Jara for her endless patience, warm humor, and invaluable help with research in Mexico City.

I thank *Art Criticism*, *Dance Research Journal*, and Oxford University Press for granting permission to include previously published material in this book.

An earlier version of portions of Chapters 3 and 4 first appeared as "Passion and Angst: Postwar Identity in Two Dances by Anna Sokolow," *Art Criticism* 25, nos. 1&2 (2010): 131–152. © 2010 State University of New York at Stony Brook. Reprinted with permission. An earlier version of portions of the Preface, Introduction, and Chapter 1 first appeared as "Inevitable Designs: Embodied Ideology in Anna Sokolow's Proletarian Dances," *Dance Research Journal* 45.2 (August 2013): 5–23. © 2013, Cambridge University Press. Reprinted with permission. An earlier version of portions of Chapter 3 appeared as "*Kaddish* at the Wall: The Long Life of Anna Sokolow's 'Prayer for the Dead,'" in *Dance on Its Own Terms: Histories and Methodologies*, eds. Melanie Bales and Karen Eliot, 2013, Oxford University Press, reproduced with permission of Oxford University Press. An earlier version of portions of Chapter 4 first appeared as "Queer Spaces in Anna Sokolow's *Rooms*," in *Queer Dance: Meanings and Makings*, ed. Clare Croft, 2017, Oxford University Press, reproduced with permission of Oxford University Press.

Last, but certainly not least, I thank my parents Judy and Herb Kosstrin for being my stalwart champions and my sisters Julie Tuczynski and Katie Griffin and their families for making life worth living. Finally, I thank Ali Potvin, book steward extraordinaire and simply the best partner a person could have.

ABBREVIATIONS

92Y:	92nd Street Y Educational Department Records
Biblioteca, CENART:	Biblioteca de las Artes, Centro Nacional de las Artes, Mexico City
BICLM:	The Ohio State University Billy Ireland Cartoon Library & Museum
BPL Microtext:	Boston Public Library Microtext Department
CENIDID, CENART:	Centro Nacional de Investigación, Documentación e Información de la Danza "José Limón," Biblioteca de las Artes, Centro Nacional de las Artes, Mexico City
DLI:	Collection of the Israeli Dance Archive at the Beit Ariela Library, Tel-Aviv
DD, OSU:	The Ohio State University Department of Dance
DNB:	Collection of Dance Notation Bureau, New York City
DNBX:	Dance Notation Bureau Extension Office, The Ohio State University
Dorot, NYPL:	Dorot Jewish Division, The New York Public Library
FOIPA No. 1138496-000:	U.S. Department of State, FOIPA No. 1138496-000, Sokolow, Anna. Obtained under Freedom of Information Act Exemptions (5 USC 552/552a).
HTC:	Harvard Theatre Collection
JRDD, NYPL:	The Jerome Robbins Dance Division of the New York Public Library for the Performing Arts
Juilliard:	The Juilliard School Archives
LNA:	Lexis-Nexis Academic
MAD, NYPL:	New York Public Library Manuscripts and Archives Division

MD, LOC: Music Division, Library of Congress, Washington, DC

MD, NYPL: Music Division, New York Public Library for the Performing Arts

Microforms, NYPL: The Microforms Section of The New York Public Library

NRSV: Coogan, Michael D., ed. *The New Oxford Annotated Bible, New Revised Standard Version With the Apocrypha: An Ecumenical Study Bible*, 4th ed., 1965. Reprint, New York: Oxford University Press, 2010.

PBA: Acervo Histórico del Palacio de Bellas Artes, Mexico City

PQHN: *ProQuest Historical Newspapers*

SDF: Sokolow Dance Foundation, Attleboro, MA

SIBL, NYPL: The New York Public Library Science, Industry, and Business Library

Introduction

In 1934, Anna Sokolow scraped together enough money to voyage 5,000 miles from Manhattan to Moscow. She went to perform and to visit her boyfriend and artistic collaborator Alex North, who was studying music composition at the Moscow Conservatory. Like other young American Communists, Sokolow wanted to experience the Soviet Communist experiment. In a letter home to her sister Rose Bank, she described the Red Army parading through Red Square alongside army tanks and workers waving red flags celebrating the return of Stratonauts, scientists who tested the earth's upper atmosphere in hot-air-balloon-powered metal capsules.[1] Sokolow's palpable excitement in her letter suggests that the communal mingling of workers, children, and the army presented the ideological system she admired.[2] Sokolow grew up with communist values in New York's immigrant

---

1. Anna Sokolow to Rose Bank, June 21, 1934, hand-transcribed from the original letter by Larry Warren, Larry Warren Collection on Anna Sokolow and Lester Horton, MD, LOC. Sokolow dedicated a section of her *Suite of Soviet Songs* (1936), called "Lullaby (a song about the Soviet stratosphere flight)," to this event. Program, *Anna Sokolow and Dance Unit*, 92nd Street Y, April 5, 1936, 92Y. Jewish excitement for the USSR predated what Janice Ross calls Stalin's "campaign to liquidate what remained of Soviet Jewish culture" from 1946 to 1953. Ross, *Like a Bomb Going Off: Leonid Jakobson and Ballet as Resistance in Soviet Russia* (New Haven: Yale University Press, 2015), 61. For Stratonauts, see "Russian Ascent to the Stratosphere," *Science* 78, no. 2024 (1933): 328; "Findings of Stratosphere Flyers Surprise Scientists," *The Science News-Letter* 25, no. 672 (1934): 116–117; "Analysis of Stratosphere Air Verifies Pre-Flight Estimates," *The Science News-Letter* 25, no. 679 (1934): 228; and "Radio Enabled Scientists to Aid Stratosphere Flyers," *The Science News-Letter* 28, no. 763 (1935): 325–326.

2. American Communism in New York contained factions relating to local politics that did not necessarily map onto Russian Bolshevik or Menshevik ideology. Sokolow's connections in the USSR, Mexico, and the United States suggest that her desire to marry art and politics in the service of revolution aligned with Bolshevism led by Vladimir Lenin as opposed to Menshevism led by Leon Trotsky. Sokolow choreographed pageantry for Lenin commemorative meetings in New York and was romantically involved with muralist David Alfaro Siqueros's assistant Ignacio

Russian Jewish community. This trip to the USSR reinforced her idea of communist ways of being. At the time, Soviet Premier Josef Stalin's cult of personality was in full swing and his purges were not yet fully underway. The Soviet government mediated information about the famine and collectivization that claimed millions of Ukrainian lives and covertly sent citizens to the Gulag's network of prison camps.[3] But for visiting Communists like Sokolow, the Park of Culture and Rest where she performed, the visitor food card that subsidized her meals, and the spectacle of the Red Army presented communist utopia in action.

In shared spirit with Soviet artists such as David Burliuk and Vladimir Mayakovsky, who made art in the service of revolution, Sokolow aimed to marry art and politics. Like many who flocked to Moscow, Sokolow did not stay. In New York, she translated the physical, emotional, and political power of her idealized Soviet Moscow into dances for social change to fuel a revolution that never came.[4] This trip initiated transnational conversations in Sokolow's dances that underscored her choreographic beginnings in an American Jewish Communist context and expanded among international communist networks within the Jewish Diaspora.[5]

Honest Bodies: Revolutionary Modernism in the Dances of Anna Sokolow traces Sokolow's efforts for a social revolution in her choreography long after her 1934 Sovietophile romanticism faded. In this book, I argue that Sokolow's choreography and its revolutionary spectatorship enabled the international circulation of American dance modernism through communist and Jewish channels of the international Left in the early and mid-twentieth century. I consider Sokolow as a transnational artist in order to position her communist sympathies and Jewish identity in a global landscape, which further reveals the political function of her dances within historical moments of ideological struggle, ethnic definition, and nation formation. The porousness of how Sokolow's and her dancers' physicalities

---

Aguirre in Mexico. As an attempted Trotsky assassin, Siqueros was not a Menshevik; as a close associate of Siqueros and a frequenter of Lenin pageants, Sokolow was likely not a Menshevik either.

3. See Anne Applebaum, *The Gulag: A History* (New York: Anchor Books, 2003); Véronique Garros, Natalia Korenevskaya, and Thomas Lahusen, eds., *Intimacy and Terror: Soviet Diaries of the 1930s*, trans. Carol A. Flath (New York: New Press, 1995); and Walter G. Moss, *A History of Russia: Volume II, Since 1855* (New York: McGraw-Hill, 1997).

4. I base this comment on sentiments from American Communist Party leader Rose Chernin. Kim Chernin, *In My Mother's House: A Daughter's Story* (New York: Harper & Row, 1983), 154–155, 191.

5. Nadine George-Graves's term "diasporic spidering" helps explain the dynamic exchange of communist and socialist influence in the early twentieth-century Jewish Diaspora. Predicating this idea on black identity as a performative act and active process within the African Diaspora, George-Graves defines diasporic spidering as a lateral, interconnected circulation and recirculation of influence among a global diasporic web as opposed to a unidirectional flow between one point of origin and points in a diaspora. George-Graves, "Diasporic Spidering: Constructing Contemporary Black Identities," in *Black Performance Theory*, eds. Thomas F. DeFrantz and Anita Gonzalez (Durham: Duke University Press, 2014), 33–44.

signified—their honest bodies—tracked the cultural residue of these influences through Sokolow's dances.

Sokolow's work evinced communist discourse in three ways: Her and her dancers' physiques displayed aesthetic markers of their training practices that indicated links with social movements; her choreography manifested revolutionary tropes; and critical responses to her concerts shows how spectators engaged with these ideas. By following international communist discourse through Sokolow's dances, we see how American dance similarly circulated its own catalog of aesthetic values. *Honest Bodies* reanimates this history to articulate Sokolow's prominence in international leftist and Jewish circles, why her choreography resonated so widely, and how anticommunist quieting of these values affected her career during postwar American Jewish assimilation. In this Introduction I argue for Sokolow's leftist transnationalism to position her choreography within it, I figure her dancing body from archival evidence to ground the book's analysis, and I define Jewish cultural and aesthetic elements in Sokolow's work to explain how her dances' Jewish signifiers engendered their meaning-making processes.

The development of Sokolow's choreography in international contexts redefined American modern dance. Approaching Sokolow's work in light of political and artistic ideology circulated through the Americas, along with North American influence in Israel, complicates midcentury constructions of the category "American." From Mexico, Sokolow understood that formalism and indigeneity exist on a continuum, and that modernism could thus include ethnic elements like Jewishness. Sokolow's engagement within a 1930s–1940s Mexican leftist milieu expanded how she could be leftist, American, and modern when leftist affiliations in the United States called one's "American" loyalties into question. Israel allowed Sokolow to be Jewish and communist when postwar assimilation and McCarthyism inhibited this position in the United States, and American Jews actively distanced themselves from their socialist pasts to avoid discrimination.[6] These influences contributed to an American modernism that people at the time considered to be universal and unmarked by specific cultural or political designations.

By defining how Sokolow's choreography worked through communist ideals, this book changes how we understand American modernism as a transnational phenomenon through dance. Sokolow's spectatorship and actions demonstrate the circulation of communist ideologies through concert dance choreographies in the United States, USSR, Mexico, and Israel in the early to mid-twentieth century.[7] Her leftist allegiances are no secret in the field of dance studies. Dance scholarship, including studies by Mark Franko, Lynn Garafola, Ellen Graff, and Stacey Prickett, have detailed Sokolow's work with the revolutionary movement, and dance

6. Rona Sheramy, "'Resistance and War': The Holocaust in American Jewish Education, 1945–1960," *American Jewish History* 91, no. 2 (2003): 301–303.

7. See Victoria Phillips Geduld, "Performing Communism in the American Dance: Culture, Politics and the New Dance Group," *American Communist History* 7, no. 1 (2008): 43.

historians Gay Morris and Rebekah Kowal have shown how Sokolow grappled with restraints from communist-effacing postwar American modernism.[8] In this book, I show how Sokolow's communist and Jewish allegiances enabled her mobility among the transnational Left and how international communist ideology traveled through her choreography. In doing so, I build on Mexican historical scholarship by Barry Carr, Friedrich Katz, and Daniela Spenser that details how communist dialogues circulated through American, Soviet, and Mexican intellectual and political discourses by bringing dance into this conversation as a mode of knowledge production.[9] I expand the US–USSR–Mexico triangle to include Israel as a geographical point through which Sokolow's dances engaged revolutionary spectatorship to show its hemispheric, Jewish, and American political implications.

Honest Bodies locates Sokolow's activities within a global circulation of communist ideals that redefined what it meant to be American. In the 1920s–1930s, communist ideologies reinforced American egalitarianism and social programs in the face of economic strife, and political candidates embraced them in cities like New York. In the 1940s–1950s, Second Red Scare proponents deemed communism un-American. Sokolow's fellow artists found themselves on trial before HUAC for their revolutionary actions. Although the FBI and the CIA followed Sokolow closely from the 1930s to the 1970s, she was never called before HUAC.[10] Public accusations of Communist ties had repercussions like blacklisting, passport revocation, and long-term unemployment, so Sokolow and her contemporaries understandably downplayed Sokolow's communist connections in the Red Scare's aftermath.[11] Sokolow's Cold War reframing of her own reputation by denying Communist affiliations, or narratives proffered by others that she merely reacted emotionally to the status quo,[12] do not diminish the role of communist principles in her work. I do not intend to further what Spenser calls the fetishization of communism and espionage

8. Franko, *Dancing Modernism/Performing Politics* (Bloomington: Indiana University Press, 1995); ibid., *The Work of Dance: Labor, Movement, and Identity in the 1930s* (Middletown, CT: Wesleyan University Press, 2002); Lynn Garafola, ed., *Of, By, and For the People: Dancing on the Left in the 1930s,* Studies in Dance History V, no. 1 (Society of Dance History Scholars, 1994); Graff, *Stepping Left* (see Preface, n2); Stacey Prickett, "From Workers' Dance to New Dance," *Dance Research: The Journal of the Society for Dance Research* 7, no. 1 (1989): 47–64; ibid., "Dance and the Workers' Struggle" (see Preface, n7); Gay Morris, *A Game for Dancers: Performing Modernism in the Postwar Years, 1945–1960* (Middletown, CT: Wesleyan University Press, 2006); and Rebekah J. Kowal, *How To Do Things With Dance: Performing Change in Postwar America* (Middletown, CT: Wesleyan University Press, 2010).

9. Carr, *Marxism and Communism* (see Preface, n9); Katz, *Secret War in Mexico* (see Preface, n9); and Spenser, *Impossible Triangle* (see Preface, n9).

10. FOIPA No. 1138496-000; Susan Viscuso, Information and Privacy Coordinator, Central Intelligence Agency, to Hannah Kosstrin, January 28, 2011, in the author's possession; and Viscuso to Kosstrin, July 28, 2011, in author's possession.

11. During this time, Larry Warren researched his *Rebellious Spirit* biography.

12. Warren, *Rebellious Spirit,* 37 (see Preface, n2); and Sanya Shoilevska Henderson, *Alex North, Film Composer* (Jefferson, NC: McFarland & Company, 2003), 14–15.

within Cold War narratives[13] or to oversimplify Sokolow's case by suggesting that all communist activity can be explained by whether a person was called to testify. Instead, I show how Sokolow's and her dancers' honest bodies determined their own political subjectivity through signifying their relationships to social, aesthetic, and legislative politics in her dances.

My work began with a fascination with Sokolow's choreography and Jewishness. I saw *Rooms* (1954) in college and was drawn to it for its defiant vulnerability. At the time I, a secular American Jew raised in the Reform movement, was thrilled to see a Jewish choreographer making any kind of work. Why did discussions of her choreography obscure her Jewishness and celebrate her modernist alienation, I wondered, when Jewish organizations celebrated Sokolow, seated in front of her chamseh-covered apartment wall in the documentary *Anna Sokolow: Choreographer*, as a Jewish cultural figure?[14] Is there a distinction between Jewish work and choreographers making work while being Jewish? These categories shift, but these questions pose points of articulation for Jewishness in the United States, other points in the Diaspora, and Israel. Sokolow's hybridity of Jewishness and modernism came together in her technical practice and choreography. In the following section I explain how I flesh out these elements from archival evidence by incorporating Sokolow's movement training and critical response to her performances to render her dancing body within its time to analyze her work.

REVIVING SOKOLOW'S DANCING BODY

Sokolow's dancing body—a radical body, a Jewish body, a female body, a modern dance body—played a significant role in her ability to navigate critical, political, raced, and gendered boundaries with her revolutionary work. *Honest Bodies* shows how the choreography lived through Sokolow's and her dancers' bodies, how reaction to it was informed by contemporary sentiment, and how her teaching and dancing bod(y)(ies) generated a discursive legacy for a range of choreographic styles.[15]

13. Daniela Spenser, "Standing Conventional Cold War History on Its Head," in *In from the Cold: Latin America's New Encounter with the Cold War*, eds. Gilbert M. Joseph and Daniela Spenser (Durham: Duke University Press, 2008), 382–383.

14. *Anna Sokolow: Choreographer*, VHS, produced and directed by Lucille Rhodes and Margaret Murphy (1980; Pennington, NJ: Dance Horizons Video, 1991).

15. I build on a Foucaultian framework of discourse analysis that assumes threads of discussion can exist and be historicized, furthered by Judith Butler's assertion that performance is a discourse of power that materializes through bodily actions, and Diana Taylor's argument that the lack of label for the kind of discourse that theatrical performance creates does not illegitimize its existence. Michel Foucault, "What Is an Author?" in *Language, Counter-Memory, Practice: Selected Essays and Interviews by Michel Foucault*, ed. Donald F. Bouchard (Ithaca: Cornell University Press, 1977), 113–138; Butler, *Bodies That Matter: On the Discursive Limits of "Sex"* (New York: Routledge, 1993), 187, 224–230; and Taylor, *The Archive and the Repertoire: Performing Cultural Memory in the Americas* (Durham: Duke University Press, 2003), 6. I build on Manning's analysis in *Modern Dance, Negro Dance* (see Preface, n14) of how

Sokolow's dancing body was the only constant in her work as she traveled around the northeastern United States and Mexico City in the 1930s and 1940s, and her teaching body carried her kinesthetic knowledge to Europe, South America, Israel, and East Asia for the rest of her career. Sokolow developed a way of performing that relied on a sense of strong weight, diverse dynamic range, vulnerability, and open-endedness.

Critical commentary from the 1930s helps figure Sokolow's dancing body by describing her as a technical and compelling performer. Critics wrote high praise for Sokolow's "hex dance" duet with Anita Alvarez in the "Dedication" section of Graham's *Panorama* (1935), which critic Edna Ocko noted was Graham's first work based in social action that resonated with the leftist movement.[16] Ocko highlighted this duet as "some of the finest dancing of the evening," as well as a *New Theatre* 1935 dance highlight.[17] John Martin later noted in the *New York Times* that Sokolow performed Graham's *Four Casual Developments* "with delightful comedy and skill."[18] The most exciting description of Sokolow's choreography comes from the 1930s leftist press. Owen Burke, a *New Masses* dance critic and one of Sokolow's biggest champions, provided evocative weekly reviews of Sokolow's work. Other critics and Sokolow's classmates and teachers commented on her technical dexterity and charismatic persona. One noted in *American Dancer* in 1937 that Sokolow "impresses one by her force and vigor and by her sincerity."[19] That year, Margery Dana noted in the *Daily Worker* how Sokolow's petite frame could dominate the space: "On a sudden burst of music, something happens. The stage and auditorium both seem filled with portentous action and electric energy."[20] Sokolow moved, according to accounts, with an impressively broad dynamic range. Fellow Graham dancer Dorothy Bird remembered that Sokolow was "secure on her feet, so agile, so in balance, and so fast!"[21] In 1932, Bird said, their Henry Street Settlement and Neighborhood Playhouse acting teacher Laura Elliot informed the class, "only she [Sokolow] possessed the knack of being sufficiently objective, while remaining in touch with her feelings."[22] These comments spurred a reputation that drew broad spectatorship to Sokolow's work and provided credibility for her choreographic career.

the discourse of critical reviews from various publications determined how audiences and critics constructed the racial and social positions of the works and their choreographers.

16. Edna Ocko, "Martha Graham's 'Panorama,'" *New Theatre* (September 1935): 27.

17. Ocko, "Martha Graham's 'Panorama,'" 27; and ibid., "Dancers, Take a Bow," *New Theatre* (February 1936): 24.

18. John Martin, "New Recital Given by Martha Graham: Dancer and Her Group Present Program of Wide Variety at Guild Theatre," *New York Times*, March 15, 1937, 16. PQHN.

19. "Anna Sokolow and Dance Unit, Y. M. H. A., February 28," *American Dancer*, no month, 1937, n.p., Anna Sokolow Clippings, JRDD, NYPL.

20. Margery Dana, "Dancing to the Tune of the Times: Young Anna Sokolow Among the Leading Modern Dancers of America," *Daily Worker*, November 10, 1937, 7.

21. Bird and Greenberg, *Bird's Eye View*, 67 (see Preface, n5).

22. Ibid., 87.

A performance I saw demonstrated the charisma of Sokolow's stage persona in the absence of film of her performing in the 1930s, and served as an example of how contemporary performance dialogues with archival evidence. At the Sokolow Theatre/Dance Ensemble's 100th Birthday Tribute Concert on February 14, 2010, at the 92nd Street Young Men's/Young Women's Hebrew Association (YM/YWHA, or "Y") on Manhattan's Upper East Side, Charis Haines's command of performance and clarity of movement in *Preludes* (1981), a solo Sokolow made for Haines's teacher Tonia Shimin,[23] recalled the power critics described so often in Sokolow's performances.[24] In her dancing, Haines was petite and muscular, tender yet fierce. She poured her weight with crisp clarity into different pools of support as if through a fiber-optic funnel. Her pristine tiny, quick footwork complemented a cross-body tension that played against swooping turns and deepening spins. She was strong but not tense, yielding into softness as she sank into wrapped shapes. Her shatteringly precise leg beats and arm threads preceded generous full-body *pliés*. Haines was charismatic and articulate, with her discerning focus encompassing a combination of joy and an understanding of worldly sorrow. Watching Haines gave me a new understanding for what it might have been like to see Sokolow dance. Haines's performance recalled Sokolow's embodiment, reinforcing the importance of recognizing how dancers' individual physicalities and performance qualities distinctly signify dances' meanings.

Engaging a work's full meaning necessitates specific language to describe how the bodies form the choreography in that space and time. My argument here is influenced by the limits of onstage colorblindness that dance theorist Susan Leigh Foster calls "simply(?) the doing of it" in the work of postmodern choreographers and life partners Bill T. Jones and Arnie Zane. The materiality of Jones's black body and Zane's white, Italian-Jewish body together in their playful, poignant duets that referenced nothing outside themselves necessarily invoked the political importance of how "they are dancing together, *intimately* [original emphasis]" because of the way mainstream American culture trains audiences to read bodies as raced, gendered, and classed entities against an established norm.[25] When we look at photographic images of dancing, how do we read what we see? In a picture of *Case History No.—* (1937) (central photo of Figure 1.5 in Chapter 1) Sokolow lands a jump with her knee tracking over her toes, in a physical moment valued as "good technique"

23. Anna Sokolow, *Preludes*, restaged by Tonia Shimin, performed by Charis Haines, *Sokolow 100th Birthday Tribute*, presented by Sokolow Theatre/Dance Ensemble, February 14, 2010, 92nd Street YM/YWHA, New York City.

24. Dancer and choreographer Ze'eva Cohen, who danced with Sokolow in Tel Aviv and New York and knew her since the early 1960s, and who also witnessed Haines's 2010 performance, agreed that Haines came close to embodying Sokolow's performance abilities and style. Cohen in phone conversation with the author, September 14, 2010.

25. Susan Leigh Foster, "Simply(?) the Doing of It, Like Two Arms Going Round and Round," in *Continuous Replay: The Photographs of Arnie Zane*, ed. Jonathan Green (Cambridge: MIT Press, 1999), 114.

within the American modern dance tradition. These images contain a Jewish body aesthetically aligned with white modern dance during a time when Jews were targets of racialized language that "Othered" their bodies.[26] As Foster's insistence that the viewer grapple with how Jones and Zane dancing intimately upset institutionalized racism and heteronormativity on American stages, we cannot ignore Sokolow's Jewish body's prominence during a time that American society marked working-class Jews as second-class citizens, even when discussions about choreography in abstract language highlighted Sokolow's disciplined modern dance look.

To revive Sokolow's dancing body, I flesh out her choreography from archival evidence to understand the political stakes of her work.[27] I aim to make dance descriptions I assemble from historical crumbs in still images, program notes, critical reviews, financial reports, or a sentiment scribbled on the back of a publicity photograph read as immediately as contemporary performance. I work to convey the movement I read in a Labanotation score, a twentieth-century movement notation system that shows where bodies go in space and time, as effortlessly as my description of a live or filmed dance.[28] I hope to invoke in my reader the palm-clammy excitement and empowered rage that Sokolow produced in her audiences to convey the implications of spectatorship amid the time's political environment.

I analyze Sokolow's dances to create a written record in dialogue with kinesthetic evidence to display how her dances were sites for Jewish and communist aesthetics. For this, I integrate what performance theorist Diana Taylor discerns as the archive and the repertoire with what dance theorist Priya Srinivasan calls the bodily archive to show how the residue of physical practice generates transnational discourse. In the archive, knowledge takes the form of written evidence, and in the repertoire, modes of bodily transmission evidence embodied knowledge.[29] Taylor argues that performance can remap the Americas into a complete hemisphere that rematerializes histories lost through colonization and a devaluation of knowledge production originating

26. See Howard Eilberg-Schwartz, ed., *People of the Body: Jews and Judaism from an Embodied Perspective* (Albany: State University of New York Press, 1992); and Rebecca Rossen, *Dancing Jewish: Jewish Identity in American Modern and Postmodern Dance* (New York: Oxford University Press, 2014).

27. I build on the methods Susan Manning, Ann Cooper Albright, and Nadine George-Graves introduce for assembling and analyzing dances from archival sources and for gaining a kinesthetic understanding of the work through ethnographic and practical means. Manning, *Ecstasy and the Demon: The Dances of Mary Wigman* (Minneapolis: University of Minnesota Press, 2006); Albright, *Traces of Light: Absence and Presence in the Work of Loïe Fuller* (Middletown: Wesleyan University Press, 2007); and George-Graves, *Urban Bush Women: Twenty Years of African American Dance Theater, Community Engagement, and Working It Out* (Madison: University of Wisconsin Press, 2010). I build on Melanie Bales and Karen Eliot's assertion for a dance-focused methodology wherein theoretical and historical conclusions grow from the dance's materiality. Bales and Eliot, eds., "Introduction," in *Dance on Its Own Terms: Histories and Methodologies* (New York: Oxford University Press, 2013), 3–7.

28. See Hannah Kosstrin, "Notation Score as Embodied Documentary Presence: A Response to Amelia Jones' 'Presence in Absentia,'" *The International Journal of Screendance* 2 (2012): 44–47.

29. Taylor, *Archive and Repertoire*, xvii, 19–25.

outside a Eurocentric conception of evidence. I engage Taylor's assertions about the transnational location of knowledge in performance forms' mobility to ascertain how Sokolow's dances bridged hemispheric tensions between the United States and Mexico, and between the United States and Israel, by circulating leftist ideology that connected these geographical areas, at least politically. Combining the archive with the repertoire, Srinivasan defines the bodily archive as "the discourses of living, breathing texts produced by these dancing bodies" in which dancers' physiques generate repositories of definable, and traceable, kinesthetic influences.[30] Physical residue, or kinesthetic markings left by training and choreographic practices, reappears in dancers' performances and in traits of local dance scenes. By embracing the conventions of their ephemerality, these dance performance elements can be quantified.[31] This kind of kinesthetic evidence is as consistent as archival evidence, but, like archival evidence, must be understood within its historical context. This book's discourse analysis comes from physical characteristics of Sokolow's and her dancers' historical bodies in motion as well as from reviews, theoretical discussions, historical progressions, and my own kinesthetic interaction with the material.[32]

My embodied knowledge becomes part of my renderings of Sokolow's choreography. Sokolow trained in Martha Graham's codified technique and taught Graham technique classes. With her powerful, stark, fiery movement, Graham portrayed weighty matters through women's bodies that were too powerful to be diminutively feminized and not as overtly harsh as to appear masculine[33] (Figure 0.1). Sokolow utilized elements of Graham's technical base in her choreography without imitating it.[34] I trained in this movement vocabulary and other styles of modern dance that developed in the mid-twentieth century. In

30. Priya Srinivasan, *Sweating Saris: Indian Dance as Transnational Labor* (Philadelphia: Temple University Press, 2012), 67–71, 186n10.

31. For ephemerality and performance, see Rebecca Schneider, *Performing Remains: Art and War in Times of Theatrical Reenactment* (Abingdon: Routledge, 2011); Harmony Bench, "Dance and Digitality: The Twice-Ephemeral" (paper, Congress on Research in Dance and Society of Dance History Scholars joint conference, University of Iowa, Iowa City, IA, November 15, 2014); José Estéban Muñoz, "Gesture, Ephemera, and Queer Feeling: Approaching Kevin Aviance" in *Dancing Desires: Choreographing Sexualities On and Off the Stage*, ed. Jane C. Desmond (Madison: University of Wisconsin Press, 2001), 423–442; and Amelia Jones, "Material Traces: Performativity, Artistic 'Work,' and New Concepts of Agency," *TDR* 59, no. 4 (2015): 18–35.

32. My focus on moving bodies as generators of discourse and the historian's role in kinesthetically rendering dances is further informed by Susan Leigh Foster, "Choreographies of Gender," *Signs* 24, no. 1 (1998): 1–33; and Ann Cooper Albright, "Tracing the Past: Writing History through the Body," in *The Routledge Dance Studies Reader*, 2nd ed., eds. Alexandra Carter and Janet O'Shea (London and New York: Routledge, 2010), 101–110.

33. Marcia B. Siegel, "Art, Inspiration, and the Body: The Emergence of Modern Dance," in Bird and Greenberg, *Bird's Eye View*, xvii.

34. Anna Sokolow, interview by Theresa Bowers, November 27, 1978, transcript, 17, "Bennington Summer School of the Dance: Reminiscences of Anna Sokolow," Columbia University Oral History Collection, New York, NY; and Patricia Shirley Allen, "Young Modern: Anna Sokolow Goes Forward," *The American Dancer* (February 1938): 13.

Figure 0.1: Dorothy Bird and Ethel Butler practice Graham technique at the Bennington School of the Dance, mid-1930s. Photographer unknown. Photo courtesy of Estate of Dorothy Bird Villard.

Figure 0.2: *Anti-War Trilogy*. Dancers (left to right): Florence Schneider, Celia Dembroe, Marie Marchovsky, Rose Levy, Eleanor Lazarus. Photo by Alfredo Valente. Courtesy of the Sokolow Dance Foundation and Richard Valente.

1930s photographs of Sokolow's performances, I recognize the spiraling uses of the back, the vector-like power that comes from initiations through abdominal contractions, and the strong weight and energetically bound flow necessary to execute the Graham vocabulary. This aesthetic visually manifests in photographs such as Sokolow's group in *Anti-War Trilogy* (1935) (Figure 0.2), a dance that

Figure 0.3: Sokolow improvising. Photographer unknown. Courtesy of the Sokolow Dance Foundation.

premiered as *Anti-War Cycle* (1933) and won second prize in a 1934 Workers Dance League competitive recital, or a spiral through the back, as in a photograph of Sokolow improvising that affects the positions and actions of Sokolow's and her dancers' heads, limbs, and torsos (Figure 0.3). Sokolow transformed her Graham training into choreography that recalled elements of Graham's movement and women's power while breaking thematically from Graham's Protestant subjects. By engaging my embodied knowledge of this dance genre, my writing assumes the responsibility of portraying the movement from the inside out and from the outside in.

In addition to engaging the Graham technique, I construct the historical presence of Sokolow's physical practice and choreography from her work with Louis Horst's composition classes, the Stanislavsky Method, and George Balanchine's style of ballet to give a sense of the movement influences that engendered her physical form. Sokolow met Horst, a Denishawn musician and composition teacher who worked with Graham, at Henry Street on New York's Lower East Side and then became his summer teaching assistant at the Bennington School of the Dance. Horst's dance composition led his students to embrace abstraction and a contention that an artist could transcend time and place through the universality of formalist art.[35] Through Horst's influence and the domain of Bennington's invited choreographers known as the Big Four—Graham, Doris Humphrey, Charles Weidman, and Hanya Holm—bolstered by *New York Times* critic John Martin, these formal elements came to define modern dance in the early to mid-twentieth century, and aligned Sokolow's work with modern dance abstraction. Sokolow credited Horst's mentorship with finding her choreographic voice, facilitating her incorporation of music with movement, teaching her to use the rhythm of a piece of music to dictate the structure, weight, and theme of a dance, and guiding her to find her inner purpose.[36] Sokolow cemented her compositional methods within leftist circles by pairing Horst's training with the gut impetus of Stanislavsky's inner motivation and the rhythmic precision of Balanchine's technique. A regular at the School of the American Ballet, the training ground for Balanchine's New York City Ballet, Sokolow considered Balanchine's experiments integral to her dance training.[37] She took classes with Muriel Stuart and Anatole Oboukoff (who once threw her out for taking class barefoot).[38] Sokolow was a lifelong admirer of Balanchine's work,[39] which, like Sokolow's aspirations, blended modernist, balletic, and Africanist influences.

Sokolow's revolutionary spectatorship summoned the interplay between her dancing body and how audiences perceived her work. Concert dance audiences represent a spectrum of political, aesthetic, raced, and gendered subjectivities. Audience members who recognize dances' thematic or aesthetic codes understand the work differently than those who do not see the references. Dance historian Susan Manning's use of Tirza True Latimer's and Patricia Simons's term "cross-viewing" offers a framework for explaining spectatorship among Sokolow's hybrid audiences. Cross-viewing is a spectatorial situation in which audience members notice the way other audience members interact with the performance that may differ from their own negotiations with the material. Spectators who cross-view, Manning explains, "catch glimpses of subjectivities from social locations that differ from their own" and experience cross-fertilization of cultural values.[40] In Sokolow's concerts, audiences

35. See Louis Horst and Carroll Russell, *Modern Dance Forms in Relation to the Other Modern Arts* (Princeton, NJ: Princeton Book Company, 1987).

36. Anna Sokolow, interview by Barbara Newman, December 2 and 12, 1974, and May 11, 1975, transcript, 43–47, Oral History Archives, JRDD, NYPL; and Anna Sokolow, quoted in Anna Kisselgoff, "In Anna Sokolow's Dance, Her Beliefs," *New York Times* December 2, 1975, 46, n.p., Alan M. and Sali Ann Kriegsman Collection, MD, LOC.

37. Sokolow foresaw a joining of ballet and modern dance into one form. Ruth Ann Heisey, "Anna Sokolow—Interview," *Dance Observer* (December 1937): 77.

38. Anna Sokolow, interview by Marlene Burns Harding, January 27, 1992, A/V Collection, JRDD, NYPL; and Bird and Greenberg, 189–190.

39. Anna Sokolow to George Balanchine, November 24, 1964, Folder bMS Thr 411 (1765), Barbara Horgan and the George Balanchine Trust, 1992 March 25, George Balanchine Archive, The Houghton Library, Harvard University.

40. Manning, *Modern Dance, Negro Dance*, xvi, 224n10. Manning and Foster further demonstrated that performance production elements, from venue to genre to critical reception, contextualize or frame a performance. Manning, *Modern Dance, Negro Dance*, xviii-xix, and

who came for the politics experienced modern dance aesthetic philosophies, and those who came for the dance saw or missed nuanced social, gendered, and political codes, but by noticing their fellow audience members' reactions they found themselves part of a larger political artistic community. At Sokolow's 1930s–1960s productions, workers saw themselves onstage; middle-class audiences attended dances for workers' rights; racially mixed audiences witnessed the indictment of an antilynching bill filibuster within a predominantly African American production; non-Jewish audiences viewed work with Jewish themes; Soviet audiences found her work too bourgeois; Mexican audiences considered folklore revolutionary but American audiences pejoratively called it ethnic dance; and Israeli audiences found catharsis in a no-holds-barred representation of the Holocaust that Diaspora audiences more hesitantly accepted. Sokolow's work fostered the transnational Left by providing audience members a shared experience as they watched her dances and one another.

Many of Sokolow's works, like *Kaddish* (1945) or *Rooms*, have fifty-year lifespans that negotiated changes in spectatorship and dancers' physiques. Some choreographic elements remained consistent over time, and some changed with the passage of roles from one dancer to another. Sokolow often recombined and retitled dances based on the concert situation or the dancers performing the work,[41] and audiences saw choreographies variantly, depending on the contexts in which they viewed them. In the following section, I focus on the Jewishness in Sokolow's dances to show how, despite diverse readings by spectators from myriad social and historical positions, it defined the form and politics of her work.

FROM THE *KISHKES*: JEWISHNESS AND REVOLUTIONARY MODERNISM

The Jewishness in Sokolow's work drives the interplay I highlight among the functions of communism, modernism, and gender in her dances. Dance ethnographer Deidre Sklar's assertions about acting from the *kishkes*, a Yiddish expression that means with conviction, resonates for me in articulating the urgency and from-the-gut earnestness inside Sokolow's dances.[42] In telling the story of this book, I center Sokolow's Ashkenazi (Central and Eastern European; Yiddish) cultural elements of thematic and movement characteristics that contribute to a broad definition

Susan Leigh Foster, *Reading Dancing: Bodies and Subjects in Contemporary American Dance* (Berkeley: University of California Press, 1986), 59–65.

41. Morris, *A Game for Dancers*, 94, and Anadel Lynton (Mexican-based dancer, choreographer, dance scholar), in discussion with the author, June 20, 2009.

42. Deidre Sklar, "The Embodied I-Thou of Fieldwork," (keynote lecture, Performance Ethnography: Explorations in Theory and Practice, Oberlin College, Oberlin, OH, April 24, 2015). *Kishkes* translates as intestines or entrails; literally, "guts."

of Jewishness in dance.[43] Sokolow's cultural traditions informed her practice and her work with and without overt Jewish thematic material. Jewish signification appeared in Sokolow's choreography, the spectatorship and cultural assimilation surrounding her work, and the dynamic identity process that Sokolow's dancing ignited. Whether a dance is more or less Jewish, depending on audience makeup, rests on where the meaning-making lies: Is a dance inherently Jewish, or does audience interaction with the work and its historical context determine its Jewishness? A combination of these scenarios occurred with Sokolow's work. In this section I work through the categories of communism, modernism, Jewishness, and gender to show how their significations operated together in Sokolow's dances.

Communism

Sokolow's views reflected the socialist loyalties of her immigrant Eastern European Jewish community in New York. Many of these Jews supported belief systems connected to Marxism as part of *Yiddishkeit* (Eastern European Jewish culture). Yiddishkeit had socialism and egalitarianism at its core in opposition to the late nineteenth-century capitalist Russian monarchy, which pursued anti-Semitic policies including confining Jews within the boundaries of the Pale of Settlement and sanctioning violent pogroms against them.[44] Eastern European communist ideology's rhetoric of international solidarity gave Jews hope for sovereignty and a sense of transnational peoplehood in European countries that did not present, as would the United States, the potential for Jews to form a community of identity within a nation–state.[45] By Jewish peoplehood, I refer to the early twentieth-century American social project with roots in late nineteenth-century Europe that encompasses Jews' imagined connection to other Jews inside and outside their social or geographic milieu, through the felt commonality of ethnicity, shared experiences of persecution, and often, but not always, religion.[46] As such, Russian Jewish

43. In the Diaspora, Ashkenazim share characteristics that differ from those of Jews of Mediterranean, Arabic, or African descent.

44. The Pale of Settlement was the designated area, beginning in 1791, where Jews in the Russian Empire were legally allowed to settle.

45. Karen Brodkin, *How Jews Became White Folks and What That Says about Race in America* (New Brunswick and London: Rutgers University Press, 1998), 104–109; Dan Diner and Jonathan Frankel, "Jews and Communism: The Utopian Temptation," in *Dark Times, Dire Decisions: Jews and Communism*, ed. Jonanthan Frankel (New York: Oxford University Press, 2004), 3–4, 11; Arnold Eisen, "Four Questions Concerning Jewish Peoplehood—And Just as Many Answers," in *Jewish Peoplehood: Change and Challenge*, eds. Menachem Revivi and Ezra Kopelowitz (Boston: Academic Studies Press, 2009), 4–8; and Noam Pianko, *Jewish Peoplehood: An American Innovation* (New Brunswick: Rutgers University Press, 2015), 27–34.

46. Riv-Ellen Prell, "Against the Cultural Grain: Jewish Peoplehood for the 21st Century," in *Jewish Peoplehood*, 122; and Pianko, *Jewish Peoplehood*, 3, 19–27.

immigrants brought socialism as political action to New York in the late nineteenth and early twentieth centuries.[47] Some were Communist Party members, whereas others aligned themselves with socialist values of equality for all people. This cultural position in which Jewishness and socialism intertwined generated an activist worldview. The transnational revolutionary discourse that I observe in Sokolow's dances originated in this Eastern European Jewish context in which Jewishness was inextricable from socialism.

The changing critical reception of Sokolow's work reflects the assimilation of her generation from the marginalized working class into the American middle class from the 1920s to the 1950s.[48] Sokolow was a member of the "second generation" of American Jews, the mainly secular children of the Eastern European (Ashkenazi) Jewish immigrant wave that settled mostly in New York from 1881 to 1914.[49] We can expand this "second-generation" definition to include Jews settled in eastern cities in the Americas—New York, Baltimore, Mexico City, São Paulo, Bogotá, and Buenos Aires—to engage a common Atlantic connection between these Diaspora communities. Their shared values, especially socialism, are pertinent for considering Sokolow's work in Mexico, and place Sokolow in a hemispheric Jewish communist context.[50]

For many working-class American Jews of Eastern European heritage, like Sokolow, socialist values were central to their identification as American Jews living in enclaves like the Lower East Side during the late nineteenth and early twentieth centuries. But Depression-era New York Jews' leftist political allegiances did not break cleanly along party lines. Many Jews believed in socialist ideals but found the Communist Party too theory oriented and insufficiently rooted in practical social action. Politics related to kosher meat boycotts, food cost protests, or rent strikes were neighborhood specific.[51] If politics broke down by neighborhood, Sokolow's various 1930s residences near Manhattan's Union Square, which housed the Communist Party USA headquarters, offices of the Communist papers *New Masses* and *Morgen Freiheit* [Yiddish, *Morning Freedom*], and the workers' bookstore, put her in the center of American and Ashkenazi Jewish communist ideology in action (Figure 0.4). In 1936 Sokolow and her romantic partner, musician Alex North (born Isadore Soifer), lived on West 16th Street between 5th and 6th Avenues, a

47. For Jewish cosmopolitanism and the Left, see Moshe Halbertal, "On Modern Jewish Identities," in *Jewish Peoplehood*, 45–47; and Prell, "Against the Cultural Grain," 117–119.

48. See Brodkin, *How Jews Became White Folks*.

49. Deborah Dash Moore, *At Home in America: Second Generation New York Jews* (New York: Columbia University Press, 1981), 4–5; Beth S. Wenger, *New York Jews and the Great Depression: Uncertain Promise* (Syracuse: Syracuse University Press, 1999), 7. Wenger extends the term to include the idea of "a cultural generation" from the 1920s through the postwar era.

50. For hemispheric studies, see Diana Taylor, *Archive and Repertoire*, xiii–xix.

51. Wenger, *New York Jews and the Great Depression*, 103–135.

Figure 0.4: Communist Party Headquarters Union Square, 1930s; Charles Rivers Photographs and Scrapbooks; TAM 260; Box 1; Item 4; Tamiment Library/Robert F. Wagner Labor Archives, New York University.

block and a half from Union Square. (Their earlier shared dwellings included a West 12th Street communal loft and an apartment on East 13th Street between 2nd and 3rd Avenues, both within a few blocks of Union Square and the Yiddish Theater District.)[52] Sokolow's and North's neighborhood allegiances intertwined with their political and aesthetic affinities into an embodied American Jewish and revolutionary existence. At the time, Graham's studio was near Union Square at the corner of West 13th Street and 5th Avenue, so Sokolow's associations with dance modernism were similarly geographically entrenched.[53]

52. *List of Enrolled Voters* 1936, 56 (see Preface, n11); and Warren, *Rebellious Spirit*, 38. Coincidentally, their 16th St. apartment was next door to what is now the Center for Jewish History.
53. Graff, *Stepping Left*, 6–7.

Modernism

The revolutionary modernism in Sokolow's choreography drove her dances' meanings and aligned her with artists across the international Left. Revolutionary modernism was a 1930s proletarian art movement that challenged capitalist modernist bourgeois notions of an avant-garde.[54] It encompassed proletarianism, egalitarianism, unity in the face of oppression, and an active dismantling of hierarchy within an aesthetic marriage of experimental form and anticapitalist content. Sokolow's work embraced Mexico's centrality of the folk as proletariat in a postrevolutionary society, and the collectivity and idealized agrarianism at the core of Israeli socialist Zionism. Within the 1930s revolutionary dance movement, Sokolow's aesthetic affinities combined a stark formalism from what Graff calls Graham's "bourgeois" technical base and choreography with an American Marxist-affiliated belief that abstract art forms could portray social statements,[55] along with an alignment with the working class, a sense of alienation, and a from-the-gut conviction to galvanize audiences to enact social change after seeing the work.[56] Revolutionary modernism attracted American leftist artists in the 1930s, particularly those who hailed from Yiddish backgrounds.[57] Although revolutionary modernism in dance was not solely Jewish, it reflected the socialist values of New York's immigrant Jewish community because of large numbers of Eastern European and Eastern European–descended Jews in the revolutionary movement.[58]

Sokolow's training history tracks her relationship to Jewish developments in modernist dance. Like many 1930s dancers who were children of Eastern European Jewish immigrants, Sokolow began dancing in afternoon settlement house dance classes. She first studied at the Emmanuel Sisterhood of Personal Service on East 82nd Street in 1919, and in 1925 transferred to Henry Street, where modern dance leaders Graham, Horst, Humphrey, Blanche Talmud, and Weidman were on the

54. Michael Denning, *The Cultural Front: The Laboring of American Culture in the Twentieth Century* (New York: Verso, 1997), 121–122.

55. Graff, *Stepping Left*, 10; and Serge Guilbaut, "The New Adventures of the Avant-Garde in America: Greenberg, Pollock, or from Trotskyism to the New Liberalism of the 'Vital Center,'" trans. Thomas Repensek, *October* 15 (1980): 64.

56. See Graff, *Stepping Left*; Edna Ocko, "The Revolutionary Dance Movement," *New Masses*, June 12, 1934, 27, BICLM; and Marjorie Church, "The Dance in the Social Scene," *Dance Observer* (March 1937): 27. See also Matei Calinescu, *Five Faces of Modernity* (Durham: Duke University Press, 1987), 95–97 and 125–132.

57. Ruth Jennison, "Combining Uneven Developments: Louis Zukofsky and the Political Economy of Revolutionary Modernism," *Cultural Critique* 77 (2011): 146. For shared characteristics of revolutionary modernism among Jewish composers in Europe, see James Loeffler, "From Biblical Antiquarianism to Revolutionary Modernism: Jewish Art Music, 1850– 1925," in *The Cambridge Companion to Jewish Music*, ed. Joshua S. Walden (Cambridge: Cambridge University Press, 2015), 179–182.

58. See Julia Foulkes, "Angels 'Rewolt!': Jewish Women in Modern Dance in the 1930s," *American Jewish History* 88, no. 2 (2000): 233–252; Linda Tomko, *Dancing Class: Gender, Ethnicity, and Social Divides in American Dance, 1890–1920* (Bloomington and

faculty under the direction of the German-American Jewish sisters Alice and Irene Lewisohn.[59] Sokolow's Henry Street training, including American Delsartism, Graham technique, ballet technique, and Horst's dance composition, defined American dance modernism. At Henry Street, Sokolow performed in pageants written by Irene Lewisohn that featured allegorical, mythological, and biblical themes, compositionally incorporated music visualization, and employed large architectural sets. Students provided onstage support for teachers who performed, including Graham, Humphrey, Talmud, Weidman, and Benjamin Zemach.[60] Sokolow's professional trajectory from settlement house dance classes to Graham company member and workers' choreographer was similar to that of other Jews who began dancing at the settlement house.

Through shared political allegiances and training practices with second-generation dancers in the 1930s, Sokolow's experience of modernism was entwined with Jewishness. Many of these women went from settlement house technique classes into Graham's and Humphrey's companies.[61] These Jewish dancers engendered a reciprocal relationship between their embodiment of Graham's and Humphrey's movements and the development of these techniques. Revolutionary work in the 1930s contained scarce religious themes, but Jewish choreographers enacted their cultural Jewishness by performing for social justice. Dance historian Naomi Jackson noted, "radical dance *was* a kind of Jewish dance [original emphasis]" because of the predominant numbers of Jewish women of Eastern European descent who led the leftist dance movement and the cultural values of social justice they embodied in their dance for social change.[62] Many revolutionary dancers associated with the New Dance Group also trained at Hanya Holm's studio. By way of these configurations of Jewish dancers working with Graham, Humphrey–Weidman, and Holm by day, and choreographing proletarian dances by night, Jewish, revolutionary, and modernist values converged in Big Four and revolutionary choreographies.

Indianapolis: Indiana University Press, 1999); Manning, *Modern Dance, Negro Dance*; and Naomi Jackson, *Converging Movements: Modern Dance and Jewish Culture at the 92nd Street Y* (Hanover: Wesleyan University Press, 2000). In *Kiev: Jewish Metropolis, A History, 1859–1914* (Bloomington: Indiana University Press, 2010), Natan Meir argued that an urban space can become a Jewish city, despite discrimination against Jews, because of Jewish production in infrastructure. Jewish presence in modern and revolutionary dance played a similar role.

59. Warren, *Rebellious Spirit*, 3–16. See also Tomko, *Dancing Class*.

60. Program, *Tocatta and Fugue in D Minor*, 92nd Street YM/YWHA, April 26–27, 1931, Folder 16; Irene Lewisohn's notebook containing notes for *Tocatta and Fugue in D Minor*, Folder 16; Program, *Israel*, Manhattan Opera House, May 4–6, 1928, Folder 9; *Israel* scenario notes, Folder 9; and *A Burmese Pwe* scenario notes, 1925–1926, Folder 4, all in Neighborhood Playhouse Scenarios, 1914–1931, JRDD, NYPL; William W. Yates, "Neighborhood Playhouse Presents *A Pagan Poem*," *The Dance Magazine* (May 1930): 53–54; Jewish Women's Archive, "Elsa Pohl, Anna Sokolow (center), and unknown dancer as 'Beauty, Reason and Folly' at the Emanuel Sisterhood," <http://jwa.org/node/8957> (June 17, 2010).

61. Foulkes, "Angels 'Rewolt!'" 239.

62. Jackson, *Converging Movements*, 176.

Revolutionary modernism persisted in Sokolow's work despite its 1940s eclipse by a new American modernism associated with Greenbergian formalism that aesthetically defined the American vanguard in terms of form for form's sake. Critics and presenters inside and outside the United States read Sokolow's work as American because of its abstraction. American anticommunist sentiments during and after World War II and the increasingly conservative values of the postwar American middle class shifted public perceptions of modernism from a combination of formalism and social consciousness to encompassing abstract expressionism.[63] In the 1940s to the 1960s, American dance modernism relied on a sense of professionalism coupled with a perceived universalism through abstraction, whiteness, and a visual resonance of bodies trained in prominent choreographers' techniques that disciplined bodies into recognizable physiques.[64] Early and mid-century modern dance utilized an articulating, arcing, and spiraling torso; bare feet that incorporated flexed and extended ankles;[65] and a weighted relationship with gravity in floorwork sequences and downward-pulling jumps. Many modern dance practitioners also incorporated the lengthened shapes, articulate limbs, and gravity defiance of ballet movement. Sokolow's revolutionary impetus challenged the universalist constraints of postwar modernism.

Sokolow's postwar dances aligned aesthetically with abstracted dance modernism, but revealed devastating emotional portraits of people unable to engage in intimate relationships. Whereas Graham's choreography contained what Manning called "mythic abstraction," which effaced references to race by signifying epic themes larger than individual dancers,[66] Sokolow's work, as Kowal argued, presented "ordinary action," or movements based on quotidian concerns, in which abstracted movements heightened dancers' individual subjectivities.[67] Postwar choreographers worked to stay within the "rules" of the "game of modernism," as Morris detailed, by employing abstract choreography that appeared to reference nothing outside itself so as not to fall outside the norm and rouse suspicion in an era of surveillance.[68] Consequently, modern dance audiences received choreography that delivered thematic content by means of abstracted, instead of mimetic, movement vocabularies as universal. The perceived universalism in Sokolow's choreography, and her role as a Graham technique teacher,

63. See Morris, *A Game for Dancers*, xv–xvi, 3–5; Sally Banes and Noël Carroll, "Cunningham, Balanchine, and Postmodern Dance," *Dance Chronicle* 29 (2006): 51; and Guilbaut, "New Adventures," 61–78.

64. See Morris, *A Game for Dancers*; Kowal, *How To Do Things with Dance*; and Clare Croft, *Dancers as Diplomats: American Choreography in Cultural Exchange* (New York: Oxford University Press, 2015).

65. Alice Helpern, "Martha Graham's Early Technique and Dances: The 1930s, A Panel Discussion," *Choreography and Dance* 5, part 2 (1999): 13.

66. Manning, *Modern Dance, Negro Dance*, 118.

67. Kowal, *How To Do Things With Dance*, 86–116.

68. Morris, *A Game for Dancers*.

aligned in time with the American Jewish community's midcentury assimilation into whiteness.

After the Holocaust, Sokolow gained widespread recognition amid upward economic mobility for assimilating American Jews. As they increasingly moved from cities to suburbs in the postwar period, Jews experienced new (to them) advantages of white privilege as they became socially and politically Caucasian and found themselves having to choose how far to distance themselves from Yiddishkeit to blend into their suburban neighborhoods, away from tight-knit urban Jewish communities.[69] Although Sokolow's 1930s Yiddishkeit-influenced ideals remained in her 1950s work, her choreography, like *Lyric Suite* (1953), looked more like the whiteness of abstract expressionism that defined midcentury modern dance.[70] Sokolow's Jewishness manifested in the layered yet dissonant structures and open endings with many answers in her works. Even through the conceits of modern dance abstraction, Sokolow's Jewishness underpinned the structures and political statements of her work.

Jewishness (in Choreography)

The Jewishness in Sokolow's choreography functioned as spectatorial practice and historical categorization. Her dances' unresolved endings reflected Jewish modes of teaching through questioning,[71] drew her audiences into dialogue with her assertions, and pressed them to finish the dances with their actions outside the theater. In 1967 Sokolow expounded, "I never gave an answer to what I did. They used to say 'you must finish it' and I would say 'well, who knows what the finish is.' I still don't finish anything because I don't feel that anything ever ends."[72] Sokolow's refusal to offer solutions to problems in her choreographic representations of oppressive authoritarian power or the neglected poor insisted that spectators draw their own conclusions. She often ended dances with a question or accusation, once remarking

69. Matthew Frye Jacobson, *Whiteness of a Different Color: European Immigrants and the Alchemy of Race* (Cambridge, MA and London: Harvard University Press, 1998), 94–95, 103–112, 187–188; Deborah Dash Moore and S. Ilan Troen, eds., "Introduction," in *Divergent Jewish Cultures: Israel and America* (New Haven, CT: Yale University Press, 2001), 20–21; Daniel J. Elazar, "Changing Places, Changing Cultures: Divergent Jewish Political Cultures," in *Divergent Jewish Cultures*, 319–331; Brodkin, *How Jews Became White Folks*, 144–145, 185; and Alisa Solomon, "Balancing Act: *Fiddler*'s Bottle Dance and the Transformation of 'Tradition,'" *TDR* 55, no. 3 (2011): 21–30.

70. Morris, *A Game for Dancers*, 5–8; and Graff, *Stepping Left*, 167. See also Manning, "*Ausdruckstanz* Across the Atlantic," in *Dance Discourses*, eds. Franco and Nordera, 54 (see Preface, n15).

71. Judith Brin Ingber asserts that many scholars "in classic Talmudic fashion, answer questions by asking others." Ingber, "Introduction: Coming into Focus," in *Seeing Israeli and Jewish Dance*, ed. Ingber (Detroit: Wayne State University Press, 2011), 1.

72. Anna Sokolow, quoted in "Talking to *Dance and Dancers*," *Dance and Dancers* (July 1967): 18.

about the ending of *Rooms,* in which the dancers' fates are unclear, "That's the Jew in me. Ask the world a question, and you get no answer."[73] This comment replicates the structure of Sokolow's favorite childhood Yiddish song, *"Fragt die Velt an Alte Kashe"* ["The World Asks an Old Question"], which portrays a cycle of questions unanswered, or questions returned with a question, or questions returned with meaningless rhythmic syllables.[74] Her comment also suggests the notion of "the world" standing in for a god and human bystanders silent in the face of Jewish suffering during the Holocaust and other events. By demanding viewers' engagement to complete the onstage action, Sokolow implicated her spectators in the indictment at hand to spur social change.

Beyond its revolutionary roots, Sokolow's choreography manifested historical markers of Ashkenazi Jewishness in posture, weight, and impetus. Ashkenazi influence was prominent among Jewishness in midcentury American concert dance. This kind of Jewishness encompasses dance that uses Jewish cultural history as a narrative, references based on Jewish spirituality, or biblical stories as themes; dance that teaches through questioning; dances with unresolved endings or accusatory statements open for discussion; dances that use irony, satire, Borscht Belt comedy, or other nuances as part of a work's meaning; and dances for social change through a contemporary interpretation of the Jewish religious tenet of *tikkun olam* [repairing the world], which many American Jews took up as social justice in the twentieth century.[75] Dance historian Rebecca Rossen has demonstrated that the act of dancing is a mode of Jewish identity formation through her term "dancing Jewish," a dynamic identity process dependent on historical contexts through which a person knows Jewish identity by dancing. Rossen argues, "Jewishness is not a matter of essences, but rather a repertory of images, themes, and frames that signify 'Jewish.' "[76] For Sokolow, dancing revolutionary was dancing Jewish. Her dances signified both.

Dance studies modes provide additional ways of identifying Jewishness in Sokolow's movement. Rossen's "dancing Jewish" expands the mid-twentieth-century assertions of dancer Felix Fibich, who defined Jewish dance between opposing tensions that represent "the Jewish soul, which is torn between joy and sadness," and movement that grows "from the guts."[77] Many dancers and critics discussed Sokolow's choreography as coming from the "gut." Beyond the emotion and *kishkes* conviction this phrase references, Sokolow deepened the emotional imperatives of the Graham technique's torso contractions with movement originated from

73. Anna Sokolow, quoted in *Anna Sokolow: Choreographer.*

74. Warren, *Rebellious Spirit,* xiv.

75. Ashkenazi American Jewishness specifically relates to Jewish identity in the United States for Jews of European descent. Jews from the Mediterranean, Middle East, and Africa have intersecting but different embodied traditions.

76. Rossen, *Dancing Jewish,* 3.

77. Felix Fibich, quoted in Judith Brin Ingber, "The Unwitting Gastrol: Touring the Soviet Union, France, the United States, Canada, Israel, South America, Europe, and Back to Poland,"

her abdominal core and prominent spirals through the back. Traceable Ashkenazi movement influences include movement that comes from the *kishkes*, postures that reference Yiddish theater tropes, a particular sensitivity to the hands' surfaces with a sense of yielding weight in the palm, and specific gestures from Jewish rituals.[78] Dance theorist Hannah Schwadron employs choreographic analysis to show how American Jewish women feminist and comedic performers' work challenges normative Jewish representation.[79] The emphasis of *Honest Bodies* on the function of bodies in motion expands Jewish studies corporeal discussions focused on stationary bodies or individual body parts for evidence in a variety of textual representations.[80] This book shows that choreography is the conduit for a historical understanding of Sokolow's social commentary by centering dance performance and women's dancing bodies as the locus for Jewish content.

Gender

For Sokolow, dancing Jewish contained her communist sensibilities along with physical, emotional, and thematic opposing tensions that spoke to a particularly female experience of midcentury American Jewishness. Sokolow's movement choices, thematic material, and critical reception contained a defining American Jewish tension of navigating the space between competing forces. American Jews faced strain between religious observance and secularism, retaining tradition or assimilating, and blending into the American mainstream while retaining elements of difference. Jewish women bore the brunt of this ambivalence. For the women of Sokolow's generation, as American and Jewish studies scholar Riv-Ellen Prell demonstrated, acculturation into US society dictated an embrace of sameness to "displace their fear of being different and their tensions around joining and staying in the middle class" amid the United States' prevailing cult of white womanhood.[81]

in *Seeing Israeli and Jewish Dance*, ed. Ingber (Detroit, MI: Wayne State University Press, 2011), 51; and Felix Fibich, quoted in *The Joyce Mollov Memorial Lecture and Performance*, VHS. Presented by the Continuing Education Program and Center for Jewish Studies at Queens College, Queens College Theater, Flushing, New York, November 4, 1990, JRDD, NYPL.

78. See Ingber, "Introduction," 7–8; and Karen Goodman, *Come Let Us Dance: Two Yiddish Dances, Heritage, Style, and Steps* (2002; Teaneck, NJ: Ergo Media, 2005), DVD.

79. Hannah Schwadron, "White Nose, (Post) Bawdy Bodies, and the Un/dancing Sexy Jewess" (PhD diss., University of California Riverside, 2013).

80. See Eilberg-Schwartz, ed., *People of the Body*; Daniel Boyarin, Daniel Itzkovits, and Ann Pellegrini, eds. *Queer Theory and the Jewish Question* (New York: Columbia University Press, 2003); and Barbara Kirshenblatt-Gimblett, "The Corporeal Turn," *Jewish Quarterly Review* 95, no. 3 (2005): 447–461.

81. Riv-Ellen Prell, *Fighting to Become Americans: Assimilation and the Trouble between Jewish Women and Jewish Men* (Boston: Beacon Press, 1999), 8, 13. See also Barbara Welter, "The Cult of True Womanhood: 1820–1860," *American Quarterly* 18, no. 2 (1966): 151–174.

Sokolow's negotiation of this tension between universality and specificity enabled her work to cross boundaries in its critical reception. Critics' language in reviews engendered Sokolow's mobility among hierarchies based on gendered notions of performative power.

Broad 1930s critical acclaim in the United States afforded Sokolow, as a young, working-class, left-wing female Jewish choreographer, the freedom to move among political and artistic circles that the label "revolutionary" or "modern" would have denied her. American reviewers in the 1930s, discussing Sokolow's dances in publications including the leftist and communist *New Masses*, *Daily Worker*, and *New Theatre*, the mainstream *New York Times* and *Boston Herald*, Louis Horst's dance-specific *Dance Observer*, and the black press' leftist *New York Amsterdam News*, make clear that her dances attracted a wide range of concert dance-goers and suggest that she built her dances more effectively than her contemporaries. This strength came from the way women in her dances dismantled hierarchical systems. Critics alternated between writing about Sokolow's onstage personas as male by referring to Sokolow's characters as "he," subsuming Sokolow into a universalist understanding of maleness as the norm, or their comments evidenced how Sokolow's choreography upended normative representations of and actions by women. Parallel responses across constituencies continued in reviews of her work through the 1960s. These spectatorial interactions included Sokolow's own gender presentation as part of her leftist politics.

Sokolow's challenges to normative gender roles in her choreography demonstrate how individual bodies can shift performance expectations. Her actions controlled the stage space by defining it through her direct interactions with it and with the audience. She positioned her and her dancers' bodies as empowered onstage subjects instead of voyeuristic objects. The way Sokolow took a direct control over the space read as unspecifically gendered (i.e., male) and, more often than not, deflected a sexualized gaze away from her and her dancers' bodies. This differs from Graham's presentation of herself onstage, which became increasingly erotic after her initial Puritan experiments; critics considered Graham's work transcendent but decidedly female and sexualized.[82] Sokolow's gendered presentation in her work shows how she navigated spaces of onstage power by taking on the male control of space. This presentation occurred in her own performances of piercing satire of a (male) politician in *Histrionics* (1933); a homeless teenager in *Case History No.—*, which critics read as male; appropriating men's ritual power by wearing *tefillin* (men's phylacteries) in *Kaddish*, as she led mourning for the Holocaust in a role Jewish tradition forbade women to take up in the 1940s; and in the group works *Strange American Funeral* (1935), in which her dancers became workers in a metal

---

82. Croft, *Dancers as Diplomats*, 105–142; and Mark Franko, *Martha Graham in Love and War: The Life in the Work* (New York: Oxford University Press, 2012).

refinery, and in *Rooms'* nonconforming sexual desires. Even after a chronic back condition cut Sokolow's performing career short in the early 1950s and changed the way she built dances by relying on performers' input, her work retained a sense of gendered agency.[83]

CIRCULATING BODIES

Sokolow choreographed until the 1990s, but for historical and thematic reasons *Honest Bodies* ends in 1967, when her work was most ascendant. She had her first standing company in the United States since her 1930s Dance Unit; leading companies like the Joffrey Ballet, Alvin Ailey American Dance Theater, and Boston Ballet performed her work in their repertories;[84] television and Broadway producers employed her; and the concertgoing public considered her a voice of the counter-cultural rebellion. In 1967 Sokolow experienced acute mental distress during her disastrous gig as the first choreographer of the musical *Hair*, and she slipped into a severe depression.[85] This episode reflected shifting choreographic preferences and a changing Left, and it affected Sokolow's place in the dance and political fields. From her first presentation at the Neighborhood Playhouse in 1931 through becoming a recognized American voice of alienation by 1967, Sokolow's formidable choreography exposed the inner workings of humanity in a way few choreographers did or have done ever since.

My choice to end this book in 1967 is also framed by the Six Day War/1967 Arab–Israeli War in the Middle East, which marked the end of the Israeli social–democratic experiment.[86] The war resulted in the Israeli military occupation and annexation of the Sinai Peninsula, the Gaza Strip, the West Bank, East Jerusalem, and the Golan Heights. Israeli nationalist ideology shifted from the inward-focused socialist Zionism that fostered Sokolow's work to outward-looking concerns about

83. In 1943, Sokolow badly injured her back before a performance and was out of commission for a week. It never fully healed. Anna Sokolow to Rose Levy, (postmark) June 21, 1943, Larry Warren Collection on Anna Sokolow and Lester Horton, MD, LOC.

84. Sokolow staged *Rooms* for the Joffrey and Ailey companies in the 1960s. She made *Opus '65* for Joffrey in 1965. Robert Joffrey to Helen Alkire, March 8, 1978, Sokolow Dance Foundation. In a form letter that he used to solicit choreographers, Ailey listed Sokolow's work as an example of what his company kept in repertory. Alvin Ailey to Herbert Ross, March 3, 1969, and Alvin Ailey to Todd Bolender, April 30, 1969, Box 118, Folder 17, the Alvin Ailey Collection, MD, LOC. The Boston Ballet performed Sokolow's repertory in the 1950s–1970s. Doris Hering (dance critic), in discussion with the author, August 29, 2008, New York City.

85. Warren, *Rebellious Spirit*, 237–239; Jim May (Sokolow Theatre/Dance Ensemble Artistic Director), in discussion with the author, October 14, 2009, New York City; Ze'eva Cohen (dancer, choreographer; Lyric Theatre and Anna Sokolow Dance Company member) in discussion with the author, October 11, 2009, New York City.

86. See Ari Shavit, *My Promised Land: The Triumph and Tragedy of Israel* (New York: Spiegel and Grau, 2015), 397–406.

Israeli borders. As Israel studies historian Nina Spiegel has shown, Israeli culture contained inherent tensions since European Jews settled in Palestine in the late nineteenth century.[87] The cultural complications that the wars after 1967 introduced, in which the Israeli government was the aggressor and retaliator, changed the social milieu. Given this timeline, I locate the revolutionary modernism in Sokolow's work from 1931 to 1967.

Honest Bodies examines dances from the early 1930s to the late 1960s to illustrate how they reflect political and identity discourses by locating Sokolow within a global terrain. World War II's seismic shifts reverberate through all the chapters. I organized the book thematically, instead of chronologically, according to the dance premiere dates, to allow for contrapuntal play between thematic groupings of Jewishness, communism, modernism, and gender. This thematic organization within an overall chronological progression aligns Sokolow's choreographic actions, and these categories, with historical succession. Like a kaleidoscope, each chapter locks into focus dances that embody its thematic grouping. Table 0.1 includes a list of these dances by premiere date for chronological reference. Although the book focuses on dances that premiered from 1933 to 1967, I consider a wide view of Sokolow's career. Because of the study's scope, the book does not include analysis of Sokolow's theater work, but references it as context for her choreography, artistic process, and political implications. The book contains the following chapters.

Chapter 1 argues that Sokolow's 1930s proletarian and anti-fascist choreographies spoke to an increasingly vibrant conversation through predominantly Jewish channels of the transnational Left by means of shared ideologies of egalitarianism and antiracism as they made space for women in these conversations. The 1930s was Sokolow's most fruitful decade, and the chapter discusses a catalog of her work, including: *Histrionics* (1933); *Speaker* (1935); *Four Little Salon Pieces* (1936); *Strange American Funeral* (1935); *Case History No.—* (1937); *Excerpts from a War Poem* (*F. T. Marinetti*) (1937); *Façade—Exposizione Italiana* (1937); *Slaughter of the Innocents* (1937); "Filibuster" from *The Bourbons Got the Blues* (1938); *Dance of All Nations* (1938); and *Sing for Your Supper* (1939). These dances match the succession of American Communism throughout the 1930s, from the initial proletarian statements to aligning with the Popular Front against Fascism, from Jewish–Black alliances across the American Left, and leftist cries against the American government as it began to prosecute communist-affiliated activities.

Chapter 2 follows the alignment of Sokolow's choreography with postrevolutionary Mexican political values within transnational communist and Jewish discourses during her early years in Mexico City. First, the chapter engages how *The Exile* (1939), Sokolow's indictment of the Third Reich's treatment of Jews, reflected the precarious position of Holocaust refugees in Mexico. It explains how

---

87. Spiegel, *Embodying Hebrew Culture*, 1–20 (see Preface, n9).

Table 0.1. CHRONOLOGICAL LIST OF SOKOLOW'S
DANCES BY PREMIERE DATE DISCUSSED
IN THIS BOOK

Title of Dance	Premiere
Histrionics	1933
Speaker	1935
Strange American Funeral	1935
Four Little Salon Pieces	1936
Case History No.—	1937
Excerpts from a War Poem (F. T. Marinetti)	1937
Façade—Exposizione Italiana	1937
Slaughter of the Innocents	1937
"Filibuster" from The Bourbons Got the Blues	1938
Dance of All Nations, Lenin Memorial Meeting	1938
Sing for Your Supper	1939
The Exile (A Dance Poem)	1939
Don Lindo de Almería	1940
El renacuajo paseador [The Fable of the Wandering Frog]	1940
Lament for the Death of a Bullfighter	1941
Kaddish	1945
Mexican Retablo	1946
Lyric Suite	1953
Rooms	1954
Bullfight	1955
Session for Six	1958
Opus '58	1958
Opus Jazz 1958	1958
Session for Eight	1959
Opus '60	1960
Dreams	1961
Opus '62	1962
Opus '63	1963
Forms	1964
Odes	1964
Opus '65	1965
Time+	1966
Hair: The American Tribal Love-Rock Musical	1967
Los Conversos [The Converts]	1981

Sokolow's dance highlighted contemporary persecution of Jews within a longer history of continuous Jewish exile that connected Europe, North America, and South America. Second, the chapter argues that Mexican modernism's reliance on indigeneity fed Sokolow's revolutionary modernism in the choreography she made there with the collaborative company La Paloma Azul [The Blue Dove], including *Don Lindo de Almería* (1940) and *El renacuajo paseador* [*The Fable of the Wandering Frog*] (1940).

Chapter 3 argues that US critical reactions to Sokolow's Mexican works *Wandering Frog* and *Lament for the Death of a Bullfighter* (1941) displayed differences between Mexican and American modernism. Critics read the dances as ethnic instead of revolutionary within an anticommunist American critical discourse of ethnic and ethnologic dance. The resonance of Sokolow's choreography among the 1930s transnational Left fell flat in the wartime aftermath of American demonization of Communism and a shift in US dance coverage from leftist to more mainstream newspapers and magazines. This spectatorial mismatch ended in a loss of nuance in the public readings of her dances, but created space for dances like *Kaddish* (1945) to be transgressive while appearing universal. *Kaddish* and *Mexican Retablo* (1946) display Sokolow's feminist subversion of ritual in reaction to the Holocaust. They account for a human tragedy she railed against and publicly mourned in its aftermath.

Chapter 4 shows how Sokolow's early Cold War choreography veiled social(ist) challenges to the status quo under the façade of American modernism. *Lyric Suite* (1953) laid bare sexual discontent in the guise of universal abstraction; *Rooms* (1954) portrayed gay people's and Jews' experiences among those of society's untouchables in tenement houses; and the *Opus* series (1958–1965) cemented the political significance of the Old Left meeting the New Left through ironic uses of compositional elements drawn from jazz, as Africanist elements like these signaled Americanness, even during the continued subjugation of the African American community at the onset of the Civil Rights Movement. Sokolow's assimilation into concert dance whiteness through these works' critical reception, I argue, reflected the American Jewish community's postwar assimilation from racially marked to Caucasian. Sokolow's work evidences the role of leftist Jews in crafting definitive images of midcentury Americana as they publicly rewrote their 1930s leftist actions into normative postwar American activities during the Second Red Scare.

Focusing on Sokolow's work in Israel, Chapter 5 highlights tensions between American Jewishness and Israeliness through critical response to her dances *Dreams* (1961), *Opus '63* (1963), *Forms* (1964), and *Odes* (1964). I introduce the term "*sabra* physicality" to describe the performative qualities of defiant vulnerability that dancers in Sokolow's Israeli company Lyric Theatre introduced into her oeuvre. With financial support from the American Fund for Israeli Institutions (America–Israel Cultural Foundation), Sokolow belonged to North American influences building Israeli art and cultural institutions while postwar alliances formed between the United States and Israeli governments. Like Chapter 2, Chapter 5 shows Sokolow's role in disseminating American modern dance through the bodies of her students abroad. The ways students performed Graham's technique and Sokolow's choreography changed American modernism. Photographs of Sokolow's technique classes in New York, Mexico City, and Tel Aviv appear interchangeable as dancers fit their bodies into Graham's seated, angled fourth position of the legs, or hollow out their abdomens into visceral torso contractions.[88] In a reversal of what Srinivasan accounts for as the "kinesthetic legacy that Indian dancers left on white bourgeois women, such as [Ruth] St. Denis,"[89] Sokolow's kinesthetic imprints circulated American cultural values through training Mexican and Israeli dancers' bodies into American modern dance physicality.

The Epilogue poses questions mediating the politics of dances' residue.

Honest Bodies reinforces how the intertextuality of Sokolow's dances makes for political resonances beyond their identity markers. A cyclical, instead of linear, understanding of time and memory within Jewish culture and religious texts supports how meaning emerges in Sokolow's dances.[90] By peeling back the layers of *The Exile* to reveal the Book of Isaiah within a Holocaust-induced cry to rise up, *The Wandering Frog* exposing the workings of Colombian poet Rafael Pombo within Mexican modernism, or the quintessentially alienating *Rooms* unveiling queer subjectivities, and seeing how proletarian dances like *Strange American Funeral* or anti-racist revue dances like "Filibuster" aligned with the timbre of the era's political cartoons, it becomes evident how Sokolow's sophisticated artistic–political work operated in nuanced ways that engaged a broad audience spectrum. Certainly, the majority of Sokolow's audience members did not catch all the ways in which her dances made meaning. But for those witnesses for whom her work fully resonated, and for us looking in on her work with historical distance, the effectiveness of her dances comes chillingly into focus. Sokolow was prophetic in the sense of biblical Hebrew prophets: She observed, commented on, and made poignant meaning of current events.[91] Decades before critic Clive Barnes bestowed on Sokolow the moniker "prophet of doom,"[92] Sokolow's intertextual dances grounded in cultural references posed questions so that her audience members might go out to repair the world's ills.

Amid early twenty-first-century surges in nativist movements, terrorizing extremism, and fear-mongering born from economic fears and racial discrimination that become virulent anti-intellectualism and righteous violence, Sokolow's story

---

88. For photographs of Sokolow's classes, see Walter Sorell, "We Work Toward Freedom," *Dance Magazine* (January 1964): 53; Warren, *Rebellious Spirit*, plate 5; Instituto Nacional de Bellas Artes/Secretaría de Educacion Pública, *50 Años de Danza en el Palacio de Bellas Artes* (México: Instituto Nacional de Bellas Artes, 1986), 78, 148; and Chapter 5, Figures 5.2 and 5.3.

89. Srinivasan, *Sweating Saris*, 72.

90. See Yosef Hayim Yerushalmi, *Zakhor: Jewish History and Jewish Memory* (Seattle: University of Washington Press, 1982), 1–12; Yael Samuel, "Meredith Monk: Between Time and Timelessness in *Book of Days*," *Nashim: A Journal of Jewish Women's Studies & Gender Issues* 14 (2007): 9–29; and Lynn Kaye, "Fixity and Time in Talmudic Law and Legal Language," *Journal of Jewish Thought and Philosophy* 23, no. 2 (2015): 127–160.

91. I thank Lynn Kaye for this articulation.

92. Clive Barnes, "Dance: Anna Sokolow, Poet of Chaos," *New York Times*, November 14, 1968, 54.

snaps into focus with parallels to contemporary politics. The importance of her relationship to communist ideals pales in comparison with what she accomplished with these principles. She moved masses of people at a moment when it was crucial to do so. Her leading voice as a leftist, a woman, and a Jew challenged hegemonic power structures. Her inextricably linked work, identity, and political actions surface a significant transnational US historical moment with multiple points of articulation for others in similar circumstances across this swath of history.

CHAPTER 1
Dances of All Nations

Choreographing Communism

Aphotograph of Anna Sokolow's Dance Unit puts the viewer in the middle of the action (Figure 1.1). Some dancers are tangled in a heap on the floor, some try to get up, and others menacingly encircle the fallen and poise to go in for the kill. Sokolow's dances, like this one, portrayed masses rising up against capitalist power structures or dangerous workings of totalitarian regimes. Sokolow's 1930s New York concerts enacted revolutionary ideology through an American communist agenda of workers' rights, egalitarianism, racial equality, and anti-fascism. Her dances brought physicality into dialogue with political conversations in print and at rallies through abstracted, instead of mimetic, movements. The hybridity of communism, Jewishness, and challenges to a gendered status quo in her dances stemmed from American Jewish proletarianism that existed alongside aesthetic modernism from the fledgling American modern dance and revolutionary dance scenes, and manifested transnational leftist values.

This chapter traces how the revolutionary modernism in Sokolow's choreography connected her to communist and Jewish artistic political circles in Europe, Mexico, and the Soviet Union. Sokolow's choreographies aligned with the American Popular Front's shifting ideological position during the 1930s from proletarianism to anti-fascism.[1] Her work defined American dance in terms of these

---

1. The Popular Front was not affiliated with the American Communist Party, but many people associated with it were Communists or fellow travelers, and the American Communist Party adapted Popular Front ideology in 1935. The Popular Front's accompanying cultural apparatus, which Michael Denning labels the Cultural Front, including the arts, entertainment, literature, and advertising, brought the arts to the political front lines as it was the "laboring of American culture." Denning, *The Cultural Front*, xvi–xviii, 50 (see Introduction, n54). See also Lynn Garafola, "Writing on the Left: The Remarkable Career of Edna Ocko," *Dance Research Journal* 34, no. 1 (2002): 56; Lynne Conner, "'What the Modern Dance Should Be': Socialist Agendas

Figure 1.1: Anna Sokolow's Dance Unit in performance, late 1930s. Photographer unknown. Larry Warren Collection on Anna Sokolow and Lester Horton, Box 1, Music Division, Library of Congress, Washington, DC.

values. I argue that Sokolow's dances expanded the political statements women could make regarding class and race in a 1930s communist milieu that, through its egalitarian claims, usurped women into an oft-assumed male-gendered whole. Sokolow's onstage embodiment of Jewishness and female-gendered women's power through satire subverted this patriarchy. I build from Susan Foster's assertion about kinesthetic empathy's spectatorial properties that "the viewer's rapport is shaped by common and prevailing senses of the body and of subjectivity in a given social moment as well as by the unique circumstances of watching a particular dance,"[2] to show how Sokolow's work manifested the US Depression-era social environment and connected audiences to concerns among the international Left. *New Masses* dance critic Owen Burke insisted that dancers and audience members had a joint social responsibility,[3] and the revolutionary spectatorship in which Sokolow's audiences engaged emotionally provided a catalyst for social action.

in the Modern Dance, 1931–1938," in *Crucibles of Crisis: Performing Social Change*, ed. Janelle Reinelt (Ann Arbor: The University of Michigan Press, 1996), 238–240; Franko, *Dancing Modernism/Performing Politics*, 27 (see Introduction, n8); and Phillips Geduld, "Performing Communism," 56 (see Introduction, n7).

2. Susan Leigh Foster, *Choreographing Empathy: Kinesthesia in Performance* (London and New York: Routledge, 2011), 2.

3. Owen Burke, "The Dance," *New Masses*, April 6, 1937, 29, BICLM.

Sokolow's popularity exemplifies how her work resonated with audiences' aesthetic values shaped by their social environment. She was a highly acclaimed soloist in the Martha Graham Dance Company from 1930 to 1939 and concurrently presented choreography with her own left-oriented Theatre Union Dance Group starting in 1933. Sokolow formed this group under the auspices of the Theatre Union, which, also established in 1933, answered workers' desires to have aesthetically accessible theatrical performances that reflected their concerns.[4] Sokolow's artistic goals aligned with this sentiment, and her group's first performances were for workers' unions.[5] She filled her group with dancers from Graham's company and school,[6] with the purposes, as she stated in press materials, of "perform[ing] revolutionary dances at all labor organizations," "producing revolutionary dances for performance," and "[raising] the standard of proletarian dancing."[7] In 1935 Sokolow changed the group's name to Dance Unit. Its first Broadway performance was in 1937 at the Guild Theatre on West 52nd Street under the auspices of the Communist organ *New Masses*,[8] which Alex North's brother Joseph North edited and which financed Sokolow's performances.[9] Sokolow widened her performance venues to include workers' halls, the Jewish cultural institution and modern dance venue of the 92nd Street YM/YWHA in the Upper East Side's middle- and upper-class Jewish neighborhood,[10] and Broadway houses.

As Sokolow's influence grew, she reached a progressive audience that included leftists and various politically affiliated modern dance attendees by employing concrete thematic movements that blended abstraction with mimesis into clear metaphors of tangible ideological concepts. Her appearances in centrally located Broadway theaters engendered a broader audience than her concerts in Columbus Circle's workers' theaters or at the 92nd Street Y.[11] Her dances' recognizably communist themes transformed immigrant Jewish traditions into a secular medium for the American workers' cause. By invoking the contemporary Jewish tenet of repairing the world through her engagement in secular social action, Sokolow performed leftist cultural Judaism allied with other minorities who challenged social

4. Rose Morrison, "Review of Broadway Stage," *New Voices* (October 1938): 6, Microforms, NYPL.

5. Cynthia Lyle, *Dancers on Dancing* (New York: Sterling, 1979), 141.

6. Warren, *Rebellious Spirit*, 44 (see Preface, n2).

7. Program Notes, *Workers Dance League Presents for Benefit of "Daily Worker" Recital— Leading Revolutionary Dance Groups*, January 7, 1934, Workers Dance League Programs, JRDD, NYPL; *New Dance: Special Recital Issue* (January 1935): 6, Workers Dance League Programs, JRDD, NYPL; and *Workers Dance League Bulletin—Festival Issue, Souvenir Program*, June 1934, Box 69, Folder 25, Sophia Delza Papers, JRDD, NYPL.

8. Program, *Dance Concert Debut by Anna Sokolow and Dance Unit*, Guild Theatre, November 14, 1937, Martha Hill Papers, Juilliard.

9. Warren, *Rebellious Spirit*, 38.

10. See Jackson, *Converging Movements* (see Introduction, n58), for the role of modern dance at the 92nd Street Y and the role of the 92nd Street Y in the development and patronage of modern dance in the twentieth century.

11. See Jackson, *Converging Movements*, 10, 72–73.

injustices.[12] Her dances easily fit among widely embraced ideologies of proletarian-ism and anti-fascism. Burke wrote in 1937, "She is still a dancer young in years, but her dances are among the most significant, mature, sensitive, and profound. . . .One doesn't any longer expect student work from Sokolow—and one doesn't get it."[13] Sokolow met the onstage challenge for revolutionary choreographers to present dances that answered concert dance aesthetic demands and remained "legible" to workers' audiences in union halls.[14] Had Sokolow's content appeared too bourgeois or not fully proletarian, leftists would have rejected her.[15] Conversely, if her work did not subscribe to modernist compositional norms, the then-emerging mod-ern dance establishment would have ignored her. Sokolow's negotiations among these interests garnered her widespread recognition in the communist havens of New York, Moscow, and Mexico City.

The era's dance critics played an important role in registering the legibility of Sokolow's work across constituencies and mediating public dialogue about modern and revolutionary dance. Two of the most influential voices in the 1930s discussion defining concert dance were John Martin and Edna Ocko. Martin, who was largely responsible for Graham's artistic prominence, valued professional technical train-ing and formalist craft, and identified modern dance through the lenses of abstrac-tion and universalism. A well-known critic of left-wing ideology, Martin refused to address political content in the revolutionary dances he reviewed in *The New York Times*.[16] Ocko, one of the era's definitive dance critics and a champion of the rev-olutionary dance movement, defined concert dance professionalism as a marriage of technical ability, craft, and social message.[17] Critics in the dance-focused *Dance Magazine*, *The American Dancer*, and *Dance Observer* addressed issues defining mod-ern and revolutionary dance along similar lines. Combined critical support enabled Sokolow to reach multiple representational spheres. The most detailed description of revolutionary dance, especially of Sokolow's choreography, comes from the left-ist press. This attention exemplifies the importance of concert dance, and Sokolow's work, to the revolutionary cause.[18]

12. See Wenger, *New York Jews and the Great Depression*, 110 (see Introduction, n49) for the role of *tikkun olam* in Depression-era protests by Communists in Jewish neighborhoods.

13. Owen Burke, "The Dance: Bennington, Vermont," *New Masses*, August 31, 1937, 29, BICLM.

14. Manning, *Modern Dance, Negro Dance*, 63 (see Preface, n14).

15. The 1930s leftist press categorized dancemakers by their ideological and choreographic affiliations, between what leftist critics labeled "bourgeois" and revolutionary dancers. "Bourgeois" choreographers included Graham, Humphrey, Weidman, and Holm, who devel-oped codified techniques and contended that an artist could transcend time and place through the universality of formalist art. Graff, *Stepping Left*, 10 (see Preface, n2).

16. See Edna Ocko, "The Dance Congress," *New Theatre* (July 1936): 23.

17. She also wrote under the pseudonyms Edna Poe, Marion Sellars, Elizabeth Skrip, Eve Stebbins, and Frances Steuben in leftist publications including *New Theatre* and *New Masses* as well as in mainstream papers. Garafola, "Writing on the Left," 56.

18. Although the *Freiheit, Jewish Daily Bulletin*, and *Jewish People's Voice* advertised the Yiddish Theater, Henry Street performances, and touring companies such as the Ballets Jooss, they

Sokolow's Graham training was her vehicle for intervention in the revolutionary movement. She believed that the codified dance vocabularies promulgated by Martha Graham, Doris Humphrey, Charles Weidman, and Hanya Holm (the "Big Four") provided useful technical bases for revolutionary dance. In her December 1, 1936 lecture, "The Revolutionary Dance," in John Martin's lecture–demonstration series at the New School for Social Research, Sokolow aligned the revolutionary dance movement with the working class and noted that "revolutionary dance is concerned not so much with building a new system [of dance technique] as with making use of the excellent equipment provided in systems now being taught."[19] Similar to many leftist dancers, Sokolow viewed Graham's technique as a means to an end.[20] She chose Graham-trained dancers for her Dance Unit "so that," Sokolow told *American Dancer* writer Patricia Shirley Allen, "they speak the same dance language."[21] Some revolutionary dancers' agitation–propaganda work displayed limited technical training, but many left-wing modern dancers like Sokolow built their proletarian dances with defined technical vocabularies.[22] Her work initially looked too much like Big Four modern dance for *Dance Observer* critic Henry Gilfond to group her with her Workers Dance League (WDL) colleagues. In 1934 he wrote that Sokolow's "work can hardly be termed 'red'" because her choreography was less mimetic than the other WDL compositions on the concert, so presumably contained more "art" and less propaganda.[23] Prior to the American Communist Party's adoption of the Soviet edict of socialist realism that resulted in revolutionary dancers using "bourgeois" compositional tools for their revolutionary choreographic methodologies,[24] it was an insult to be termed "red" in the press because the label denoted a lack of technical training.[25] Sokolow used her proletarian allegiances in conjunction with her Graham training by grounding her dances in conceptions of "the people."[26] Later in her career Sokolow deviated from Graham's aesthetic, but in 1938 Sokolow "made it very clear that she does not depart technically from the Martha Graham school. She considers that she was trained in this method, that it is her instrument. It is in the *application* of technique that she tries to express

carried few dance reviews, and scarce of Sokolow—though assimilating Jewish progressives interested in concert dance surely read English-language Communist papers like the *New Masses* and *Daily Worker* that regularly covered her work.

19. Anna Sokolow, quoted in Marjorie Church, "The Dance in the Social Scene," 27 (see Introduction, n56).

20. See Prickett, "Dance and the Workers' Struggle," 55 (see Preface, n7).

21. Anna Sokolow, quoted in Allen, "Young Modern," 13 (see Introduction, n34).

22. Stacey Prickett, "'The People': Issues of Identity within the Revolutionary Dance," in *Of, By, and For the People: Dancing on the Left in the 1930s*, 15 (see Introduction, n8).

23. Henry Gilfond, "Workers' Dance League, Civil Repertory Theater, November 25th, 1934," *The Dance Observer* (December 1934): 89.

24. Graff, *Stepping Left*, 9–10.

25. Ocko, "The Dance Congress," 23.

26. See Owen Burke, "Anna Sokolow and Other Dancers," *New Masses*, December 7, 1937, 28, BICLM, and Anna Sokolow, interview by Margaret Lloyd, "Dance Is for People, Part II," no source, May 16, 1942, Anna Sokolow Clippings, JRDD, NYPL.

originality [emphasis added]."[27] As a revolutionary, Sokolow used Graham's technical scaffolding to fight for humanity in specific contexts by using contemporary subjects instead of following Graham's reliance on the pathos of humanity through Eurocentrist archetypes.[28]

In the field of revolutionary dance, in which groups of bodies made collective proletarian statements through mass dancing, Sokolow instead told individual stories that hit with a stronger impact. She employed modern dance compositional tools, especially those of Humphrey and Holm, in choreographing groups made up of individuals: Margery Dana noted in the *Daily Worker* in 1937 that Sokolow "thinks both solo and group dancing are important, and by group dancing she does not mean just mass dancing, but the expression of individuals in a group."[29] Sokolow's haunting, urgent work with relatable characters had a foretelling quality. Her nonlinear, open-ended storytelling, her Graham training, and her revolutionary allegiances earned her notable success across US critical divides and made her dances compelling to a range of audience members. These qualities highlighted Sokolow among her leftist US contemporaries and excited proletarian audiences in Mexico City, which boasted socialist circles that US leftists closely followed.[30] Sokolow's dances featured proletarianism and anti-fascism that resonated internationally as they manifested American Jewish leftist cultural tropes of social action through both sincere and parodic narratives.

I begin this chapter with the parodic solos *Histrionics* (1933), *Speaker* (1935), and *Four Little Salon Pieces* (1936) to show how Ashkenazi Jewish women's stage performances undergirded Sokolow's satire. The chapter continues with a collection of Sokolow's projects to show how her choreography reflected the changing faces of the American Left between 1933 and 1939, and how these choreographies connected Sokolow's audience members to the international Left. These dances include the proletarian works *Strange American Funeral* (1935) and *Case History No.—* (1937); the anti-fascist dances *Excerpts from a War Poem (F. T. Marinetti)* (1937, also known as *War is Beautiful*), *Façade—Exposizione Italiana* (1937) and *Slaughter of the Innocents* (1937); the 1938 Lenin Memorial Meeting pageant *Dance of All Nations*; the antiracist Negro Cultural Committee revue *The Bourbons Got the Blues* (1938); and the Federal Theater Project revue *Sing for Your Supper* (1939).

27. Allen, "Young Modern," 13.
28. See Heisey, "Anna Sokolow—Interview," 77 (see Introduction, n37).
29. Dana, "Dancing to the Tune of the Times," 7 (see Introduction, n20).
30. Between 1934 and 1937, *New Masses* ran articles about Mexican muralist art and Mexican working-class politics. These include David Alfaro Siqueiros, "Rivera's Counter-Revolutionary Road," May 29, 1934, 16–19; Charles Wedger, "Toward the Mexican Crisis: Millions of Peons— Millionaire Rulers—An Explosion Preparing," September 3, 1935, 11–14; Stephen Alexander, "Art: Orozco's Lithographs," November 19, 1936, 29; Vincente Lombardo Toledano, "Greeting from Mexico," May 5, 1936, 14; Toledano, "Trotsky in Mexico," February 2, 1937, 6–7; and Joseph Freeman, "Trotsky in Coyoacan," March 23, 1937, 14–16. All BICLM.

For Sokolow, satire was a particularly Ashkenazi Jewish narrative device th
cyclical critique and feminist refusals of gendered hierarchies.[31] Crowned
queen of satire" by *Daily Worker* critic Louise Mitchell,[32] Sokolow's acuity al
with Jewish women's humor and Yiddish theater traditions in which performers portray a tension between two emotions at the same time, as their words or eyes say one
thing and their body postures reveal another. By intertwining humor and political
values in her work, Sokolow built her revolutionary platform with Jewish signifiers.
Revolutionary dance offered a dual viewing experience and acculturation process for
Jewish dancers and proletarian audiences of Sokolow's generation. After the 1910s,
Jewish performers did not engage in specific tropes that accentuated their Jewish
bodies, like late nineteenth-century to early twentieth-century vaudeville performers did, overemphasizing Jewish body stereotypes through costuming and makeup.
Instead, early to mid-twentieth-century performers expressed their Jewishness in
implicit ways,[33] Americanizing their names or performing for social change. For
Jewish musical comedienne Fanny Brice, for example, who was born Fania Borach
on the Lower East Side and grew up in New Jersey, Jewish expression manifested
in an overperformance of Yiddishness in body postures—resting the weight on
the back leg and slouching while shrugging the shoulders, palms up, and opening
the eyes wide with feigned innocence, as if to give the Yiddish expression "*Nu?*"—
accompanied by an overpronounced Yiddish accent.[34] In considering American
Jewish women entertainers Brice, Sophie Tucker, Joan Rivers, Bette Midler, and
Barbra Streisand as social reformers, historian June Sochen argues that these femi-
nists' performances root them in Jewish tradition: "Indeed, these women humorist/
performers juxtapose three powerful themes that pervade Jewish culture: a strong
interest in social justice, self-deprecatory humor, and a satiric tongue."[35] Through
embodying stereotypical behavior, Brice aligned herself with audiences who identified with and laughed self-deprecatingly at her Yiddishisms; these actions distinguished her as American, separate from the immigrant experience.[36] Sokolow's satire
similarly rehearsed this assimilation through parody as a vehicle for social change.

31. See Schwadron, "Un/dancing Sexy Jewess," 163–164 (see Introduction, n79).

32. Louise Mitchell, "New Dance Unit Is Tops," *Daily Worker*, March 3, 1937, n.p., Anna
Sokolow Clippings, JRDD, NYPL.

33. Harley Erdman, *Staging the Jew: The Performance of American Ethnicity, 1860–1920* (New
Brunswick: Rutgers University Press, 1997), 159.

34. Erdman, *Staging the Jew*, 158; and Franko, *Work of Dance*, 161. Leo Rosten explained
nu: "*Nu* is the verbal equivalent of a sigh, a frown, a grin, a grunt, a sneer. It is an expression of
amusement or recognition or uncertainty or disapproval. It can be used fondly, acidly, tritely,
belligerently. . . . It can convey pride, deliver scorn, demand response." Rosten, *The Joys of
Yiddish* (New York: Pocket Books, 1968), 271–272.

35. June Sochen, "From Sophie Tucker to Barbra Streisand: Jewish Women Entertainers as
Reformers," in *Talking Back: Images of Jewish Women in American Popular Culture*, ed. Joyce
Antler (Hanover: Brandeis University Press, 1998), 71.

36. See Sochen, "Sophie Tucker to Barbara Streisand," 71 and Erdman, *Staging the Jew*, 158.

By carrying the work of performers like Brice onto the concert stage, Sokolow's satire connected revolutionary dance to Jewish tradition. Sokolow lampooned social conventions and public figures in funny parodies and distressing scenarios that read clearly at home and abroad. In Moscow, one critic gave Sokolow's 1934 concert a lukewarm reception because her American citizenship denoted a connection to capitalism, her dance showed no connection to Russian classical ballet conventions, and her calls to revolution fell flat. Yet this critic embraced her satirical dances: "The artist better unmasks (let us remember her parodies) than affirms."[37] In New York in 1934, Edna Ocko yoked satire and social action when she called for satire as a "trenchant weapon" in the class struggle, but warned of ineffective satire's danger of reproducing, instead of indicting, bourgeois society.[38] Sokolow hit her mark. Ocko welcomed Sokolow's caustic characterizations of politicians and the bourgeoisie in revolutionary dance, and the more mainstream Henry Gilfond listed Sokolow's burlesque capabilities as something that distinguished her among other choreographers.[39] Writing in the Workers Dance League monthly publication *New Dance*, Simon Hall celebrated Sokolow's humor for offering a break from the more "brooding" dances on a program about social injustices and elevating the folk (such as Sophie Maslow's *Themes from a Slavic People*). He ventured, "When revolutionary dancers become fully conscious of the power latent in humor, satire, and burlesque what weapons will be forged!"[40] Humor made Sokolow's social statements relatable, even palatable, to audiences who wanted to hear them and for audiences who needed convincing. As Norma Roland noted in *New Theatre* in 1936, Sokolow's wit was "a surer way to the hearts and minds of people than many another."[41] The language in these reviews acculturated Sokolow's Jewish satire into a widely legible American social–art product.

Critics excitedly discussed how funny the solos *Histrionics, Speaker*, and *Four Little Salon Pieces* were without giving a clear picture of what they looked like. *Histrionics* dismantled Graham's own choreographic pathos to undermine the seriousness of Broadway modern dance. Critics' reviews implied that nothing escaped Sokolow's scrutiny; she brought, according to Ocko, a "penetrating sense of the ridiculous" to bear.[42] Hall reported with glee, "What cutting humor! And despite its form of uproarious burlesque, what pathos *Histrionics* contains! [. . .] How expertly she cut to the heart of both the pathos and rottenness in the Broad-way [*sic*] dance

37. V. E. G., "Anna Sokolow," *Sovetskoe Iskusstvo* [*Soviet Art*], July 17, 1934, n.p., Larry Warren Collection on Anna Sokolow and Lester Horton, MD, LOC, trans. Ali Potvin.

38. Edna Ocko, "The Dance," *New Masses*, December 4, 1934, 30, BICLM.

39. Edna Ocko, "The Dance," *New Masses*, March 5, 1935, 27, BICLM; and Henry Gilfond, "Anna Sokolow and Dance Unit, Theresa Kaufmann Theatre, Sun. Eve., April 5, 1936," *Dance Observer* (May 1936): n.p., Anna Sokolow Clippings, JRDD, NYPL.

40. Simon Hall, "The Solo Recital," in *New Dance: Special Recital Issue*, January 1935, 4, Workers Dance League Programs, JRDD, NYPL.

41. Norma Roland, "Dance Reviews," *New Theatre* (May 1936): 30.

42. Ocko, "The Dance," *New Masses*, March 5, 1935, 27.

arena. How we laughed at the sordid sorry tale she told."[43] Sokolow's biographer Larry Warren's description that Sokolow "portrayed a Shakespearean actor, in Hamlet-style garb, making a mockery of overstated and insincere performance in the commercial theater" reinforces Sokolow's charade of theatrical establishment conventions.[44] A tirade by Ballets Russes choreographer Michel Fokine in *Dance Magazine* following a 1931 New School lecture–demonstration of Graham's work reads like fodder for such satire: "The arms would either hang limply or be raised with elbows turned outward. . . . The fists were clenched, and the movements of the body and head were jerky and abrupt. This seems to be a cult not only of sadness but of ill humor, crossness."[45] From this description one can imagine how Sokolow's exaggerated movements twisted Graham's oeuvre into parody.

In *Speaker* and *Four Little Salon Pieces*, Sokolow mocked elite society members through disarming caricatures. Capitalizing on exaggerated elocution gestures, *Speaker* was a send-up of extreme politicians who fancied their own importance. In this portrait Norma Roland saw a "sincere, radical orator," and Gilfond, a "demagogic stump politician."[46] Figure 1.2 shows how Sokolow punctuated hyperbolic gestures with powerful turns or weighted full-body balances, and how she slinked slyly backward, extending a hand as if to retract it quickly and trick the person who reached for it. Her piercing glare confirms a distrustworthiness that, like Brice's feigned innocence with upturned palms and shrugged shoulders, portrays a dichotomy between the body presenting one reality and the eyes revealing another. Sokolow's focus on extremists and corrupt politicians called out members of the ruling class. In an era of social and economic strife such soapboxers seemed insignificant but posed a threat if they succeeded in moving the masses. Sokolow must have distressed her audience with the gravitas of her portrayal, for critic Louise Mitchell reported in the *Daily Worker* that the dance "struck hard and fast like a trip hammer."[47] Although the politician Sokolow portrayed was powerless, her satire showed the serious implications of such a demagogue.

Similarly, in her stinging parody of upper-class women's mannerisms in *Four Little Salon Pieces* (Figure 1.3), Sokolow showed how remaining blind to society's problems by cocooning oneself in a parlor was as damaging as grandstanding for extremist views. Donning a chiffon dress and hair ribbon, Sokolow, with what Roland highlighted as her "distinctive poker-face humor," made fun of "debutante" mannerisms and what Martin identified as "social affectation."[48] Sokolow may have flitted around the stage, mocking upper-class women's expected comportment. As

43. Hall, "The Solo Recital," 5.

44. Warren, *Rebellious Spirit*, 63.

45. Michel Fokine, "A Sad Art," *The Dance Magazine* (May 1931): 29.

46. Roland, "Dance Reviews" (May 1936): 30; and Gilfond, "Anna Sokolow and Dance Unit" (May 1936).

47. Mitchell, "New Dance Unit Is Tops."

48. Roland, "Dance Reviews" (May 1936): 30; and John Martin, "Dance Debut Here by Anna Sokolow," *New York Times*, November 15, 1937, n.p., Anna Sokolow Clippings, JRDD, NYPL.

Figure 1.2: Anna Sokolow in *Speaker*. Left: Photograph by Ralph Samuels, 1936. Samuels photo courtesy of Sokolow Dance Foundation. Right: No photographer credited, *Dance Observer* cover, December 1936.

with the stump politician, the *Salon* woman's gestures and posture denoted her characterization. By assuming characters that were likely not Jewish in *Speaker* and *Salon*, Sokolow called attention to her own Jewish (communist, working-class) body. A chilling truth undergirded *Salon*'s irony: If women spent time upholding frivolous social norms rather than challenging threats to the nation's class system, the real-world demagogues could prevail.

DANCING FOR JUSTICE IN *STRANGE AMERICAN FUNERAL* AND *CASE HISTORY NO.—*

Although Sokolow's comedic sarcasm buttressed her work, some of her dances, like *Strange American Funeral* (1935) and *Case History No.—* (1937), relied on sincere and personally resonant portrayals of societal ills to fulfill their social justice imperatives. Sokolow's Graham lineage complicated her representation in these dances by aligning her with whiteness. The physical appearance of a modern dance–trained body enabled working-class Jewish dancers like Sokolow to appear visually American (white) instead of off-white,[49] and Sokolow's work with Graham

49. Rebecca Rossen, "Hasidic Drag: Jewishness and Transvestism in the Modern Dances of Pauline Koner and Hadassah," *Feminist Studies* 37, no. 2 (2011): 339. See also Croft, *Dancers as Diplomats*, 66–67 (see Introduction, n65).

Figure 1.3: Anna Sokolow in *Four Little Salon Pieces*. Photographer unknown. Courtesy of Sokolow Dance Foundation.

afforded her a status that revolutionary Jewish dancers who did not dance for a Big Four company could not claim.[50] *Boston Herald* critic William T. Chase, Jr. opined, for example, that a dancer's training with Graham or Humphrey–Weidman "practically assured one of a certain competence of technique."[51] But Sokolow's position

50. Rossen, "Hasidic Drag," 337–339. See Erdman, *Staging the Jew*; Jacobson, *Whiteness of a Different Color* (see Introduction, n69); Brodkin, *How Jews Became White Folks* (see Introduction, n45); and Moore and Troen, eds., *Divergent Jewish Cultures* (see Introduction, n69) for the intersection of Jewishness with race and ethnicity in the early to mid-twentieth century.

51. William T. Chase, Jr., "The Theater: Repertory, *New Dance League*," *The Boston Herald*, April 11, 1936, 14, Dance Clippings, New Dance League Folder, HTC.

differed from her leftist and Jewish contemporaries who utilized the transcendence of whiteness to map black experience through their female bodies as a way to align themselves with the plight of oppressed peoples.[52] As Jews in the United States were not culturally considered white until after World War II, this kind of identity circulation through whiteness became a mode of assimilation. Sokolow engaged jazz music to create an urban atmosphere with which she identified,[53] and she was part of Communist Jewish–Black coalitions through the International Workers Order,[54] but she did not portray portraits of African American struggle. Sokolow fit uneasily into these categories, where her dances represented strife that recalled her own history instead of generalized experience from a social or ethnic position that differed from her own. Her interventions in *Strange American Funeral* and *Case History* inserted women into the social spaces of steel mills and back alleys in order to use modern dance's abstraction to bring a Jewish feminist–driven dignity to workers and the poor.

In *Strange American Funeral*, Sokolow furiously accused the capitalist establishment of the wrongful deaths of hundreds of miners and steel workers. This popular dance, which premiered in a New Dance League (NDL) Festival at the Park Theatre in Manhattan's Columbus Circle on June 9, 1935, indicted workplace safety violations as it spoke to a multifaceted audience.[55] Dancers' progressions through shifting geometric formations displayed the community's experience of loss, anger, and chaos, and empowered the masses to rise up against oppressive power structures. The ten women of Sokolow's Dance Unit stirred sentiments of social unrest through patterns of increasing intensity; *New Masses* dance critic Stanley Burnshaw pointed to the "constant freshness and 'inevitableness' with which the dancers flow from one design into another" as their bodies inscribed indelible etchings in space. Imagery in the movement and textual accompaniment transformed flesh into steel and human into machine,[56] showing the human toll of modernity's scientific progress. Sokolow considered the piece as reinforcing the worker's cause.[57] The dance's haunting tone clearly separated the oppressed worker from the establishment against which Sokolow railed. As the performers swarmed around the stage in an

52. Manning terms this convention "metaphorical minstrelsy," wherein white and Jewish dancers like Helen Tamiris in *Negro Spirituals* (1928–1944) performed nonwhite themes as universal, whereas critics like Martin criticized black dancers presenting the same themes for the specificity of the material. See *Modern Dance, Negro Dance*, 10–12, 35, 63.

53. Anna Sokolow, quoted in Jean Battey, "The Dance—Choreographer Works Slippers Off Dancers," *The Washington Post*, January 18, 1967, n.p., Alan M. and Sali Ann Kriegsman Collection, MD, LOC.

54. See, for example, advertisement for Annual Fiesta of the International Workers Order Pageant, *New York Amsterdam Star-News*, March 28, 1942, 17. PQHN.

55. Sokolow's Workers Dance League changed its name to the New Dance League in April, 1935. This name change reflected an expanded leftist and anti-fascist political identity and a shift from a local to national organization.

56. Franko, *Work of Dance*, 116.

57. Warren, *Rebellious Spirit*, 66, and Program, *New Dance League June Dance Festival*, June 9, 1935, Workers Dance League Programs, JRDD, NYPL.

exhorted mass of mechanized bodies to agitate for workers' rights, the abstraction of the movement allowed them to portray men and women workers, and attract workers' revolutionary and mainstream audiences.[58]

Strange American Funeral was rooted in the workers' plight and spoke to audiences across class lines. Sokolow culled the libretto and musical accompaniment for this dance from her leftist art and literature circles. She based the dance on the poem "Strange Funeral in Braddock" by Michael (Mike) Gold, a *New Masses* founder, revolutionary dance supporter, and one of a group of writers who defined proletarian literature,[59] and set it to leftist composer Elie Seigmeister's musical rendition of the poem. Gold's verse narrates the story of Jan Clepak, an Eastern European immigrant steel worker in Pennsylvania who daydreams at his puddling trough and plunges to his death in the molten metal when he falls through a broken guardrail.[60] An accompanying program note asserts that Clepak was "a worker who was caught in a flood of molten ore—whose flesh and blood turned to steel."[61] The poem's haunting refrain patters, "Listen to the mournful drums of a strange funeral./ Listen to the story of a strange American funeral!"[62] Gold juxtaposes the imagery of Clepak as a "soft man" who mused about his family's future and Braddock's rolling hills, with the hard metal of his occupation and the hardened version of his body at his death. Clepak's widow proclaims, "I'll make myself hard as steel, harder!/I'll come some day and make bullets out of Jan's body/and shoot them into a tyrant's heart," taking her revenge by piercing a businessman's squishy organs with pieces of Clepak's steeled body.[63] Gold's Pennsylvania steel industry scenario, where Frederick Winslow Taylor tested punishing systems for worker productivity, set immigrant bodies, perceived by white American citizenry as racially inferior and physically effeminized, against American modernity's progressive mechanization.[64] Clepak's metallization, after falling out of step with Taylorized efficiency, heightened Sokolow's exposure of inhumane working conditions, while it highlighted modernist alienation and immigrant tensions within these scenes.

Sokolow brought the fervor of proletarian mass meetings to the concert dance stage with her translation of an activist-charged text through women's bodies. She created choreographic potency in this dance through layering geometric formations. This progression matched the build in the musical intensity, which in turn reflected the poem's typography wherein the letters of the refrain became larger

58. In modernist abstraction, "The strong women stood for Everyman." Deborah Jowitt, *Time and the Dancing Image* (Berkeley: University of California Press, 1988), 191.

59. See Denning, *Cultural Front*, 200–205; and Granville Hicks et al., eds., *Proletarian Literature in the United States: An Anthology* (New York: International Publishers, 1935).

60. Michael Gold, "Strange Funeral in Braddock," in Program, *New Dance League June Dance Festival*, June 9, 1935.

61. Program, *Anna Sokolow and Dance Unit*, YM/YWHA Theresa L. Kaufmann Auditorium, April 5, 1936, 92Y.

62. Gold, "Strange Funeral in Braddock."

63. Ibid.

64. Franko, *Work of Dance*, 22.

down the page as Clepak's body mutated from flesh to steel.[65] Musicologist Carol J. Oja described the music's "melodic angularity, disjunct rhythms, and spiky dissonance" that depicted Clepak's violent accident; Gold's poem was to be chanted by crowds gathered at mass meetings, and the pace and increasing intensity of Elie Seigmeister's musical score mimicked the rhythmic build of such chanting.[66] Based on the dance's premiere on a NDL program in a workers' theater, it is not unthinkable to imagine similar audience participation at the concert.

The solemnity of fated wrongful death resonated throughout the dance. The piece opened with a funeral cortege: A group of women clad in long utilitarian dresses, their heads bound by black hairnets, held a dancer aloft as they slowly traversed the stage while singer Mordecai Bauman ominously rang out the refrain: "Listen to the story of a strange American funeral!"[67] Burnshaw reported that Bauman's eerie amplified voice in his recitation of Gold's poem provided "a strange quality supremely attuned to the needs of the dance."[68] The rest of the piece was a narrative flashback that portrayed Clepak's grisly death and workers' anger in response to it. In demonstrating their resistance against workplace supervisors and the businessmen who ran these mills, who appeared in the form of what Martin described as "two pompous masked figures representing directors [who] enter[ed] the scene" halfway through the piece,[69] the dancers strained against one another's locked arms, portraying a necessity to break free. The architectural formation in Figure 1.4 suggests the visual repetition of workers toiling line by line and replicates critic Muriel Rukeyser's 1935 report in *New Theatre* of a "solid steel block of dancers, locked at the elbows, coming heavily downstage."[70] Ensuing group-movement patterns wove through each other until, Burnshaw noted, the dance "achieve[d] a summit of militancy and accusing power" that produced a growing force fed by outrage with each new worker's death.[71]

By using Gold's poem as a libretto with Seigmeister's score and staging the politics of labor relations, Sokolow aligned herself with a message all too familiar to her audience. The trope of funerals for miners who died on duty appeared often in *New Masses* during the mid-1930s. Such a funeral was tragic yet dignified. In Emery Balint's 1934 short story "Miner's Funeral," the funeral was an event of pride and belonging; there was a sense of loyalty when the person was a union member.[72] In

---

65. Hicks et al, quoted in Carol J. Oja, "Composer with a Conscience: Elie Seigmeister in Profile," *American Music* 6, no. 2 (1988): 179.

66. Oja, "Composer with a Conscience," 173, 178, 163.

67. Warren, *Rebellious Spirit*, 65; and Oja, "Composer with a Conscience," 161–162.

68. Stanley Burnshaw, "The Dance," *New Masses*, January 7, 1936, n.p., Anna Sokolow Clippings, JRDD, NYPL.

69. John Martin, "The Dance: With Words," *New York Times*, June 30, 1935, 4X.

70. Muriel Rukeyser, "The Dance Festival," *New Theatre* (July 1935): quoted in Graff, *Stepping Left*, 69.

71. Stanley Burnshaw, "The Dance: Finale to a Brilliant Season," *New Masses*, July 2, 1935, 43, BICLM.

72. Emery Balint, "Miner's Funeral: A Short Story," *New Masses*, January 16, 1934, 16–19, BICLM.

Figure 1.4: Dance Unit in *Strange American Funeral*. Photographer unknown. Larry Warren Collection on Anna Sokolow and Lester Horton, Box 1, Music Division, Library of Congress, Washington, DC.

a political cartoon titled "Miner's Homecoming," two men lift a lifeless body onto a bed as the small house fills with family and friends looking on.[73] Clepak's steel worker story shares with the miner trope a culture of active unions in physically demanding and dangerous jobs.

Contemporary reviews lacked substantial movement description of *Strange American Funeral*, even though critics dedicated significant space to its coverage. Most writers expounded on the importance of the narrative's gruesome outcome and commented on Sokolow's ability to affect the masses with her choreography. Gilfond and Marjorie Church, both writing in *Dance Observer*, acknowledged it as a singularly significant, emotionally compelling, and politically effective dance.[74] Many critics in leftist publications also praised the work. Ocko highlighted *Strange American Funeral* as one of *New Theatre*'s best dances of 1935 alongside Graham's *Panorama*.[75] Louise Mitchell echoed the work's enduring power when she wrote of its resonance two years later in *Daily Worker*: "Dances with the choreographic strength of 'Strange American Funeral' grow in intensity with each repetition."[76]

73. Herb Krackman, "Seeing America First: IV—Miner's Homecoming," *New Masses* February 2, 1937, 7, BICLM.

74. Gilfond, "Anna Sokolow and Dance Unit" (May 1936); and Marjorie Church, "Anna Sokolow and Dance Unit, Major Subscription Series, YMHA, Sunday, February 28, 1937," *Dance Observer* (April 1937): 41, Anna Sokolow Clippings, JRDD, NYPL.

75. Ocko, "Dancers, Take a Bow," 24 (see Introduction, n17).

76. Mitchell, "New Dance Unit Is Tops."

Choreographer Jane Dudley considered *Strange American Funeral* Sokolow's best revolutionary dance.[77] Even though Martin's complaints that the work "was inchoate and pointless"[78] revealed his opposition to Sokolow's leftist thematic material,[79] he nevertheless noted: "Many individual passages of her composition were superb not only in their integrity of feeling but in their boldness of imagination."[80] This resonance shows Sokolow's empathy with contemporary sentiment.

Lively debates among critics and dancers about the definitions, missions, and aesthetics of modern and revolutionary dance in 1930s dance periodicals informed how Sokolow's audiences interacted with her work. Points of interest included how choreographers should craft propaganda by concert dance standards and embody social protest, and how revolutionary dancers could not simply "put on" proletarian airs for leftist work, but had to live or convincingly portray the working-class experience.[81] For example, Chase scolded Humphrey–Weidman dancer and leftist choreographer Bill Matons for appearing energetically too well fed in a solo about hunger.[82] To this end, Gold expounded in 1935, "Real proletarian writers must, essentially, understand the class struggle."[83] Ocko echoed this statement when she wrote that revolutionary dancers had to embody their proletarian themes: "Working-class ideology, no matter how thinly sketched, cannot be superficial integument slipped on to any skeleton of a dance technic [*sic*], nor can it be an innovation in movement imposed on to an idea that becomes revolutionary by annotation."[84] To be considered revolutionary, a choreographer had to present a marriage of proletarian content with technical prowess; it helped if the choreographer came from a working-class background. Sokolow fulfilled this spectatorial desire in the autobiographical *Case History No.—*. Compositionally, she engaged the Stanislavsky Method's reliance on personal experience by incorporating her own history of growing up poor to feed her performance of juvenile delinquency.[85] She needed to make a realistic characterization if the audience was going to believe the work and react to its social message.

Whereas in *Strange American Funeral* Sokolow projected one incident as an example of workers' issues, in *Case History No.—* she generalized the plight of impoverished youth in Manhattan's poorest neighborhoods through her solo

77. Dudley, interview by Wormser, 6 (see Preface, n8).
78. Martin, "The Dance: With Words," 4X.
79. Franko, *Work of Dance*, 114–117.
80. John Martin, "New Dance League Holds 3D Festival: Park Theatre is Crowded for Performances in Evening and Afternoon," *New York Times*, June 10, 1935, n.p., Dance Clippings, New Dance League Folder, HTC.
81. In "Art and Propaganda," *Dance Observer* (December 1936): 109, 113, Dane Rudhyar argued that art must be embodied to be vital; otherwise, it is propaganda.
82. Chase, "The Theater: Repertory, *New Dance League*," 14.
83. Irving Weisser, "Face to Face with Michael Gold," *New Voices*, August 1935, 9. Microforms, NYPL.
84. Ocko, "The Revolutionary Dance Movement," 27 (see Introduction, n56).
85. Graff, *Stepping Left*, 70–72.

body. She premiered *Case History* on a Dance Unit program on February 28, 1937, at the 92nd Street Y, and it became one of her signature solos. It appeared at Sokolow's Broadway debut at the Guild Theatre in November 1937,[86] and on countless programs through 1943 in various New York venues and for audiences of workers, artists, and intellectuals in Mexico City's opera house Palacio de Bellas Artes.[87] A program note from the 1937 premiere reads, "A study of a majority of case histories shows that petty criminals usually emerge from a background which begins with unemployment and follows its course from street corner to pool room, from mischief to crime."[88] To a musical score by Wallingford Riegger, Sokolow performed a portrait of a poor child like her, as the perceived universalism of the dance allowed her to subvert class and gender expectations through androgyny that emerged onstage.

Sokolow occupied this dance's rough, urban space rarely attributed to women's habitation, yet because she lived in tenements as a child, she knew this area well.[89] Her classed and ethnic familiarity with these spaces denied her white womanhood's femininity, but allowed her to make proletarian statements. As this dance answered Gold's and Ocko's call for choreographers to understand their dances' social material from the inside out, it reinforced Sokolow's ability to transcend gendered specificity while portraying the working-class struggle. Sokolow embodied these youths' gritty existence with a polished focus that showcased her technical range, emotional depth, and fiery, scrappy performance charisma. Dance Unit dancer Aza Bard remembered Sokolow's heart-wrenching performance of the abandoned child's alienation.[90] Exhibiting concentrated power, oppositional tension, and a broad dynamic range, Sokolow portrayed, as critic Margery Dana noted in the *Daily Worker*, "the sordid playground—perhaps a street in 'Hell's Kitchen'—of the children of the poor."[91]

The dance's flying shapes, arrested motion, and pained solitude manifested this child's decrepit world with such tangibility that it laid bare the humanity of the class struggle. Riegger's two-piano score begins in a minor key that conjures dingy alleys that are dark because their close-together buildings block out the sun.[92] The piano

86. Program, *Dance Concert Debut by Anna Sokolow and Dance Unit*, Guild Theatre, November 14, 1937, Martha Hill Papers, Juilliard.

87. Program, *Anna Sokolow y su Cuerpo Ballet*, Palace of Fine Arts, April 18, 1939, Collection of Patricia Aulestia, PBA; and Program, *La Paloma Azul*, Palace of Fine Arts, September 20, 1940, Item GP-DF00163, CENIDID, CENART.

88. Program, *Dance Recital by Anna Sokolow and Dance Unit of the New Dance League*, YM/YWHA Theresa L. Kaufmann Auditorium, February 28, 1937, 92Y.

89. See Graff, *Stepping Left*, 71.

90. Aza Bard Mackenzie, interview by Larry Warren, 1987, transcript, 13, Larry Warren Collection on Anna Sokolow and Lester Horton, MD, LOC.

91. Margery Dana, "Anna Sokolow and Unit Seen In New Solo and Group Dances," *Daily Worker*, March 1, 1939, 7.

92. Wallingford Riegger, "Case History No.—," score, 1937, MD, NYPL, transcr. Mont Chris Hubbard.

Figure 1.5: Anna Sokolow in *Case History No.—* (1937). Photographs by Barbara Morgan. I determined the order of the images by proof numbers, but this is not necessarily the order of the dance. Barbara and Willard Morgan Photographs and Papers, Library Special Collections, Charles E. Young Research Library, UCLA.

repeats sets of notes that amble forward and backward on themselves, as if they narrate a kid meandering through the neighborhood. One movement sequence included what Marjorie Church described in *Dance Observer* as a "slow, walking [movement motif], forward and back, which suggested miles of city streets traversed, corners paused at and finally turned, cups of coffee now and then in grubby little dives."[93] Sokolow addressed her audience members over her left shoulder, as her cold stare accused them of causing her misery and at the same time appealed for help.[94] The photographs in Figure 1.5 offer a glimpse of frozen moments from the dance. Sokolow bends her body into a midair crescent as she sadly gazes into space; she whips her left arm behind her body as she hovers just above the ground; and prone, she painstakingly peels her limbs off the floor, wringing her body as she exposes her vulnerable ventral surface that, along with her face, were previously

93. Church, "Anna Sokolow and Dance Unit, Major Subscription Series, YMHA, Sunday, February 28, 1937," 41.

94. Photograph in Sali Ann Kriegsman, *Modern Dance in America: The Bennington Years* (Boston: Hall, 1981), 264.

smashed into the floor. Sokolow's dirty bare feet in these images verify her embodiment of the material, as if she wandered shoeless through New York City.

Sokolow employed syncopated rhythms in the music and movement along with what Burke called "a neurotic bravado" to construct an unstable cityscape.[95] The music jumps between high and low octaves with notes that land just off the beat. Suddenly, the score transposes a generic ragtime phrase into deeper tones and a minor key that gives it a twisted, sarcastic feeling, suggesting that something commonplace has gone awry. The ensuing chords are subdued by comparison; lower notes heavily advance as higher ones fall like raindrops on Sokolow's head as she trudges ever onward. The piece ends abruptly after a few frantic musical measures, as if in midsentence, insisting that the audience members rectify this strife. Burke wrote in *New Masses* that the dance was "[i]ntense in structure, literally tearing away at space in a nervous staccato rhythm, dominated by a desire for security."[96] In one photograph, Sokolow takes off: She quickly shifts her weight onto her bent left leg, leaving her right leg behind, as her left elbow slices behind her and she focuses intently into the palm of her right hand. The opposing tensions and displaced joints through Sokolow's body, from her torso bent over the right side of her waist, and from her cocked right wrist to her flexed left hip and knee, resemble the polycentrism and ephebism that Brenda Dixon Gottschild identifies as part of the Africanist aesthetic in American dance.[97] *Case History* portrayed a metropolitan America where Eastern European–immigrant, Southern European–immigrant, and Africanist influences met in expressions of the class struggle as it addressed problems of poverty in the city's poor and immigrant neighborhoods.

Case History exposed the dark underbelly of a city failing to protect its poorest, most vulnerable members. These young people, Sokolow implied, have no choice but to lurk in alleys and engage in illegal behavior. Church reported that the "sense of futility and the growing despair in the youth become the force which drives him toward defiant and anti-social acts."[98] Mitchell's comments that she saw "the countless [delinquents] who never got a chance, whose only crime was being born into a society that breeds them and then destroys them like gutter rats" mirror Sokolow's accusations that city negligence generated case files numerous beyond account.[99]

Critical response to *Case History* contained gendered language conventions that labeled Sokolow as male, instead of as female, to make her social indictment.[100] Sokolow wore a tweed skirt and fitted black shirt, and the program note

95. Owen Burke, "The Dance," *New Masses*, March 16, 1937, 28, BICLM.
96. Owen Burke, "Dances for Spain and China," *New Masses*, February 15, 1938, 30, BICLM.
97. Brenda Dixon Gottschild, *Digging the Africanist Presence in American Performance: Dance and Other Contexts* (Westport, CT: Praeger, 1998), 14–16.
98. Church, "Anna Sokolow and Dance Unit, Major Subscription Series, YMHA, Sunday, February 28, 1937," 41.
99. Mitchell, "New Dance Unit Is Tops."
100. Critics' language determined that Sokolow's portrayals of or as women did not resonate as universally powerful as did her "everyman" portrayals. See Clare Croft, "Feminist Dance

does not denote the gender of the youth she portrayed, but many critics referred to Sokolow as a young man. In one such *Daily Worker* review, Mitchell wrote of Sokolow's performance of these petty criminals' "boyish bravado, their willfulness, frustration, desperation, the hunted suspect, the third degree, the cringing boy killers, the last mile."[101] Critics like Mitchell portray Sokolow as a male thug and not as a prostitute, a female archetype who also wandered those streets. The diminution of Sokolow's female gender reflects communist tropes of presenting gender-neutral (male) ranks of comrades, and it also reflects the 1930s convention of white and Jewish women choreographers to transcend the specificity of their race and gender in performance to make an appeal to universality.[102] When reviewers assigned her a female characterization, moreover, it was of a child who showed brief promise to escape before succumbing to the streets' immorality. Russian immigrant artist David Burliuk, writing in New York's *Russkii Golos* [*The Russian Voice*], reported that Sokolow "shows us a young girl on Avenue B on the East side noticing a light-winged butterfly flying on the green freshness of nature in urban hell, or the history of an older 16-year-old girl, taking the path of vice, the lure of destruction."[103] Riegger's score is generally ominous, but when it briefly stops and the key becomes major, it lilts along, as if Sokolow found the butterfly that could liberate her from her hell, but uncertainty returns in broken minor-keyed chords and dissonant clashes that confirm the dismal reality for boy and girl alike. These critics' comments suggest that women needed to become part of the (male) collective to make widely applicable statements and could not make them as women. Using this dance to point to social injustices, Sokolow nevertheless presented an American portrait in the criminals she portrayed.

In the aftermath of solos such as Graham's *Frontier* (1935) that presented a hearty woman of heroic femininity surveying the vast horizon as a synecdoche of mythic Americana ideals, Sokolow's solo portrayed an urban, immigrant outsider that contrasted presentations of fabled white pioneers pushing west. In *Case History*, Sokolow's outsider status highlighted her own intersectionality of being Jewish, leftist, and poor. Sokolow felt alienated from Graham's Puritan, ethics-based stories of pioneers on the Western plains, because of her own family's immigrant, Northeastern urban history. She departed from Graham's Americana to present the working poor as American archetype. Sokolow noted to this end in 1975, "I was not Americana. I never was and that's it. That's her [Graham's] background and it

Criticism and Ballet," *Dance Chronicle* 37, no. 2 (2014): 195–217, for a feminist call to ballet criticism that argues for reviews to enable women's agency through their movement description and sentence structure choices.

101. Mitchell, "New Dance Unit Is Tops."

102. See Manning, *Modern Dance, Negro Dance*, 12; and Jowitt, *Time*, 191.

103. David Burliuk, "In the World of Art," *Russkii Golos* [*The Russian Voice*], n.d. 1943, Larry Warren Collection on Anna Sokolow and Lester Horton, MD, LOC, trans. Ali Potvin.

was not my background."[104] Sokolow instead found inspiration in urban landscapes for which she found the structure and instrumentation of jazz music an appropriate fit.[105] This further distinguished her from Graham, who upheld the racist reasoning that jazz was vulgar.[106] For Sokolow, jazz's African American origins, musical intensity, and prominence among marginalized populations spoke to her conception and experience of a people's "America."

Sokolow believed that jazz created expressions of Americanness within the pace of modernity and the reflection of the urban metropolis. Later in life, she said: "Jazz is what I feel to be the music of our time and also the sound that I was brought up in. I was brought up in a neighborhood where there was jazz all the time . . . I always felt it was an important American expression in music."[107] In the 1930s, Sokolow engaged swing, blues, and ragtime, and with artists like Louis Armstrong, Count Basie, Duke Ellington, Ella Fitzgerald, Billie Holiday, and Lena Horne. In the late 1930s through the early 1940s, Sokolow worked with these musicians on projects like *Bourbons Got the Blues* in 1938 and a 1943 fundraising concert to elect Benjamin J. Davis, Jr., an African American Communist who represented Harlem, to the New York City Council.[108] Many dance composers with whom she worked in the 1930s blended jazz influences with modernist compositional elements like transposition, which caused dissonance in sound, like in *Case History*, and many of these artists aligned with the Left. Sokolow's connection to jazz within proletarian work reinforced her use of folk elements to make populist statements,[109] and it linked African American and Jewish coalitions through leftist ideology. For some African Americans, communism provided an avenue to collectively fight oppression. Sokolow inserted her modern dance body into communist and black spaces with *Case History* as a way to highlight, instead of efface, the cry of the working poor. *Case History*'s jazz score, sentiment of working-class alienation in urban environs, and androgynously gendered spaces served as a study about urban alienation and isolation for *Rooms* (1954), which I discuss in Chapter 4.[110] *Case History* fed Sokolow's later work in terms of American urbanity and gender performance.

Sokolow's work linked diverse audiences with its revolutionary spectatorship. Her choreography enabled middle-class audiences to examine proletarian issues within a familiar aesthetic context of modern dance. John Martin's support of

104. Anna Sokolow, quoted in Kisselgoff, "In Anna Sokolow's Dance, Her Beliefs," 46 (see Introduction, n36).

105. Anna Sokolow, interview by Barbara Newman, December 2 and 12, 1974, and May 11, 1975, transcript, 127, Oral History Archives, JRDD, NYPL.

106. Graham did not approve of Horst allowing Sokolow to use jazz music in her student composition studies. Agnes de Mille talks about Anna Sokolow, May 31, 1974, Oral History Archive, JRDD, NYPL.

107. Anna Sokolow, quoted in "Talking to *Dance and Dancers*," 18 (see Introduction, n72).

108. "Radio, Stage, Screen Stars To Pace Cast of Victory Show," *The Pittsburgh Courier*, October 16, 1943, 19, PQHN.

109. See Denning, *Cultural Front*, 284, 320; and Kriegsman, *Bennington Years*, 199.

110. Warren, *Rebellious Spirit*, 70.

Sokolow continued onto the 92nd Street Y's stage, where cultural director William Kolodney entered into a partnership with Martin in 1934 to build a home for modern dance at the Y.[111] In this alliance, Kolodney refused to present most leftist Jewish choreographers, but he included Sokolow. Her involvement at the Y, as a teacher and frequent performer, evidenced Kolodney's negotiations between what the Y's Jewish community wanted and what Martin preferred,[112] and demonstrated how Sokolow was leftist enough for progressive middle-class Jewish audiences who attended the Y and Graham–resonant enough for Martin's modern dance–defining aesthetics. The Y's audiences carried mixed political views and valued a combination of social and modernist content. For the proletarian audience in Columbus Circle, however, *Strange American Funeral* and *Case History* spoke to contemporary issues of workers' rights and justice for the poor while embodying these subjects in a way that was central to the goals of revolutionary dance.

Sokolow's late 1930s dances aligned with shifting Popular Front sentiments as her proletarian actions blended with an anti-fascist agenda. The aesthetics of Sokolow's and other leftist artists' proletarian work influenced that of their anti-fascist work.[113] This shift from proletarianism to anti-fascism was reflected in the field's organizations when Sokolow's Workers Dance League changed its name to the New Dance League in April 1935. This name change reflected an expanded leftist and anti-fascist political identity and a shift from a local to national organization. Further developments included a training school, a broadening in the organization's mission to embrace anti-fascism, and, according to Nadia Chilkovsky in the NDL's organ *New Theatre*, "a mass development of the American dance to its highest artistic and social level, for a dance movement that is against war, fascism, and censorship."[114]

Two events from 1935 to 1937 in which figures from across concert dance united under the anti-fascist banner reflected the seriousness of the European totalitarian threat that played out in Sokolow's, and others', choreography. In 1935–1936 the NDL organized a boycott of the International Dance Festival scheduled alongside the July 1936 Berlin Olympics in Nazi Germany. The NDL circulated a petition at its dance concerts asserting the festival's organization by German dance leaders Mary Wigman and Rudolf Laban, who taught courses in Nazi ideology, discredited the festival's stated goals of cultural unity through dance.[115] Sokolow

111. Jackson, *Converging Movements*, 57 and 257n8.

112. Jackson shows Martin's animosity toward Jewish dancers despite his instrumental role in establishing the dance program at the 92nd Street Y. Jackson, *Converging Movements*, 59, 64–67, 138–142. Martin's aggression toward leftist dance may have been a disagreement in ideology or latent anti-Semitism.

113. See Denning, *Cultural Front*, 374.

114. Nell Anyon (Nadia Chilkovsky), "The New Dance League," *New Theatre* (April 1935): 28. See also "What is the New Dance League," and "New Dance League School," Folder 906, Box 23, Bessie Schönberg Papers, JRDD, NYPL.

115. Petition, The New Dance League, Folder 906, Bessie Schönberg Papers, JRDD, NYPL. In an indictment of Wigman, Laban, and Gret Palucca for their allegiances to Hitler, Ocko

was among the first people to sign onto the boycott, along with dancers and choreographers Miriam Blecher, Sophia Delza, Elsa Findlay, Graham, Humphrey, Esther Junger, Polly Korchien, Ruth Page, Gluck Sandor, Tamiris, Weidman, and Benjamin Zemach; impresarios Sol Hurok and Lincoln Kirstein; dance editor Paul Love; musician Riegger; and director Max Reinhardt.[116] Modern and revolutionary dancers again joined forces in May 1937 when they formed the American Dance Association (ADA), which merged the NDL, the Dance Guild, and Tamiris's Dancers' Association. The ADA foregrounded anti-fascism and a belief, according to Burke, that "the audience, no less than the dancer, must have his part in the making of the organization and the molding of its policies."[117] Burke often waxed rhapsodic in 1937, writing in June about an ADA performance to benefit the Medical Bureau to Aid Spanish Democracy: "Both the dancers and the dance audience continue to demonstrate a social responsibility and a clear recognition of the tie-up between art and the social set-up," and again in September, "It is difficult to recall a year more crowded with dance material of such excellence; and at no time in recent dance history have dancers been so immersed in organizational activities of a general and social economic nature."[118] Sokolow's dances *War Poem*, *Façade*, and *Slaughter* fueled Burke's excitement and the American Left's indictment of European Fascist regimes. Through resonances with the work of German choreographer Kurt Jooss and Ballet Russe choreographer Léonide Massine, as I show in the next section, these dances connected Sokolow to communist conversations across the international Left and show how choreography circulated transnational ideology.

CRUMBLING FAÇADES: GENDER AND ANTI-FASCISM

Sokolow's proletarian and anti-fascist dances' appearances together reflected leftist choreographic conversations that blended proletarian and anti-fascist activism.

---

implored New York dancers to sever ties with the Wigman school although many leftist dancers had trained in and taught Wigman technique. Ocko acknowledged the loyalties with which dancers, herself included, found themselves at odds since the Wigman technique was integrated into American leftist dance. Her conclusion, "let us not permit sentimentality and emotional ties to obscure our vision," spoke to the emotional difficulty of the situation, and how a theatrical dance form could be implicated in international politics. Edna Ocko, "The Swastika is Dancing," *New Theatre* (November 1935): 17.

116. Emanuel Eisenberg, "Danse Macabre," *New Theatre* (May 1936): 37.

117. Owen Burke, "The Dance," April 6, 1937, 29. The ADA's executive board boasted Fanya Geltman, Holm, Horst, Humphrey, Bessie Schönberg, and Tamiris among others. Anne Dodge (ADA executive secretary) to John Krimsky (chairman of the World Fair Entertainment Committee), October 6, 1937, Folder 3, Box 679, New York World's Fair 1939/1940 and Incorporated Records, MAD, NYPL.

118. Owen Burke, "The Dance," *New Masses*, June 8, 1937, 28, BICLM; and ibid., "The Dance," *New Masses*, September 14, 1937, 31, BICLM.

New York concertgoers at Dance Unit performances from 1937 to 1939 saw *Strange American Funeral* and *Case History* alongside *Excerpts from a War Poem* and *Slaughter of the Innocents*. The latter compositions clarified American leftist views of 1930s regimes in Italy, Spain, and Germany. Dance concerts boasted hard-hitting dances following the 1936 National Dance Congress that brought modern and revolutionary dancers together under the banner of anti-fascism, racial equality, and employment assurances for dancers.[119] Sokolow's dances ideologically dismantled European Fascism and implored audience members to respond to totalitarian atrocities.

Sokolow's references to European dictators Benito Mussolini, Francisco Franco, and Adolf Hitler in her anti-fascist dances reflected a trend for communist artists outside Europe to conflate these dictators after these men allied themselves against Communism.[120] In this section I discuss Sokolow's contribution to anti-fascist discourse in *Excerpts from a War Poem* and *Façade—Exposizione Italiana*, two group works that condemned Mussolini's Italian fascist ideals, and *Slaughter of the Innocents*, a solo in which Sokolow portrayed mothers' plights who lost children in Franco's Spanish Civil War bombings. *War Poem* and *Façade* were Sokolow's first dances to play out her biting choreographic voice through men's and women's bodies, as Sokolow added four men to her Dance Unit for her February 28, 1937 concert at the 92nd Street Y.[121] In *Slaughter* and *The Exile (A Dance Poem)* (1939), a solo based on Sol Funaroff's poem "The Exiles" that yearned for Jewish vitality before Jewish displacement under Hitler that I discuss in Chapter 2, Sokolow exposed gendered points of contention by pushing against what critics considered acceptable for representations of power through women's bodies onstage.

Sokolow's anti-fascist work reproduced an anti-fascist aesthetic that labor historian Michael Denning identified in the work of leftist artists like playwright Orson Welles.[122] Denning defined the anti-fascist aesthetic to include an exaggerated performance of power by feckless prop dictator characters while employing Julius Caesar archetypes as metaphors, mostly for Mussolini, but also for Franco, Hitler, or American anti-Left business leaders or media moguls like J. P. Morgan or William Randolph Hearst. Denning identified two main elements of Welles's anti-fascist aesthetic to be "the portrait of the great dictator and the reflection on showmanship and propaganda."[123] This linking of European totalitarian dictators with American capitalist tycoons solidified US proletarianism's connection to anti-fascism.

119. Ocko, "The Dance Congress," 23–24; Henry Gilfond, "Dance Congress and Festival," *Dance Observer* (June-July 1936): 1; and "Resolutions," *Dance Observer* (June-July 1936): 64–65.

120. See Giuseppe Finaldi, *Mussolini and Italian Fascism* (Harlow, England: Pearson Longman,

ı, *Rebellious Spirit*, 71.

ng, *Cultural Front*, 375.

84.

War Poem and *Façade* embodied anti-fascist parodic showmanship by portraying a prop Caesar through hyperbole and archetypal characters. After a bloody nineteenth-century reunification of Italy and widespread devastation after World War I, Mussolini declared himself the modern reincarnation of Caesar to unite Italians under the mythology that they were heirs to a great empire.[124] Theater historian Günter Berghaus noted how Fascist Party ideology propagated a belief that "under the guidance of Mussolini, Rome could fulfill its historic mission in the modern world."[125] In the United States, foreign correspondent journalist George Seldes suggested in his 1935 book *Sawdust Caesar* that Mussolini was inconsequential despite modeling himself on Caesar's actions. History will not remember Mussolini as a great Caesar, Seldes intoned, but as a pale imitation.[126] Sokolow's poignant, ironic performance through *War Poem*'s and *Façade*'s caricatures engaged audiences' visceral reactions to these political events.

Sokolow's dances' satirical anti-fascist aesthetic countered the fascist aesthetic of mechanization and conformity. In *War Poem*, Sokolow twisted the words of Italian Futurist poet F. T. Marinetti's work "War is Beautiful" into a piercing satire of Fascist Italy in the years preceding World War II.[127] Burke wrote in *New Masses* that the Dance Unit's February 28, 1937 premiere of this work at the Y presented "A vigorous satire on the trumpeted Fascist philosophy and the decadent and destructive manifestations of it[. T]he composition [portrays] a series of swift analytical sketches, searching, precise, a thoroughly effective ironic statement—anti-war, anti-Fascist."[128] The futurism to which Sokolow responded engaged the work in a transatlantic modernist conversation. Modernist theorist Carrie Preston noted that Futurists like Marinetti sought "an aesthetics of shock" within the machinery and alienation that marked their genre's modernity.[129] Sokolow's response to Marinetti's shock modernism with *War Poem*'s automaton figures that destroy humanity challenged the fascist aesthetics of a world ruled by war machines.[130] For Marinetti, machines posed an aesthetic solution for his desired anarchic social revolution that combined art and politics.[131] Marinetti and other Futurist poets glorified a

124. Günter Berghaus, *Futurism and Politics: Between Anarchist Rebellion and Fascist Reaction, 1909–1944* (Providence: Berghahn Books, 1996), 9–10. See also Finaldi, *Mussolini*, 85.

125. Berghaus, *Futurism and Politics*, 10.

126. George Seldes, *Sawdust Caesar: The Untold History of Mussolini and Fascism* (New York: Harper & Brothers, 1935).

127. Warren, *Rebellious Spirit*, 68.

128. Owen Burke, "The Dance," *New Masses*, March 16, 1937, 29, BICLM.

129. Carrie J. Preston, *Modernism's Mythic Pose: Gender, Genre, Solo Performance* (New York: Oxford University Press, 2011), 7.

130. Marinetti's shock modernism was part of interwar European modernism that featured a martial mechanization of bodies and intermingled human flesh with metal. Its Futurist and proto-fascist aesthetics highlighted machines as solutions to humanity's problems, along with Cubist imagery fracturing that reflected a splintering of society. See Hal Foster, "Prosthetic Gods," *Modernism/Modernity* 4, no. 2 (1997): 5–38; and Kate Elswit, *Watching Weimar Dance* (New York: Oxford University Press, 2014).

131. See Berghaus, *Futurism*, 9.

hyperbolic enthusiasm for war, fascism, and violence, retained an anti-intellectual stance against libraries, museums, and academies, and propagated hatred against women and feminism.[132] He believed extreme violence was necessary to remake society.[133] Even though Mussolini was suspicious of Marinetti and the futurist movement because of its revolutionary connections, Futurists aligned themselves with Italian fascism because they believed a political–artistic alliance was possible, even ideal, between fascism and futurism.[134] Sokolow countered fascism with anti-fascism in *War Poem*'s musical score and choreography. Alex North's opening musical bars presage an epic battle between opposing ideological forces.[135] A storm brews through sounds of metallic rumbles of thunder followed by scurrying, whirling piano notes. Rapid-fire ascents and descents that frantically fold forward and backward through dissonant peaks and valleys and end in sharp-edged, sustained pauses[136] prompted Burke to reinforce in *New Masses*, "No dancer has dealt more keenly, more ironically with the hypocrisy of the Fascist 'civilizers.'"[137] The contradiction between the storm and the stillness enabled Sokolow's satire.

War Poem undermined Marinetti's "War is Beautiful" by employing the material it criticized. The concert program listed *War Poem*'s five sections, all quotations from Marinetti's poem's stanzas that featured destructive, exaggerated imagery, including

a. "War is Beautiful."
b. "War is Beautiful because it fuses in Strength, Harmony and Kindness."
c. "War is Beautiful because it realizes the long dreamed of metalization [*sic*] of the human body."
d. "War is Beautiful because it symphonizes pauses choked by silence, the perfumes and odors of putrification and creates the spiral smoke of burning villages."
e. "War is Beautiful because it serves the greatness of our great fascist Italy."[138]

132. F. T. Marinetti, "Manifesto of Futurism," in *Poems for the Millennium: The University of California Book of Modern & Postmodern Poetry*, eds. Jerome Rothenberg and Pierre Joris (Berkeley: University of California Press, 1995), 198.

133. Berghaus, *Futurism*, 57.

134. Ibid., 9–12. Soviet futurist artists like Mayakovsky and Burliuk diverged from Italian futurism by tying their political statements to communist, not fascist, ideology.

135. North's unfinished handwritten musical score gives the dance temporality and suggests movement lines that are otherwise a mystery. In the score North noted movement cues and orchestration suggestions. The score is written for percussion and four-hands piano, which is likely how North and pianists Charlotte Homer or Jesus Duron played it for performances. According to North's widow, Anna Hollger North, there are no extant recordings of North's scores for Sokolow's dances. Michael McDonagh, "An Interview with Anna North," *The Cue Sheet: The Newsletter of the Society for the Preservation of Film Music* 16, no. 3 (2000): 18.

136. Alex North, "Anti-War Poem," score, n.d., Larry Warren Collection on Anna Sokolow and Lester Horton, MD, LOC, transcr. Mont Chris Hubbard.

137. Burke, "The Dance," March 16, 1937, 29.

138. Program, *Dance Recital by Anna Sokolow and Dance Unit of the New Dance League*, 92nd Street YM/YWHA, February 28, 1937, 92Y.

Marinetti advocated dismantling poetic and theatrical conventions to i poetry from structures and syntax.[139] His apocalyptic prescriptions include(his poetry with images of fire, mechanical violence, and annihilation, and hi in his "Manifesto of Futurism" that war is "the world's only hygiene."[140] Alo anti-Semitic European discourses that claimed Jews were physically degenerate disease carriers,[141] Marinetti's martial imagery of killing people as a hygienic solution recalls ethnic cleansing like that of Hitler's Final Solution. Sokolow enacted Marinetti's imagery to forewarn the horrors such realization would wreak on humanity.

This imagery took hold in *War Poem*'s archetypal trio of characters, Strength, Harmony, and Kindness, as personifications of these attributes taken from Marinetti's verse: "War is Beautiful because it fuses in Strength, Harmony, and Kindness." Reviewers term these dancers the "three graces" or the "three Roman ideals."[142] They represented a fascist Italian tripartite: Mussolini; the historical ghost of Caesar's dominance; and Mussolini's political adversary, the futurist-allied fascist poet Gabriele D'Annunzio. In Anton Refregier's costumes, they each wore a color of the Italian flag—red, white, or green. According to Burke, they denoted the personalities of "Il Duce's Italy," while moving in "stylized mechanical gestures"[143] that recalled Marinetti's idealized "metallization of the human body." As Strength in Figure 1.6, Lew Rosen looks like a superhero in dark, footless tights, a shirt with pompous-looking poufy long sleeves, and a cape. He is, according to Burke, "bull-like 'Strength' in red (Mussolini)."[144] The most defining parts of Grusha Mark's costume are a white downward-pointing triangular smock and elbow-length conical white wristcuffs. She represents "the pale glory-that-was-Rome 'Harmony' in white (emasculate Caesar)."[145] Allen Wayne wears a white sash over a long-sleeved bodysuit, anchored with a large heart pinned to his chest, to become "the romantic heart-on-the-breast 'Kindness' in green (Gabriel D'Annunzio [sic])."[146] These figures' bright costumes stood out against the masses dressed in black. Marchlike snare drum rolls announced the trio's onstage arrival in the dance's second section before these characters destroyed humanity for the duration of the piece. *Daily Worker* critic Louise Mitchell noted, "All human and constructive elements are ruthlessly destroyed by the savagery

139. Rothenberg and Joris, *Poems*, 193–194, 208.
140. Marinetti, "Manifesto of Futurism," 198.
141. See Sander L. Gilman, "The Jewish Body: A Foot-note," 223–241, and Jay Geller, "(G) nos(e)ology: The Cultural Construction of the Other," 243–282, both in *People of the Body* (see Introduction, n26).
142. See Burke, "The Dance," March 16, 1937, 29, and Church, "Anna Sokolow and Dance Unit, Major Subscription Series, YMHA, Sunday, February 28, 1937," 41, for "three graces" references, and Louise Mitchell, "New Dance Unit is Tops" for the "three Roman ideals" reference.
143. Burke, "The Dance," March 16, 1937, 29.
144. Ibid.
145. Ibid.
146. Ibid.

Figure 1.6: Strength, Harmony, and Kindness, *Excerpts from a War Poem (F. T. Marinetti)* (1937). Dancers, left to right: Lew Rosen, Grusha Mark, and Allen Wayne. Uncredited photograph, *Daily Worker*, November 10, 1937. People's World Daily News, peoplesworld.org.

and deception of Fascist ideals."[147] In *Dance Observer* Marjorie Church described how these three "step delicately and meltingly through a safe little routine which serves as a mask for the brutalities to come."[148] Sokolow parodied these historical figures, using ridiculousness to warn of their power. Church wrote that Sokolow "plucked [Fascism] mercilessly apart, line by line, exposing a ruthlessness, a savagery, and a masochistic blindness underlying this viewpoint which are appalling in their implications."[149] Sokolow implied that futurist destruction yielded an impotent Italy and a dangerous new world order.

Sokolow choreographically aligned herself with the aesthetic zeitgeist through her use of allegory and archetypes to expose the dangers of European totalitarian regimes. *War Poem* and *Façade* reflected themes from Kurt Jooss' *The Green Table* (1932) and Léonide Massine's symphonic ballets (1933–1936) within the transnational Left. *Green Table*, subtitled "A Dance of Death in Eight Scenes," was a poignant

147. Mitchell, "New Dance Unit is Tops."
148. Church, "Anna Sokolow and Dance Unit, Major Subscription Series, YMHA, Sunday, uary 28, 1937," 41.
ˌ. Ibid.

antiwar piece in which racketeering bureaucrats plot out war from the safety of their headquarters. Massine's symphonic ballets' music visualizations manifested anti-fascist messages through allegory and archetypal characters. *War Poem*'s February 1937 premiere came on the heels of Massine's return performances of *Symphonie Fantastique* (1936) with Col. Wassily de Basil's Ballet Russe in November 1936. The previous four years of Massine's New York tours of *Les Présages* (1933) and *Choreartium* (1935), alongside Jooss' *Green Table*, certainly influenced Sokolow as her dances germinated. Sokolow was in the *corps* of Massine's 1930 staging of *The Rite of Spring* in New York,[150] so prior to Massine's mid- to late-1930s tours with the Ballet Russe companies,[151] Sokolow knew Massine and likely attended his concerts. The socialist Jewish circles in which Sokolow traveled embraced the productions of Jooss, Massine, and other Ballets Russes–influenced companies like that of Serge Lifar during their 1930s New York tours, as *Morgen Freiheit* and *New Masses* often featured reviews of their work. *War Poem* and *Façade* were satirical like *Green Table* and they employed an archetypal allegory for anti-fascist meaning-making like Massine's symphonic ballets. The triangulation of Sokolow's, Jooss', and Massine's choreographies highlighted revolutionary spectatorship among their cross section of the international Left that included revolutionary choreographies across modern and ballet lexicons.

With its three dominant archetypal figures, *War Poem* resembled Massine's symphonic ballets, especially *Les Présages* (1933), which was set to Tchaikovsky's Fifth Symphony, featured good triumphing over evil, and toured New York in December 1933.[152] Chief among the similarities between *War Poem* and *Présages* were the way archetypal figures drove the works' allegory and foreshadowed destruction and the architectural formations of the dancers' bodies in the space.[153] Because *Présages* ran at West 44th Street's St. James Theater, a regular NDL haunt, NDL audiences likely aligned politically with *Présages* and participated in its revolutionary spectatorship. The ballet's title translates roughly as "the omens" and the work referenced *The Green Table*.[154] Reporting on a July 1933 London performance of *Présages* for the *New York*

150. Warren, *Rebellious Spirit*, 29–31.

151. See Vicente García-Márquez, *Ballets Russes: Colonel de Basil's Ballets Russes de Monte Carlo 1932–1952* (New York: Knopf, 1990), xvi–xvii for a chronology of the Ballet Russe companies' names and artistic directors after Serge Diaghilev's 1929 death.

152. John Martin, "New Ballet Russe Warmly Greeted," *New York Times*, December 23, 1933, 18, PQHN; and ibid., "Ballet Russe Offers New Composition," *New York Times*, December 27, 1933, 23, PQHN. See also García-Márquez, *Ballets Russes*, 51–63; and Judith Chazin-Bennahum, *René Blum & The Ballets Russes: In Search of a Lost Life* (New York: Oxford University Press, 2011), 133–134.

153. For Massine's symphonic ballets, see Nancy Reynolds and Malcolm McCormick, *No Fixed Points: Dance in the Twentieth Century* (New Haven, CT: Yale University Press, 2003), 119–122; and Janet Sinclair, "Choreartium Born Again," *Dance and Dancers*, October 1991, 12–15.

154. Janice Berman, "Dance: Memories of Massine," *Los Angeles Times*, May 3, 1992, http://articles.latimes.com/print/1992-05-03/entertainment/ca-2006_1_ballets-russes. Accessed December 11, 2014.

Times, critic F. Bonavia saw "Groups of dancers scurrying across the back of the stage in ordered anarchy" before a "final paean of triumph"—moments that return in Sokolow's *War Poem*.[155] *Présages* reportedly contained fascist salutes and goose stepping in the movement and visual elements of abstracted swastikas,[156] all of which, like Sokolow's use of Marinetti's verse, foreshadowed the danger of, rather than upheld the ideology of, what they signified.[157]

Sokolow further compositionally affiliated with European anti-Nazi work by means of her dances' resonance with *Green Table*. Jooss' ideals aligned with Joseph Lewitan's leftist dance journal *Der Tanz*. Lewitan, a Zionist dance writer and immigrant Russian Jew living in Germany and stripped of his nationality when the Nazis deemed him and other Jews stateless in 1935,[158] made space in *Der Tanz* for theoretical discussions and reportage about Jewish dance in addition to essays about German expressive dance.[159] According to Susan Manning, Jooss' leftist associations were legible to contemporary German viewers: first, through the characters that audiences read as Nazi figures of the Gentlemen in Black (the bureaucrats around the war table), and the Profiteer, who like a vulture picks his way through the dead characters' belongings; and second, through Jooss's reading of *Die Weltbühne*, a leftist theater magazine edited by prominent German Jewish anti-fascist satirist Kurt Tucholsky.[160] Jooss' reputation accompanied him to New York, where the Jewish socialist community knew his politics. 1933 *Morgen Freiheit* advertisements

155. F. Bonavia, "Ballet Season in London: Monte Carlo, Serge Lifar and Camargo Society Troupes Give Performances," *New York Times*, July 30, 1933, 117. PQHN.

156. Berman, "Dance: Memories of Massine."

157. John Martin noted the influence of *Symphonie Fantastique* (1936), which toured New York in October–November 1936, on *Façade*. He observed that "the group moves in a kind of surréaliste attitudinizing, and one is reminded forcibly of Massine's handling of a similar problem in the pastoral movement of the 'Fantastic Symphony.'" John Martin, "The Dance: New Blood: Esther Junger, Jose Limon and Anna Sokolow in Bennington," *New York Times*, August 29, 1937, 8X, Anna Sokolow Clippings, JRDD, NYPL.

158. In the early twentieth century, Zionism was a modern nationalist movement, aligned with Eastern European Jewish socialism, and based in a desire for Jewish sovereignty at a time when other nineteenth-century and early twentieth-century European nationalist movements excluded Jews. Zionism did not yet have a religious connotation or assumed connection to the modern state of Israel, which did not yet exist. Reuven Firestone, "One Holy Land, Three Holy Peoples: Islamic, Christian, and Jewish Regard for the 'Holy Land' and Its Impact on the Current Conflict" (lecture, Columbus Jewish Community Center, Columbus, OH, January 18, 2015). For Lewitan see Marion Kant, "Joseph Lewitan and the Nazification of Dance in Germany," in *The Art of Being Jewish in Modern Times*, eds. Barbara Kirshenblatt-Gimblett and Jonathan Karp (Philadelphia: University of Pennsylvania Press, 2008), 349.

159. Kant, "Lewitan and Nazification," 338–339. *Der Tanz*'s content, and Lewitan's Jewishness, prompted Mary Wigman to attack *Der Tanz* as a Jewish publication in a letter to Josef Goebbels's Ministry of Propaganda in 1935. Kant, "Lewitan and Nazification," 349.

160. Manning, *Ecstasy*, 164 (see Introduction, n27); "Tucholsky, Kurt (1890-1935)," in *The Crystal Reference Encyclopedia* (West Chiltington: Crystal Semantics, 2005), and "Tucholsky, Kurt," in *The Columbia Encyclopedia* (New York: Columbia University Press, 2013), both Credo Reference. Manning notes that "The Nazis correctly interpreted Jooss' leftist leanings" and "harassed the choreographer." Manning, *Ecstasy*, 165.

for *Green Table* suggest that the dance, as well as Jooss' politics, aligned with leftist Jewish discourse.[161] The Ballets Jooss toured the United States with *The Green Table* four times between 1933 and 1937, and enjoyed enthusiastic reception and widespread coverage in prominent newspapers including the *New York Times*, *Washington Post*, and *Los Angeles Times* that spoke to the broad concertgoing public. In an effort to widen Jooss' audiences and protect his reputation, Martin often pointedly mentioned that Jooss did not support Third Reich ideology and that Jooss worked with many Jews in his company.[162] Sokolow's incorporation of a Death archetype connects *War Poem* to *Green Table*'s anti-fascism, and joins her New York audiences to Jooss' in the United States and Europe through revolutionary spectatorship.

Death functions as an inevitable force throughout *War Poem* and replaces Caesar as the mythic power. The first section of the dance introduces a creeping thematic melody in a single piano line that foreshadows doom. In his description of the *War Poem* musical score, composer Mont Chris Hubbard noted, "the preponderance of snare drum and tambourine rolls and the sepulchral clangs of the piano give the impression of a death march or execution, while a triangle provides a bit of whimsy. But the lack of either melody or harmony, and the lack of variation in tempo, leave it strangely emotionless."[163] This musical line recalls the archetypal Death character's musical theme in *Green Table*, where Death, a hybrid soldier–skeleton, claims soldiers and civilians in a haunting, macabre refrain. Dance theorist Kate Elswit has noted of this character's liminal nature: "Jooss' Death occupied the dual roles of a soldier—one who brings death to others and one who is susceptible to it."[164] The characters Strength, Harmony, and Kindness propel *War Poem* in their archetypal death roles. Similar to Jooss' Death, they foreshadow social destruction, but Sokolow aligned them with Futurism's fascist aesthetic by portraying them as mechanical puppets and soulless automatons. Whereas Jooss' Death's mortality made him the most human character in *Green Table*, the lack of emotional pull from Strength, Harmony, and Kindness relegates them to the inhuman realm of cold, futurist machines. These archetypes deliver the dance's satire: Sokolow juxtaposed a Fascist Italy of cultural leadership with the results of fascist destruction all around

161. Advertisements in *Morgen Freiheit*, October 29, 1933, 7 and November 5, 1933, 7, Dorot, NYPL, trans. Ali Potvin and Hannah Kosstrin.

162. John Martin, "The Dance: A European Ballet Star," *New York Times*, September 24, 1933, X2; John Martin, "The Dance: Coming of Jooss Ballet," *New York Times*, October 29, 1933, X4; John Martin, "The Dance: Art of Jooss," *New York Times*, November 5, 1933, X2. See also "Ballet Jooss Here for a Tour," *New York Times*, October 29, 1933, N3, and "Jooss Says Dance is Not Propaganda," *New York Times*, November 11, 1933. All PQHN. Jooss fled Nazi Germany in February 1933, under cover of departing for this tour. Lilian Karina in Lilian Karina and Marion Kant, *Hitler's Dancers: German Modern Dance and the Third Reich*, trans. Jonathan Steinberg (New York: Berghahn Books, 2003), 45.

163. Mont Chris Hubbard, written notes to author accompanying s~~ October 2011, in author's possession.

164. Elswit, *Watching Weimar Dance*, 11.

Beyond the inefficacy of a sawdust Caesar, *War Poem* intoned that Mussolini's begat his own destruction.

War Poem's fourth section contained its dramatic climax, in which the three totalitarian automatons wended through the swirling onstage chaos. In Marinetti's verse, war harmonizes destruction, and its ruins form an aesthetic landscape: "War is Beautiful because it symphonizes pauses choked by silence, the perfumes and odors of putrification and creates the spiral smoke of burning villages." This devastation culminated with "terrorized women" running all over the stage around "distorted" bodies.[165] Burke called this scene "a series of single and duo figures of disintegration—hurried, frantic, utterly futile efforts to bolster the diseased 'culture' which faces an inevitable and running destruction."[166] At one point, Harmony, in profile to stage left, commanded the stage by mimicking a fascist salute, while her other arm pointed low in front of her. Strength and Kindness folded on the floor at her feet. Other dancers' bodies littered the stage. Some embraced, some made disfigured shapes, one lay prone, and one focused on something on the floor by his foot, perhaps a dead body or shrapnel.[167] Strength and Kindness rose as Harmony traversed the stage to hover over the prone body, slicing her arms to alternate their position. Strength drew his cape across his chest as Kindness stood at attention and stepped forward, while a frightened, cowering woman joined the solitary man to gaze, frightened, at the destruction on the ground (Figure 1.7). Strength, Harmony, and Kindness calmly continued their mechanized movements through the piece's final section as the world crumbled into ruin around them. The group incorporated movement themes from elsewhere in the dance, as Burke noted, "all four preceding phrases are harmonized in a brilliant choreographic structure."[168] This weaving, Church detailed, "form[s] a picture of distortion, in which human values are crushed by the very symbols which pretended to idealize those values."[169] Fascist ideals blindly ruin humanity. Caesar's Rome is gone.

The aftermath of this fury in the dance's final section compositionally reinforced Sokolow's and North's proletarian and anti-fascist allegiances, and thematically juxtaposed Marinetti's "War is Beautiful because it serves the greatness of our Fascist Italy" with the onstage carnage that instead suggested Fascist Italy's glory disappeared. From the frantic counterpoint and tremulo triangle, the melody emerges as a slowed-down, regal-sounding reprise of the archetypal theme from the first section of the piece. This section lacks a musical climax; instead, references to other sections of the score pass through before the music unexpectedly fades away. Siegmeister noted that North's score "used all the resources of contemporary

---

165. Church, "Anna Sokolow and Dance Unit, Major Subscription Series, YMHA, Sunday, February 28, 1937," 41.

166. Burke, "The Dance," March 16, 1937, 29.

167. Photograph by Will Weissberg, SDF.

168. Burke, "The Dance," March 16, 1937, 29.

169. Marjorie Church, "Anna Sokolow and Dance Unit, Major Subscription Series, YMHA, Sunday, February 28, 1937," 41.

Figure 1.7: Dance Unit in *Excerpts from a War Poem (F. T. Marinetti)* (1937). "War is Beautiful because it symphonizes pauses choked by silence, the perfumes and odors of putrification and creates the spiral smoke of burning villages." Photography by Will Weissberg, NYC. Courtesy of Sokolow Dance Foundation.

music to deliver a savage attack on Fascist barbarism."[170] The dance's end in a whimper, instead of with a grand gesture, offered no direct solution to the problems it presented.

Sokolow's leftist coalition further manifested through her collaboration in *War Poem* with North. Their common backgrounds and compositional strategies contributed to their shared artistic–political goals. Like Sokolow, North was born in 1910 to Russian Jewish immigrants and raised by a widow committed to education and culture who provided for the family. Sokolow's and North's concerns for the human condition attracted them to New York's leftist activities in the 1930s. After meeting at a 1932 union hall dance performance,[171] their shared interest in jazz music connected them to the Popular Front, which considered jazz the new American folk music and a social practice.[172] Fellow leftist musician Siegmeister, who scored Sokolow's *Strange American Funeral* in 1935 when North studied in Moscow, highlighted the strength of

170. Elie Seigmeister, *The Music Lover's Handbook* (New York: William Morrow, 1943), 770, quoted in Henderson, *Alex North*, 22 (see Introduction, n12).

171. Henderson, *Alex North*, 14.

172. Denning, *Cultural Front*, 284, 320; and Robert Walser, ed., "Preface," in *Keeping Time: Readings in Jazz History* (New York and Oxford: Oxford University Press, 1999), vii-viii.

Sokolow's and North's camaraderie. Frustrated with many concert dancers' attitudes that music was "auxiliary" in relation to their movement, Siegmeister wrote, "It can only be through the close collaboration of musician and dancer on a status of complete equality, seeking a common objective, based on a pro-labor, anti-war, and anti-fascist ideology. The product [must] be . . . an equilibrium in which the best energies of both artists have room to expand," and he cited Sokolow's collaboration with North in the Dance Unit as one such example.[173] Martin, referencing the November 14, 1937 Dance Unit Broadway debut, wrote, "North . . . is an invaluable collaborator. His music has vitality and imagination and that rarest of attributes, a feeling for movement."[174] Fifty years later, after scoring films, plays, and dances (for Sokolow and others) and receiving fourteen Academy Award nominations, North called "functional music," his stage and screen compositions, the most satisfying to compose.[175]

Sokolow's and North's shared compositional strategies answered the American Communist movement's mid-1930s imperative to co-opt bourgeois techniques for revolutionary statements.[176] Sokolow applied the techniques she learned with Graham and Horst, and North the virtuosic composition he studied at The Juilliard School and the Moscow Conservatory, in the service of their proletarian and anti-fascist work. Sokolow expanded Graham's lexicon of contractions and spirals with movements that portrayed her own content. As Horst's assistant, Sokolow employed choreographic structures he taught based in classical and modern musical forms. One example for North is the final musical movement of *War Poem*. It begins with a fugue, a mathematically virtuosic compositional form. North embellished this technical base through rhythmic experimentations informed by his jazz work.[177] Sokolow's and North's use of Africanist elements like syncopation, juxtaposition, tonal play, and angularity connected them compositionally to the New York Left's social values and continued in *Façade* and *Slaughter*.

In *Façade*, as in *War Poem*, Sokolow stripped Caesar-like dictators of their power. She unveiled a failed Roman Empire and horrors in Spain, where Franco's and Hitler's forces firebombed the Basque town Guernica three months before *Façade*'s premiere. A program note connects Fascist Italy to the Spanish Civil War:

> Behind the glittering front of the Exposizione Italiana fascism offers its trumpeted wares to the Citizen: the glories of yesterday's Caesars and the Caesar of today. The Citizen scans the statues and fountains, the pillars and marble. . .watches the martial youth. . . the Fruitful Woman. . . .But truth, where is its booth at the Exposizione, the Citizen cries in the Fantasmagoria? Where are the bleeding men of Guadalajara . . .?[178]

173. Elie Siegmeister, "Music for the Dance," *New Theatre* (October 1935): 10–11.
174. John Martin, "Dance Debut Here by Anna Sokolow."
175. Charles Champlin, "Alex North: A Score for Reticence," *Los Angeles Times*, August 23, 1984, 1, 8. PQHN.
176. See Graff, *Stepping Left*, 58.
177. Thank you to Mont Chris Hubbard for this articulation.
178. Program, *New Masses Presents Anna Sokolow and Dance Unit*, Alvin Theatre, February 26, 1939, Martha Hill Papers, Juilliard.

Mainstream and leftist critics received *Façade* as they had *War Poem*, praising Sokolow's fascist indictment, her portrayal of the victims' humanity, and her effective yet understated satire. Margery Dana summed it up in the *Daily Worker*: "The stature of the comment grows as the dance progresses, the resolution being in the nature of a profound warning to take stock of our own honesty lest we fall into the fascist [*sic*] trap."[179]

Façade echoed international interwar-period artistic response to European fascism. Sokolow premiered it in the Vermont State Armory in Bennington, Vermont, on August 12, 1937, at the Bennington Summer School of the Dance.[180] Pairing *War Poem* (*War is Beautiful*) with *Façade*, American critics noted *Façade*'s pain through its satire as distinct from *War Poem*'s rage. Gilfond noted in *Dance Observer*, "It is as bitter as *War Is Beautiful*, and what it may lack in anger, compared with the former work, it makes up for with the deeply moving human quality of hurt."[181] Burke asserted, "*Façade* has less anger than *War Is Beautiful*, but a more poignant human quality for all its bitterness."[182] *Façade*'s humanity appeared in Sokolow's Citizen character that universalized suffering by drawing the audience into its midst. As the Citizen, Sokolow stood on a raised box, surveyed the wreckage, and then descended to address the audience members from the edge of the stage. By insisting that they, too, must recognize the destruction, Sokolow implicated her audience members as witnesses to these atrocities and as empowered members of society who could do something about it when they left the theater.

As did *War Poem*, *Façade* hit with an emotional and politically charged impact similar to *Green Table*. When the Dance Unit performed *Façade* in Mexico City in 1939, moreover, critic Armando de Maria y Campos averred in the daily paper *Hoy* that *Façade* was "undoubtedly" inspired by *The Green Table*.[183] By means of their choreographic allegiances to Jooss and Sokolow's political alliances in the NDL and ADA, her anti-fascist dances evidenced transnational communist discourse circulating through them.

In *Façade*, things fall apart when Sokolow reveals the Potemkin Village–like charade of Italy's sawdust Caesar. One reviewer wrote in response, "When the citizens

179. Dana, "Anna Sokolow and Unit Seen In New Solo and Group Dances," 7.

180. Kriegsman, *Bennington Years*, 71. Sokolow, José Limón, and Esther Junger were choreographic fellows at Bennington in the summer of 1937. Sokolow restaged *Façade* for her Dance Unit and they performed it for the next couple seasons.

181. Henry Gilfond, "Workshop and Fellow Concerts, August 12-13-14, 1937, Vermont State Armory, Bennington, VT," *Dance Observer* (August–September 1937): 79.

182. Burke, "The Dance," August 31, 1937, 29.

183. Armando de Maria y Campos, "El Ritmo del Teatro: Ana Sokoloff y su Grupo en el Escenario de Bellas Artes," *Hoy*, April 22, 1939, 53, CENIDID, CENART. "Indudablemente que el ballet 'Fachada de Exposición Italiana' que acabamos de verle a 'Ana Sokoloff y su Grupo' está inspirado ed 'La Mesa Verde', como 'Raro Funeral Americano', de la misma Ana Sokoloff, música de Elie Siegmeister, lo está en 'Pavane por une Infante Défunte', de Kurt Joos, música de Ravel; las fotografías que de ambos ballets tengo delante no delante no dejan lugar a duda. La visita de los ballets de Joos a Estados Unidos ha sido utilísima a los discípulos de Martha Graham."

seek to dig beneath the shining exteriors of these highly-touted virtues, comes the rebellion."[184] The five sections of *Façade*, "Spectacle," "Belle Arti," "Giovanezza," "Prix Femina," and "Fantasmagoria," satirized aspects of Italian Fascist culture, including what one critic described as "maternity, athletic skill, victory and the love of victory, culture (but, of course, with a capital C)."[185] According to critic Margaret Lloyd, "Spectacle" "illustrated the pomp and pageantry of Mussolini's nefarious regime."[186] In "Belle Arti," three women wearing long skirts and light-toned belted tunics with white headbands represent what Gilfond described as "Greekish statuary and Florentinish oil."[187] Reflecting a patriotic fascist paean to youth, "Giovanezza" displayed competitive athleticism.[188] Dancers wore white t-shirts strapped by medium-toned, perhaps red, sashes; the women sported kilts and the men, bloomers. In Figure 1.8, they lunge forward en masse, each onto one leg as they punch an arm forward and extend the opposite leg behind, in an exaggerated run and a competition of strength. The presentation of bodies in this photograph resonates with the images in Leni Riefenstahl's *Olympia*, a filmic celebration of the 1936 Berlin Olympics funded by the Third Reich's Ministry of Propaganda that triumphed unity, commonality, and physical, healthful beauty.[189] The film did not premiere until 1938 and did not reach the United States until 1940,[190] and is based on German instead of Italian propaganda, but the arena that Sokolow created in "Giovanezza" recalls Riefenstahl's portrayal of healthy athletic bodies competing under the Nazi cause. The women in the trio "Prix Femina" could have been a dismantled Greek chorus in their ankle-length pinkish dresses with puffy long sleeves and flowers gracing their arms, necklines, and hair (Figure 1.9). They circled the stage, twisted their torsos, and extended their arms as they glided through the space.[191] Although these dancers, reported by Gilfond to appear "weak and beaten to a meek and unquestioning acceptance,"[192] suggested women's oppression under Mussolini, their presence opposed the anti-woman sentiment of Futurists such as Marinetti.

184. No author, no source, April 1939, Box 12, Folder 6, Katharine Wolfe Papers, JRDD, NYPL.

185. Ibid.

186. Margaret Lloyd, *The Borzoi Book of Modern Dance*, reprint (New York: Knopf, 1949; New York: Dance Horizons, 1974), 217. Citations are to Dance Horizons edition.

187. Gilfond, "Workshop and Fellow Concerts," 79. Costume descriptions are based on photograph by Will Weissberg, SDF.

188. Burke, "The Dance: Bennington, Vermont," 29; Gilfond, "Workshop and Fellow Concerts," 79; and Sokolow, interview by Newman, transcript, 107.

189. "Festival of Beauty," *Olympia*, directed by Leni Riefenstahl (1938; Venice, CA: Pathfinder Home Entertainment, 2006), DVD.

190. "2 Delegates Decry Venice Film Awards: Choice of German Picture Irks U.S. and British Envoys," *New York Times*, September 2, 1938, 21; "Sidelights of the Week," *New York Times*, September 4, 1938, 38; Jack Munhall, "Two-Hour 'Olympia,' Slated for Run Here, Termed Useful for Track and Swimming Students; Propaganda is Cut," *The Washington Post*, January 30, 1940, 17; and "Bankhead Hit And New Films On Horizon: 'The Little Foxes' At National Monday; Other New Bills," *The Washington Post*, February 1, 1940, 11.

191. This description is based on photos by Will Weissberg, SDF.

192. Gilfond, "Workshop and Fellow Concerts," 79.

Figure 1.8: Dance Unit in *Façade—Esposizione Italiana*, "Giovanezza." As the Citizen, Sokolow surveys the athletic competition of (left to right) Aza Cefkin (Bard), Allen Wayne, Rebecca Rowen (Stein), Kathleen O'Brien, Lew Rosen, and Daniel Nagrin. Photography by Will Weissberg, NYC. Courtesy of the Sokolow Dance Foundation.

Sokolow's Citizen character signaled larger anti-fascist modernist currents in which her choreography took part. Particularly, Hanya Holm's *Trend* (1937) premiered at Bennington the same weekend as *Façade* and integrated anticapitalist with anti-Nazi critique. Sokolow's Citizen functioned similarly to Holm's *Trend* character whose singular actions commented on events from within the dance instead of functioning as a charismatic unifying leader.[193] In the Citizen role, Sokolow portrayed a cultural seer. Dressed in black, she surveyed the dance's events from her standing perch on a raised platform. The dark background of the stage space nearly swallowed her petite form. Critics' comments about her male-resonant, stoic presence positioned her as a soothsayer.[194] Dana narrated, "like the very Truth itself, [the Citizen] dominates the scene in tense and watchful stillness,"[195] and Martin noted, "It is this central role which holds the work together, and Miss Sokolow's performance of it is magnificent for its stillness and strength."[196] Sokolow's body was

193. Manning, "*Ausdruckstanz* Across the Atlantic," 52–53 (see Introduction, n70).
194. As the Citizen, Lloyd wrote, Sokolow "symboliz[ed] the people," and thus her body represented the bodies of throngs of men and women. Lloyd, *Borzoi Book*, 217.
195. Dana, "Anna Sokolow and Unit Seen in New Solo and Group Dances," 7.
196. Martin, "The Dance: New Blood," 8X.

Figure 1.9: Ruth Freidman and Sasha Spector in *Façade—Esposizione Italiana,* "Prix Femina." Photograph by Barbara Morgan. Barbara and Willard Morgan Photographs and Papers, Library Special Collections, Charles E. Young Research Library, UCLA.

a barometer for signaling societal inner turmoil when things ruptured. In the midst of the futurist rapture of "Fantasmagoria," the Citizen "is so twisted, tormented and brow-beaten that he walks on his head" and "climbs walls—backwards."[197] After the "cultural façade disintegrates like a worm-eaten pillar," Sokolow emerged as an "accusing and protesting figure."[198] In a movement trope that Sokolow repeated in her choreography through the 1980s, she broke the theatrical fourth wall to implore audience members to fully grapple with the problems she exposed: Gilfond reported that she "walks forward into the audience [. . .and] demands recognition of what is happening, demands that the audience take cognizance of what she had said."[199] As members of society reading daily headlines that matched the world of Sokolow's dance, audience members found themselves emotionally implicated as bystanders to the real consequences of European Fascism. Yet, continuing to label

197. Gilfond, "Workshop and Fellow Concerts," 79, and Burke, "The Dance: Bennington, Vermont," 29. According to Gilfond, Sokolow was good at walking on her head.
198. Burke, "The Dance: Bennington, Vermont," 29.
199. Gilfond, "Workshop and Fellow Concerts," 79.

Sokolow's Citizen in male terms, critics could not sufficiently theorize Sokolow's resonances with universalism for the women in her anti-fascist work. In *Slaughter of the Innocents*, Sokolow's role as a mother reaffirmed women's centrality to these kinds of indictments. Critics' refusals to address Sokolow's presentation of power in a female role as transcendent reinforced modernist invisibilization of women's themes.[200]

Slaughter of the Innocents, Sokolow's only anti-fascist dance in which she portrayed a distinctly female character, displayed mothers' compassion as part of universalizing statements. Although the statement Sokolow made with *Slaughter* aligned with her pointed satire, the embodiment of it diverged. Instead of being a gender-unassigned (read: male) everyperson skeptically surveying the scene, or a choreographer whose ideas were present but whose body was not, in *Slaughter* Sokolow was a mother, an expected role for women. *Slaughter* was an emotionally intense solo focused on women and children Spanish Civil War victims,[201] in which Sokolow "turned continuously" and embraced an imaginary dead baby,[202] as she "express[ed] a Spanish mother's anguish on losing her child."[203] Sokolow drew on motherhood, a woman's role highlighted by many nationalist agendas, instead of everyman statements. Critics' responses circumscribed Sokolow's performance within normative gender expectations that did not have the far-reaching power of the Citizen. Reviewers commented on the compositional voids in this piece, yet pointed to its conviction and strength, because of Sokolow's powerful portrayal of a mother avenging her baby's wrongful death. As feminist writer Adrienne Rich asserted that motherhood is inscribed within patriarchal systems of power,[204] so too did critics treat *Slaughter* as a separate kind of representation from Sokolow's Everyman in dances like *Case History* or *Façade*. By highlighting mothers' painful losses of their children during war, Sokolow referenced a trope that easily matched her anger with her gender. In *Slaughter* Sokolow was an Everymother, a position that connected her to women across tragedy-torn areas. *Slaughter*'s anti-fascist stance gave voice to Spanish women who needed to be heard.

In *Slaughter*, Sokolow mobilized emotional qualities assigned to women in the service of anti-fascism. Burke noted that her performance "projects through tortured understatement a profound sympathy and understanding [. . .and] has the quieting effect of great sorrow rather than . . . the qualities that dynamically move out of her poignant anti-fascist blasts."[205] Photographs suggest more tenderness and

200. Dixon Gottschild's term "invisibilized" represents how US institutional racism erased acknowledgment of Africanist influences in American cultural phenomena. *Digging*, 2.

201. Warren, *Rebellious Spirit*, 71.

202. Warren, *Rebellious Spirit*, 71; and Larry Warren to Jerome Robbins, July 20, 1989, Box 539, Folder 2, Jerome Robbins Papers, JRDD, NYPL.

203. Jerome D. Bohm, "Anna Sokolow and Group Give Dance Recital," *New York Herald Tribune*, November 15, 1937, n.p., Anna Sokolow Clippings, JRDD, NYPL.

204. Adrienne Rich, *Of Woman Born: Motherhood as Experience and* (New York: Norton, 1976), 13–14.

205. Burke, "Anna Sokolow and Other Dancers," 28–29.

Figure 1.10: Anna Sokolow in *Slaughter of the Innocents*. Photographer unknown. Courtesy of the Sokolow Dance Foundation.

introspection than in *Façade*, but they also portray gradations of rage. At one point in the dance, Sokolow plunged into a lunge and smashed her left fist into her right palm overhead, with anguish apparent through her gnashed teeth as the reddish vertical bands stretching across the surface of her white burlap bodice, designed by her sister Rose Bank, evidenced muscular and emotional strain (Figure 1.10). In another moment, she beseeches,[206] and in a third she stands, displacing her right hip sideways, as she rests her head in the cradle of her arms, which cross at the

206. Photograph by Barbara Morgan, Barbara and Willard Morgan Photographs and Papers, Library Special Collections, Charles E. Young Research Library, UCLA.

Figure 1.11: Anna Sokolow in *Slaughter of the Innocents*. Photograph by Barbara Morgan. Barbara and Willard Morgan Photographs and Papers, Library Special Collections, Charles E. Young Research Library, UCLA.

wrists above her head. While her facial expression in Figure 1.11 is calm, it is unclear if this is a moment of sorrow or resolve. This coexistence of competing emotions in Sokolow's performance of a mother losing a child complicated her straightforwardly rabid anti-fascist statements in her other dances. Church wrote that the solo "is an expression of mature understanding, a plea for the preservation of human values which are fast falling asunder."[207] Critics' language portrayed Sokolow as a woman, instead of as an everyman, but tried to reconcile *Slaughter*'s womanness to apply to all. For Burke, *Slaughter* was "touched with the passion and warmth of woman's (and man's) fraternal and human compassion for an understanding of the people."[208] It remains unclear if the emotional power critics identified in the solo relied on the fact that Sokolow portrayed a vengeful, reproachful mother or whether she simply gave a compelling performance.

207. Marjorie Church, "Anna Sokolow and Dance Unit," *Dance Observer* (December 1937): 127.
208. Burke, "Anna Sokolow and Other Dancers," 28–29. See also John Martin, "Here by Anna Sokolow"; and Margery Dana, "Anna Sokolow and Dance Unit i Debut," *Daily Worker*, November 20, 1937, 7.

Slaughter represented the Spanish Civil War reports that filled the leftist press. The war lasted from 1936 to 1939 and saw Fascist forces overthrow Spain's Second Republic, which formed after the Spanish monarchy fell in 1931. The war began when Fransicso Franco, a Hitler- and Mussolini-backed Fascist who represented conservative traditionalists, initiated a military uprising against the Republican national government led by the Communist and Socialist Spanish Popular Front after February 1936 elections. During the war, the Spanish Loyalists, who were loyal to the Republican government and backed by Stalin, lost to Franco's forces.[209] The American Left's support of the Spanish Loyalists aligned with its anti-fascist stance. A 1936 *New Voices* article titled "Spain and Democracy Are Bleeding" ran the following lines about Franco's military dictatorship: "These fascist-minded capitalists lost all respect for democratic government and constitutional procedure. In their stead they resorted to the most bloody and relentless war that any Western European nation has experienced in decades."[210] In May 1938 the *Daily Worker* ran an article about a group of Mexican aid workers who, with the support of Mexican President Lázaro Cárdenas, brought terrorized Spanish orphans to a new school in Veracruz.[211] These sentiments ran through *Slaughter of the Innocents*. These reports, and leftist dancers' sentiment, however, did not show knowledge of how the rhetoric connected to Stalin's Gulag. According to dance historian Giora Manor, "Only years later did it become known that all of the people sent by the USSR to help the Republican armies in Spain . . . were sent to hard labor camps in Siberia after returning home as heroes."[212] At the time, leftists championed the USSR and were unaware that Stalin committed atrocities like the other totalitarian dictators.

Sokolow employed her *Slaughter* imagery, which represented the opening scenes from Herbert Kline's Loyalist documentary *Heart of Spain* (1937) featuring wailing mothers during a Madrid bomb attack,[213] to humanitarian ends. North's score for the film was Sokolow's inspiration.[214] The film, made for CBC Canada to showcase Canadian doctor Norman Bethune's Spanish blood donation program, focused more on blood donations for soldiers than on civilian victims.[215] Scenes

209. "Spanish Civil War," in *The New Dictionary of Cultural Literacy, Houghton Mifflin*, (Boston: Houghton Mifflin, 2002), "Spanish Civil War and Latin America," in *Iberia and the Americas: Culture, Politics, and History* (Santa Barbara, CA: ABC-CLIO, 2005), and "Spanish Civil War," in *The Columbia Encyclopedia* (New York: Columbia University Press, 2013), all Credo Reference.

210. No author, "Spain and Democracy Are Bleeding," *New Voices* (September 1936): 5, Microforms, NYPL.

211. Henry L. Gage, "Spanish Orphans' 'Road to Life,'" *Daily Worker*, May 6, 1938, 7.

212. Giora Manor, *Brother, Can You Spare a Dance? Dances Red, Pink & Naïve in America in the Thirties* (Israel: Mishmar Haemek, 1985), 21. JRDD, NYPL.

213. *Heart of Spain*, directed by Herbert Kline and Gez Karpathi (Frontier Films, 1937), http://vimeo.com/41585756. Accessed December 14, 2014.

214. Warren, *Rebellious Spirit*, 71.

215. "Herbert Kline, Filmmaker, 89; Recorded Crises in 30's Europe," *New York Times* February 17, 1999, C23, PQHN; Kevin Thomas, "3 Curiosities from 1921-37," *Los Angeles*

showed doctors delivering blood to wounded soldiers in warfront hospitals as cannons exploded outside. The heart of Spain consisted of civilian volunteers who donated blood to save soldiers' lives fighting Fascism. The film narrated mothers as life-giving and soldier-supporting everyday heroes. Sokolow's dance instead gave voice to mothers who mourned.

For Sokolow, the heart of Spain was the women's and children's lives lost in civilian bombings instead of the men's lives saved on the front lines, or volunteers who donated blood. In Mexico City, where Sokolow's audiences included Spanish émigrés who fled Franco, critic Lya Kostakowsky wrote in the leftist *El Popular* that the dance "represents the tragedy of a Spanish mother who in an open field and under a cloudy sky encounters the fascist airplanes with a terrible dead child in her arms, [while] inside us is a protest that makes the hands crisp making us feel the bondage, the savagery of what Franco represents in Spain."[216] *Heart of Spain* begins as three fighter planes roar over Madrid. People run for cover and clutch babies to their chests as a bomb falls and buildings crumble. Images of Hitler and Mussolini flash across the screen before the bomb shatters and exploding sound mixes with a woman's blood-curdling scream. Men pull dead children from a crater in the street as a woman's inconsolable sobs fill the soundscape. North's ominous-sounding score begins as the camera pans over the torn structures of bombed-out buildings, rows of coffins, and Loyalist and Fascist propaganda posters. Dancing these images in Figure 1.12, Sokolow weaves her arms around each other, cradling her invisible baby; she spins, arrests her own motion, and throws her arms forward and up, as if addressing the bombardiers; she draws her hand away from her heart, and pulses quietly with the vulnerable front surface of her torso exposed. In this solo, Sokolow mourned the loss of civilian life in anti-fascist military fighting by continuing to dance American leftist headlines.

Heart of Spain resonated with American leftist audiences. The film screened in theaters across the United States from August through December 1937, mostly at fundraising events for organizations like the Washington, DC–based American Friends of Spanish Democracy that featured introductions by doctors leaving for Spain to treat soldiers on the front lines. Much of the private US aid to Loyalist Spain came through donations to these organizations, which funded American hospitals in Spanish cities like Córdoba and Madrid. Some monies came from the concert-dance-going public. A handful of concerts, including Sokolow's, collected

Times, August 21, 1976, B8, PQHN; and Tom Vallance, "Obituary: Herbert Kline," *The Independent* (London), February 18, 1999, 6. LNA.

216. Lya Kostakowsky, "La Juventud de Anna Sokolow," *El Popular*, April 27, 1939, 3, Microforms, NYPL, trans. Alejandra Jara de Marco and Hannah Kosstrin. ". . .nos representa la tragedia de una madre española, que en campo abierto y bajo un cielo nublado se en cuentra a merced de los aviones fascistas con un terrible niño muerto, entre los brazos, dentro de nosotros se levanta una protesta, quo hace que las manos se crispen, haciéndonos sentir la cadena posada, el salvajismo de lo que Franco representa en España."

Figure 1.12: Anna Sokolow in four photographs of *Slaughter of the Innocents* by Barbara Morgan. Barbara and Willard Morgan Photographs and Papers, Library Special Collections, Charles E. Young Research Library, UCLA.

money for or donated proceeds to the Medical Bureau to Aid Spanish Democracy, a New York–based organization that supported American doctors in Spain loosely affiliated with the American Friends of Spanish Democracy.[217] *The New York Amsterdam News* ran a preview of a December 1937 *Heart of Spain* screening at the Community Church Auditorium at 550 W. 110th Street, just south of Harlem, under the auspices of the Medical Bureau to Aid Spanish Democracy. The preview highlighted a scene of Harlem Hospital nurse Salaria Kee, the sole African

217. No author, "'Heart of Spain' To Be Exhibited On Wednesday," *The Washington Post*, August 22, 1937, A5; No author, "Friends of Spain To Show Movie Of Strife Tonight," *The Washington Post*, August 25, 1937, 11; No author, "Organizer to Describe Hospital Work in Spain," *The Washington Post*, August 25, 1937, 14; Betty Walker, "Medical Aid to Spain," *The Washington Post*, September 25, 1937, 6; No author, "News of the Screen," *New York Times*, October 27, 1937, 47, all PQHN; and Irving Kolodin, "Two Dancers Give Recitals: Zahava Appears in Guild; Sokolow in Alvin," no source, February 27, 1939, n.p., Anna Sokolow Clippings, JRDD, NYPL.

American medical personnel in Spain. This announcement reinforces anti-fascist activism across Jewish, white, and black contingents of the American Left.[218] Sokolow's European anti-fascist dances fueled her ensuing American Communist statements that targeted fascism and racism at home.

PARTY PAGEANTRY FOR ANTIRACISM AND ANTI-FASCISM

Back in the United States context, Sokolow's work in Communist productions outside concert dance exemplified her political reach across the New York Left. Her *Dance of All Nations* at the New York State Committee for the Communist Party's 1938 Lenin Memorial Meeting at Madison Square Garden, her "Filibuster" in the Negro Cultural Committee's revue *The Bourbons Got the Blues* (1938), and her choreography for the Federal Theatre Project (FTP) musical revue *Sing for Your Supper* (1939) brought her into a Communist-affiliated arena beyond revolutionary and modern concert dance circles. These projects evidenced her broad appeal as a communist artist who could move public masses as well as concert dance-goers. Sokolow's circulation among Communist-affiliated venues, whose productions embodied the antiracism and anti-fascism Sokolow upheld in her choreography, displayed the broad spectatorial avenues through which committed audiences connected with revolutionary ideology.

Sokolow and North continued their revolutionary collaboration for audiences across the English- and Yiddish-speaking Jewish and African American segments of the New York Left in the pageant *Dance of All Nations* for thirty-five performers at the January 19, 1938 Lenin Memorial Meeting, which Sokolow choreographed and North scored.[219] The Communist Party in the United States and Mexico held annual meetings for Vladimir Lenin in the 1930s–1940s to commemorate the anniversary of his death. US meetings featured mass dances alongside prominent Communist speakers, including Earl Browder, Roy Hudson, "Mother" Ella Reeve Bloor, and others who held Communist Party office. The 1938 meeting packed a capacity crowd of 20,000 into Madison Square Garden.[220] The event's print advertisements in the *Daily Worker, Morgen Freiheit,* and *New York Amsterdam News* featured Lenin's face, announcements of Sokolow's *Dance of All Nations,* the rally's other entertainment, a "Chorus of 800 Voices," and a short play, *Today in America.*[221] Sokolow's top billing reinforces dancing bodies' centrality to communist spectacle.

218. No author, "Film From Spain to Show Miss Kee," *New York Amsterdam News,* December 25, 1937, 3, PQHN.

219. "Directing for Lenin Memorial," *Daily Worker,* January 17, 1938, 7.

220. "Memorial at Madison Sq. Garden Jan. 19 to Honor Lenin," *Daily Worker,* January 14, 1938, 2; and "20,000 Jam Garden for Lenin Rally," *Daily Worker,* January 20, 1938, 1, 4.

221. *Daily Worker,* January 14, 1938, 8; *Morgen Freiheit,* January 18, 1938, 2 and January 19, 1938, 6, Dorot, NYPL; and *The New York Amsterdam News,* January 15, 1938, 10, PQHN.

Figure 1.13: *Dance of All Nations.* Photographer unknown. *Daily Worker,* January 21, 1938. People's World Daily News, peoplesworld.org.

In *Dance of All Nations,* Sokolow deployed the revolutionary trope of mapping communist ideology through women's bodies. These masses remained part of a united force of female-bodied everypeople instead of individual women. Sokolow used the group en masse to portray a sense of harmony through uniting nations across the globe. A photograph of the dancers in tableaux features a throng of women in short-sleeved, knee-length dresses with wide skirts highlighted by two dark vertical stripes[222] (Figure 1.13). The phalanx of performers look over their right shoulders, and the dancers flanking the formation hold out large flags at a 45° angle. Newspaper reports neglect description of the dance, but the pageant likely shared sentiments with *Today in America,* which, the *Daily Worker* reported, "depict[ed] the swift gathering of the progressive forces in the US towards an American People's Front."[223] It is unclear if Sokolow employed only concert dancers or if her cast included performers from union houses or IWO lodges. Her choreography reinforced topics of the evening's speeches, including protest of the

222. Photograph accompanying "20,000 Honor Memory of Lenin at Madison Square Garden Mass Meeting," *Daily Worker,* January 21, 1938.
223. "Memorial to Lenin to Hear Hudson, Ford," *Daily Worker,* January 17, 1938, 2.

1938 Wagner Van-Nuys Anti-Lynching Bill filibuster, and support for peace efforts against Fascism in Europe and Japanese aggression in China.[224]

In the shadow of domestic actions like the Wagner Van-Nuys filibuster, the American Left linked racism and fascism within communist and anti-fascist discourse, while the Right used anti-fascism to justify racism. Demagogic rhetoric took over the US Senate in the late 1930s, resulting in laws that upheld racial oppression. Sokolow's fight for civil rights continued in her activism with the Negro Cultural Committee, a leftist organization focused on coalition building and advancing cultural and political opportunities for African Americans.[225] Along with cultural leaders Juanita Hall, John Houseman, Langston Hughes, Rex Ingram, Larry Jackson, Gladys Stoner, John Velasco, Orson Welles, and Frank Wilson, Sokolow's membership in the Negro Cultural Committee exemplified Denning's assertion that the New York Left had "some of the most visible alliances across racial lines of the period"[226] and demonstrated how Sokolow lived her communist values of racial equality. Sokolow became a valued artist and activist member of the black leftist community, as performance reviews attest. During World War II, she taught technique classes and repertory for the Negro Dance Company, which was formed in autumn 1942.[227] She retained her ties with the African American community in the postwar period and hired black dancers into her company when performing opportunities for black concert dancers were otherwise limited.

In her choreography for the Negro Cultural Committee musical revue *The Bourbons Got the Blues*, a send-up of the 1938 antilynching bill filibuster, Sokolow's satire became a swift indictment of American institutionalized racism in a dance that was too horrifying to be funny. Bourbons were white supremacist, cotton baron Southern Democrats who rose to power in state governments during Reconstruction and idealized an antebellum system of slavocracy. Their political opponents invoked France's Bourbon dynasty in this epithet.[228] *Bourbons* premiered on May 8, 1938, at Manhattan's Mecca Temple on West 55th Street between 6th and 7th Avenues in Midtown. This centrally located Shriners' lodge

224. "20,000 Jam Garden for Lenin Rally," 1, and Roy Hudson, "Leninism Shows the Way to Democracy, Peace and Prosperity," reprinted in *Daily Worker*, January 21, 1938, 4.

225. "Negro Artists to Present Social Revue Sunday Night," *Daily Worker*, May 6, 1938, 7; and "Broadway Celebrities In Satire," *New (Norfolk) Journal and Guide*, April 9, 1938, 16. The FBI followed the Negro Cultural Committee as a Communist organization. Case File, Anna Sokolow, March 16, 1951, US Department of State, FOIPA No. 1138496-000.

226. Denning, *Cultural Front*, 15.

227. "Fashionables Turn Out for Negro Dance Company Party," *New York Amsterdam Star-News*, October 17, 1942, PQHN; and "Dance Company Plans Recitals," *New York Amsterdam News*, November 28, 1942, PQHN.

228. David M. Kennedy, *The American People in the Great Depression: Freedom From Fear: Part I* (New York: Oxford University Press, 1999), 30–31; and "Bourbons," in *The Great American History Fact-Finder* (Boston: Houghton Mifflin, 2004), Credo Reference.

spoke to the social and economic prominence of the production at the time; in the late 1930s many theatrical productions aligned with anti-fascism rented its large auditorium.[229] It is notable that the Negro Cultural Committee engaged Sokolow, and not a black choreographer, to make dances for this revue. Leftist white and Jewish choreographers continued to draw from black themes for their 1930s dances, while in a complicated relationship the revolutionary movement included black dancers in its activities yet excluded them from its leadership ranks.[230] In its *Bourbons* coverage, the leftist press highlighted "Filibuster" over the production's other scenes that black artists directed, and black critics' triumphing of Sokolow's dance as "little short of sensational" reinforced her popularity within this milieu.[231] Sokolow's commitment demonstrates her passage through leftist constituencies by means of revolutionary activities, and highlights a complex relationship between Jewish and black activists in the leftist movement.[232]

The leftist and black presses' hailing of *Bourbons* as one of the time's most important and searing musical revue political indictments reinforces satire's efficacy for challenging political hierarchies. Mainstream newspapers' conspicuous omission of *Bourbons* reviews suggests that the performance's association with communism and improved race relations were perceived as dangerous.[233] *Bourbons'* celebrity-filled team included Negro Theatre producers Houseman and Welles, Works Progress Administration (WPA) Theatre Project writers Carlton Moss and Dorothy Hailparn, Broadway performer Juanita Hall conducting the Negro Melody Chorus, and a cast featuring Georgia Burke, Rex Ingram, Thurman Jackson, Canada Lee, Frank Wilson, and Duke Ellington, whose original musical composition for this production, "There'll Come a Day," was reportedly his first work of social protest.[234] The show's abolitionist themes emphasized black Communists' importance as civil rights activists in the class struggle. As a member of the production team, Velasco

---

229. Since 1943 this building has been under the city's jurisdiction as the theater City Center. Christopher Gray, "Streetscapes/City Center; From Shriners' Mecca Temple to Mecca for the Arts," *New York Times*, April 11, 1999. A flyer in Yiddish, likely from the late 1930s, announces Sokolow and her group on an anti-fascist Jewish program at the Mecca Temple. Flier, "Come Greet the Jewish Volunteers Who Fought Against Fascism," December 4, no year, RG 1477, YIVO Institute for Jewish Research, trans. Kalman Weiser.

230. Manning, *Modern Dance, Negro Dance*, 66.

231. "'Bourbons Got Blues' Proves Clever Show: Frank Wilson, Georgia Burke Ace Performers; Ballet Is Sensational," *The New York Amsterdam News*, May 14, 1938, 16, PQHN.

232. See Manning, *Modern Dance, Negro Dance*, 1–113.

233. Although he previewed this event, John Martin's review of it does not appear in the paper. Martin, "The Dance: Opera Again: Philadelphia Ballet Engaged by Chicago Company—News of the Week," *New York Times*, May 8, 1938, 164.

234. "Mecca Temple To Be Scene of Big Show," *The New York Amsterdam News*, April 30, 1938, 16; "'Bourbons Got The Blues' Hits Boards Sunday: To Present Social Satire With Brilliant Cast at Mecca Temple Downtown," *The New York Amsterdam News*, May 7, 1938, 16; "Duke Writes Song for Congress Benefit Show," *The Baltimore Afro-American*, May 7, 1938, 11; and "'Bourbons Got Blues' Proves Clever Show," 16. All PQHN.

told a reporter early in the rehearsal process that the revue was an upsurge against discrimination.[235] Scenes included Frank Wilson as Denmark Vesey planning his 1822 Charleston slave insurrection, Rex Ingram as Frederick Douglass delivering Douglass's 1852 Fourth of July Oration underscoring racial inequities amidst celebrations of Independence Day freedoms,[236] Georgia Burke's portrait of a domestic worker in what one *New York Amsterdam News* reviewer labeled the "Bronx 'slave market,'" and Thurman Jackson as what the same reviewer described as a "burlesque of a white southern minister."[237] Burke concluded in *New Masses* that the revue "[said] in monologues, music, and dance that 'Uncle Tom is dead.'"[238] The Negro Cultural Committee gave this performance as a fundraising benefit for the New York chapter of the National Negro Congress, an advocacy and civil rights group who lobbied for—and, according to one *New York Amsterdam News* reporter, was instrumental in securing—President Franklin Delano Roosevelt's support for the Wagner Van-Nuys Anti-Lynching Bill.[239]

Sokolow's dance about this legislation, one of many antilynching bills that failed in the US Houses of Congress over a span of decades, marked her continued Jewish–leftist challenges to American institutionalized racism. The House of Representatives proposed the Wagner Van-Nuys Anti-Lynching Bill in 1934, and passed it in April 1937, after a horrific mob burning of two black men in Duck Hill, Mississippi.[240] Southern senators blocked the bill in the US Senate because it imposed federal rules on local governance of racially motivated felonies; for white supremacists like Theodore Bilbo of Mississippi and Allen Ellender of Louisiana it represented a Reconstruction Era meddling of the North in Southern affairs that trumped state's rights and upset the Jim Crow racial imbalance for the unilateral power of whites.[241] In their six-week-long filibuster of the bill from January to February 1938, Bilbo and Ellender led Democratic and Republican Southern senators in wielding the power of their majority so that Roosevelt feared losing legislative support in the Senate and did not publicly support the bill.[242] Articles and editorials about the filibuster filled the leftist press. One *Daily Worker* political cartoon portrays a black man's body bound and hanging from the US Senate building as white senators in suits and fedoras look on, smoking cigars (Figure 1.14).

---

235. "Broadway Celebrities In Satire," *New (Norfolk) Journal and Guide*, April 9, 1938, 16, PQHN.

236. For Douglass' speech: http://www.pbs.org/wgbh/aia/part4/4h2927.html. Accessed September 13, 2015. Vesey's revolt was thwarted by Charleston authorities.

237. "'Bourbons Got Blues' Proves Clever Show," 16.

238. Owen Burke, "Filibuster and the National Negro Congress," *New Masses*, May 24, 1938, 31, BICLM.

239. "'Macbeth' Producers Join Negro Cultural Committee: Houseman, Welles Aid Musical at Mecca Auditorium," *The New York Amsterdam News*, April 9, 1938, 21.

240. Kennedy, *Great Depression*, 342.

241. Ibid.

242. Ibid., 342–343.

Figure 1.14: "Lynch Filibuster" by Fred Ellis. *Daily Worker*, November 18, 1937. People's World Daily News, peoplesworld.org.

Bourbons took the Senate and, by extension, the president, to task. In "Filibuster," Sokolow's dance for forty performers that closed the *Bourbons* revue, her criticism became a danced political cartoon that carried abolitionist sentiment into contemporary politics.[243]

Sokolow's blistering statements in "Filibuster" resonated widely. A critic for the *New York Amsterdam News* reported, "the ballet proved to be one of the most mirth-provoking and at the same time graphic portrayals of one of the most shameful

243. *Bourbons* was similar to the Living Newspaper performance form that theatricalized headlines for social action and the name of the FTP wing that staged these productions. See Denning, *Cultural Front*, 78, 368–370.

events in contemporary national history."[244] In this dance, Sokolow portrayed US senators filibustering the antilynching bill as spoiled children playing with an array of toys instead of working together to end racial injustices. "The satire would have been a lot funnier," Burke concluded, "if the situation were less acutely real and demanding of the protest the ballet called for."[245] The widespread popularity of and interest in this performance, not just across the white, Jewish, and black segments of the New York leftist community, but also in Baltimore, Chicago, Pittsburgh, and Norfolk, Virginia, suggest that theatrical productions were effective platforms for the people's voice and that a broad segment of society deeply opposed the legacies of slavocracy.

Sokolow achieved the "Filibuster" effect through satirical costuming and movements and with a sound score culled from government records. The senator characters wore masks created by the FTP's designer Howard Bay, which reviewers could only describe as "satirical."[246] The masks, photographs of which have not surfaced, likely served a similar function to those of the corrupt politicians in Jooss' *Green Table*, which exaggerated the characters' features while concealing the performers' identities (similar to the foremen in *Strange American Funeral*) and tied *Bourbons* into international anti-fascist artistic discourse. Layered into "Filibuster"'s onstage chaos that Burke reported as "the austere Washington Senate turned into a marble-shooting, kite-flying, toy-pistol-toting kindergarten," the Federal Theatre Radio Division personality Tommy Anderson became the off-stage Voice of the Filibuster, reading transcripts from the Congressional Record of Bilbo's and Ellender's Senate floor speeches through the theater's speaker system.[247] Burke described the sensation of this accompaniment, which must have been overwhelming in its aural competition with North's musical score, "the hyp-notized and hypnotizing Senators Bilbo and Ellender pour forth (through an off-stage loud speaker) an almost incredible rush of obscene pro-fascist garbage to kill the Anti-Lynching Bill."[248] The horror portrayed by Sokolow indicted senators who tapped into national isolationist fears of an advancing Third Reich, by conflat-ing fascism with deep lines of racism to justify racially motivated murder. Sokolow held up a mirror to society that was too frightening to ignore and too painful to be funny. "Filibuster" hit home by speaking a piercing truth to power and drawing on

244. "'Bourbons Got Blues' Proves Clever Show," 16.

245. Burke, "Filibuster and the National Negro Congress," 31.

246. "Negro Artists to Present Social Revue Sunday Night," 7; "'Bourbons Got The Blues' Hits Boards Sunday: To Present Social Satire With Brilliant Cast at Mecca Temple Downtown," *The New York Amsterdam News*, May 7, 1938, 16, PQHN; and "'Satiric' Masks to Be Worn In Show," *The Pittsburgh Courier*, April 30, 1938, 20, PQHN.

247. Burke, "Filibuster and the National Negro Congress," 31; "Mecca Temple To Be Scene Of Big Show," *The New York Amsterdam News*, April 30, 1938, 16, PQHN; "'Bourbons Got Blues' Proves Clever Show," 16; and unknown author in *Time Magazine*, May 16, 1938, quoted in Warren, *Rebellious Spirit*, 76.

248. Burke, "Filibuster and the National Negro Congress," 31.

communal values of social justice while using humor as a way to stomach the realities of the legislative status quo.

The following year, the US government's censure of the FTP musical *Sing for Your Supper* demanded new stakes for Sokolow's revolutionary projects. The show premiered on April 24, 1939, at the Adelphi Theater on West 54th Street between 6th and 7th Avenues, near to both Broadway and the Garment District. Its sketches commented on unemployment, the workers' plight, a desire for peace in the face of impending war, and the inability of government to serve its citizens.[249] The performance characterized the US government as out of touch with current events by plunking a rhythmically and tunefully inept Uncle Sam caricature into a musical revue that portrayed him as out of step with the wills of the people.[250] Sokolow based "The Last Waltz" dance on a final moment of cultural freedom before the Nazis invaded Vienna.[251] *Daily Worker* reviewer John Cambridge reacted to its thematic clarity by reporting the number was a "most effective statement of the condition of Europe in 1939."[252] As "Filibuster" focused on an unjust US context, "The Last Waltz" grappled with escalating European tensions.

Ensuing political events confirmed that the US Houses of Congress and the leftist movement were out of sync. *Sing for Your Supper* was popular, but Congress censured it two months after it opened and then cut funding for the FTP, ending it on June 30, 1939.[253] The Dies Committee attacked the FTP and *Sing for Your Supper* in particular. Dance historian Jeanne Lunin Heyman reported the committee "charged that the Federal Theater was a hotbed of Communism, and that its propagandistic art did not justify its continuation as a public relief program."[254] FTP director Hallie Flanagan was called before the Dies Committee in 1938 and denied communist leanings in the production, but as a left-aligned revue that criticized the government, *Sing for Your Supper* became an early lightning rod for accusations of communism in the performing arts. Sokolow cut her ties with the revue before the controversy. She resigned from the FTP on March 31, 1939, on the premise of

249. Program, *Federal Theatre (A Division of the Works Progress Administration) presents Sing for Your Supper*, Adelphi Theatre, Box: Programs, Folder: Sokolow, Anna (Programs—1930s Only), JRDD, NYPL; Phillips Geduld, "Performing Communism," 39; and Hallie Flanagan, *Arena: The History of the Federal Theatre* (1940; New York: Benjamin Blom, 1965), 365–367.

250. "Federal Theatre Fall Schedule," *New Voices*, September 1938, 6, Microforms, NYPL; and Phillips Geduld, "Performing Communism," 39.

251. Warren, *Rebellious Spirit*, 79. Because of regulation rules, Sokolow worked with Federal Theatre dancers instead of her Dance Unit in this production. Warren, *Rebellious Spirit*, 78–79. The show had two dance ensembles: a Modern Dance ensemble, and a Negro Tap ensemble. Program, *Sing for Your Supper*. It is unclear if Sokolow choreographed only for the Modern Dance ensemble or if she staged all ensemble choreography.

252. John Cambridge, "Enthusiastic Performance of 'Sing for Your Supper,'" *Daily Worker*, April 26, 1939, 7.

253. Flanagan, *Arena*, 334.

254. Jeanne Lunin Heyman, "Dance in the Depression: The WPA Project," *DanceScope* 9, no. 2 (1975): 39.

having completed her choreographic responsibilities to *Sing for Your Supper* and in preparation for her Mexico tour.[255] The Dance Unit crossed the US border into Mexico in mid-April and were deep in residency activities there before *Sing for Your Supper* premiered April 24.

Sokolow found a welcoming public in Mexico City, which provided a work environment to continue making revolutionary art with governmental support instead of governmental scrutiny. Dances like *Case History* and *Façade* established Sokolow as a revolutionary choreographer in Mexico City. Her 1939 tour expanded into a ten-year exchange within Mexico City's Jewish and communist art and social circles. As opposed to American modernism that refused nonwhite markers, Mexican modernism embraced formalist elements with ethnic references. Sokolow's work there expanded the boundaries of American modernism.

255. "'Henry IV' to End Its Run Tonight," *New York Times*, April 1, 1939, 17, PQHN.

CHAPTER 2

Revolutionary Exile in Postrevolutionary Mexico City

Jewishness and Mexican Modernism

By 1939, Sokolow led New York's revolutionary dance movement and soloed for Martha Graham, twin positions that landed her an invitation to Mexico's Instituto Nacional de Bellas Artes (INBA) [National Institute of Fine Arts]. After a four-day train ride from New York City to Laredo, Texas, a several day-long detention at the United States–Mexico border because Sokolow's and her Dance Unit dancers' visitors' permits were unarranged, and an additional few days on the train from Laredo to Mexico City once their visa situation was rectified, it took them about two weeks to get to Mexico City in April 1939.[1] Carlos Mérida, a painter, political intellectual, and INBA Dance Department director, sponsored Sokolow's residency. His letter of offer provided transportation from the Mexican border to Mexico City,[2] but Sokolow and her company had to find their own way into Mexico. Sokolow's difficulties crossing the border related to stories of Jewish exile she would experience in Mexico City: first, with sharp declines in North American visas for Holocaust refugees; and second, with Jewish Spanish Civil War exiles who became her artistic collaborators.

Sokolow's dances engaging political representations of Jewishness and Mexican folklore connected her to an uneasy history of Jewishness within Mexico's national race discourse *mestizaje* that privileged European and indigenous creolization. Sokolow's time in Mexico City from 1939 to 1945 was circumscribed by international political and local cultural elements related to revolutionary modernism,

---

1. Warren, *Rebellious Spirit*, 82–83 (see Preface, n2).
2. Ibid., 82.

Jewishness, race, aesthetic optics, and refugees. She worked under government and private auspices when the Mexican government limited Holocaust refugee immigration. Since the Mexican government asserted that Ashkenazi Jews were antithetical to *mestizaje* because they were neither of Hispanic origin nor indigenous to the Mexican region, yet Jewishness was central to Mexico City's communist bohemian art circles, Jewishness had a complicated relationship to Mexican nationalism.[3] *Mestizaje* was a communist, anti-fascist ideology, but it nevertheless countered contemporaneous racial discrimination in German National Socialist ideology. Sokolow was not a refugee or political exile, but her search for receptive revolutionary audiences between New York and Mexico City during the war continuously put her on and took her off the US government radar.[4] Her dances magnified an exile trope that reflected Jewish geopolitical events connected to the Holocaust. In this chapter I argue that the interrelation of *mestizaje* and Jewishness in Sokolow's choreography evidences her negotiation of communism, modernism, and Jewishness between Mexico City and New York audiences while the Mexican and US governments marginalized Jews through restrictions on Holocaust refugee immigration. Sokolow's mediation of Jewishness under *mestizaje* highlights Jewish assimilationist actions in Mexico City and New York and a hemispheric discussion of how mid-twentieth-century American modern dance intervened in international Jewish and leftist discourses.

The 1939 Mexico trip recalls political sentiments Sokolow experienced during her 1934 Moscow excursion, the story with which this book began, as a popular artistic sojourn to a communist metropolis. Mexico, however, became Sokolow's revolutionary artistic home in a way that the USSR could not have been. Whereas Muscovite audiences considered Sokolow a "product of decadent capitalism" because of her American origin and her issue-driven dances,[5] the Mexican public celebrated Sokolow's proletarian background and lent her elite status as a Graham dancer. When Soviet audiences chased her down after a Foreign Workers Club

3. Daniela Gleizer, *Unwelcome Exiles: Mexico and the Jewish Refugees from Nazism, 1933–1945,* trans. Susan Thomae (Leiden, The Netherlands and Boston: Brill, 2013), 38; Adina Cimet, *Ashkenazi Jews in Mexico: Ideologies of Structuring a Community* (Albany: State University of New York Press, 1997), 28–30; and Rick A. López, "Anita Brenner and the Jewish Roots of Mexico's Postrevolutionary National Identity," in *Open Borders to a Revolution: Culture, Politics, and Migration,* eds. Jaime Marroquín Arredondo, Adela Pineda Franco, and Magdalena Mieri (Washington, DC: Smithsonian Institution Scholarly Press, 2013), 123–130.

4. The FBI, likely working with the CIA, sent informant Ann Remington to Mexico City in 1939 to report on Sokolow's and North's activities. In 1943, reports on Sokolow's FBI security card track her relationship with Ignacio Aguirre, whom the FBI identified as being acquainted with Communist circles. The FBI continually canceled and reinstated her security card. Memo, from SAC, New York to director, FBI, 4/30/51, Alto Case: Espionage—R (Bufile 65-43302), RE Los Angeles report [of] 3/7/51; Security Card: SOKOLOW, Anna, Villalongin [illegible], Mexico, D.F., August 14, 1943; and Security Card: Sokolow, Anna, 160 West 73rd Street, New York City, August 14, 1943. FOIPA No. 1138496-000.

5. Anna Sokolow, quoted in Leonard Dal Negro, "Return from Moscow: An Interview with Anna Sokolow," *New Theatre* (December 1934): 27.

performance, Sokolow reported her surprise that they wanted to see more acrobatics and "pretty curved movements" and that her technical demonstration "had something of the effect usually attributed only to gentlemen who pull rabbits out of hats."[6] Much to Sokolow's dismay, Soviet audiences desired spectacular feats rooted in classical ballet's hierarchical pyrotechnics instead of provocative choreography that united the workers of the world. Sokolow did not know that in 1917 Lenin declared ballet a substitute for religion to disseminate the government's postrevolutionary propaganda to a largely illiterate public.[7] Just as Lenin's decree transformed an elite art form into a populist vehicle, the Mexican government employed modernist visual art as revolutionary propaganda during and after its revolution (1910–1917). Mexican audiences' enthusiasm for Sokolow's proletarian themes and modernist aesthetic, and her own embrace of Mexico's sentiment of folk elements signifying revolution, expanded her work's aesthetic politics through the spectatorship and collaborations in which she participated.

During Sokolow's first tour to Mexico City, she and her Dance Unit performed her proletarian repertory. In subsequent years there, Sokolow presented her proletarian solos and wove Mexican folklore into her new dances for herself and for the group of Mexican dancers in her short-lived company La Paloma Azul [The Blue Dove]. Her new choreographies reflected Mexican and Spanish cultural themes replete with *mestizaje*'s Euro-dominant tensions. Sokolow enjoyed favorable receptions to these dances in Mexico, but New York critics could not read these dances' revolutionary codes. Sokolow's transnational navigation of this spectatorship demonstrates blind spots that emerged for audiences as her dances crisscrossed national borders.

By incorporating specific, if appropriated, imagery in sets, costumes, and movement from Latin American folklore, set to music by Mexican and Spanish composers, Sokolow's Mexican choreographies became part of a history of *mestizaje* cultural products. In the 1920s, Minister of Education José Vasconcelos envisioned *mestizaje* as part of a mythical *Raza Cósmica* [Cosmic Race] that would form the bedrock of a powerful political future.[8] Through miscegenation and eugenics Vasconcelos imagined a *mestizo* nation purified of what he considered indigenous weakness and in which Hispanism (Europeanness) eclipsed indigenousness.[9] He disseminated this propaganda in urban districts and sent teachers into Mexico's rural areas to teach them.[10] During the postrevolutionary era, *mestizaje* became a nationalist point

6. Ibid.

7. Ross, *Like a Bomb Going Off*, 37–39 (see Introduction, n1).

8. Tace Hedrick, *Mestizo Modernism: Race, Nation, and Identity in Latin American Culture, 1900–1940* (New Brunswick, NJ: Rutgers University Press, 2003), 4, 6.

9. Nancy Leys Stepan, *"The Hour of Eugenics": Race, Gender, and Nation in Latin America* (Ithaca, NY: Cornell University Press, 1991), 147–149; David Craven, *Art and Revolution in Latin America, 1910–1990* (New Haven, CT: Yale University Press, 2002), 54; and Cimet, *Ashkenazi Jews*, 19.

10. Michael C. Meyer, William L. Sherman, and Susan M. Deeds, *The Course of Mexican History*, 8th ed. (Oxford: Oxford University Press, 2007), 499–501.

of pride through reclaiming indigeneity independent of Cosmic Race ideology. *Mestizaje's* ideological racial democracy remained a myth, as ethnomusicologist Sydney Hutchinson articulated, "that only mask[s] discrimination and prejudice."[11] By whitewashing indigenous influences and silencing Africanist contributions, European elements eradicated them and retained the hierarchy of European over indigenous. At the height of the national project to assimilate Mexico's indigenous population during President Lázaro Cárdenas' administration (1934–1940),[12] *mestizaje* rearticulated *indigenismo* (heightening indigenous elements), a pan-Latin American elite discourse glorifying a mythological pre-Columbian past while devaluing contemporary indigenous populations.[13] According to historian Rebecca Earle, "The goal of *indigenismo* under Cárdenas was therefore [as Guillermo de la Peña wrote] not to 'indianize Mexico but to mexicanize the Indian.'"[14] Sokolow's La Paloma Azul dances in the years following Cárdenas's presidency reflected indigenist goals because they enveloped folk themes into US modern dance aesthetics. Privileged access to funding and considerations of whiteness provided Sokolow a position of power over local choreographers as she used Mexican folkloric elements to revolutionary ends.

Sokolow's *mestizaje* work aided her own assimilation because, as a Graham exponent, she stood for the American artistic establishment even though her revolutionary goals aligned her with Jewishness. I frame this chapter's discussion using religious and political exile in Mexico during the Holocaust as outlined by Mexican historian Daniela Gleizer to show how assimilation was important for Sokolow in a Mexican wartime climate of anti-Semitism,[15] antirefugee sentiment, and heightened *indigenismo*. Gleizer shows how the Mexican government's refusal to recognize Jewish refugees from the Holocaust as political exiles resulted in denying them entrance to Mexico, whereas the government accepted political refugees of any heritage from concurrent crises like the Spanish Civil War.[16] The government's refusal of Jewish Holocaust refugees as political exiles raised the stakes of Sokolow's work with Jewish political origins.

To explain Sokolow's shifting relationship to these discourses, I begin the chapter with Sokolow's entrée into Mexican nationalism via communist currents. I follow with a discussion of *The Exile (A Dance Poem)* (1939), an anti-Nazi solo

---

11. Sydney Hutchinson, "The Ballet Folklórico de México and the Construction of the Mexican Nation Through Dance," in *Dancing Across Borders: Danzas y Bailes Mexicanos*, eds. Olga Nájera-Ramírez, Norma E. Cantú, and Brenda M. Romero (Urbana: University of Illinois Press, 2009), 208.

12. Earle, *The Return of the Native: Indians and Myth-Making in Spanish America, 1810–1930* (Durham: Duke University Press, 2007), 189.

13. Joanne Hershfield, "Screening the Nation," in *The Eagle and the Virgin: Nation and Cultural Revolution in Mexico, 1920–1940*, eds. Mary Kay Vaughan and Stephen E. Lewis (Durham: Duke University Press, 2006), 259, 266.

14. Earle, *Return*, 189.

15. Gleizer, *Unwelcome Exiles*, 46, 53–55.

16. Ibid.

Sokolow made in New York and toured to Mexico, to show how tropes of exile in Jewish memory and in relation to the US and Mexican governments' treatment of Holocaust refugees heightened Sokolow's anti-Nazi statement in the dance. I then turn to the collaborative production *Don Lindo de Almería* (1940) and the group dance *El renacuajo paseador* [*The Fable of the Wandering Frog*] (1940),[17] two works Sokolow made in Mexico, to show how Sokolow defied nationalist rhetoric that Jews could exist only outside *mestizaje*. These dances and their receptions display the entwining of Mexican nationalism, international communist discourse, and the Holocaust in Sokolow's compositions and revolutionary spectatorship. Her choreography was legibly revolutionary to Mexican audiences, and her INBA teaching imprinted a US physique into her Mexican dancers' kinesthesia.

SOKOLOW AND MEXICAN NATIONALISM

Sokolow's introduction into Mexico's postrevolutionary milieu began with her repertory, like *Case History No.—*, that embodied the government's artistic–political goals to foreground proletarian concerns. In the 1930s, the Mexican government negotiated its cultural program between the political ideology of Soviet Communism and the economic unfolding of the US Depression.[18] Revolutionary action through artistic processes was part of Cárdenas's agenda,[19] so under the aegis of revolutionary art funding that supported muralists such as painter Diego Rivera,[20] the Secretaría de Educación de Pública (SEP) [Secretary of Public Education] engaged revolutionary dancers like Sokolow. Public buildings featured murals and frescoes with images of collective working-class and indigenous identities to unite a largely agrarian, rural nation around new national ideals of industrial progress, modernity, and a government by the people. Public art was part of national educational goals tied to cultural production as an urban extension of the Mexican Revolution; the government sent phalanxes of women teachers into rural areas to disseminate nationalist ideals for industry, child rearing, and hygiene.[21] The government strove to join Mexico's disparate

17. *El renacuajo paseador* translates as *The Fable of the Wandering Tadpole*. Sokolow presented it in English as the *Wandering Frog*. The character is a young person poised on adolescence. Unattributed translations are my own.

18. Spenser, *Impossible Triangle*, 193 (see Preface, n9).

19. Tortajada Quiroz, *Frutos de Mujer: La Mujeres en la Danza Escénia* (México: Teoría y Práctica de Arte, 2001), 356.

20. Magnolia Flores (Ballet Independiente artistic director) in conversation with the author and Alejandra Jara de Marco, March 26, 2010, Mexico City.

21. Craven, *Art and Revolution*, 31–32; Mary Kay Vaughan, "Nationalizing the Countryside: Schools and Rural Communities in the 1930s," in *The Eagle and the Virgin: Nation and Cultural Revolution in Mexico, 1920–1940*, eds. Vaughan and Lewis (Durham, NC: Duke University Press, 2006), 157–175; and Stephanie J. Smith, "Educating the Mothers of the Nation: The Project of Revolutionary Education in Yucatán," in *The Women's Revolution in*

factions under a postrevolutionary national identity that elevated indigenous culture and the *pueblo* (Mexico's peasant and working classes). Imagery of peasants taking up arms together across Mexico's rural regions stood for Mexico's visual sentiment that folklore signified revolution.[22] Because the *pueblo* was indigenous or of *mestizo/a* (mixed European and indigenous) descent, venerating it defined indigenousness as proletarianism in national ideology and enabled politicians to claim that Mexico was a society of the people. Racial equality was not a daily reality, and folk forms were elevated only through blending them with European or criollo influences. Rivera's and other painters' works, like those of Frida Kahlo who blended indigenous and Europeanist imagery into feminist renderings of magic realism, were prominent in Mexican visual culture. Mexican audiences read revolutionary signs in Sokolow's dances like *Case History*, which, like Rivera's and Kahlo's painting, made *pueblo* activities archetypal and centered the proletariat in postrevolutionary discourse.[23] For a nation in which the arts reinforced political ideology, Sokolow could rally the masses around government propaganda and give Mexico a hemispheric cultural edge with the onset of World War II.

Sokolow was one of many dance artists from outside Mexico City who influenced its concert dance scene. Prior to her arrival, the ballet-focused concert dance community thrived under the SEP's auspices. Ballet teachers in the 1920s–1930s included American and Russian immigrants, in addition to Mexican-born dancers.[24] Sokolow's fellow New York leftist choreographer Si-Lan (Sylvia) Chen toured Mexico City in October 1938 amid Mexican interest in the US revolutionary dance movement. Mexican critic Armando de Maria y Campos noted in the daily newspaper *Hoy* that Chen's performance, sponsored by the Chinese Red Cross at the Palacio de Bellas Artes (Palace of Fine Arts, Mexico City's opera house), addressed working-class concerns.[25] Chen's and Sokolow's invitations to Mexico City reflect late 1930s incentives to bring politically conscious American modern dance to Mexico City, when the government sought American practitioners of the so-called new dance.[26] This was good timing for US leftist dancers, as the Dies Committee's installation had quelled their political choreography.

Mexico, 1910–1953, eds. Stephanie Mitchell and Patience A. Schell (Lanham, MD: Rowman & Littlefield, 2007), 37–51.

22. Ballet Folklórico de México's *Revolución* retains this imagery. *Ballet Folklórico de México de Amalia Hernández*, presented by Columbus Association for the Performing Arts, September 22, 2015, Capitol Theatre, Riffe Center, Columbus, OH.

23. Craven, *Art and Revolution*, 64.

24. José Luis Reynoso, "Choreographing Politics, Dancing Modernity: Ballet and Modern Dance in the Construction of Modern Mexico (1919–1940)" (PhD diss., University of California–Los Angeles, 2012), 154–209.

25. Campos, "El Ritmo del Teatro: Ana Sokoloff y su Grupo en Escenario de Bellas Artes," 53 (see Chap. 1, n183).

26. Tortajada Quiroz, *Fruto de Mujer*, 345.

SEP engaged Sokolow along with Waldeen Falkenstein, another revolutionary American Jewish dancer who became known as Waldeen, to teach American modern dance at INBA. Sokolow did not stay permanently in Mexico, but Waldeen did. Her consistent presence offered security, and she trained generations of modern dancers. Many historical sources compare the two as opposing forces in the Mexican dance scene, most notably with Sokolow focusing on universal themes in her choreography and Waldeen centering folkloric aesthetics in hers.[27] The diminutive nicknames for their students, "las Sokolovas" and "las Waldeenas," reinforced this rivalry and deepened the indigenist discourse surrounding both choreographers' work. Notably, the Mexican government brought Sokolow and Waldeen to Mexico amid national debate about the status of Jewish refugees, even though the SEP brought them as revolutionary dancers and not as Jews. Their engagement by Mérida highlights their status as government guests amid national fears of Jewish refugee immigration. Sokolow's and Waldeen's communist ideals justified their presence in Mexico, where the government welcomed people it deemed defenders of humanitarian values, many of whom were Jewish.[28]

As Mexico struggled for international political prominence, the government capitalized on Sokolow's stature as a modern dancer and communist artist to disseminate its agenda. Sokolow and the Mexican government's mutual interest dated back to at least 1937. While a Choreography Fellow at the Bennington School of the Dance in the summer of 1937, Sokolow led conversations with groups of interested dancers gathered on the lawn about the Communist cause in Mexico City and Franco's oppression of Spanish Loyalists.[29] Like many American Communists, Sokolow sent money to Mexico to support these causes.[30] She likely took notice of Mexico City in the mid-1930s, when US Communist papers including *New Masses* associated Mexico City with Moscow as a metropolis through which international communist politics circulated.[31] Mexico's early twentieth-century social revolution made the country attractive as a destination for US Communists and "fellow travelers" in the 1930s.

27. Tortajada Quiroz, *Frutos de Mujer*, 340–402; Warren, *Rebellious Spirit*, 97–100; Waldeen Falkenstein, "Orígenes biológicos y filosóficos de la danza," *Revista Plural* XV-IX, no. 177 (1986): 38–41, reprinted in *La Danza en México: Visiones de Cinco Siglos* Volume II, eds. Maya Ramos Smith and Patricia Cardona Lang (México: Escenología, A.C., 2002), 525–530; Colombia Moya, "Waldeen, ¡feliz cumpleaños!" *La Jornada*, April 4, 1993, reprinted in *La Danza en México*, eds. Smith and Lang, 669–670; Colombia Moya, "Waldeen, ¡hasta siempre!" *La Jornada*, August 21, 1993, reprinted in *La Danza en México*, eds. Smith and Lang, 671; *50 Años de Danza en el Palacio de Bellas Artes*, 39–41, 60–62 (see Introduction, n88); and Jim May, discussion (see Introduction, n85). See also Reynoso, "Choreographing Politics."

28. Daniela Gleizer, e-mail message to the author, July 16, 2015.

29. Helen Alkire (dancer, choreographer, teacher) in discussion with the author, April 13, 2010, Orient, OH.

30. Ibid.

31. Advertisements in *New Masses* through the 1930s announced tours to Russia and to Mexico. See also Weisser, "Face to Face with Michael Gold," 9 (see Chap. 1, n83).

Mexico City enabled Sokolow to work freely in a social environment she sought, and her stature as a preeminent modern dance choreographer of Graham lineage brought international attention to Mexico City's burgeoning concert dance scene.[32] Sokolow's reputation similarly attracted Mérida, as her work aligned with his political–artistic circle's goals.[33] In 1937, he proposed to the Congreso de la Liga de Escritores y Artistas Revolucionarios [Congress of the League of Revolutionary Writers and Artists] to establish a modern dance training program for INBA modeled on Martha Graham's school and, specifically, Sokolow's work: Dance focused on social issues that used a fully expressive body and stressed the collective over the individual.[34] INBA sought artists to train its students in US modern dance techniques, and Mexico's government media outlets initially used Sokolow as an example of what Mexican high-art dance could become. By linking working-class issues and anti-fascist sentiments with signifying movements and collective groups made up of individuals, Sokolow's choreography embodied the goals of the artistic and intellectual Mexican left. Mérida's daughter, Ana Mérida, danced with Sokolow in Mexico and became a prominent figure in Mexican concert dance. Mérida perhaps considered his daughter's career when he connected with Sokolow in New York through their mutual friend Emilio Amero, a Mexican muralist living in Manhattan who was Sokolow's neighbor. They met backstage at The New School in March 1939 after a Theater Arts Committee concert, where Mérida invited Sokolow to Mexico City.[35] Sokolow left town a few weeks later after resigning from *Sing for Your Supper*.[36] In Mexico, Sokolow was considered a revolutionary dancer and a modern dancer at the same time. Her choreography generated intellectual discourse within its revolutionary spectatorship that connected Mexican audiences to international artistic–intellectual bourgeois and revolutionary conversations across the United States, the USSR, and Mexico.[37]

Sokolow's SEP-sponsored concerts at Mexico's national opera house, as opposed to New York's privately run workers' institutions, the Y, or Broadway theaters, shows the nationalist role of her work in Mexico. Her Dance Unit's concert program series from April to May, 1939, at the Palacio de Bellas Artes featured her New York

32. Antonio Luna Arroyo, *Ana Mérida en la Historia de la Danza Mexicana Moderna* (México: Publicaciones de Danza Moderna, 1959), 22.

33. Warren, *Rebellious Spirit*, 81. See also Anadel Lynton, *Anna Sokolow*, Cuadernos 20 (Ciudad de México: INBA, Dirección de Investigación y Documentación de las Artes, CENIDI-DANZA, 1988), 12–13.

34. Tortajada Quiroz, *Frutos de Mujer*, 357–358.

35. Warren, *Rebellious Spirit*, 81.

36. The Dance Unit likely left New York on Monday, April 3. Warren notes that the dancers were "bleary-eyed from the previous night's performance in Boston." Warren, *Rebellious Spirit*, 82. Revolutionary dance concerts occurred on Sundays. Sokolow was scheduled to begin residency activities in Mexico on April 15. "'Henry IV' to End Its Run Tonight," 17 (see Chap. 1, n255).

37. See Katz, *Secret War in Mexico* (see Preface, n9); and Carr, *Marxism and Communism* (see Preface, n9).

repertory and was extended because of popular demand. Leftist and mainstream Mexican newspapers covered her performances and the audiences of workers, artists, and intellectuals shared Sokolow's beliefs and embraced her work. To reciprocate, Sokolow dedicated her performances on May 13–14, 1939, to *trabajadores de Mexico* (Mexico's workers) and to the Mexican proletariat, respectively.[38] The Dance Unit returned to New York after the six-week run, but Sokolow stayed, under contract with the SEP through January 1940.[39]

Despite Sokolow's ideological alignment with Mexican art and political culture, the Dance Unit tour was plagued by miscommunications, according to the dancers as they told their memories to Larry Warren. Beyond the dancers' struggles to breathe in Mexico City's high altitude and a lack of funds to cover their daily expenses, the impresario who funded the Dance Unit's travel was a Mussolini-aligned Fascist and thought the Dance Unit was a Russian ballet company because of Sokolow's name.[40] This impresario, who Warren does not name, "was quite vexed to find that his Russian ballerina had turned out to be a barefoot social reformer."[41] He reportedly yelled "Viva Benito Mussolini!" after the Dance Unit performed *Façade—Exposizione Italiana* and withheld profits because of his opposition to Sokolow's work.[42] It is unclear where Mérida was during these events. Regardless, the left-aligned segments of the Mexican public comprised the majority of Sokolow's audiences.

Mexican newspaper reports employed postrevolutionary sentiments to demonstrate how Sokolow's proletarianism engendered *mestizaje*-type mixing. Mexican critics linked Sokolow to Graham and to Isadora Duncan in an effort to legitimize Mexico's dance scene in the eyes of the elite by connecting it to artistic advances in Euro–American concert dance.[43] After seeing her 1939 Mexican debut, critic Carlos González Peña wrote in *El Universal* that Sokolow "unites tradition and modernity," the mingling at the heart of *mestizaje*.[44] The leftist paper *El Popular's* full-page interview with Sokolow in the week of the Dance Unit's 1939 premiere introduced Sokolow as "La Gran Danzarina Rusa" [The Great Russian Dancer].

38. Advertisement, "Palacio de Bellas Artes: Mayo 13, Anna Sokolow y su Ballet," *El Popular*, May 13, 1939, Microforms, NYPL; and Advertisement, "Palacio de Bellas Artes: Mayo 14, Anna Sokolow y su Ballet," *El Popular*, May 14, 1939, Microforms, NYPL.

39. Warren, *Rebellious Spirit*, 93, and Tortajada Quiroz, *Frutos de Mujer*, 361.

40. Warren, *Rebellious Spirit*, 83–84.

41. Ibid., 84.

42. Ibid.

43. See, for example, Luna Arroyo, *Ana Mérida*, 21–23; "La Danza Moderna de Anna Sokolow," *El Popular*, April 17, 1939, 5, Microforms, NYPL, trans. Alejandra Jara de Marco and Hannah Kosstrin; and Armando de María y Campos, "El Ritmo de Teatro: Ana Sokoloff y su Grupo en el Escenario del Bellas Artes," *Hoy*, April 22, 1939, 53, CENIDID, CENART.

44. Carlos González Peña, *El Universal*, no date, quoted in Luna Arroyo, *Ana Mérida*, 22. "Una artista que reúne en sí tradición y modernidad." For *mestizaje* and artistic nationalism, see Marco Velásquez and Mary Kay Vaughan, "*Mestizaje* and Musical Nationalism in Mexico," in *The Eagle and the Virgin*, eds. Vaughan and Lewis, 95–118.

Although this announcement likely points to the communication failure that led the producer to believe he was getting a Russian ballet troupe, the "Russian" moniker marks a connection among Soviet (Russian)–Mexican–American Communist discourse. This interview aligned Sokolow with *mestizaje*. Sokolow said that, instead of folklore, she incorporated the full spirit of a place into her work.[45] The interview further quoted Sokolow: "Technically, American modern dance shows clear Negro and indigenous influences."[46] *El Popular*'s inclusion of this assertion, which departed from Sokolow's US interviews during this time, displayed how Sokolow's brand of modern dance resonated with *mestizaje* by incorporating indigenous forms into elite culture.

Mexico City's artistic communist social circles provided Sokolow refuge for her communist activities. Mexico City was an intellectual and artistic metropolitan harbor for what art historian David Craven called the "left-wing dissidents from the intelligentsia of the Americas."[47] It centered art in a way the US proletariat did not. Sokolow reported her reverence for the Mexican Electrical Union to the *Daily Worker*, where, she said, "cultural workers are considered as essential to the union as anybody else."[48] Sokolow became involved in international communist conversations in Mexico City through her associations with Rivera, Kahlo, muralist David Alfaro Siqueiros, and artists associated with the Taller de la Gráfica Popular (TGP) [People's Graphic Workshop]. In Mexico, her work's social values aligned with governmental priorities instead of fighting them.

The connection between Mexican muralists and US leftist dancers exemplifies the international nature of communist currents. Sokolow shared artmaking techniques, ideology, and reciprocal influence with the muralists and TGP members. These artists watched Sokolow's rehearsals and welcomed dance as a vehicle for disseminating revolutionary ideas.[49] Moreover, just as Sokolow employed Graham's "bourgeois" dance technique to make her proletarian statements, Rivera and Mérida used their European training to elucidate Mexican proletarian content[50] without

---

45. "La Danza Moderna de Anna Sokolow," 5.

46. Ibid. "Técnicamente, la danza moderna norteamericana muestra claras influencias negras e indígenas." I have translated "negras" as "Negro" because of the historical specificity of the term. In the United States during the 1930s, many African American concert dancers termed their choreography "Negro dance" to differentiate their work from more commercial jazz dance; in the 1960s, this term was replaced with "black dance." Manning, *Modern Dance, Negro Dance*, xiii-xiv (see Preface, n14). The term Negro was specific to the 1930s US social context. In Mexico, the term Negro has been used to denote a person of Africanist origin; there was not a shift from "Negro" to "black" in Mexican Spanish as there was in American English. I thank Jose Luis Reynoso and Stephanie Smith for helping me sort this out.

47. Craven, *Art and Revolution*, 71.

48. Anna Sokolow, quoted in Beth McHenry, "Anna Sokolow: Trip to Mexico," *Daily Worker*, September 20, 1943, 7.

49. Lloyd, "Dance Is for People, Part II" (see Chap. 1, n26); and Warren, *Rebellious Spirit*, 89.

50. Desmond Rochfort, "The Sickle, the Serpent, and the Soil: History, Revolution, Nationhood, and Modernity in the Murals of Diego Rivera, José Clemente Orozco, and David Alfaro Siqueiros," in *The Eagle and the Virgin*, eds. Vaughan and Lewis, 55.

upholding *mestizaje's* racist underpinnings. The artists' methods paralleled the US revolutionary dance movement, specifically of those, like Sokolow, who were part of a Big Four dance company and created art with establishment techniques and proletarian content.

Even though the Mexican Revolution predated the Bolshevik (Russian) Revolution and the Mexican Communist movement, while Sokolow was in Mexico, different communist ideologies divided society. Mexico City, like New York, was home to a rift between the bourgeois Left and the working class.[51] The American leftist press followed Mexican events in the 1930s, like the Mexican press followed the Russian Revolution in the 1910s–1920s,[52] and Russian revolutionaries followed the Mexican Revolution. After the US Communist Party adopted anti-fascist ideology and the Popular Front line in 1934, the Mexican delegation to the Communist International (ComIntern) followed suit in 1935.[53] ComIntern ideology was not widely popular, but Mexican Communism flourished in Mexico City's art circles.[54] By 1939 communism was more of an ideological basis for Mexican muralists than active political membership was.[55] After the Mexican government granted Leon Trotsky asylum in 1937, Mexico City Communists split along Leninist (Bolshevik) and Trotskyist (Menshevik) lines. Rivera and Kahlo harbored Trotsky in the Coyoacán arts district. An ideological rift between Trotskyist artists like Rivera and Leninist artists like Siqueiros culminated in Siqueiros's assassination attempt on Trotsky in May 1940, which preceded Soviet agent Ramón Mercader's (aka Jacques Mornard) murder of Trotsky on August 20, 1940.[56] During this time Sokolow was acquainted with Rivera and Kahlo,[57] but befriended artists mostly affiliated with Siqueiros. Ignacio "Nacho" Aguirre, Sokolow's collaborator and romantic partner after she and Alex North separated, was Siqueiros's assistant and a TGP member.[58] Sokolow was likely a Leninist because of her American Communist Bolshevik affiliations and participation in New York Lenin meetings. During her 1950s social trials Sokolow denied having social relationships with these artists as I show in Chapter 4, yet her inclusion with them puts her at the heart of this vibrant, tumultuous, and prominent political–artistic community.

51. See Carr, *Marxism and Communism*, 47–79.

52. Spenser, *The Impossible Triangle*, 113.

53. Olcott, *Revolutionary Women in Postrevolutionary Mexico* (Durham: Duke University Press, 2005), 109.

54. Spenser, *Los Primeros Tropiezos de la Internacional Comunista en México* (México, DF: Centro de Investigaciones y Estudios Superiores en Antropología Social, 2009), 255.

55. For example, the Partido Communista Mexicano [Mexican Communist Party] expelled Rivera in 1929. Craven, *Art and Revolution*, 21.

56. Exhibition plaques in Museo Casa de Leon Trotsky [Trotsky Museum], Coyoacán, Mexico City, March 23, 2010; "Man Who Assassinated Trotsky Dies in Havana," *Los Angeles Times*, October 20, 1978, B13; and Craven, *Art and Revolution*, 69–71.

57. Jim May, discussion.

58. Sokolow, interview by Newman, transcript (see Chap. 1, n106); and Warren, *Rebellious Spirit*, 88. See also Lynton Snyder, *Anna Sokolow*, 13.

Sokolow's Mexico City social associations with Jewish political and artistic circles reinforced her revolutionary connections. Mexico City's embedded Jewish presence since the Conquest includes Sephardic (Spanish) influence by means of crypto-Judaism and *conversos* (Jews forced to convert to Catholicism during the Spanish Inquisition who privately continued Jewish traditions), in addition to European and Eastern European Ashkenazi Jews who immigrated to Mexico during the nineteenth and early twentieth centuries. The Mexican Ashkenazi Jewish community harbored leftist activism that supported Sokolow's political and artistic needs, especially in the shadow of the Holocaust. According to sociologist Adina Cimet, the Jewish Left had a strong Mexican presence in the 1930s–1940s, and, like the New York Jewish Left of the 1920s–1930s, it included sympathies from across the Marxist spectrum.[59] Sokolow's relationships with prominent Mexican Jewish families included social organizer Lilly Weissenberg,[60] and Sokolow's most influential collaborators, writer José Bergamín and musician Rodolfo Halffter, were Spanish Jewish exiles from the Spanish Civil War and became connected to Mexico City's communist circles.[61] The 1939 Nazi–Soviet Pact broke many factions along ideological lines, as it did in the United States, and the Mexican government displayed general ambivalence toward Jews.[62] This included denying entry to European Jewish refugees with corrupted documentation they unknowingly acquired from European consulates[63] and Mexican government officials falsifying Latin American passports originating in Germany.[64] Sokolow's *Exile*, in which she spoke specifically as a Jew for all Jews, registered the social tensions of Mexico's changing 1930s definitions of and privileges associated with who could be an exile.

RECLAIMING THE GARDEN IN *THE EXILE*

Sokolow's *Exile*, a prophetic anti-fascist intertext woven of Jewish history, spirituality, and cultural texts, magnified the American and Mexican governments' refusal of Jewish Holocaust refugees before the beginning of World War II. The twelve-year Nazi threat girded Sokolow's anti-fascist dances, from the January 30, 1933 rise of the Third Reich, through the Allied liberation of the Nazi concentration camps from January to April 1945, to Germany's surrender to the Allies on May 7, 1945, and in the displaced-persons camps that housed survivors with no place to

59. Cimet, *Ashkenazi Jews*, 78–84, 138.

60. No author, "'Cocktail' en Honor de Anna Sokolow," *El Universal*, no date, Folder: Sokolow Ana, CENIDID, CENART.

61. Alberto Dallal, *La Danza en México México en el Siglo XX* (Xoco, CP, Mexico, DF: Dirección General de Publicaciones, 1997), 131, 141; and Raquel Tibol, *Pasos en la Danza Mexicana* (Ciudad Universitaria, México, DF: Universidad Nacional Autónoma de México, 1982), 19.

62. Cimet, *Ashkenazi Jews*, 139–150.

63. Kennedy, *Great Depression*, 417 (see Chap. 1, n228).

64. Gleizer, *Unwelcome Exiles*, 211.

go through the late 1940s. Sokolow's work spoke to a Jewish leftist discourse that existed between Mexico City and New York, her dances reflecting her changing relationship to the implications of the Holocaust and the role of ritual in the face of racial persecution by governments on both sides of the Atlantic. In the anti-fascist dances *War Poem, Façade—Exposizione Italiana,* and *Slaughter of the Innocents* that I discussed in Chapter 1, Sokolow drew on communist politics to connect with people persecuted by totalitarian regimes in Italy and Spain. In *Exile,* she employed these tactics to speak for her own threatened Jewish Diaspora by portraying a violent disruption of Eden. She premiered the solo on her Dance Unit's *New Masses–*sponsored concert at the Alvin Theatre in New York on February 26, 1939, about a month before she departed for Mexico. She first performed it in Mexico City on April 29, 1939, the same day *El Popular* ran the headline "HITLER PROVOCA LA GUERRA" ["HITLER INCITES WAR"] after Hitler's April 28 speech to the Reichstag in which he refused to comply with Roosevelt's April 15 telegram imploring Hitler and Mussolini to commit to a decade of nonaggression.[65] My discussion of *Exile* in New York and Mexico City as Sokolow performed it from 1939 to 1948 positions the dance hemispherically and shows how the choreography shuttled leftist and Jewish ideology across national borders.

As a sibling solo to *Slaughter of the Innocents, Exile* presented another kind of lost innocence through Sokolow's portrayal of idyllic Jewish life before the rise of the Third Reich and then the Nazis' destruction of it. *Exile'*s premieres followed years of Jewish persecution in Germany and its occupied territories before Hitler's September 1, 1939, invasion of Poland that started the war in Europe. Rebecca Rossen traced how Sokolow used *Exile* as a seed for her 1943 work *Songs of a Semite,* wherein Sokolow took up a female Jewish banner to march against Jewish persecution.[66] Sokolow performed *Exile* with a tenderness absent from her other anti-fascist work. She alternated between moments of darting, flight-infused power on the ground, and spiraling, gently turning revolutions on her feet as if under the shadow of a looming dark force. In a series of photographs, she propels herself across the floor with a spring from her back hand, looking over her shoulder in fear. Soon thereafter, in a moment in which it is unclear if Sokolow is falling or getting up, she balances on one folded leg, as her outstretched hands reach toward the ground and she looks behind herself with trepidation.[67] She sweeps a dark cape through the space, bunches it into a knot, spreads it in front of her torso, and then allows it to swirl around her as she rotates (Figure 2.1). This solo's juxtapositions between strength and vulnerability reflect Jews' treacherous experiences during the

65. "Hitler Provoca la Guerra: Los pactos con Londres y Varsovia eran sus compromisos de Pax," *El Popular,* April 29, 1939, 1.

66. Rossen, *Dancing Jewish,* 68–75 (see Introduction, n26).

67. These descriptions are based on a series of photographs by Barbara Morgan, ca. 1941, of Sokolow in "I had a garden," Barbara and Willard Morgan Photographs and Papers, Library Special Collections, Charles E. Young Research Library, UCLA.

Figure 2.1: Anna Sokolow in "I had a garden" from *The Exile*. Photograph by Barbara Morgan. Barbara and Willard Morgan Photographs and Papers, Library Special Collections, Charles E. Young Research Library, UCLA.

Holocaust, including those persecuted in Europe and escapees denied refuge by countries' refusal to abolish quotas.

Exile came in the wake of 1937–1938 US reports about the Nazis' systematic displacement of European Jews and during increased anti-Semitism in the United States as the government refused Jewish refugees. Through the 1930s, Roosevelt, despite his organization of a July 6, 1938 international conference on the Jewish refugee crisis and various efforts to extend refugee visas, ultimately did not raise the US quota for Jewish immigrants and instead upheld the quota terms of the 1924 National Origins Act, denying asylum to many European Jews.[68] Anti-immigration-propelled legislation continued in HR-5643, a bill generated by Alabama Representative Sam Hobbs in May 1939, which proposed US detention centers for immigrants lacking documentation from their country of origin.[69] This affected Holocaust refugees stripped of their citizenship by the Nazis. The Hobbs Bill fueled the Left's insistence to mobilize against nativist forces, fearing Fascist influence in the US government.[70]

68. Kennedy, *Great Depression*, 410–416.

69. HR 5643, 76th Cong., 1st sess. (July 10, 1939), *Cong. Rec.* 761 (July 11, 1939), *Lexis-Nexis Congressional*, http://congressional.proquest.com.proxy.lib.ohio-state.edu/congressional/docview/t01.d02.76_hr_5643_ras_19390711?accountid=9783 (accessed July 16, 2013).

70. Adam Lapin, "Concentration Camp Bill to Go Before House; Open Fight on Fascist Measure," *Daily Worker*, April 27, 1939, 1–2. See also editorial, "Defeat the Bill for Concentration Camps," same issue.

The English and Yiddish leftist presses stated that Jewish persecution in Europe signaled a call to action for the labor movement and that anti-fascist sentiments must transform into fighting anti-Semitism.[71] Sokolow's *Exile* reflected this proletarian call to fight anti-Semitism with her anti-fascist work.

Sokolow's choreographic contemporaries made similar statements to *Exile*. From 1937 to 1939, US leftists presented dances about the Nazi persecution of Jews alongside choreographies about Spanish and Italian Fascism. The New Dance League's April 25, 1937 farewell concert at the St. James Theater featured, among others, Jane Dudley's *Under the Swastika* (music by Alex North), Miriam Blecher's *Advance Scout—Lincoln Battalion* about American volunteers who fought for the Loyalists in Spain, and Lily Mehlman's *Spanish Woman* consisting of the sections "Lullaby for a Dead Child" and "*No Pasarán*" ["They Shall Not Pass"] with thematic similarities to Sokolow's *Slaughter of the Innocents*.[72] On a January 15, 1939 Modern and Theatre Dance Recital at the Mecca Temple, Blecher presented *Three Jewish Songs* with the sections "Austria—The Day After," "Poland—In the Shop," and "Biro-Bidjan—In the Field," and José Limón presented *Three Dances of Death*, wherein, according to program notes, "The first is German; the second, Italian; the third, Spanish."[73] Sokolow's prophecies rang prominently among this choreographic trend. In Mexico, to which we now return, Sokolow's *Exile* was additionally significant as it refracted Mexico's policies toward Jews.

By labeling herself the exile, Sokolow engaged a history of Jewish exilic persecution while she used the stage as a venue of empowerment in the face of desolation. Her April 1939 arrival in Mexico followed long government debates about the status of Jews fleeing Hitler and whether to accept them into Mexico as refugees. As Gleizer demonstrates, the status of exile in Mexico in the 1930s was closely tied to government privilege: "Not only did an exile receive privileged treatment along with this title; exile status legitimized the causes of his flight and entailed that the government act accordingly by protecting him."[74] The Mexican government did not protect Jews fleeing the Holocaust, however, because they were rarely seen as political refugees. Despite Mexico's official policy granting exile status to political refugees of any religious persuasion, Gleizer notes that the Mexican governments

71. See Blanche Holzer, "Review and Comment: Professor Mamlock," *New Voices* (June 1937): 15, Microforms, NYPL; Michael J. Quill, "Anti-Semitism Goes Hand-in-Hand With Reaction," *Jewish People's Voice*, April 1938, 2, Dorot, NYPL; M. J. Olgin, "What Is That Jewish Culture, Anyway?" *Morgen Freiheit*, January 20, 1938, 6, Dorot, NYPL; M. J. Olgin, "Ban Anti-Semitic Propaganda," *Morgen Freiheit*, April 25, 1939, 6, Dorot, NYPL; and political cartoon featuring an old religious Jew carrying a swastika as if he bore a cross, Jewish People's Committee, "Petition Our Government to Grant Right of Asylum to Refugees from Nazi Persecution," *Jewish People's Voice*, June 1938, 3, Dorot, NYPL.

72. Program, *The New Dance League presents a Solo Recital*, April 25, 1937, New Dance League Programs, JRDD, NYPL.

73. Program, *Modern and Theatre Dance Recital*, January 15, 1939, Folder: Sokolow, Anna (Programs—1930s Only), JRDD, NYPL.

74. Gleizer, *Unwelcome Exiles*, 7.

of Presidents Cárdenas and Manuel Ávila Camacho (1940–1946) did not widely accept stateless Jews seeking asylum from Nazi-controlled Europe and refused to define their legal status. Anti-Semitism within *mestizaje*'s mythological racial equality (Jews were neither Hispanic nor indigenous and so complicated the Cosmic Race) led to distinguishing these Jews from political refugees by labeling them "racial refugees" in the 1940s.[75] The anti-immigrant argument against accepting so-called undesirable refugees like European Jews was that they were perceived as non-assimilationist and non-Spanish-speaking and therefore could not participate in *mestizaje* and become Mexican. The argument for accepting them was a reworking of Mexico's refugee legislation to include Jews as racial refugees alongside political refugees like Spanish Loyalists who fled the Spanish Civil War.[76] Sokolow's Mexican choreographies *Don Lindo de Almería* and *El renacuajo paseador* that I subsequently discuss, moreover, showed that she later artistically aligned with *mestizaje*.

Exile's persecution resonances were rooted in its intertextual poetry as well as in its choreography. Jewish-born Communist poet Sol Funaroff's poem "The Exiles," which he wrote for Sokolow's *Exile*,[77] articulates a prophetic cyclical history of Jewish life and oppression.[78] American literature scholar Alan Wald referred to Funaroff as a "poet–seer" who blended revolutionary politics into his palimpsestual poems to reframe established texts with his leftist consciousness.[79] Funaroff based "The Exiles" stanzas' imagery in verses from the books of Isaiah, Daniel, Lamentations, and the Song of Songs, all from the texts of the Hebrew Bible. Understandings of time in the Hebrew Bible are cyclical instead of chronological; thus, events have new meanings in their telling. Readers learn from events multiple times as they reappear, and readers can understand their own times as expressions of biblical events' recurrence.[80] Funaroff's characterization in "The Exiles" of the Jews as the "people of the grass" came from Popular Front poet Walt Whitman,[81] and it gave a sense of the scale of the Jewish Diaspora. By making sense of current events in terms of paradigmatic and cyclical biblical situations and connecting these references to the Popular Front, Funaroff yoked Jewish memory and social action in this poem, as did Sokolow in the dance.

Exile's musical accompaniment furthered the poem's nostalgic underpinnings despite the secular nature of its anti-Nazi comment. North arranged the music, listed alternately on programs as "traditional Palestinian folk music" (Palestine here

75. Ibid., 1–12.

76. Ibid., 85–200.

77. Program, *New Masses presents Anna Sokolow and Dance Unit*, February 26, 1939, Martha Hill Papers, Juilliard; and Warren, 77.

78. Sol Funaroff, "The Exiles," published in *New Masses*, January 18, 1944, 16–17. www.unz.org/Pub/NewMasses-1944jan18-00016. Accessed January 23, 2015.

79. Alan M. Wald, *Exiles from a Future Time: The Forging of the Mid-Twentieth-Century Literary Left* (Chapel Hill, NC: The University of North Carolina Press, 2002), 204–212.

80. Yerushalmi, *Zakhor,* 1–10 (see Introduction, n90).

81. Wald, *Exiles*, 214.

references the Jewish community in British Mandate Palestine), "traditional Jewish music," and "traditional folk music."[82] The music's origins in an idea of an epic Jewish homeland highlight the exile and provide a spiritual home for European Jews rendered stateless by Hitler, as its folk associations registered as revolutionary. In some performances, baritone Arlo Tanny spoke and sang Funaroff's poem.[83] In others, when Sokolow recited the poem while dancing, the scripture became part of Sokolow's embodiment.[84]

Funaroff's references to the book of Isaiah, an indictment of Israel in the voice of God that narrates a biblical Jewish exile after the destruction of the First Temple in Jerusalem, brings prophecy to the poem and the dance.[85] This exile experience cycled throughout ancient and modern Jewish history as Jews scattered throughout a Diaspora assimilated into cultural and national contexts, generating a Jewish people, as Funaroff says, "of all nations." By taking up textual references to Isaiah, Funaroff, and then Sokolow (through her dancing and vocality when she recited the poem while dancing), became Isaiah's prophesizing voice.

Exile engaged biblical references that envisage paradise ruined. The poem's beginning in the aftermath of dispersion reflected the Nazis tearing Jews from their livelihoods. "My people," Funaroff narrates, are "uprooted," "fugitives," and in "exile." They are refugees again, and their mourning underwrites their wandering. The poem's narrator longingly evoked descriptions of a flowering garden that represent images of social unity, plenty, bucolic beauty, and peace. The garden, which the narrator cleared of stones to plant, references Isaiah 5:2.[86] Funaroff's allusions to the garden's spices, lilies, and fruits originate in the erotic narration of the Song of Songs.[87] Song of Songs is cyclical and unending,[88] so that love is unending; but in Funaroff's poem, the cycle of uprooting the people of the grass is unending and heartwrenching. In the garden the narrator nurtured wisdom and learning "like the

82. Program, *New Masses presents Anna Sokolow and Dance Unit*, February 26, 1939, Martha Hill Papers, Juilliard; Program, *Anna Sokolow: Nuevos Ballets, Anna Sokolow y su Grupo*, April 29, 1939, Folder: Sokolow, Anna (Programs—1930s Only), JRDD, NYPL; Program, *Anna Sokolow and Alex North in a Joint Recital of Dance and Music*, February 18, 1940, 92Y; and Program, *Anna Sokolow and Group*, April 5, 1940, Bennington College, SDF.

83. Program, *New Masses presents Anna Sokolow and Dance Unit*, February 26, 1939, Martha Hill Papers, Juilliard; Program, *Anna Sokolow: Nuevos Ballets, Anna Sokolow y su Grupo*, April 29, 1939, Folder: Sokolow, Anna (Programs—1930s Only), JRDD, NYPL; and Warren, *Rebellious Spirit*, 77.

84. Warren, *Rebellious Spirit*, 305.

85. Isaiah was written in the aftermath of Babylonian King Nebuchadnezzar's 586 BCE destruction of the First Temple in Jerusalem. His actions demolished Judah, a sovereign Jewish region in the ancient Middle East that contained Jerusalem. He deported most of Judah's Jews to Babylon. NRSV, 1147. The Persian King Cyrus defeated the Babylonians in 539 BCE and returned the Jews to Jerusalem. Nebuchadnezzar's expulsion of Jews from Judah is called the exile; the Jews he evacuated were the exiles. NRSV, 966.

86. NRSV, 974.

87. 6:2-6:3 (NRSV, 956).

88. NRSV, 959.

Figure 2.2: Anna Sokolow in "I had a garden" from *The Exile*. Photograph by Barbara Morgan. Barbara and Willard Morgan Photographs and Papers, Library Special Collections, Charles E. Young Research Library, UCLA.

leaves of a story/of a tree of life, of a tree of knowledge," a reference to the Torah's guiding principles, before the tragedy.

In *Exile*'s first half, "I had a garden," Sokolow embodied Funaroff's imagery, "I had a garden, a lovely garden, /a tribe of flowers in a garden of nations, /a people of many-colored grass," through gently spiraling movements and a look of softly focused attention that gave a sense of serenity. In Figure 2.2, curvilinear shapes reoccur in Sokolow's spiraling torso, inwardly rotated shoulders, and carving arms. Her balanced distribution of weight between her feet gives a sense of equilibrium, and her indirect focus and half-closed eyes imply that she feels safe in her environment. Read within the historical context of the rise of the Third Reich and Mexico's refusal of Jews as political exiles, *Exile* reinscribed Jews as refugees displaced from a fruitful land within a history of expulsion. In the final section of his poem titled "The Road," Funaroff summons Isaiah to tell the exiles, the Jews, to gather themselves and go forth once again.[89] *Exile* was a cry to empower Jews and their allies to rise up against their own evacuation.

"The Desert" section of Funaroff's poem on which Sokolow based *Exile*'s second half, "The beast is in the garden," reads like an unfolding pogrom as an iron-clawed, fire-breathing beast burns, pillages, and tears apart the halcyon scene. Jewish learning is one of its main victims, as "the wise man is become a leper/and wisdom a disease" as the beast reduces the Jewish nation to "a heap of refuse" and stretches out in the destroyed garden, which is now "a place for beasts to lie down."[90] The

89. Funaroff's verse "Awake and sing, you that dwell in the dust, /take root in the earth, / O people of grass, /and rise again" resonates with Isaiah's proclamation of returning to Jerusalem: "You shall see, and your heart shall rejoice; /your bodies shall flourish like the / grass; /and it shall be known that the hand of the LORD is with his servants, /and his indignation is against his enemies." Isaiah 66:14 (NRSV, 1056). See also Isaiah 32:9–32:20 and 47:1. Rossen notes that this section echoes the Book of Judges. Rossen, *Dancing Jewish*, 69.

90. Funaroff, "The Exiles."

beast in the garden recalls the ten-horned beast in the biblical figure Daniel's prophetic dream during the Jews' exile in Babylon. The horrifying beast, with "teeth of iron and claws of bronze, . . . stamped what was left with its feet,"[91] represented a kingdom to wipe out the rest of the world.[92] The end of "The Desert," wherein "The beast of nations lies down in the field, / the garden is a desolation, / a place for beasts to lie down in," comes back to Isaiah and to Lamentations. Isaiah says, "But wild animals will lie down there," where "there" is Babylon during the biblical Jewish exile.[93] The final poem of Lamentations portrays similar violence as it describes the First Temple, and the independent nation of Judah, destroyed by the Babylonians,[94] "which lies desolate; jackals prowl over it."[95]

Funaroff's haunting destruction imagery from Daniel, Isaiah, and Lamentations recalls *Kristallnacht* [Night of Broken Glass], the devastating German pogrom that took place on November 8–9, 1938. The perpetrators of this government-sanctioned attack burned, smashed, defaced, and pillaged Jewish synagogues, businesses, and homes in Germany, Austria, and the Sudentenland in Nazi-occupied Czechoslovakia. Nazi Party officials, along with members of the *Sturmabteilungen* (a Nazi paramilitary organization known as the SA or Storm Troopers) and Hitler Jugend (Hitler Youth, or HJ) carried out this massive hate crime. Sokolow premiered *Exile* three months after *Kristallnacht*, one week after an anti-Semitic, pro-Aryan German American Bund rally at Madison Square Garden,[96] and two weeks after the introduction of the Wagner–Rogers refugee aid bill in the US Senate and House of Representatives that proposed that the United States admit an additional 20,000 refugee children over two years (the bill was later defeated in July 1939).[97] In late 1938–early 1939 the Mexican government was divided regarding Jewish refugees: Cárdenas briefly loosened immigration policy, whereas Minister of the Interior Ignacio García Téllez refused Jewish immigration on the basis of their presumed nonassimilation into *mestizaje*.[98]

In Sokolow's *Exile*, Hitler's foot soldiers were the fire-breathing beast that burned and smashed its way through the heart of Jewish livelihood in the garden of the established and assimilated metropolitan German Jewish community. Sokolow sounded the alarm to learn from histories of the Jews who preceded her, so that her exile was cyclical. "The beast is in the garden" embodied a sense of fighting persecution on behalf of a people. The snapping swiftness of Sokolow's kick in Figure 2.3 sends her skirt billowing as she fights the dual beasts of the Nazis and closed

---

91. Daniel 7:19 (NRSV, 1248).
92. Daniel 7:23 (NRSV, 1249).
93. Isaiah 13:21 (NRSV, 988).
94. See NRSV, 1147.
95. Lamentations 5:18 (NRSV, 1158).
96. Rossen, *Dancing Jewish*, 71.
97. http://www.ushmm.org/outreach/en/article.php?ModuleId=10007698. Accessed August 17, 2016.
98. Gleizer, *Unwelcome Exiles*, 148–149.

Figure 2.3: Anna Sokolow in "The beast is in the garden" from *The Exile*. Photograph by Barbara Morgan. Barbara and Willard Morgan Photographs and Papers, Library Special Collections, Charles E. Young Research Library, UCLA.

borders. Particularly striking in the image on the right is the intensity in Sokolow's face and the depth of her skirt's flair. Sokolow's strong performance deepened her social comment. One New York critic remarked on Sokolow's haunting qualities and powerful presence that the dance was "tragically powerful, deeply moving, and was danced with a dramatic intensity that bound the audience to Miss Sokolow completely."[99] This ability to affect the audience transformed Sokolow's choreographic blueprint into actions they might take outside the theater to stop the genocide. By prophetically aligning biblical destruction, Nazi atrocities, and Sokolow's female honest body dancing onstage, *Exile* indicted *Kristallnacht* in a millennia-old history of Jewish persecution.[100]

In New York, *Exile* drew reviews with mixed comments on Sokolow's performance, the movement that purveyed seemingly secular, social-protest content and assertions about its Jewish context. Rossen has noted that leftist choreographies like *Exile* avoided literal references in favor of universalizing experience,[101] yet critics saw Jewish markers in the dance. It is unclear if the music, movement, or poem most explicitly elucidated Jewishness for these critics across the political spectrum, as the program listed no explanatory note about the dance's thematic material. Margery Dana wrote in the *Daily Worker* that *Exile* "sprang from a depth of sincere feeling that amounted to passion. In movement that was completely lyric, and characterized by the utmost simplicity and delicacy, portrayed both the tragedy and the question of the persecuted Jewish race."[102] Another critic wrote about

99. No author, "Anna Sokolow, YMHA Dance Theatre, Feb 18," no source, no date, no page. Anna Sokolow Clippings, JRDD, NYPL.

100. I consider here Meredith Monk's works *Quarry* (1976) and *Book of Days* (1988), which feature a young woman visionary who gathers generations of Jewish history into one poignant moment of understanding.

101. Rossen, *Dancing Jewish*, 71.

102. Dana, "Anna Sokolow and Unit Seen In New Solo and Group Dances," 7 (see Chap. 1, n91).

Sokolow's February 18, 1940 performance at the 92nd Street Y, "The theme is the Jew in his happier Biblical existence, and his life under modern European oppression. . .Greatly heightening the effect was the traditional Hebrew music."[103] Despite the indigenist tone, this critic notably read Jewish specificity instead of universality. It is unclear how the music heightened the effect, if the critic thought the intended effect was protest or generic Jewish representation. Depending on their recognition of or their aesthetic affinities with the dance's Jewish codes, music, or poem, audience members found various meanings in the dance based on their social position and their political stance in relation to anti-Nazism.

In Mexico, *Exile* became a beacon for Jewish audience members who felt powerless in the shadow of the Holocaust. Although reviews of Sokolow's April 29, 1939, concert at Bellas Artes in which she presented *Exile* have not surfaced, critical response shows how this work resonated deeply in Mexico City at the end of the war. Taken by Sokolow's sharp statements and the physical power she exerted onstage, Mexican critic José Herrera Petere exclaimed in 1945 in *El Nacional* (reprinted in the Jewish periodical *Tribuna Israelita*) a cry that echoes the Mexican sentiment of her work: "Yes, Jews: the beast is in the garden; but everybody, all the world's moral passion, all the world's military force, we return the people to their garden and crush the beast forever." He continues: "Thank you, dance of Anna Sokolow; thank you Hebrew burning bush never extinguishing; thank you Mexico, for making me understand and feel this truth once again!"[104] The notion of speaking out reflects a history of social action that was knit into Jewish secular culture. In *Exile* Sokolow railed against the Jewish Diaspora's destruction. Six years later, when she presented *Exile* and her Holocaust memorial solo *Kaddish* together, she brought audience members like Petere through hell to catharsis. The new dances Sokolow made in Mexico reflected Mexican nationalism through folklore-as-revolutionary aesthetics. Jewish audiences were sympathetic, and the Holocaust persisted as an undercurrent. I now turn to two of Sokolow's dances forged in a Mexican context to show how these choreographies entangled American and Mexican modernism by resonating with the indigenist values of *mestizaje*.

LA PALOMA AZUL: CHOREOGRAPHING *MESTIZAJE*

The folkloric opera-house-scale works that Sokolow choreographed in Mexico caused audiences to confront an internalized tension between *mestizaje* and

103. No author, "Anna Sokolow, YMHA Dance Theatre, Feb 18," no source, no date, no page. Anna Sokolow Clippings, JRDD, NYPL.

104. José Herrera Petere, "¡Aleluya! en México," *El Nacional*, August 24, 1945, reprinted in "What the Mexican Press Says," *Tribuna Israelita*, September 15, 1945, 23, Dorot, NYPL. "Sí, judíos: la bestia está todavía en el jardín; pero todos, toda la pasión moral del mundo, toda la fuerza militar del mundo, devolveremos a los pueblos su jardín y aplastaremos a la bestia para

American influence. Her *Don Lindo de Almería* project and La Paloma Azul company (both 1940) provided collaborative endeavors with artists who shared her political and aesthetic goals. These projects began with her INBA teaching, where she trained the students of prominent ballet teachers Nellie and Gloria Campobello, many of whom became her Sokolovas, in Graham technique. While there, Sokolow directed these women in the Campobellos' Nuevo Grupo Mexicano de Danzas Clásicas y Modernas [New Mexican Group of Classical and Modern Dance] under her name.[105] The Sokolovas, mostly young teenagers, came from conservative Catholic families; many of their parents were suspicious of Sokolow's Graham technique and observed Sokolow's classes and rehearsals to keep an eye on her influence on their children.[106] On October 11 and November 16, 1939, Sokolow gave technical demonstrations with her students in the Palacio de Bellas Artes' Green Room, followed by her performances of her existing solo repertory.[107] Through these government-sponsored events, Sokolow's students demonstrated their new Graham training, and the INBA Dance Department displayed how their Mexican youth embodied US modern dance technique. Critical response demonstrated nationalistic pride for INBA students studying with a North American dancer and embodying a form associated with high training standards. José Barros Sierra, for example, confirmed in *Hoy* these demonstrations' effect: "In the short time that she had to work with the group of young Mexicans, Anna Sokolow achieved notable results."[108] Unwittingly, the Sokolovas represented the Mexican government's *mestizaje* by melding their Mexican bodies into US modern dance technique. Las Sokolovas danced in Sokolow's productions for the following two years, as the politics of her work and presence shifted.

Repurposing Elitism in *Don Lindo de Almería*

Sokolow's first large-scale new production under SEP's auspices, *Don Lindo de Almería*, blended Spanish and Mexican elements with proletarian goals. With José Bergamín's libretto and Rodolfo Halffter's musical score, *Don Lindo* was the first

siempre./¡Gracias, danza de Anna Sokolow; gracias, ardiente zarza hebrea que nunca te apagas; gracias, México, por haberme hecho comprender y sentir esta verdad una vez más!"

105. Nigel Dennis, "Prólogo: Historia de *Don Lindo de Almería* (1926–1940–1986)," in José Bergamín, *Don Lindo de Almería (1926)*, ed. and prologue by Nigel Dennis (Valencia, Spain: Pre-Textos y Ministerio de Cultura, 1988), 52.

106. Tortajada Quiroz, *Frutos de Mujer*, 360.

107. Invitation, *Técnica moderna de la danza*, El Departamento de Bellas Artes, October 11, 1939, Folder GP-MF01751, Biblioteca, CENART; and Invitation, *Demonstración Técnica*, El Departamento de Bellas Artes, November 16, 1939, Folder GP-MF01776, Biblioteca, CENART.

108. Jose Barros Sierra, "Música," April 6, 1940, 6, CENIDID, CENART. "En el poco tiempo que tuvo para trabajar con un grupo de jóvenes mexicanos, Ana Sokolov logró realmente resultados notables."

of a handful of productions in which Sokolow mixed Mexican folk and national-ist influences with American-modernist abstraction during her Mexican tenure. Featuring the artistic collaborators and dancers who later formed La Paloma Azul, *Don Lindo* presented Sokolow's INBA students as El Grupo Mexicano de Danzas Clásicas y Modernas, and premiered on January 8–9, 1940, at the populist venue Teatro Fabregas.[109] Sokolow drew the attention of the dance community and the artistic intellectual elite, especially what art collector MacKinley Helm described as "refugee intellectuals" in the audience made up of mostly Jewish Spaniards who fled Franco, because of her collaboration with Bergamín and Halffter.[110] The *Don Lindo* premiere was a social event that brought these artist intellectuals, like Mérida, Helm, and many painters who created the scenery, programs, and publicity posters, together to see and be seen.

A popular event for Mexico City's leftist artistic–intellectual elite, *Don Lindo* unmasked Porfirian decadence and parodied Francoist nationalism through a comedy of errors that unfolded against a grandiose orchestral score.[111] Don Lindo was a prominent family's disappointing son. This half-hour-long production that Bergamín alternately described as a *mojiganga* or a *zarzuela*, a masquerade or a musi-cal comedy, portrayed a series of Don Lindo's antics and manifested traces of cul-tural mixing from the commercial centers of Andalusia.[112] Barros Sierra described the production as a "masquerade of Andalusian customs," wherein, program notes explain, "many figures common to popular Spanish life [were] reduced to stereo-types."[113] The work progressed through satirical non-sequitur episodes that had the slapstick comedic pacing of a Charlie Chaplin film. The narrative goes some-thing like this: characters encounter one another in a town square, a bullfighter marries a schoolgirl, Don Lindo somehow causes tumult, the marriage falls apart, Don Lindo escapes on a pig, and the bullfighter reunites with his bride. The motley crew of characters included Three Mulatas, a Santera, a Young Girl, Three Moresque Priests, a host of bullfighters, a Couple of Rural Policemen, and a set-piece cocka-too, donkey, pig, and Saint Anthony statuette that, the program notes assert, "do

109. Program, *Don Lindo de Almeria*, Teatro Fabregas, January 9, 1940, Folder GP-MF 01820, Biblioteca, CENART.

110. MacKinley Helm, *Modern Mexican Painters* (New York: Harper & Brothers, 1941; repr., New York: Dover, 1974), 157.

111. Rodolfo Halffter, *Don Lindo de Almería*, José Ramón Encinar (conductor), Orchestra of the Comunidad de Madrid, *Rodolfo Halffter: Don Lindo de Almería, La madrugada del panadero (The Baker's Dawn) (Ballet Suites)*, iTunes album, (P) 2006 Naxos Music Library. The Mexican Revolution overthrew Porfirio Díaz's elite government (1876–1911), referred to as the Porfiriato. For Halffter's music and Francoist nationalism, see Eva Morela Rodríguez, *Music and Exile in Francoist Spain* (Surrey: Ashgate Publishing, 2016).

112. For libretti of *Don Lindo* from specific nights of the performance during the fall 1940 season of La Paloma Azul, see Bergamín, *Don Lindo*.

113. Barros Sierra, "Música," April 6, 1940, 6. ". . .mojiganga de costumbres andaluzas. . ."; Program, *Don Lindo de Almeria*, January 9, 1940. "En estas escenas se ven muchas figuras habit-uales de la vida española popular reducidas a jeroglífico. . ."

not dance."[114] Set pieces of lush tropical plants and the larger-than-life cockatoo in a birdcage in front of a palm tree, along with musical themes that denoted characterization, evoked the production's setting on the colonial southeastern coast of eighteenth-century Spain. The dramatic action portrayed elite Spanishness.

The collaborators' proletarian allegiances suggest they incorporated Spanish stereotypes to challenge elitism, but critics' desires for authenticity show how Eurocentrism persisted on the Left. *Don Lindo*'s colonial Mediterranean setting encouraged audience desires to identify the dance as belonging to that imagined geographical and historical location. Although the production took place in the Spanish southeast, Spanish Loyalist playwright and poet Federico García Lorca, writing to close friend Bergamín in 1935 of the first libretto, found the work's tropical air more characteristic of Cádiz on Spain's southwest coast than the environment of the southeast.[115] Bergamín based the work in Andalusian themes, but reportedly he did not want it to depict local folk traditions as exotic.[116] In a reflection of the importance of representations of Spanish or Mexican vernacular elements to Mexican modernism,[117] critics considered production elements acceptably authentic and did not quibble over regional specificity. María y Campos wrote of the "truly extraordinary quality" of the January 8 premiere, which he felt reproduced an "authentic" Spanish quality and that the production also presented "the finest of Mexican culture." He noted that the dancers, including Alicia Reyna and Ana Mérida, "danced with absolute mastery of technique and beautiful grace, in the interpretation of the delicious theme, establishing itself as the first—the only—of this category which has formed in Mexico."[118] Bergamín's and Halffter's Spanish origins provided the sense of cultural authenticity these critics sought, and Sokolow's choreography read as elite through the dancers' Graham-trained physiques that fashioned recognizable Europeanist dance–technical shapes within the dance's colonial condition.

Bergamín's choice of Sokolow as choreographer reflects the artistic and intellectual elite's push to Westernize Mexican productions. Bergamín, Halffter, and Sokolow created a distancing effect by portraying exaggerated stereotypes of characters of

114. Program, *Don Lindo de Almeria*, January 9, 1940. "La cacatúa, el burro, el cochino y San Antonio no bailan."

115. Armando de Maria y Campos, "El Ritmo del Teatro: Don Lindo de Almaria, Ballet de Rodolfo Halffter, Jose Bergamin y Anna Sokoloff, Con Decorado y Trajes de Antonio Ruiz, se Estrena en México con Bailarina Mexicanas y Constituye un Soberbio Triunfo Escénico," No source, February 17, 1940, 63, CENIDID, CENART. See Warren, *Rebellious Spirit*, 91, for Bergamín's friendship with García Lorca.

116. Warren, *Rebellious Spirit*, 91–92.

117. Hedrick, *Mestizo Modernism*, 9, 31.

118. María y Campos, "El Ritmo del Teatro," February 17, 1940, 63. "El Grupo de Anna Sokoloff—Rafael Gutiérrez Lejarza, un perfume que baila; Floriza Ruiz Velázquez, Alicia Reyna, Alba Betanzos, Marta Bracho, Josefina Luna Montalvo, Ana María Mérida, Juan Ruiz—, bailó con dominio de técnica absoluto y gracia fina, en la interpretación del delicioso argumento, consagrádose como el primero—único—de esta categoria que se ha formado en México."

color through European-sounding modernist orchestration and abstracted, even balletic, poses. The press reflected this impulse toward modernist universalism. María y
Campos wrote that *Don Lindo* "[was] not a simulation or popular falsification by artifi-
cial folklore, but by direct and real creation of form: by authentic creation."[119] This colonialist belief that artists could use abstract movement as a vehicle to access authenticity
mirrored similar 1930s–1940s claims in US modern dance.[120]

Don Lindo made space for Jewishness and the Spanish African diaspora to exist
within *mestizaje*, even as cultural mixing undergirded the dance's Europeanist framing. The Moresque Priests, who recalled Andalusia's crypto-Muslim cultural mixing, the Mulatas, who manifested racial mixing, and the Santera, who suggested
Caribbean religious practices, represented currents of cultural and racial mixing
between Spain and its colonies in Mexico and the Caribbean. The piece opens with
the Three Mulatas buying burritos from a vendor to the sounds of cheerful violins,
suggesting people coming into the streets of a quaint town.[121] The Santera enters
to pray at a niche in the wall that holds Saint Anthony, when a minor-scale clus-
ter of lilting cello notes suggests mischief is afoot. Taking their cue, the little bullfighters arrive to quick, rhythmic strings and swift clicks of wood blocks that imply
approaching horses. The music's call and response evokes two groups advancing
and retreating, which develops into the following section's racing phrases. It is
perhaps here where the bullfighters—one matador, cape draped over forearm, is
flanked by four "mounted" bullfighters (sans bulls) in brocaded jackets and knee-
length knickers—advance toward the Three Mulatas, who don ruffled skirts and
colorful vests. Two peek coyly underneath their classically curved, ruffle-covered
arms at the advancing suitors, while the one in the middle drops her arms and slides
her foot along the floor toward the bullfighters, teasing them.[122] The Mulata characters exemplify what dance theorist Melissa Blanco Borelli argues were Mexican
cinema's popularization of sexualized images of mulata rhumba dancers as seduc-
tive and disenfranchised within Cuban-themed films from 1935 to 1959.[123] *Don
Lindo*'s young performers came from elite families and retained a distanced purity
from the sexed and raced mulata role that they embodied, yet they invited a voyeuristic gaze by serving as temptresses. The bullfighters, four "Picadores" and one

119. María y Campos, "El Ritmo del Teatro," February 17, 1940, 63. "Y esto no por una sim-
ulación o falsificación popular, por artificioso folklorismo, sino por directa y ral creación de
forma: por auténtica creación. . ."
120. See, among others, Graff, *Stepping Left* (see Preface, n2); Manning, *Modern Dance, Negro
Dance*; and Rossen, *Dancing Jewish*.
121. Bergamín, *Don Lindo*, 93.
122. Photograph in Program, *Concierto y Tres Bailes del Grupo de Danzas Clasicas y Modernas
dirigido por Ana Sokolow*, Teatro de Bellas Artes, March 23, 24, 27, 1940, Item GP-D00966
9032, Biblioteca, CENART.
123. Melissa Blanco Borelli, "'¿Y ahora qué vas a hacer, mulata?': Hip Choreographies in the
Mexican *Cabaretera* Film *Mulata* (1954)," *Women & Performance: A Journal of Feminist Theory*
18, no. 3 (2008): 215–216.

"Torevillo" as listed in the program, were performed by four women and one man because of the dancers available to Sokolow in her group. While the cross-cast young-women-as-men bullfighters stride toward the Mulatas, each with a left arm strongly bent in front of the torso to match the stride of their right foot, however, the dancers perform an air of confidence misaligned with their young age. They embody Spanish colonialism as their advances project racial and classed assumptions onto the Mulatas within *mestizaje* that erased the Mexican African Diaspora as it refused Jewishness.[124]

As the proceedings continue with a Moresque Priest officiating at the wedding of the virile matador to the (presumably white) Young Girl, they reinforce mulatas' subordinate societal position of being acceptable for sensual pleasures but not for marriage. Some kind of silly confrontation happens as the Moresque Priests tell a superstition of finding a husband by knotting one's scarf.[125] "Maybe that's why they all sneeze loudly," Bergamín narrates in the libretto, as if to illustrate by means of slapstick comedy the need for producing one's handkerchief. Suddenly the Young Girl has a knotted kerchief and is ready to marry the main bullfighter.[126] The dance's swirling chaos pauses for the wedding's long-bowed musical phrases, parts of which sound similar to Igor Stravinsky's score for George Balanchine's ballet *Apollo* (1928). One can imagine the young betrothed moving toward each other with measured steps, bright eyes, and bated breath, yet this is only a brief respite from the *zarzuela*'s shenanigans.

Don Lindo's frolicking ghosts a history of Jewish expulsion from Spain even though it does not feature Jewish characters. Bergamín and Halffter fled Jewish persecution under Franco's dictatorship.[127] Jewish and Muslim religious and intellectual study flourished in Andalusia from the tenth through the twelfth centuries where they influenced each other.[128] In the eleventh to fifteenth centuries, Andalusia bustled with Jewish and Muslim populations. Between the mid-thirteenth century and the fifteenth-century Spanish Inquisition, pejorative representations of Jews and Muslims in popular sources denoted rising prejudices against them. Between 1492 and 1502, the Spanish monarchy forced Jews and Muslims to convert to Catholicism or face expulsion from Spain. Jews who stayed under conversion were

---

124. See Anita Gonzalez, *Jarocho's Soul: Cultural Identity and Afro-Mexican Dance* (Lanham, MD: University Press of America, 2004).

125. Bergamín, *Don Lindo*, 93.

126. Ibid., 94. "Tal vez por esto estornudan estrepitosamente todos, y cuando el pañuelo es anudado por la colegiala, vuelve a aparecer en escena el torerito, conducido entre cuatro picadores, como dice la copa del pañuelo que tuvo la novia de Reverte."

127. See Chaim U. Lipschitz, *Franco, Spain, the Jews, and the Holocaust* (New York: Ktav Publishing, 1984), 16–17.

128. Joel L. Kraemer, *Maimonides: The Life and World of One of Civilization's Greatest Minds* (New York: Doubleday, 2008), 44–48.

called *conversos* or *anusim*, and Muslims, *moriscos*; many privately retained their Jewish and Muslim traditions.[129] Caricatures of these people appear in the forms of *Don Lindo*'s Moresque Priests. These characters' capricious roles contain racial complications, yet the idea of concealing cultural identity for personal safety in Spain points to Jews' experiences in 1930s–1940s Europe. A May 1941 order from Franco to Spanish provincial governors demanded a list of Jews living in their provinces, which he used to gain access to the Axis powers.[130] Bergamín and Halffter left Spain for Mexico in the late 1930s, when Franco aligned himself with and received military aid from Hitler,[131] and the Mexican government welcomed Spanish but not Holocaust exiles. Reading *Don Lindo* in the context of these trials elicits the dance's irony in its environment.

Don Lindo's discordant final section reaches an apotheosis that suggests elites have the privilege of running away from their problems. Cymbals interrupt choppy-sounding actions, and booming tympani ominously mark out a march to the end underneath perky violins interrupted by sharp dissonant notes. The increasing furor evokes continuing antics as the policemen frantically try to keep order among the clash. An ascending trill on the violins suggests this is the moment Don Lindo mounts the pig before it flies him into the clouds as a comic reference to his philandering. The string instruments create a melancholically triumphant umbrella of sound as all of the characters might have grouped around the stage, shaken from their infighting, to watch his ascent. Don Lindo may have been his family's disappointment, but he does not have to clean up his mess. With this conclusion, Sokolow reinforced her proletarianism with this piece's assertions about race and privilege.

Proletarian Folklore in *El renacuajo paseador*

The production of *Don Lindo* laid the groundwork for La Paloma Azul, a collective endeavor focused on an alliance of the arts,[132] whose dances like *El renacuajo*

129. Teofilo F. Ruiz, "The Other 1492" (lecture, Phi Beta Kappa 43rd Triennial Council, Palm Beach, FL, August 4, 2012). See also Teofilo F. Ruiz, *Crisis and Community: Land and Town in Late Medieval Castile* (Philadelphia: University of Pennsylvania Press, 1994). Alicia Gojman de Backal specifies that in fourtheenth- and fifteenth-century Spain and Portugal, *conversos* referred to Jews who voluntarily converted to Christianity, and *anusim* referred to Jews who were forcibly converted. Gojman de Backal, "*Anusim* Women in Mexico," *Shofar* 18, no. 1 (1999): 8.

130. Giles Tremlett, "General Franco Gave List of Spanish Jews to Nazis," *The Guardian* (June 20, 2010). http://www.guardian.co.uk/world/2010/jun/20/franco-gave-list-spanish-jews-nazis.

131. Cary Nelson, "The Spanish Civil War: An Overview," 2001. http://www.english.illinois.edu/maps/scw/overview.htm.

132. Dennis, "Prólogo," 54.

paseador [*Wandering Frog*] contained folklore that easily signified revolution. After Sokolow's SEP contract expired in January 1940, INBA director Celestino Gorostiza formed the Ballet Bellas Artes. Concert programs continued to list it as El Grupo Mexicano de Danzas Clásicas y Modernas. Sokolow worked with this company through spring 1940, except when she returned to New York for a February concert run.[133] With El Grupo, Sokolow presented classical suites with music by French composers, including Jean-Baptiste Lully and Jean-Philippe Rameau, and a revival of *Don Lindo*.[134] During her February absence, Bergamín and Halffter secured the patronage of socialites Adela Formoso de Obregón Santacilia and Carlos Santacilia for La Paloma Azul.[135]

Sokolow's April 1940 return to Mexico City after her winter stay in New York prompted critical dialogue that surfaced a tension in her work and circumstances surrounding her employment. Barros Sierra lamented the January 1940 termination of her SEP contract and accused the Mexican government of failing to provide Sokolow with the resources she needed. Barros Sierra's sarcastic comments, "promises that were made were always postponed until tomorrow, for 'tomorrow' has become synonymous with abandonment, with procrastination, with the admirable Mexican laziness,"[136] characterize Mexico as culturally subordinate and point to a middle-class desire to meet a new influx of Euro–American influence while reconciling long-standing prejudices directed at Mexico's *mestizo* heritage. Although I have not found evidence that Sokolow applied to the Mexican government for exile status, it is worth noting that in January 1940, the number of refugee visas shrank because of a new requirement that political exiles needed permission ahead of time from Mexico's Ministry of the Interior to enter the country.[137] It is a coincidence that SEP terminated Sokolow's contract then, but her choreography and the geopolitical events surrounding her employment pointed to international ramifications for Holocaust refugees at the beginning of the war.

Funding patterns surrounding La Paloma Azul reflected these tensions. The company lasted for one season at the Palacio de Bellas Artes, from September to October 1940. Although it was not solely a vehicle for Sokolow's choreography, with this company, Sokolow performed her existing 1930s solo repertory, and she choreographed a handful of new group dances based in Mexican folkore, including

---

133. Tortajada Quiroz, *Frutos de Mujer*, 361; and Warren, *Rebellious Spirit*, 93.

134. Program, *Concierto y Tres Bailes del Grupo de Danzas Clásicas y Modernas dirigido por Ana Sokolow*.

135. Tortajada Quiroz, *Frutos de Mujer*, 361; and Warren, *Rebellious Spirit*, 93.

136. Barros Sierra, "Música," April 6, 1940, 6. "Si nuestros edificos, nuestras presas y nuestros caminos se quedan frecuentemente truncos, no hay razón para que a nuestros ballets no les suceda lo mismo. Dígalo si no Ana Sokolov que salió de México decepcionada porque las promesas que se le hicieron quedaban siempre aplazadas para mañana, para ese 'mañana' que ha acabado por convertirse en sinónimo del abandono, de la dejadez, de la admirable pereza mexicana."

137. Gleizer, *Unwanted Exiles*, 178–179.

the popular *Wandering Frog*. The group's mission was to make collaborative performances. La Paloma Azul's member artists named the company after a cantina where they gathered, which was also the title of a Mexican folk song.[138] The company's slogan, "Las artes hice mágicas volando," or "I transformed the arts into flying magic," came from the poem "Belardo á Amarilis" by Renaissance-era Spanish poet Lope de Vega and conveyed the group's goals.[139] Although Paloma Azul had patronage from the Santacilias, they struggled to support the fall 1940 season and turned to SEP for funding. A series of telegrams and letters between Adela Formoso with Rodrigues Lozano, director of the National School of Plastic Arts, and Agustín Leñero, the president's personal secretary, regarding the September–October 1940 performances of La Paloma Azul, discuss the urgent need for written financial commitment from Gonzalo Vásquez Vela, the Secretary of Education, to support the performance.[140] Vásquez Vela's approval of the funding shows the government's ongoing interest in Sokolow's work.[141] Against the background of Mexico's refusal of Jewish refugee immigration, Sokolow's government support suggests that her work upheld Mexican values.

Sokolow incorporated a sensibility for vernacular regionalism that was important to Latin American modernism into *Wandering Frog*.[142] Similar to that of *Don Lindo*, the linear narrative of *Wandering Frog* more closely resembled a story ballet or an archetypal Graham piece than the character- or issue-driven political statements of Sokolow's 1930s choreography. Unlike *Don Lindo*, *Wandering Frog*'s regional folkloric elements signaled to audiences that it was Mexican and revolutionary. *Wandering Frog* premiered on October 4, 1940, at the Palacio de Bellas Artes. Mexican composer Silvestre Revueltas's orchestral score for *Wandering Frog* indicates onstage actions, with Mexican regional folk musical themes interrupted by dissonant clashes.[143] Mérida designed the elaborate body-transforming costumes and opulent sets. Large costumes of generously sweeping skirts, wide jackets, full-body animal suits, and fully encased, papier mâché head masks—all made to look like the cats, frogs, and mice in the story—hid dancers' bodies (Figure 2.4). The costumes' animal heads, and the large prop duck that was likely papier mâché as well, follow in a Mexican folk art tradition of *cartonería*, large papier mâché objects

138. Warren, *Rebellious Spirit*, 93.

139. Program, *La Paloma Azul*, Palacio de Bellas Artes, October 15, 1940, Collection of Patricia Aulestia, PBA; and Warren, *Rebellious Spirit*, 94. Thank you to Jeannine Murray-Román for helping me identify the poem and define the translation.

140. Adela F. Obregon Santacilia and Rodrigues Lozano to Agustín Leñero, April 24, 1940, and July 4, 1940, Folder "Ana Sokolow," Biblioteca, CENART.

141. Agustín Leñero to Gonzalo Vásquez Vela, July 16, 1940, and Gonzalo Vásquez Vela to Agustín Leñero, July 20, 1940. Folder "Ana Sokolow," Biblioteca, CENART.

142. See Hedrick, *Mestizo Modernism*, 31.

143. Silvestre Revueltas, *El renacuajo paseador*, David Atherton (conductor), London Sinfonietta, *Silvestre Revueltas: Centennial Anthology 1899–1999, 15 Masterpieces*, compact disc, RCA, (P) 1999 BMG Entertainment.

Figure 2.4: Rin Rin Renacuajo, *The Fable of the Wandering Frog*, Mexican production. Photographer unknown. Larry Warren Collection on Anna Sokolow and Lester Horton, Box 1, Music Division, Library of Congress, Washington, DC.

and characters with oversized heads used during holiday festivals.[144] Concert dances like *Wandering Frog* that incorporated folk themes differed from traditional or regional folk dances. The concert-based *danzas nacionalistas* [nationalist dances], prominent during the Mexican postrevolutionary era in the companies of Sokolow and Waldeen, were a genre distinct from the *bailes folklóricos* or *bailes regionales* of participatory regional folk dances.[145] These theatrical *danzas nacionalistas* became a vehicle for enveloping modernism into nationalist sentiment.

In an alliance of the arts, *Wandering Frog*'s scenery, musical score, libretto, and choreography came together in a production of folkloric and modernist elements that represented what literature and gender studies scholar Tace Hedrick terms "*mestizo* modernism." Hedrick's concept of *mestizo* modernism helps explain how Sokolow's dances functioned in the environment of Mexican modernism that relied on a continuum of autochthonous elements, social action, and abstracted form. *Mestizo* modernism, Hedrick argues, connected a mythic indigenous past to industrial progress that included all of postrevolutionary Mexico's imagined races instead of the rupture central to European and American modernism.[146] *Mestizo*

144. See Susan N. Masuoka, *En Calavera: The Papier-Mâché Art of the Linares Family* (Los Angeles: UCLA Fowler Museum of Cultural History, 1994), 1, 102, 119.

145. Olga Nájera-Ramírez, "Staging Authenticity: Theorizing the Development of Mexican *Folklórico* Dance," in *Dancing Across Borders*, 279.

146. Hedrick, *Mestizo Modernism*, 25–28.

modernism focused on, Hedrick asserts, "a concern with a sense of the ancient in combination with the modern—a mestizaje that called for race mixing but was simultaneously indigenist,"[147] and it applies to the work of artists like Rivera and Kahlo. *Mestizo* modernist tenets resonate with Mexican dance historian Raquel Tibol's 1956 assertion, which I discuss in the next chapter, that modernist form comes from a blending of indigeneity and social action. *Mestizo* modernism's reliance on the continuity of ethnicity and form enabled Sokolow's revolutionary modernism to be a continuum of Jewish proletarianism and modernist formalism. Considering Hedrick's definition of *mestizo* modernism, the stakes of exile connected ethno–political displacement with a way for modernism to absorb, instead of deflect, ethnically marked elements. In turn, *Wandering Frog* embodied Mexican postrevolutionary nationalist ideology as it challenged government positions against Jewish exile by showing that Jews could make *mestizaje* art.

Written by Rafael Pombo, a nineteenth-century Colombian poet popular throughout Latin America, the *Wandering Frog* was a fable that, with Pombo's other children's stories and life lessons featuring animals, was still beloved in the early twentieth century.[148] Prior to La Paloma Azul's production, *El renacuajo paseador* was a 1933 puppet show, for which Revueltas wrote the music.[149] The parable featured Rin Rin Renacuajo, a young frog who embarks on a solo journey despite his mother's plea for him to stay home. Mr. Mouse lures him to a party at Mr. and Mrs. Mouse's cantina, which is attacked by Mr. and Mrs. Cat. A hungry duck eats the frog as he tries to escape, and herein lies the lesson: "Mr. Mouse and Mrs. Mouse and the cats have their dinner, the duck its supper, and Mama Frog remains alone."[150] The orchestra's instruments indicate the characters as follows, according to musicologist Eduardo Contreras Soto: "The trombone represents the tadpole, and the small chamber ensemble serves to animate the walks, the party, and the cat's surprising eruption; a descending trombone scale illustrates the tadpole's sad descent into the duck's belly."[151] This narrative twist echoed the destruction in the face of contentment from many of Sokolow's earlier choreographic themes. In her concert

147. Ibid., 5.
148. See Nicolás Bayona Posada, "Rafael Pombo: Los Tres Somos el Poeta," *Revista Iberoamericana* 9, no. 18 (1945): 217–241; B. Sanín Cano, "Review of *Poesías de Rafael Pombo, Traducciones poéticas de Rafael Pombo,* and *Fábulas y Verdades de Rafael Pombo,*" *The Modern Language Review* 13, no. 2 (1918): 252–254; Lyon F. Lyday, "Review of *Biografía y bibliografía de Rafael Pombo* by Héctor Orjuela," *Hispania* 50, no. 1 (1967): 93; and bibliotecasvirtuales.com. The program notes at the Paloma Azul premiere date the story to the mid-nineteenth century. For an animated rendition of this story, see http://www.youtube.com/watch?v=jjFlohHnYFI. Accessed September 13, 2015.
149. Eduardo Contreras Soto, "Silvestre Revueltas: An Orchestral and Chamber Anthology, Centennial Commemorative Edition, 1899–1999," liner notes for *Revueltas: Centennial Anthology 1899–1999, 15 Masterpieces,* trans. Rebecca Salazar (BMG Entertainment, 1999), 12.
150. Program, *Anna Sokolow and Dance Group,* Mansfield Theatre, March 3, 1941, Martha Hill Papers, Juilliard. Other versions of the fable include just one cat.
151. Contreras Soto, "Silvestre Revueltas," 12.

program, Sokolow cemented the production within communist discourse by quoting a version of the fable fashioned in verse by García Lorca.[152]

The *Wandering Frog* follows *Don Lindo* as a *zarzuela* rife with mishaps. The first part of the musical score features Rin Rin's trombone happily ambling amid a pleasant scene set by lighthearted violins that narrate the start of a quotidian but nonetheless enjoyable adventure. Two-thirds of the way into the five-minute piece, disjunctive sounds interrupt the orderly music. Clashes denote distress as trouble enters in the form of Mr. and Mrs. Cat. One photograph of these rabble-rousers features them gleefully rearing to take off across the stage. Their hands expand through a gesture of stroking their whiskers before they continue wreaking their havoc. Rin Rin sits in front of them bent over with his big bulgy-eyed frog head in his hands.[153] Rin Rin was only too lucky to sit there, as, in no time, crying then descending trombone notes announce his fate as the duck swallows him. The score reaches a hastily unsettling yet pithy conclusion. The papier mâché duck that enacted this final dramatic moment solidified Mexican cultural elements as significant factors in this dance. Because of some kind of backstage dispute, however, the stagehands refused to move the huge prop duck onstage,[154] so the opening-night performance likely missed its full bite as there was no visible duck to eat the frog.

Wandering Frog was a hilarious farce based on a familiar parable, and Sokolow depended on her audience's nuanced understanding of the narrative for the dance to be funny.[155] Mexican dancers' and critics' laudations reinforced this subtlety. Sokolova Rosa Reyna, who danced the role of one of the cats in the premiere,[156] reminisced that the piece with its character-specific movements "was fun and child-like, with divine masks and rich music."[157] Mexican critic Arturo Perucho wrote in 1947 that the dance was "full of funny jokes and great episodes," that Sokolow's choreography was "dynamic and sparkling," and that the scenery, costumes, and masks were "full of color and popular sentiment."[158] He concluded that the piece

152. García Lorca's full verse is reprinted in Luna Arroyo, *Ana Mérida*, 91.

153. Photograph in Arturo Perucho, "Ballet Moderno en Mexico," *Nuestra Musica* (1947): 177–191. See also Flier, *Three Ballets from Mexico*, Mansfield Theatre, March 3, 1941, Anna Sokolow Clippings, JRDD, NYPL.

154. Reynoso, "Choreographing Politics," 267.

155. I base this inference on the way the humor in choreographer Doug Elkins's *Fräulein Maria* (2006) depends on the audience's knowing Julie Andrews's version of *The Sound of Music* (1965) and the American cult sensation around it, along with recognizing twentieth-century concert dance historical references, in order to find *Fräulein Maria* funny. Doug Elkins & Friends' *Fräulein Maria* and post-performance talk, presented by White Bird, January 14, 2011, Newmark Theatre, Portland, OR.

156. Program, *La Paloma Azul*, Palacio de Bellas Artes, September 20, 1940, Folder GP-DF 00041, Biblioteca, CENART.

157. Rosa Reyna quoted in Lynton, *Anna Sokolow*, 16: *"El renacuajo paseador* era muy divertido e infantil, con unas máscaras divinas y una música tan rica. Los movimentos correspondían al tipo de personaje."

158. Perucho, "Ballet Moderno," 183–184: ". . . plagado de graciosas y fantásticos episodios. . . . Ana Sokolow creó una coreografía dinámica y chispeante; Carlos Mérida diseñó un decorado y unos fantásticos vestidos y mascarones, rebosantes de color y sentido populares."

"was one of the most legitimate successes of that season."[159] Raquel Gutiérrez, who danced the role of the Waiter Mouse, defined it as a perfect and delightful ballet.[160] Sokolow melded a *danza nacionalista* that appeared revolutionary through its folkloric characters and set dressing.

Reyna, moreover, connected with a sense of nationalism she found in the dance. She reflected in 1983 that Sokolow brought Mexican traditions onto the concert stage where before there were only European stories in foreign *pointe* shoes. "For me," she said, "this was a new feeling that finally we could do something Mexican in dance."[161] Reyna found Sokolow's *mestizaje*-esque blending of "something Mexican" with American concert traditions culturally reinforcing. The Mexican dance community did not retain this sentiment. In 1956, as I show in Chapter 3, Waldeen accused Sokolow of not being Mexican enough and for her dismissiveness of dance rooted in *mexicanidad*, a national cultural discourse defining Mexicanness through mythical indigenous and revolutionary folk imagery.[162] Despite Sokolow's later entanglements with *mexicanidad*, the dance's resonance as nationalist reinforces its revolutionary connections.

Sokolow's triumph with La Paloma Azul was short lived, and the company received mixed reviews. Criticism included complaints that the dancers did not perform at a professional level; support praised the dancers' technical performances. Nicolas Dorantes's assertion in *The Kenyon Review* that Sokolow "left untouched the enormous heritage from the Mexican dancing tradition" suggests the work was too Eurocentric.[163] Conversely, critic Luis G. Basurto forgave some technical flaws because of what he perceived as a short rehearsal time, noting that Sokolow was a "good dancer and perhaps better, a magnificent choreographer."[164] Larry Warren reported that critics asserted "that high expectations had been exceeded."[165] It is possible that Mexican critics bolstered Sokolow's work, even if the dances were compositionally weak, so that the Mexican government appeared strong. Although the dancers remember it fondly, not everyone supported La Paloma Azul. Mérida reported the Palacio de Bellas Artes's mysterious animosity toward the company that resulted in drastic cuts to rehearsal time and stagehands' refusal to move integral set pieces, such as *Wandering Frog*'s duck or the pig suspended on wires that was

159. Perucho, "Ballet Moderno," 184: "*El renacuajo paseador* constituyó uno de los más legítimos éxitos de aquella temporada y uno de los muchos títulos por los cuales se venera la memoria del inquieto compositor duranguense."

160. Raquel Gutiérrez quoted in Dallal, *La Danza en México*, 73.

161. Rosa Reyna quoted in Lynton, *Anna Sokolow*, 16. "Para mí era una novedad sentir que por fin podíamos hacer algo mexicano en la danza."

162. See Hershfield, "Screening the Nation," 259.

163. Nicolas Dorantes, "Mexican Letter, Mexico City, October 28, 1940," *The Kenyon Review* 3, no. 1 (1941): 133.

164. Luis G. Basurto, "Critica de Arte: El Ballet de 'La Paloma Azul,'" no source, no date, Patricia Aulestia Collection, CENIDID, CENART. "Ana Sokolow es una buena bailarina. Pero tambíen y esto resulta tal vez mejor, una magnífica organïzadora."

165. Warren, *Rebellious Spirit*, 95.

supposed to transport Don Lindo up and away at the end of the dance.[166] La Paloma Azul disbanded in 1940 when Formoso withdrew her patronage after refusing to allow Sokolow to present a dance depicting a prostitute.[167]

NEGOTIATING HEMISPHERIC AESTHETIC DIFFERENCES

Sokolow's Paloma Azul choreographies continued to be embroiled in divergent aesthetic expectations when she presented them in New York with her company there, now listed as her Dance Group or simply Group (instead of Dance Unit), the following season. Although Mexican audiences praised these dances for their technical prowess though some felt they were not Mexican enough, New York's critical establishment opposed them because they appeared too Mexican. The rift between Sokolow's critical reception in both cities points to the elements critics included in or excluded from 1940s discourses of universal art, as I show in the next chapter. Although she did not again have a standing company in Mexico City after La Paloma Azul folded, Sokolow continued to present solo concerts. After she stopped performing, she was a guest or resident choreographer for INBA and contemporary companies.

Sokolow's impermanence in Mexico stripped her of the long-term star status Waldeen enjoyed. Sokolow split her time between New York and Mexico throughout the 1940s, spending six months at a time in each place. At the start of that decade, Sokolow presented solo concerts or counted on small groups to rehearse and perform her work while she was away.[168] She did this out of necessity because of her constant moves, but felt lonely in New York because of it.[169] She later reflected that she went back and forth for too long.[170] Sokolow's romantic relationship with Aguirre gives one explanation for her travel,[171] but questions linger about how a communist artist tracked by the FBI could travel freely between the United States and Mexico during World War II. Sokolow reportedly loved Mexico City, the dancers, and her community there, but it was more important to her to remain prominent in New York than to stay in Mexico.[172] The Sokolovas joined Waldeen's company or the Ballet of Mexico City in Sokolow's absence.[173] Notably, Waldeen's historical legacy as an embodiment of Mexican nationalism through her folkloric choreography

166. Reynoso, "Choreographing Politics," 267.

167. Tortajada Quiroz, *Frutos de Mujer*, 362–363.

168. No author or title, *American Dancer*, January 1941, n.p. Anna Sokolow Clippings, JRDD, NYPL.

169. Anna Sokolow to Bessie Schönberg, August 2, 1942, Box 11, Folder 417, Bessie Schönberg Papers, JRDD, NYPL.

170. Anna Sokolow, interview by Newman, transcript.

171. Warren, *Rebellious Spirit*, 96.

172. Ibid., 95.

173. Tortajada Quiroz, *Frutos de Mujer*, 373–376.

is the inverse of the 1939 reception of these women, in which audiences perceived Waldeen as a more abstract choreographer than one of strong social conscience.[174] Audiences initially preferred Sokolow's choreography with its clear revolutionary themes.

Governmental shifts altered Sokolow's dances' reception, as political changes in Mexico in the 1940s affected artists. The government embraced ballet as it swung to the political right. The Cárdenas administration dropped modern dance, sending Sokolow and Waldeen scrambling to support their work; from 1940 to 1946 the government, under the leadership of Cárdenas and then Camacho, supported classical ballet companies including the Campobellos and the Ballet of Mexico City.[175] New York experienced similar conservative shifts, as revolutionary dance dissipated after the US government demonized Communism. Juggling Mexico's *mestizaje* nationalist aesthetics with American anticommunist desires for abstract universalism, Sokolow sojourned between Mexico City and New York for the war's duration, herself an artistic exile with no home to which to return.

174. Reynoso, "Choreographing Politics," 257.
175. Tortajada Quiroz, *Frutos de Mujer*, 373.

CHAPTER 3

The Wandering Frog That Did Not Travel Well

Jewishness, Mexicanidad, *and Ethnic Dance*

Sokolow miscalculated wartime shifts in New York critics' aesthetic expectations. She discovered the new critical establishment's values when she toured her Mexican-made dances back to the American Northeast. With the workers' movement quieted, the critics who dominated 1930s dance criticism in the *Daily Worker, New Masses, New Theatre,* and *New York Amsterdam News* were replaced with what Gay Morris acknowledged as the "exclusively white" high-art dance press corps in *Dance Magazine, Dance News, Dance Observer, The American Dancer, New York Times,* and the *Christian Science Monitor.*[1] Disconnected from international communist conversations and aligned instead with the 1940s–1950s US dance press dialogue that prized white transcendent ideals over folk-as-revolutionary themes, critics labeled Sokolow's Mexican-made dances unsophisticated. Sokolow's dances were caught between American modernist abstraction that prized universality without direct statements and Latin American modernism's continuum of ethnicity and abstraction.

Because US critics panned many of the dances Sokolow produced from 1941 to 1952, these dances are often absent from critical concert dance histories in the United States. This chapter addresses the reception of two pairs of dances, *El renacuajo paseador* [*The Fable of the Wandering Frog*] that I introduced in the previous chapter, and the solo *Lament for the Death of a Bullfighter* (1941), and the solos *Kaddish* (1945) and *Mexican Retablo* (1946), to show how the reception of a dance can determine its place in the historical record. The first two pieces engaged

---

1. Morris, *A Game for Dancers,* xxiii, 88 (see Introduction, n8).

mexicanidad to make revolutionary statements, whereas the second two dances drew heightened ethnicity from *mexicanidad*'s nationalistic values to deploy religious representations as political statements in the Holocaust's aftermath. At a moment when the US critical establishment upheld abstraction, Sokolow's highlighting of Jewishness and Catholicism as political vehicles challenged an encroaching hierarchy of whiteness in US dance.

Critics' reviews of Sokolow's dances reflected midcentury US concertgoers' fascination with ethnic and ethnologic dance.[2] Ethnic dance was a label that US dance critics assigned to performers or dance forms that appeared to originate outside the Christian Euro–American tradition. Ethnologic dance was a term assigned to non-Western dance forms danced by white practitioners with Eurocentric performance and training values. Ethnologic performers tapped into what Rebekah Kowal articulated as midcentury dance universalism wherein audiences accepted white bodies to stand in as placeholders for all bodies, even though movement that was considered universal "maintained ethnocentric biases (white, Western, Christian, heterosexual)."[3] Susan Manning connected this kind of transcendent experience to concert dance whiteness, in which critical discourses enabled white bodies to perform as culturally unmarked bodies.[4] Sokolow's work fell among these tensions because critics received her dances as containing a mix of culturally marked and unmarked elements. This uneasy transfer between Sokolow's work and its reception, I argue, is the space in which Sokolow's revolutionary modernism troubled binary expectations of US wartime and postwar audiences and, as a result, brought *mestizo* modernist and Jewish elements into American modernist discourse.

Bringing *Wandering Frog, Bullfighter, Kaddish,* and *Retablo* into conversation resurfaces the hemispheric cultural exchange between the United States and Mexico that occurred through Sokolow's dances. In this discussion, I examine wartime currents in the American Jewish community paired with the Mexican cultural and nationalist environment of *mexicanidad*, Catholicism, and women's roles. Additionally, I show how the co-constructions of Jewishness and *mexicanidad* in *Kaddish* and *Retablo* enabled these dances to resonate across constituencies and specifically for Jewish audiences in Mexico and the United States. Taken together, these four dances register compositional transitions from Sokolow's 1930s proletarian and anti-fascist dances to her vanguard modernist works in the 1950s.

---

2. See Rebekah Kowal, "Choreographing Interculturalism: International Dance Performance at the American Museum of Natural History, 1943–1952," in *The Oxford Handbook of Dance and Ethnicity*, eds. Anthony Shay and Barbara Sellers-Young (New York: Oxford University Press, 2016), 454–479; Rebecca Rossen, "Dancing Jews and Jewesses: Jewishness, Ethnicity, and Exoticism in American Dance," in *The Oxford Handbook of Dance and Ethnicity*, eds. Anthony Shay and Barbara Sellers-Young (New York: Oxford University Press, 2016), 66–90; and Yutian Wong, "Artistic Utopias: Michio Ito and the Trope of the International" in *Worlding Dance*, ed. Susan Leigh Foster (2009; New York: Palgrave Macmillan, 2011), 144–162.

3. Kowal, "Choreographing Interculturalism," 464.

4. Manning, *Modern Dance Negro Dance*, xiv–xv (see Preface, n14).

The politics surrounding the modern versus ethnic dance divide came to a head for Sokolow among her Mexican peers in the mid-1950s. I end this chapter with a confrontation between Sokolow and prominent members of the Mexico City dance community about the definition of Mexican dance during two conferences in Veracruz, Mexico, in the summer of 1956. Mexican choreographers and intellectuals found the abstract expressionism of vanguard American modernism overtaking the continuum of formalism and indigeneity of Latin American modernism. Sokolow's assertions, in which she staunchly held the line against her Mexican colleagues for the necessity of abstract dance movement to reference nothing outside itself, pointed more to the changing stakes of modern dance, ethnic dance, and revolutionary dance in the United States under the government's eradication of Communism than to any shifts in the way she made dances. She had received similar criticism in New York fifteen years prior.

THE WANDERING FROG THAT DID NOT TRAVEL WELL

Previews of Sokolow's 1940–1941 New York–area concerts promoted an intangible exoticism critics wanted in Sokolow's Mexican dances. Her tour's timing coincided with popular interest in Spanish and Latin American performers.[5] Reviews of Sokolow's concerts contain primitivist language linking her folkloric themes to juvenile ideas instead of the complex irony critics expected based on Sokolow's 1930s work.[6] These many dances included *Homage to García Lorca* (1941), which included the solo "Duelo" that became *Lament for the Death of a Bullfighter*, and *Wandering Frog*. US critics' labeling these dances immature align their values with concert dance whiteness, by privileging abstracted (white) form over nonwhite content.[7] Their reviews did not recognize the folk-as-revolutionary politics of the Mexican elements in *Wandering Frog* and other dances, including the antiwar *Vision Fantastica (after Goya)* and *Canciones para Niñas* [*Songs for Children*]. Although Sokolow's 1930s proletarian dances were culturally marked as part of the New York (Jewish) revolutionary milieu, US critics read them as modernist. Conversely, they

5. Articles in *The American Dancer* and *Dance Magazine* highlighted the flamenco dancer Amaya, various dance opportunities in Brazil and Argentina, and American ballet companies' tours of South America. Helen Dzhermolinska, "You Must See Amaya," *The American Dancer* (May 1941): 12–13, 30; Frederic Majer, "South America as a Dance Market," *Dance Magazine* (June 1941): 12; and Lincoln Kirstein, "The American Ballet in Argentina: Part II of a Travel Diary," *The American Dancer* (October 1941): 12–13, 25, 29.

6. See Earle, *Return of the Native*, 102, 117, and 131 (see Chap. 2, n12), and Anthea Kraut, *Choreographing the Folk: The Dance Stagings of Zora Neale Hurston* (Minneapolis: University of Minnesota Press, 2008), 1–24 for reception of the primitive and folk within dominant discourses.

7. Following Joann W. Keali'inohomoku's argument that dances reflect their ethnic origins, modernist dance was culturally marked in terms of its whiteness. Keali'inohomoku, "An Anthropologist Looks at Ballet as a Form of Ethnic Dance," *Impulse* (1969–1970): 24–32.

labeled the folk markings in Sokolow's Mexican dances "ethnic" instead of revolutionary. This US reception strips these dances of choreographic sophistication, yet their reception as ethnic possibly diverted attention away from the political ramifications they had as Mexican revolutionary propaganda as the United States attempted to contain Communism in fear of the war in Europe coming to American borders through Mexico.

Sokolow's only Mexican import that US critics favorably received because of its male-gendered, Euro-legible compositional material, *Bullfighter* reinforced American modernist appetites for transcendent themes reliant on Euro-resonant male characteristics. As a program note explained, "Federico García Lorca, Spanish Poet was killed by the Fascists in Spain in 1937,"[8] and the bullfighter was a metaphor for the Loyalist playwright. In her flared black matador costume accented with vibrant red lining, Sokolow invoked García Lorca fighting the bull of Franco's Spanish Nationalists and the injustice his murder by them represented. Silvestre Revueltas's haunting modernist orchestral music featured a weeping bassoon over a thicket of woodwinds and horns and aurally resonated with the opening of Igor Stravinksy's modernist trailblazer *Le Sacre du Primtemps* [*The Rite of Spring*].[9] Sokolow's inclusion of *Bullfighter* on her concerts alongside *Slaughter of the Innocents, Exile,* and her dances with folklore-as-revolutionary themes suggests that these dances constituted a revolutionary conversation in Mexico. This nuance was illegible to US critics no longer aligned with the Left.

The Spanish colonial origins and masculine traditions of bullfighting freed this dance from effeminized indigenous associations and aligned it with critics' expectations of the masculine personae in Sokolow's 1930s solos like *Case History* and *Façade.* The solo's original title, "*Duelo*" ["Pain"], with the program note, "Lament for the death of a bull-fighter," couples strength with defeat.[10] This dance demonstrates how the word *duelo* translates as duel, or mourning, in addition to pain. In a 1977 performance of "*Duelo*," Manuel Alum is a triumphant, tormented matador. He thrusts his arms overhead while his cape flares; he twists and collapses before swaying his cape aside and raising his right arm in difficult victory.[11] In a March 3, 1941 performance at New York's Mansfield Theatre on West 47th Street near Broadway, Sokolow danced, according to critic Robert Sabin, "with fierce intensity of mood and a use of costume, lighting and movement which showed that she is still

8. Program, *Anna Sokolow in Dance Recital assisted by Sylvia Gershkowitz, Pianist, Benefit of Russian War Relief, Berkshire Pines, West Copake, N.Y.,* July 25, 1942, Box 11, Folder 417, Bessie Schönberg Papers, JRDD, NYPL. Lorca was murdered on August 19, 1936, one month after the Spanish Civil War began.

9. Silvestre Revueltas, *Homenaje a Federico García Lorca,* arr. Eugenio Toussaint, Urtext Digital Classics JBCC106.

10. Program, *Anna Sokolow and Dance Group,* Mansfield Theatre, March 3, 1941, Martha Hill Papers, Juilliard.

11. *Manuel Alum Dance Company,* VHS (New York: Washington Square Methodist Church, 1977), JRDD, NYPL.

a remarkable talent."[12] Sokolow's power in the masculine role of this dance stood out. Certainly the lionization of García Lorca and sympathies for Loyalist Spain also provided support for the dance, and its portrayal of a regal, archetypal (male) individual hero enabled the solo to appear universal. There is little visual evidence of *Lament for the Death of a Bullfighter* from the early 1940s, but Sokolow's performance in a pared-down version of this dance in Shirley Clarke's 1955 film *Bullfight* gives a sense of her physicality that attracted critics' attention.

Sokolow's performance in Clarke's film retains the stage version's paired victory and vulnerability. In *Bullfight*, the camera cuts back and forth between a bullfight in an arena, where Sokolow is in the crowd, and an isolated theatrical studio space, wherein a matador-costumed Sokolow performs "Duelo."[13] Clarke, a Jewish experimental filmmaker, had danced with Graham, Holm, and Sokolow.[14] She and Sokolow collaborated on two dance films in which Clarke experimented with choreography for the camera: *Bullfight* and *A Moment in Love* (1957), a surrealist duet for Carmen Gutierrez and Paul Sanasardo.[15] The communist political import of *Bullfighter* became masked in *Bullfight*, where the film positioned Sokolow within an actual bullfight instead of the solo's enacting the bullfighter as a fascist-fighting metaphor. Sokolow and Clarke made *Bullfight* as a formalist study during Sokolow's public retreat from communism in the 1950s, yet it recalls her Loyalist politics. Sokolow's movements on film are deliberate and sustained. Alternating between being strong and noble and being gutted and slain, she is at once bull and matador. In *Bullfight*, Sokolow performed a struggle for humanitarian justice.

Bullfight's central themes of surveillance, calculated vulnerability in attack, and victory through murder continued Sokolow's refashioning of gendered performance ranges for women despite the constrictions of postwar normalcy. The painting in the film's opening credits figures Sokolow as a matador prodding a bull, even though in the film she does not touch one. The professional matador's slaying of the bull at the film's conclusion brings García Lorca a posthumous victory despite the inner turmoil Sokolow's dance phrases suggest, as if to say his death was not in vain. As the film opens, Sokolow deliberately surveys the studio space as white light pours over her black costume. The camera cuts to a bullfight arena, and Sokolow is one of the few women in the crowd, wearing a white ruffled shirt and looking around with the same even observance. The bull enters the ring; Sokolow as spectator watches as the matador crosses himself, takes tiny rhythmic steps, and taunts the

12. Robert Sabin, "Anna Sokolow and Group, Mansfield Theatre, March 3, 1941," *Dance Observer* (April 1941): 55.

13. Anna Sokolow, *Bullfight*, directed by Shirley Clarke (1955; Halcyon Films, 1975; Art Works Video, 1980), http://search.alexanderstreet.com/view/work/507142. Accessed September 15, 2015.

14. Bruce Bebb, "The Many Media of Shirley Clarke," *Journal of the University Film and Video Association* 34, no. 2 (1982): 3.

15. Lauren Rabinovitz, "Clarke, Shirley: American director," in *St. James Women Filmmakers Encyclopedia*, ed. Amy L. Unterburger (Detroit: Visible Ink Press, 1999), 88.

bull by waving his red cape. As the matador raises his sword, a woman's voice croons and the camera cuts to Sokolow in the studio space. Mostly stationary, she threads her arms through each other, lifts a bent leg to the side, and rises onto the ball of her foot before turning through a short series of jumps.[16] Suddenly, the lighting changes to deep red, and Sokolow, with her skirt repurposed into a red-edged black cape, progresses through heavier movements as a horn haunts Norman Lloyd's musical score. She dives across the floor on her knees with a thrust that recalls fighting the beast in *Exile*. She stands with a regal posture and slowly turns into the crook of her left arm before succumbing into a spiraling back fall, mimicking the ailing bull in the ring, to which the camera cuts. This moment retains a sense of García Lorca's fight before his untimely fall and positions Sokolow as a García Lorca figure in her own struggles with 1950s surveillance.

As it continues, the film represents struggle in the act of fighting through defeat. In the studio, which is now bathed in white light, Sokolow stands powerful once again. She holds up her curved right arm and looks into her elbow while holding the cape out to the side. Her ensuing counterclockwise rotations are slow and sustained until she drops to the floor as the fallen matador, and the camera cuts to the matador in the ring partially gored on the bull. Sokolow rolls her head as the camera pans around the crowd in the arena, creating a blurred view as if from the eyes of the injured matador. She drops out of the frame; the bull falls, slain, and the matador walks away, triumphant but subdued. A montage of Sokolow's poses and snapshots from the bullfight ends the film, giving Sokolow an omniscient presence as actual and metaphorical matador, bull, spectator, victim, victor, and Fascist-fighter. *Bullfighter's* masculinities interspersed potency with weakness and stood in opposition to the effeminized subordination that US critics assigned to Sokolow's folkloric pieces like *Wandering Frog*.

New York audiences unfamiliar with the *Wandering Frog* legend missed the references necessary to understand its humor and saw only a juvenile façade. Besides the nationalist sentiment lost in translation, this dance did not travel well from opera house opulence to reduction on the modern dance stage.[17] Reviews for Sokolow's March 3, 1941 concert at the Mansfield Theatre and her program on December 13, 1941, at the 92nd Street Y, reflect critics' disappointment in Sokolow's choreography and her group's performance qualities.[18] In a character-driven dance, moreover, Sokolow's thin costume reproductions detracted from the dance's impact. It

16. Earlier versions of this dance possibly contained larger movements. Because her back injury caused Sokolow to stop performing in the early 1950s, she is likely not dancing as fully as before.

17. Sokolow could not bring the original sets, costumes, cast, and orchestration with her to New York. Tortajada Quiroz, *Frutos de Mujer*, 376 (see Chap. 2, n19).

18. See Sabin, "Anna Sokolow and Group, Mansfield Theatre," 55–56; Albertina Vitak, "Anna Sokolow and Group, Mansfield Theatre, March 3," *The American Dancer* (May 1941): 17; and Lois Balcom, "Anna Sokolow, Y. M. H. A. December 13, 1941," *Dance Observer* (January 1942): 4–5.

is unclear if the critics' comments about the works' immaturity reflected a common Orientalist perception that linked folk themes and nonwhite populations to unsophisticated ideas, or if the dancers were underrehearsed or not technically proficient. Half these dancers were members of Sokolow's acclaimed Dance Unit in 1939, and it is unlikely that their technical proficiency fell so dramatically in two years' time.[19] In photographs, these dancers' bodies display an attention to detail and an understanding of weight and spatial tension characteristic of performers trained in modern dance techniques.[20] Reviews ignore the dancers' strength, but it is difficult to imagine a technically insufficient performance. They trained for the March 3 concert in Sokolow's absence, and so their performances likely differed qualitatively from those two years prior when they rehearsed daily with Sokolow.

Wandering Frog shares similarities with Sokolow's revolutionary work, but US critics saw only the folk elements that, to them, distanced the dance as Other. They described the *Wandering Frog*'s costumes and Revueltas's score in lieu of discussing the dance's movement. Although Sabin noted in *Dance Observer* the strength of *Wandering Frog*'s musical score, he was less generous about the choreography, noting the "new works were so poor choreographically and so amateurishly danced by the group that they should never have been put on the stage."[21] *Wandering Frog*'s humor and sentiment that folklore signified revolution was lost in New York. Critic Albertina Vitak echoed Sabin's sentiment. She wrote in *The American Dancer* that the dances were "limited in vocabulary. They almost suggest that Miss Sokolow works with children in Mexico?? [*sic*] Of course, it is possible that the Spanish movement has something of the native feeling when danced by the Mexican girls. It had none on this occasion."[22] Vitak's review evidences spectatorial legibility lost in translation from Mexican to American audiences, demonstrating her unfulfilled exotic expectations. She could not accept formalism with nonwhite themes and instead raced the movement based on its folkloric inspiration. These reviews' connections of nonwhite, effeminized bodies to perceived infantile themes reinforced the white patriarchal structure of the American critical establishment.

Although critics disparaged Sokolow's folkloric dances, they upheld their preferences for Sokolow's own performance persona. Vitak lamented that Sokolow did not dance enough in her Mansfield Theatre performance, contending that Sokolow

19. Program, *New Masses presents Anna Sokolow and Dance Unit*, Alvin Theatre, February 26, 1939, Martha Hill Papers, Juilliard; Program, *Anna Sokolow y su Cuerpo Ballet*, Palace of Fine Arts, April 18, 1939, Collection of Patricia Aulestia, PBA; Program, *Anna Sokolow and Dance Group*, Mansfield Theatre, March 3, 1941, Martha Hill Papers, Juilliard; and Program, *The Dance Theatre of the Y. M. H. A. presents Anna Sokolow and Group*, Theresa L. Kaufmann Auditorium, December 13, 1941, 92Y.

20. See, for example, "Anna Sokolow's group in one of the numbers from a program of dances by Miss Sokolow presented at the Mansfield Theatre, New York, March 3," *The American Dancer* (March 1941): 19.

21. Sabin, "Anna Sokolow and Group, Mansfield Theatre, March 3, 1941," 55.

22. Albertina Vitak, "Dance Events Reviewed," *The American Dancer* (May 1941): 17.

was "one of the most distinctive of the younger 'moderns.' "[23] Sokolow's solo performances addressing the Holocaust in the following years in *Kaddish* and *Mexican Retablo* returned to the kinds of solo political dances she made in the 1930s. Although critics' language a few years later did not infantilize these works, they retained a modern dance/ethnic dance tension that prevented them from articulating the impact of the works' content. Their reviews erased some of Sokolow's most poignant political statements, especially as she used religious references when abstraction did not suffice.

A KADDISH FOR THE HOLOCAUST

While US critics marginalized dances through ethnic dance labels, Sokolow joined her Jewish generation in a historical moment of unifying nostalgia toward Judaism and Jewish culture as Hitler decimated European Jewry. *Exile* and *Kaddish* chronologically bookend World War II and manifest Sokolow's advocacy during this time. Sokolow premiered *Kaddish*, her Holocaust memorial based on the Jewish mourner's prayer, at Mexico City's Palacio de Bellas Artes in August 1945, and then at Boston's Jordan Hall and New York's 92nd Street Y in May 1946. Sokolow had agitated with antiwar dances since 1933, but neither she nor the Popular Front could stop the Nazis. With *Kaddish*'s August 20, 1945 premiere, all there was left to do was mourn. *Kaddish*, along with *Exile*, proffered comments that resonated with the role of Hebrew biblical prophets, who stood outside accepted attitudes and critiqued the seats of power but also offered consolation after a tragic event.[24] After years of choreographically yelling and screaming, Sokolow's elegy in *Kaddish* brought uneasy closure for Holocaust events and challenged the traditional foreclosing of women's roles in Jewish ritual practices. *Mexican Retablo* furthered her political engagement with spirituality by expanding her religious portraiture to include Catholic penitents. Sokolow's performances of angry grief brought poignancy to these issues that enraptured audiences in New York, Boston, and Mexico City,[25] even if audience members could not read the dances' codes and US critics used the term "ethic dance" as shorthand for their content. I have previously argued for a fluid understanding of the gendered and Jewish signifiers in *Kaddish*, especially as different women in the late twentieth century performed versions of the solo tailored for them.[26] I focus this discussion on Sokolow's concerts during

23. Ibid.
24. I thank Lynn Kaye for this observation.
25. Margaret Lloyd went so far as to call the May 1946 performance "the most beautiful concert of her career." Lloyd, *Borzoi Book of Modern Dance*, 221 (see Chap. 1, n186).
26. Hannah Kosstrin, "*Kaddish* at the Wall: The Long Life of Anna Sokolow's 'Prayer for the Dead,'" in *Dance on Its Own Terms*, eds. Bales and Eliot (New York: Oxford University Press, 2013), 255–281 (see Introduction, n27).

the Holocaust's aftermath, in which women's bodies performing Jewish ethnicity provoked varied legibilities on the concert stage.

Sokolow's reconnection to her Jewish heritage in Mexico coincided with a trend: Jewish choreographers who were not religiously observant made dances with Jewish thematic material to stand in international solidarity with Jews during the Holocaust.[27] Sokolow told the *Daily Worker* in 1943 that this was the first time she felt compelled to create Jewish kinship through her work.[28] This sentiment, coupled with a shift to the right in New York and in Mexico, affected her 1940s engagement with explicit Jewish thematic material. During World War II, choreographers in the United States did not make dances about the Holocaust. According to Judith Brin Ingber, Jewish dancers who escaped the Holocaust were discouraged from putting those images into their work because the Holocaust "was a taboo to dance or to discuss."[29] Although some believe that because American artists had not seen Holocaust images, they could not create visual art in response to them,[30] others challenge the opinion that Jews, in large cities at least, did not know what was going on in Europe.[31] One way Ashkenazi American Jewish choreographers evaded this sentiment, even while fearing rising anti-Semitism,[32] was to make nostalgic dances about Eastern Europe. Graham discouraged Sokolow from making dances about Jewish ghetto life because of what she perceived as its baseness and told Sokolow instead to draw on heroines from the Old Testament,[33] which proffered a kind of universalizing (whitening) of Jewish material.[34] Although Sokolow was separated from Graham by the 1940s, some of the dances she made reflected Graham's influence, whereas others embodied a more spiritual and activist Jewishness that recalled Yiddishkeit traditions. The dances Sokolow made in response to the Holocaust during the war drew from biblical stories and figures that connected with the Jewish community's collective, if invented, memory.[35] Years before Sophie Maslow's representation of a quaint *shtetl* (Eastern European

27. Larry Warren, *Rebellious Spirit*, 104 (see Preface, n2), and Josh Perelman "Choreographing Identity: Modern Dance and American Jewish Life, 1924–1954," (PhD diss., New York University, 2008)," 273, cite Mexico as the place where Sokolow spiritually and thematically connected to her Jewish heritage.

28. McHenry, "Anna Sokolow: Trip to Mexico," 7 (see Chap. 2, n48).

29. Judith Brin Ingber, "'I Wouldn't Cross the Street to See That': Modern Dancers Who Survived the Holocaust in America," in *2004 Proceedings of Society of Dance History Scholars*, comp. Susan C. Cook (Society of Dance History Scholars, 2005), 65.

30. Matthew Baigell, *Jewish-American Artists and the Holocaust* (New Brunswick: Rutgers University Press, 1997),18.

31. Bette Roth Young, "The American Jewish Response to the Holocaust—A Reconsideration," *Midstream* (March/April 2007): 29–34.

32. Baigell, *Jewish-American Artists*, 17; and Perelman, "Choreographing Identity," 263.

33. Ze'eva Cohen, discussion, 2009 (see Introduction, n85).

34. See Rossen, *Dancing Jewish*, 62–93 (see Introduction, n26).

35. See Eric Hobsbawm, "Introduction: Inventing Traditions," in *The Invention of Tradition*, eds. Hobsbawm and Terence Ranger (Cambridge: Cambridge University Press, 1983), 1–14.

Jewish ghetto) past in *The Village I Knew* (1951),[36] Sokolow constructed traditions for metaphoric use.

In the majority of her Holocaust-era Jewish and biblically themed dances, Sokolow rewrote Jewish gender roles by centering women in positions of power. These dances, including *The Bride, Images from the Old Testament* (which debuted in Mexico City as *Canciones Semitas*, or *Semitic Songs*), and *Kaddish*, premiered in the concert that Sokolow toured from 1945 to 1946 in Mexico City, Boston, and New York. She presented the first of her dances about biblical Jewish women, *Songs of a Semite* (1943), two years prior and then never again, but her dances *Revelations* and *Semitic Songs* were reworkings of this piece that called for the mobilization of Jewish women in the face of Nazi persecution.[37] In *Songs of a Semite* (1943), she presented portraits of biblical women and a stoic procession of Jewish women leading the community, and in *The Bride* (1945), she portrayed a young Jewish bride in an imagined Eastern European village questioning the tradition of arranged marriage. Sokolow's portrayal of the "bride's apprehension and temporary mollification" produced a "sensitive portrait" that most critics were unable to articulate without reproducing the program notes in their comments.[38] In *Kaddish*, Sokolow's shift in her gendered enactment by wearing men's vestments harkens back to her portrayal of male characters in her 1930s proletarian dances, such as her portrayal of neglected lower-class youth in *Case History*. From her *Kaddish* costume of a dress belted by a *gartel* under *tefillin* (phylacteries) and her loose hair, she was a woman working in a man's space. Enacting performance as a discourse of power,[39] by acting as Jewish law forbade women to do, Sokolow made *Kaddish* a site for Jewish women to publicly stage grief.

Sokolow mobilized Jewish communal mourning in *Kaddish* as a memorial for Holocaust victims at a time when many disillusioned Jews, including Holocaust survivors, rejected a Jewish god and religion. The title of this five-minute solo references the Mourner's Kaddish, a Jewish prayer to comfort those living who commemorate those lost.[40] This prayer's Aramaic language has a pattering rhythm when spoken and a warbling quality when chanted or sung.[41] Sokolow set *Kaddish*

36. See Naomi Jackson, "Jewishness and Modern Dance in Sophie Maslow's *The Village I Knew*," in *Dancing Texts: Intertextuality in Interpretation*, ed. Janet Adshead-Lansdale (London: Dance Books, 1999), 83–103.

37. See Rossen, *Dancing Jewish*, 64–75 for an in-depth analysis of *Songs of a Semite*. See also Sydney Skybetter, "Toward *Kaddish*," *Ballet Review* 36, no. 3 (2008): 28–34; and Perelman, "Choreographing Identity," 264–266.

38. Jennie Schulman, "Modern Dance in Ethnic Style," *Dance Observer* (May 1952): 76; and David Zellmer, "Anna Sokolow: Y. M. & Y. W. H. A. May 12, 1946," *Dance Observer* (June–July 1946): 76.

39. Butler, *Bodies that Matter*, 187, 241 (see Introduction, n15).

40. Kaddish is a type of daily prayer, including a Reader's Kaddish, a Whole Kaddish, and a Mourner's Kaddish.

41. Chanting in Jewish observance is a specific way of singing the melody of prayers, based on a codified system of troches and pronunciation.

to a chanted version of the Kaddish paired with Maurice Ravel's *Deux Mélodies Hébraiques*, a breathy violin solo of minor notes and stark piano chords with expectant pauses between phrases.[42] Tapping into an emotional connection to universalism, Sokolow believed that one does not have to be Jewish to understand the Kaddish prayer.[43] She explained in 1990, "Kaddish is the Hebrew prayer for the dead, so that the theme of the dance is a prayer. How Ravel uses it, the first section is almost like someone singing it. For me, the second section is the inner feeling about it."[44] The dance was significant as a kinesthetic monument in the wake of the millions of Jewish, Roma, and gay bodies the Nazis destroyed during the Holocaust.[45] The memorial lived on in its audiences' physical memories, through their kinesthetic empathetic relationship with the dance, and in the kinesthesia and emotions of the dancers after Sokolow who performed it.

The predominant markers of gendered power in Sokolow's first performances of *Kaddish* were *tefillin*, vestments made up of a leather strap and small prayer box, worn exclusively by religious Jewish men around their left arm and head during prayer. Men must wear *tefillin* during weekday morning prayers, but not during Shabbat or the High Holidays; they have the option of wearing *tefillin* through the part of the morning service that includes the Mourner's Kaddish.[46] Today women in many denominations of Judaism pray wearing *tefillin*. But as one of the many aspects of gendered power in Jewish ritual and culture, traditional Jewish law prohibits women from doing so.[47] As a member of the secular second generation of American Jews, Sokolow participated in nonnormative gender roles.[48] Her 1930s

---

42. Margaret Lloyd noted the "wailing tones of voice" at Sokolow's Boston premiere. Lloyd, "Dance Recital Presented in Jordan Hall," *The Christian Science Monitor*, May 6, 1946, 4, BPL Microtext.

43. Anna Sokolow, quoted in *Jewish Women in Dance*, VHS, pres. International Committee for the Dance Library in Israel (1990), DLI.

44. Ibid.

45. For Holocaust memorials, see among others James Edward Young, *The Texture of Memory: Holocaust Memorials and Meaning* (New Haven, CT: Yale University Press, 1993).

46. Rabbi Shimon D. Eider, *Student Edition of Halachos of Tefillin* (Lakewood, NJ: Halacha Publications, 1985), 3, 87, 89, 99, 103, 127.

47. See Eider, *Student Edition*, 3, 87, 89, 99, 103, 127; Ann Pellegrini, *Performance Anxieties: Staging Psychoanalysis, Staging Race* (New York and London: Routledge, 1997); Miriam Peskowitz and Laura Levitt, eds., *Judaism Since Gender* (New York: Routledge, 1997); and Boyarin, Itzkovitz, and Pellegrini, eds., *Queer Theory and the Jewish Question* (see Introduction, n80).

48. Although women were the cultural guardians of Judaism, charged with keeping a Jewish home and raising Jewish children, in Orthodox and Conservative Judaism they were prevented from praying alongside men in synagogue. In Reform congregations, Jewish women gained power through their charitable work with sisterhood organizations, but they were still wholly restricted from men's prayer space. In secular American society, leftover prejudices from late nineteenth-century and early twentieth-century racialist discourses effeminized Jewish men. Jewish women were doubly alienated, as their devaluation as Other replaced Jewish men as feminized Others. See Warren, *Rebellious Spirit*, 2; Paula Hyman, *Gender and Assimilation in Modern Jewish History: The Roles and Representation of Women* (Seattle: University of Washington Press, 1995); Pamela Nadell and Jonathan Sarna, eds., *Women and American Judaism: Historical*

Workers/New Dance League leadership aligned her with many aspects of Jewish women's activism.[49] In the 1940s women were forbidden to use *tefillin*, and so Sokolow's defiance to employ them in *Kaddish* opened a space for women's power in secular American Judaism, and in its representation in modern dance. Moreover, because Jews were not allowed to have *tefillin* in concentration camps,[50] in *Kaddish*, Sokolow reclaimed *tefillin* for those who were denied them and made them a marker of religious freedom as well as gendered defiance. Although, as Naomi Jackson commented that "nothing could be farther from Jewish tradition than a woman dancing around a stage in bare feet wearing *tefillin*,"[51] *Kaddish* reoriented Jewish tradition through Sokolow's appropriation of men's vestments and prayer space in an appeal for peace. As instruments of transgressive power instead of theatrical gender play, the *tefillin* do not mimic early twentieth-century Jewish women's drag performance, wherein some dancers, including Pauline Koner and Belle Didjah, performed as men or as androgens.[52] Instead, the *tefillin* register that she is a woman doing a man's job: praying in a way from which women were excluded, and embodying a privilege from which women were barred at a moment when there were not enough people to say Kaddish for the dead. In *Kaddish*, Sokolow transgressed the assumptions associated with her position as a Jewish woman by employing male power, but not masculinity, to become a universal everyperson by reclaiming Jewish ritual to say *Kaddish* for those who had no one to say it for them.[53] Through her embodiment of male space, use of her body as a political site of ritual, and craft of *Kaddish* within the aesthetic conventions of concert dance, Sokolow twisted patriarchal traditions to suit contemporary needs.[54] She mobilized the historical strength of Jewish women

Perspectives (Hanover, NH: Brandeis University Press/University Press of New England, 2001); Alice Kessler-Harris, "Organizing the Unorganizable: Three Jewish Women and Their Union," in *American Jewish Women's History: A Reader*, ed. Nadell (New York: New York University Press, 2003), 102–103, and 111; Pellegrini, *Performance Anxieties*; and Boyarin, Itzkovitz, and Pellegrini, eds., *Queer Theory and the Jewish Question*.

49. See Brodkin, *How Jews Became White Folks*, 107 (see Introduction, n45) for gender equality ideals of the Bund, the General Jewish Labor Union of Russia and Poland, and the political leadership of women associated with Yiddishkeit. See also Kessler-Harris, "Organizing the Unorganizable"; Paula E. Hyman, "Immigrant Women and Consumer Protest: The New York City Kosher Meat Boycott of 1902," in *American Jewish Women's History: A Reader*; and Wenger, *New York Jews and the Great Depression*, 114–127 (see Introduction, n49).

50. The Nazis stripped Jews of all visual symbols of Jewish significance and replaced them with yellow Stars of David. Elie Wiesel on *The Jewish People: A Story of Survival*, PBS, June 2008.

51. Jackson, *Converging Movements*, 16 (see Introduction, n58).

52. See Rossen, "Hasidic Drag," 334–364 (see Chap. 1, n49), for a discussion of Pauline Koner's, Belle Didjah's, and Hadassah's performances in this vein. See also Erdman, *Staging the Jew*, 40–60, 133 (see Chap. 1, n33).

53. I thank Matt Goldish for this insight.

54. Riv-Ellen Prell argues that in mid-twentieth-century sociological studies, Jewish women's and men's experiences were assumed to be the same, even though the studies undervalued women's contributions to Jewish life, and as a result women's experience was written out of Jewishness. See Riv-Ellen Prell, "American Jewish Culture Through a Gender-Tinted Lens," in *Judaism Since Gender*, eds. Peskowitz and Levitt (New York and London: Routledge, 1997), 79.

within the context of revolutionary women's actions to make a dance that was a political statement and an intimate yet public prayer that became a point of pride for a healing Jewish community. Even though *Kaddish* could not bring redemption, the war was over, Hitler was dead, and by viscerally marking the Holocaust through her dance of mourning, Sokolow brought resolution.

Kaddish's movement embodied Jewishness through its elements of movement opposition, ritualistic gestures, and Sokolow's act of saying Kaddish for generations lost in the Holocaust. The dance, which critic Doris Hering called a "quavering lament,"[55] includes spiraling turns, oppositional pulls and twists through the torso, a floor section rising onto knees and hips, impatient thrusts from the gut, and contemplative moments, wherein pain meets anger and emerges with quiet hope and defiance. The movement pairs strength with vulnerability through internal turmoil from quick, weighted body rotations, labored steps, and inner direction changes.[56] According to dancer Ze'eva Cohen, for whom Sokolow made a version of *Kaddish* in the 1980s, movement similarities across *Kaddish* versions include traditional Jewish gestures for grief of beating the breast and tearing out one's hair. When a dancer performs these movements in *Kaddish*, Cohen noted, the actions are expressive of a community.[57] Although other gestures, including tearing one's collar (in reconstructions) or shielding eyes from the heavens (in a photograph of Sokolow) relate to Jewish ritual, the shapes of the full-bodied movements, from torso contractions to throwing the body over a folding waistline to recruiting limbs in the service of the back, are characteristic of the abstract shapes of midcentury American modern dance.

Sokolow's 1939–1945 experience in Mexico City provided examples for how women without political representation could change the status quo by mobilizing their bodies in public spaces. The Mexican government did not grant women suffrage until 1953, following a failed vote in 1939 during which Cárdenas's once-leftist government turned conservative. Although women were not full citizens under the law, they performed their citizenship through embodied actions in more active ways than many women in the United States at the time. These actions included politically organizing and occupying public spaces.[58] Sokolow's actions, appropriating

55. Doris Hering, "Anna Sokolow, YM & YWHA, February 1, 1948," *Dance Magazine* (March 1948): 41.

56. I gleaned this observation through embodying the movement by reading the Labanotation score of this dance. I applied my own experiences of instability, and my knowledge of the Mourner's Kaddish and the Holocaust, to inform the structure of the movement.

57. Ze'eva Cohen in phone discussion with the author, September 14, 2010.

58. See Sarah A. Buck, "The Meaning of the Women's Vote in Mexico, 1917–1953," in *The Women's Revolution in Mexico, 1910–1953*, eds. Stephanie Mitchell and Patience Schell (Lanham, MD: Rowman & Littlefield Publishers, Inc., 2007), 73–98; Olcott, *Revolutionary Women* (see Chap. 2, n53); and Jocelyn Olcott, Mary Kay Vaughan, and Gabriela Cano, eds., *Sex in Revolution: Gender, Politics, and Power in Modern Mexico* (Durham and London: Duke University Press, 2006).

men's privilege of laying *tefillin* and publicly saying Kaddish without a *minyan* (a quorum of ten men necessary to hold a public prayer service), embody this power. Indeed, critic José Herrera Petere exclaimed in a review reprinted in *Tribuna Israelita* that Sokolow's 1945 concert opened his eyes to how modern dance could be an empowering vehicle of social statement, especially for Jewish voices in the wake of the Holocaust.[59] Soloist Deborah Zall's chilling 2006 performance of *Kaddish* suggests this power.[60] Her gnarled knuckles summon otherworldly forces while her relationship with an invisible element yields a debate between two wrathful beings. Although decades removed from Sokolow's performances, Zall's moment gives a sense for the accountability Sokolow demanded from the universe and how her kinesthetic memorial was a site of remembrance and reckoning.

Photographs of Sokolow in *Kaddish* between 1945 and 1948 display the dance's transformation in the years that she performed it. The most recognizable change is the removal of the *tefillin* in later images, but what stands out is Sokolow's development in emotional gravitas and choreographic complexity. In the following photographs, it is unclear in what order these images might occur in the dance's sequential unfolding. Nor is it clear if the camera captured moments from Sokolow's *Kaddish* or staged shots for publicity.[61] These photographs by Marthe Krueger document the dance's change and demonstrate the work's dynamic and emotional range on which critics commented in their reviews. In two of Krueger's 1946 photographs, Sokolow wears a dark sleeveless tunic belted by a thick rope that harkens to the *gartel* Orthodox Jewish men wear during prayer (Figures 3.1 and 3.2). She looks grounded, with lyricism in her torso. *Tefillin* wrap tightly around her left arm. Despite the Jewish signifiers of *tefillin* and *gartel*, the abstract movement elements, such as curved limbs and an actively bent torso, relate more closely to concert dance vocabularies than to the opposition of Jewish dance.

Kaddish's secularism represents a larger current in American Jewry that addresses the Holocaust as it foreshadows the second-generation postwar assimilation. The Holocaust and its aftermath remained at the forefront of Jewish discourse in New York City during the US premieres of *Kaddish* and framed its reception.[62] Dancers like Sokolow faced an increasingly progressive Jewish audience who

---

59. Herrera Petere, "¡Aleluya! en México," 22–23 (see Chap. 2, n104).

60. *Three Dances: Deborah Zall.* DVD, performed by Deborah Zall, produced by Deborah Zall and Niramon Ross (2007). Gift of Deborah Zall.

61. Dance photographs through the twentieth century were often staged for what made an effective still image, sometimes departing from what the movement looked like in performance. Hannah Kosstrin, "Dance in Another Dimension: The Photographic Work of Lois Greenfield" (MA thesis, Ohio State University, 2003).

62. On May 12, the day of Sokolow's New York *Kaddish* premiere, the "Arts" section of the *Jewish Daily Forward* featured photographs of Polish Jews who survived the Holocaust. See "The condition of the surviving Jews in Poland is reflected in this picture," *Jewish Daily Forward*, May 12, 1946, Section 3, 1. Similar coverage appeared through at least June 2, 1946.

Figure 3.1: Anna Sokolow in *Kaddish*, 1946. Photograph by Marthe Krueger. Courtesy of the Sokolow Dance Foundation and the Marthe Krueger Estate.

expected superb modernist craft, even—or especially—in dances with Jewish thematic material.[63] In a 1948 article in the socialist periodical *Jewish Life*, critic Nathaniel Buchwald boasted of the talent of Sokolow, Sophie Maslow, and others, not because they were successful choreographers, but because they were strong artists trained by Martha Graham who were also Jewish and who used modernist techniques to create dances with Jewish themes. He named Sokolow a "characteristic example," because she "in her Jewish dances combines the technique and choreography of Graham with [Benjamin] Zemach's exaltation and intensity of emotional expression."[64] Sokolow's progressive Jewish audiences likely saw the *tefillin* as nothing more than a Jewish marker. Because Sokolow was a prominent choreographer, the *tefillin* gave her Jewish audiences a sense of pride for her visibility as a Jew in an otherwise abstract–white modernist context. In a mixed audience of Jews and non-Jews, the *tefillin* were a triumph for the Jewish community instead of a religious scandal.

63. V. Platon, "Thoughts on a Dance in Progress," *Jewish Life* 4, no. 1 (1949): 36.
64. Nathaniel Buchwald, "The Jewish Dance in America," *Jewish Life* 3, no. 4 (1948): 15.

Figure 3.2: Anna Sokolow in *Kaddish*, 1946. Photograph by Marthe Krueger. Courtesy of the Sokolow Dance Foundation and the Marthe Krueger Estate.

As well as a sign of gendered power for audience members who recognized the uncharacteristic use of the *tefillin*, I focus on them as a plain-sight ethnic marker missed by those who did not recognize the code. At the time, their absence in Jewish critical response suggests that they were a de facto, and not controversial, element of the dance. Reviews of the piece in mainstream and Jewish periodicals in Mexico City, Boston, and New York did not mention the *tefillin*.[65] In the weeks that followed Sokolow's concert at the 92nd Street Y, the *Y Bulletin* carried no reference to *Kaddish* or of any fallout from Sokolow's performance.[66] No mention appeared in the *Jewish Daily Forward* in the weeks following her concert. Perhaps

65. Herrera Petere, "¡Aleluya! en México," 22–23; Jules Wolffers, "Anna Sokolow in Dance Recital," *The Jewish Advocate* (Boston), May 9, 1946, 22, BPL Microtext; Zellmer, "Anna Sokolow: Y. M. & Y. W. H. A. May 12, 1946," 75–76; Walter Terry, "Four Solo Recitals Here Called Indicative Future of Dance," *New York Herald Tribune*, May 19, 1946, Dance Scrapbook, JRDD, NYPL.; Doris Hering, "Two Concerts," *Dance Magazine* (June 1946): 23–24, 26; and Albertina Vitak, "Anna Sokolow, May 12 at the YM&YWHA Dance Theatre, N. Y.," *Dance News* (June–August 1946): 6.

66. Steve Siegel (92nd Street Y archivist) in e-mail communication with author, January 21, 2010.

no clergy came to Sokolow's performances, and the secular Y audience created an atmosphere in which this was not a problem.[67] Orthodox Jews likely did not attend a secular modern dance performance on the Upper East Side, and the Jews in attendance did not find it blasphemous enough to be bothered.

Although the *tefillin* visually mark *Kaddish* as Jewish, the dance does not need the *tefillin* to be Jewish.[68] Jewishness resides in the movement through gestures associated with Jewish rituals and through movement characteristics with opposing tensions that resonate with American Jews' postwar negotiation of religiosity and secularity. In *Kaddish*, these tensions manifest in the movement's oppositional pulls and twists. In an early photograph of this solo, Sokolow looks out toward the camera after whipping around in a turn as her hair and skirt flair in respective orbits.[69] With elbows wide, Sokolow presses her fists together in front of her chin and contracts her abdominals as her right foot reaches for the ground. In another image, Sokolow bends her torso gently to the right.[70] Her dangling right arm and gently weighted curved left arm with upturned palm suggest reverberation through her body. The movement, with the exception of the countertension between the upper and lower halves of the body to stop the turn, appears to present shapes from midcentury concert dance that do not necessarily register as Jewish.

Although Sokolow removed *tefillin* from later versions of *Kaddish*, the Jewish elements in the movement became more pronounced than they were in versions with *tefillin*. Krueger's photographs display Jewish elements of countertension, opposition, and questioning, as well as a simultaneous reverence for and accusation toward a volatile or wrathful god, especially in the Holocaust's wake. They resonate with Jewish women's strength that harkens back to Sokolow's 1943–1945 solo

67. Local rabbis criticized Sophie Maslow for her piece *The Village I Knew* (1951) in which, during representational scenes of traditional Jewish rituals, "dancers kneel[ed] on the floor for the blessing of the Sabbath candles," and the movements of kneeling and rolling on the floor "showed the women's legs, which was considered indecent." 92nd Street Y Education Director William Kolodney invited the rabbis to see Maslow's dance. Naomi Jackson, "Jewishness and Modern Dance in Sophie Maslow's *The Village I Knew*," 91–92.

68. When Sokolow performed *Kaddish* in 1948, she removed them. In 1946, Sokolow sent the photograph labeled Figure 3.2 to Bessie Schönberg, with a note on the back inviting her to the May 12 performance in New York. Anna Sokolow to Bessie Schönberg, n.d., Box 11, Folder 17, Bessie Schönberg Papers, JRDD, NYPL. Sokolow's note to Schönberg places that photograph as existing prior to May 12, 1946. In Figures 3.3 and 3.4, Sokolow wears the *Kaddish* costume without the *tefillin*. Figure 3.3 accompanies Doris Hering's review of Sokolow's February 1, 1948, performance of *Kaddish* at the 92nd Street Y (and the original copy in the Sokolow Dance Foundation has the specifications for magazine publication written on the back), whereas Figure 3.4 is on a flyer advertising the February 1, 1948 performance at the 92nd Street Y. Hering, "Anna Sokolow YM & YWHA February 1, 1948," 41–42; and Flyer, *Dance Theatre presents Anna Sokolow in a program of New Dances Sunday Afternoon February 1st at 3:30*, 92Y.

69. Reprinted in Warren, *Rebellious Spirit*, plate 6, and in Doris Hering, *25 Years of American Dance* (New York: Rudolf Orthwine Publisher, 1954), 112.

70. Printed in Giora Manor, "Creation of Peace about Anna Sokolow in the National Homeland, 1912–2000," *DanceToday: The Dance Magazine of Israel* 2 (2000): 21.

Figure 3.3: Anna Sokolow in *Kaddish*, 1948. Photograph by Marthe Krueger. Courtesy of the Sokolow Dance Foundation and the Marthe Krueger Estate.

portraits of powerful Jewish women. In Figure 3.3, Sokolow perches on the outside edge of her thigh, bracing one arm against the ground in opposition to her floating leg, pleading through her raised eyebrows. Although this image could be from any moment of supplication, the oppositional tension suggests its Jewishness. The two halves of her body work in tandem, yet there is opposition between her low-level shape and the lightness of her weight in it. Sokolow stands in Figure 3.4, covering her eyes as she looks skyward. Her fingertips gently shield her eyes from what is above. Her face's quiet, internal expression contrasts her elbows' sharp angles. Jewishness resonates in this private movement in the absence of the *tefillin* signifier.

Sokolow's shielded focus makes this final image the most spiritual because of its resonance with aspects of Jewish ritual that include covering one's eyes. One ritual, for men and women, is during the recitation of the daily prayer *Sh'ma* that proclaims dedication to God. The shielding comes from respect for God's power. A woman's ritual is to shield her eyes while reciting the blessing over Shabbat (Sabbath) candles. Jewishness resonates in this image in the ritual of eye shielding, and in the Ashkenazi-inflected weight with which Sokolow dabs her eyelids. This nuanced weight of the hands' surfaces, as I discussed in this book's introduction,

Figure 3.4: Anna Sokolow in *Kaddish*, 1948. Photograph by Marthe Krueger. Courtesy of the Sokolow Dance Foundation and the Marthe Krueger Estate.

manifests in Eastern European Jewish folk dance. It is also familiar relative to the way many second- and third-generation Jewish women gesture conversationally, as if they resiliently hold the weight of the world in their retreating palm. Although *Kaddish* was an empowering political statement Sokolow made as a Jewish woman, non-Jewish audiences did not easily read its content.

The question of who considered *Kaddish* universal is significant when identifying mid-twentieth-century race relations and the changing racial position of Jews at the end of World War II. The white critical establishment, consisting of critics and Graham, Othered *Kaddish* and Jewish modern dancers through microaggressions. Movement description of *Kaddish* is scarce in US reviews. Although the solo concerts in which Sokolow performed *Kaddish* received wide coverage and generally high praise, critics glossed over *Kaddish* in their reviews or labeled the dance as ethnic, commenting on its relationship to Sokolow's heritage without any critical content analysis of the work. As such, critics Martha Coleman and Hering noted in 1948 that in *Kaddish* Sokolow used a "unique" movement vocabulary and style.[71] *Kaddish* presented these critics with a legibility difficulty. Unlike Sokolow's other Jewish dances of the time that were based on biblical heroines with explicit program notes, *Kaddish* was clearly Jewish through the lilting, minor chords of Ravel's score, the title of the music, and the warbly singing of the Aramaic prayer, but these critics did not understand the *tefillin*'s revolutionary statement. Specifically for Sokolow, Morris notes the friction between *Kaddish*'s Jewishness and its abstraction: "*Kaddish* therefore points up the problem of encompassing difference within the rules of modernism. [. . .By expanding inflexible modernist boundaries, Jewish dancers] challenged notions of consensus culture where difference was muted."[72] Beyond spectatorial challenges to articulating what happened in *Kaddish*, these critics and Graham did not consider Jewishness and modernism compatible. According to Mark Franko, Graham said in January 1944 "that Pearl Lang would never be a true artist because her Jewish heritage was too important to her."[73] Beyond any abstraction *Kaddish* had as part of Sokolow's choreographic composition, the "problem of encompassing difference within the rules of modernism" had more to do with dance modernism's gatekeepers than with what the work did. Sokolow's highlighting of this problem instead pointed audiences to recognize how, even in mourning, such discrimination is out of step with the consistent workings of the global community.

American Jewish critics' silence about *Kaddish*'s content suggests that, on the eve of the Second Red Scare that bound anti-Semitism with anticommunism, it was best to leave things abstract. Critic Jules Wolffers focused on the formalist aspects of Sokolow's May 4, 1946, performance in Boston's *Jewish Advocate*, simply noting that the Jewish dances on the program were "intelligently worked out."[74] In one of the last leftist dance reviews,[75] Edna Ocko wrote deftly about Sokolow's contributions to the dance field exemplified by her February 1, 1948, performance, mentioning all but *Kaddish* from that concert.[76] In one of the few reviews that discussed *Kaddish* without labeling it an ethnic dance, David Zellmer wrote that it "was emotionally compelling; all the movements flowing directly from the inspirational source."[77] Although he called Sokolow's movement sources "derivative," he ultimately praised

71. Martha Coleman, "Anna Sokolow: Y.W. and Y.M.H.A. February 1, 1948," *Dance Observer* (March 1948): 32; and Hering, "Anna Sokolow, YM & YWHA, February 1, 1948," 41.

72. Morris, *Game for Dancers*, 97.

73. Franko, *Martha Graham in Love and War*, 20 (see Introduction, n83).

74. Wolffers, "Anna Sokolow in Dance Recital," 22.

75. Morris, *Game for Dancers*, xxiii.

76. Edna Ocko, "Dance: Anna Sokolow," *Masses and Mainstream* 1, no. 1 (March 1948): 95–96.

77. Zellmer, "Anna Sokolow: Y. M. & Y. W. H. A. May 12, 1946," 76.

her performance over her choreography, while he evaluated the form ("somewhat balletic in style") and the content.[78] Zellmer, an early 1940s Graham company dancer and Air Force bomber pilot who became a dance critic and CBS news editor after the war, was not Jewish but nearly married Pearl Lang before he shipped off.[79] Perhaps because of his relationship with Lang he could read Jewish signifiers in Sokolow's dances, those he called "personally identified with herself," and did not label Sokolow's Jewish work ethnic or Other to describe it. In *Kaddish's* counterpart, *Mexican Retablo*, Sokolow employed Mexican ethno–religious traditions to get closer to the revolutionary values of *mexicanidad*. The solo introduced critical complications wherein critics read her as white but her material as ethnic.

MEXICANIDAD, JEWISHNESS, AND ETHNIC EXOTICISM

The language in Boston and New York reviews of *Mexican Retablo* suggests critics devoured the ethnic exoticism they saw in the piece. US critics heralded *Retablo* as the strongest dance on Sokolow's 1946 program. In it, Sokolow portrayed a poor indigenous woman. By using choreographic portraiture, Sokolow aligned this solo with spectatorial desires of ethnic and ethnologic dance. *The Boston Daily Globe* announced in an advertisement for the concert that Sokolow "will offer Mexican, Spanish and Jewish dances" in her performance—with no mention of modern dances, suggesting that "Mexican, Spanish and Jewish dances" were distinct from "modern dances."[80] Sokolow claimed that, after seven years of working in Mexico, *Mexican Retablo* was the first piece in which she felt comfortable embodying *mexicanidad*, even though she did not perform this dance in Mexico. She told *Daily Worker* reporter Beth McHenry in 1946, "I've always been afraid of the tourist approach. . . .I wanted to wait until I felt that I had learned and absorbed enough real understanding of Mexico and its people before attempting to interpret its life in the dance."[81] Despite Sokolow's claims of sensitivity, the dance sensationalized Mexican Catholic culture. It is unclear if this kind of exploration accompanied Sokolow's connection to her own religious heritage, or if Sokolow created this piece with the intent to capitalize on the exoticism of performing a foreign-yet-familiar religious context for American critical success. Perhaps *Retablo* was the strongest

---

78. Ibid.

79. Program, *Cappel Concert Guild Fifth Concert: The Martha Graham Dance Group*, December 18, 1941, Box 1, Folder 48, and *Starlight Chamber Music Concerts Meridian Hill Park: Martha Graham and Dance Company*, July 20 and 23, 1942, Box 1, Folder 50, the Coburn Dance Program Collection, MD, LOC; David Zellmer, *The Spectator: A World War II Bomber Pilot's Journal of the Artist as Warrior* (Westport, CT: Praeger, 1999), 64; and Franko, *Martha Graham in Love and War*, 20, 182n29. According to Ancestry.com's military records (accessed June 11, 2016), Zellmer did not have a record with the National Jewish Welfare Board.

80. No author or title, *The Boston Daily Globe*, May 2, 1946, 13, BPL Microtext.

81. Beth McHenry, "A Gifted Dancer Comes Home," *Daily Worker*, April 18, 1946, 12.

dance, technically and choreographically by critics' standards, on the program. Or, perhaps despite Sokolow's attempt to avoid "the tourist approach," the combination of her performance paired with *Retablo*'s ethnic exoticism resounded with critics and audiences desiring to experience diverse cultural representation through universalist modernist dance framing.

In contrast to their writing about Sokolow's social-justice- and Jewish-themed solos, critics report her performance in *Mexican Retablo* to be quiet, understated, and gentle. *Mexican Retablo* includes the two sections "Our Lady" and " 'Señora, save him and I will adore you on my knees until my last days.' " In "Our Lady," Sokolow tried on a performance of white womanhood in her interpretation of the Madonna, and in "Señora" Sokolow portrayed a peasant supplicant. Sokolow built the solo's two sections based on what she saw in Mexico City's cathedrals: the contrast between the elaborate images and statues of the Madonna, paired with poor indigenous women placing *retablos*, small painted religious portraits, as offerings in front of the statues.[82] A program note frames the dance: "Retablo is a painting depicting miraculous events, which record [in churches] the gratitude of those who have been saved by divine intervention."[83] A *retablo* can be any portrait, so the title *Mexican Retablo* suggests a representation of Mexicanness. Sokolow portrayed an ethnic identity more marginalized than her own Jewishness, and critics decoupled her ethnicity from that which she depicted in these solos. This situation resulted in an odd whitening through a partly transcendent portrayal critics read in the dance.

In "Our Lady," Sokolow embodied a generous mother archetype in her imagined Madonna, as she tried on a performance of whiteness complicated first by her own Jewishness and second by her portrayal of an indigenous woman in the solo's second half. In 1974, Sokolow recalled that Mexican gilded church statues of the Madonna inspired her representation of the Virgin Mary.[84] Zellmer and Hering reported that Sokolow's statuesque, regal performance resembled a stylized figurine.[85] Dressed as a carved *santo* or *bulto* (a small wooden statuette of a saint), Sokolow wore a floor-length dress with bell-shaped skirt accented with swirling designs in thick brocaded fabric, a gold-colored crown that held a white chiffon veil in place, and pearl necklaces.[86] In a series of images, Sokolow stands in a grounded position, as a lower-torso contraction brings her posture forward. She gently stretches out her arms to reach her palms downward as if connecting with a congregant. In one image, Sokolow focuses on the floor; in another, she looks

---

82. Sokolow, interview, Newman (see Chap. 1, n106).

83. *The Dance Center of the Y. M. & Y. W. H. A. Season 1945–46 presents Anna Sokolow in a Recital*, May 12, 1946, 92Y.

84. Sokolow, interview, Newman.

85. Doris Hering, "Anna Sokolow: YM & YWHA, February 1, 1948," 41, and David Zellmer, "Anna Sokolow: Y. M. & Y. W. H. A. May 12, 1946," 75.

86. http://jwa.org/media/sokolow-in-her-mexican-retablo. Accessed August 10, 2016. I thank Paul Bonin-Rodriguez for clarifying Sokolow's performance as a carved *santo*.

Figure 3.5: Anna Sokolow in "Our Lady" from *Mexican Retablo*. Photographer unknown. Larry Warren Collection on Anna Sokolow and Lester Horton, Box 1, Music Division, Library of Congress, Washington, DC.

up and out to an imagined audience; and in a third, Sokolow sends her attention out to a broadened horizon as she raises her arms, and her skirt flutters to reveal her toes.[87] Sokolow's billowing movement qualities prompted Jennie Schulman to remark in *Dance Observer* in 1952 that she "seemed, in fact, to be propelled by the wind."[88] In Figure 3.5, Sokolow could be floating on an air current as she reaches out to her followers. *Christian Science Monitor* critic Margaret Lloyd, identifying with the religious figure of Mary, received Sokolow as "a living image of

87. SDF.
88. Schulman, "Modern Dance in Ethnic Style," 76.

love."[89] By appropriating the image of Mary prominent in Mexican Catholic worship, Sokolow aligned her statements with a powerful woman figure in secular and religious Mexican culture. Sokolow was mostly still in this section, presenting a sense of reserved benevolence. Zellmer wrote in *Dance Observer* that Sokolow moved "puppet-wise in a most delicate manner, ever true to the feeling of the Holy Mother," whereas Hering, writing in *Dance Magazine,* noted in the dance the "stiff angelic sweetness of a religious portrait."[90] Both of these descriptions give a sense of emotional distance that may have been enough for Sokolow to take on a presumed whiteness through her representation of the Virgin. Sokolow's portrayal of a Catholic matriarch for a woman supplicant created a matrilineage to aid the women left behind by postrevolutionary Mexico's egalitarian rhetoric. Critics did not see the social justice Sokolow tucked into *Retablo*'s appropriative representation.

Colonialist language in reviews reinforced the critical establishment's desires for choreographies to reflect midcentury dance universalism. Lloyd described Sokolow's transcendent warmth, noting at the Boston premiere that this section "presents a madonna as a peasant might imagine her, moving with fixed arms in the style of an animated doll figure, gently tapping a foot or sweetly posturing to the familiar music of the folk, remote, unworldly, yet near to his need, bending toward him with tenderness and love."[91] Lloyd assumed that the peasant yearned for a white savior. Her comments elevated the white Christian body and suppressed the indigenous, colonized-Catholic body, despite the centrality of the Virgin of Guadalupe to Mexican Catholicism. For Lloyd, the folk elements did not signify revolution or even *mexicanidad*; they created a quaint, distant, unsophisticated world of the Other.

Sokolow's statuesque, mothering gestures and petite steps to folk music rhythms along constrained pathways in "Our Lady" upheld corporeal values of white womanhood instead of the tumultuous movement in *Kaddish* and *Exile* that defied white patriarchal expectations for how women should control their bodies.[92] Hering commented of the New York premiere, "With hands held daintily and heels tapping intermittently, she progressed through a simple floor pattern nicely colored with restraint and femininity. Here was a welcome contrast to the over-projection of dances like *Kaddish* and *The Exile*."[93] For Hering, the calm of *Retablo*'s whiteness provided a respite from the intensity of *Exile* and *Kaddish* that embodied leftist Jewish women's action through Jewish thematic material. These solos' movements

89. Lloyd, *Borzoi Book*, 221–222.

90. Zellmer, "Anna Sokolow: Y. M. & Y. W. H. A. May 12, 1946," 75, and Doris Hering, "Two Concerts," *Dance Magazine* (July 1946): 24.

91. Margaret Lloyd, "Dance Recital Presented in Jordan Hall," 4.

92. See Welter, "The Cult of True Womanhood," 151–174 (see Introduction, n81), and Julian B. Carter, *The Heart of Whiteness: Normal Sexuality and Race in America, 1880–1940* (Durham: Duke University Press, 2007).

93. Hering, "Two Concerts" (July 1946): 24.

resonated with the reported boisterous, noncontained ebullience of Eastern European immigrants that white populations perceived as threatening during the Progressive era in the United States.[94] "Our Lady" upheld white femininity, and so in this dance Sokolow could be both ethnic and white. This representational shape-shifting suggests that, through the abstracted movement that signaled midcentury dance universalism, Sokolow was malleable in how critics read her body.

Sokolow's performance in "Our Lady" shifted the cultural significations of her own earlier onstage experiences with the Madonna. In 1931, Sokolow portrayed, as Dorothy Bird remembered, "the Virgin Mary in a studio production of a medieval study" at the Neighborhood Playhouse.[95] Bird remembered how Sokolow's "angelic, oval face tipped to one side, and her delicately shaped hands fell into place with the two center fingers close together. It looked authentic, that is, if you could overlook the black dirt under her fingernails."[96] Sokolow was also in the long black-woolens-clad *corps* who attended Martha Graham's white-robed Madonna in *Primitive Mysteries* (1931). Graham based this work in her idea of how colonized indigenous populations in Mexico and the American Southwest practiced Catholicism and the resultant blending of cultures she felt it represented.[97] As opposed to the stark, reverent environment Graham created around the Virgin in *Primitive Mysteries*, Sokolow's "Lady" was generous and reflected more of a visceral presence than Graham's Puritan-inflected Virgin.

Critics' Orientalist language, that is, viewing non-Western subjects though Western cultural expectations, more directly reflected US mainstream conceptions of ethnic dance than their opinions about Sokolow's performance. Lloyd's comment that "Our Lady" was on a pedestal, "as depicted in native paintings,"[98] typifies the language critics employed to describe the work. Walter Terry's comment in the *New York Herald Tribune* that "Our Lady" contained a "sweet, stiffly moving portrait of a primitive virgin" races Mexican Catholicism, as he implied Sokolow did not portray a white virgin, but a "primitive" one—a virgin who shares the race, if not the class, of the supplicant.[99] A Mexican Madonna is no more or less "primitive" than a European or American Madonna. Furthermore, although the brown-skinned Virgin of Guadalupe figures prominently in Mexican Catholicism, in the paintings of the Virgin Mary set into elaborate cathedral walls in Mexico City, the Madonna is white. In Sokolow's 1948 repeat performance of this program, Martha Coleman enjoyed armchair tourism when she wrote that this section "gives a clue

94. Judy Burns, "The Culture of Nobility/The Nobility of Self-Cultivation," in *Moving Words, Re-Writing Dance*, ed. Gay Morris (New York: Routledge, 1996), 207.

95. Bird and Greenberg, *Bird's Eye View*, 69 (see Preface, n5).

96. Ibid.

97. Ernestine Stodelle, *Deep Song: The Dance Story of Martha Graham* (New York: Schirmer, 1984), 73.

98. Lloyd, *Borzoi Book*, 221.

99. Terry, "Four Solo Recitals."

to much of Mexican life, based as it is on the cult of the Virgin."[100] This labeling of "Our Lady" as primitive continued to feed Orientalist desires by reinforcing views that considered Latin America less sophisticated than North America.

This discourse of the primitive recalls that which surrounded reviews of Graham's *Primitive Mysteries* fifteen years prior, but critics viewed Sokolow's representation as Other while they embraced what they considered Graham's distanced, modernist depiction. Graham, like John Martin and Louis Horst, upheld a common racist belief that indigenous cultures were purified of the complications of Western society; in aligning with this view, primitivism in modern dance created a stripped-down look that aligned with modernism.[101] In 1931, Martin wrote that *Primitive Mysteries* "must be ranked among the choreographic masterpieces of the modern dance movement . . . Its simplicity of form and its evocation of the child-like religious elevation of a primitive people never falter for a moment."[102] Rehearsal of how Martin's comments reinforce Orientalist notions that associate nonwhite populations with unintelligence and unsophisticated cultural practices notwithstanding, the significance lies in the gap between how critics discussed Graham versus Sokolow in these roles. Reviews by Martin and Charles Isaacson display critical belief that *Primitive Mysteries* transcended time and place.[103] Graham presented her ideas of indigenous ritual by creating a representative distance through modernist abstraction between the autochthonous traditions and her white body.[104] By doing so, she did not become "childish," "primitive," or even effeminized through critics' writing. Conversely, critics saw Sokolow as embodying the primitiveness instead of distancing herself from it. Sokolow had a harder time separating her Jewish body from nonwhite material.

A comparison of *Retablo* with similarly themed work Graham presented contemporaneously encircles Sokolow within uneasy and pejorative conversations of being culturally marked. For *El Penitente* (1941), a trio that portrayed "the penitent, the Christ, [and] the three Marys," Graham was reportedly influenced by the "indigenous traditions" of the American Southwest.[105] Graham again appropriated indigenous material for her work by capitalizing on her distance from the tension between indigenousness and Catholicism, as exemplified by Gervase Butler's comments in *Dance Observer*. Butler averred that *El Penitente* was "an evocation of the

100. Coleman, "Anna Sokolow: Y.W. and Y.M.H.A. February 1, 1948," 32.

101. Burt, *Alien Bodies*, 162; and Horst and Russell, *Modern Dance Forms*, 57 (see Introduction, n35).

102. John Martin, *New York Times*, February 8, 1931, quoted in Agnes de Mille, *Martha: The Life and Work of Martha Graham*, reprint (1956; New York: Vintage Books, 1992), 183.

103. Charles D. Isaacson, "Dance Events Reviewed," *Dance Magazine* (April 1931): 18, 48.

104. Jacqueline Shea Murphy argues Graham's work invisibilized Indian presence while evoking its essence. Shea Murphy, *The People Have Never Stopped Dancing: Native American Modern Dance Histories* (Minneapolis: University of Minnesota Press, 2007), 148–168.

105. Gervase Butler, "Martha Graham and Group, Mansfield Theatre, Jan. 20, 1941," *Dance Observer* (February 1941): 24.

dance of atonement, the Indian mystery play which is still performed, more literally, by a religious sect in the Mexicos."[106] *El Penitente* was not transcendent like *Primitive Mysteries*, but was indigenist like *Retablo*. Comparing *El Penitente* to *Primitive Mysteries*, Butler said that *El Penitente* "is not kin to that except in its delicacy of line and effect accomplished within a small sphere of action," and noted the "illusion of the ancient race performing its ancient rites."[107] Critics' comments like these enabled Graham's whiteness to transcend Otherness in a way Sokolow's Jewishness could not. Sokolow's ethnicity connected her representationally to an Otherness wherein the West joins all the Rest together through racist assumptions that conflate non-Western contexts despite cultural distinctions. In Manning's terms, Sokolow bore the burden of representing the ethnic collective.[108] This became clear in critical response to *Retablo*'s "Señora" section.

In "Señora," Sokolow foregrounded *pueblo* poverty against the Mexican nationalist elevation of the invented epic idea of the *pueblo* but not their plight. This section manifested the predicament of a poor indigenous woman and contained an indigenist employment of folk imagery in costuming that signified Mexicanness. Sokolow's striped shirt and dark skirt recalled Mexican Tehuana dress. She draped herself in a *rebozo*, a *mestizo* woven shawl variously purposed by women across ethnicities and social classes throughout pre-Hispanic Mexican regions and New Spain including fashion, bridal gifts, and death shrouds. When Mexico's twentieth-century modernization pushed the garment out of urban aesthetics, it became associated with the underprivileged classes and the folk. Sokolow took it up in this manner. Wrapped in the *rebozo*, she moved mostly on her knees as a supplicant seeking the Madonna.[109] At one point she kneeled, raised her elbows sideways, hyperextended her back, and cupped her hands under her chin in some kind of invocation.[110] Hering remembered Sokolow dragging herself around the stage on her hips and knees during *Retablo*,[111] Terry noted a "painful and humble gluteal walk" toward "the Virgin's place" in the solo's New York premiere,[112] and at the Boston premiere Lloyd observed that the second section of the dance was "done almost entirely on the knees."[113] Kneeling appears in many Mexican contexts, but one that resonates for this discussion is the *rebozo*-draped kneeling woman central to the Michoacán November 1 dance of remembrance during the Night of the

106. Ibid.
107. Ibid.
108. Manning, "*Ausdruckstanz* Across the Atlantic," 54 (see Introduction, n70).
109. See Lloyd, "Dance Recital Presented in Jordan Hall," 4, and Zellmer, "Anna Sokolow: Y. M. & Y. W. H. A. May 12, 1946," 75. For *rebozos*, see Margarita de Orellana, Michelle Suderman, and Ramón López Velarde et al., "Rebozo: English Version," *Artes de México* 90, *El rebozo* (2008): 72–88. I thank Paul Bonin-Rodriguez for bringing this to my attention.
110. "Anna Sokolow in 'Modern Dance in Ethnic Style' *Retablo*," Box 2, Folder 23, Around the World in Dance and Song Photographs, JRDD, NYPL.
111. Hering, discussion (see Introduction, n84).
112. Terry, "Four Solo Recitals."
113. Lloyd, "Dance Recital Presented in Jordan Hall," 4.

Dead traditionally practiced by women descended from the P'urhépecha peoples. As ethnomusicologist Ruth Hellier-Tinoco argued, the Mexican government and tourist outlets promoted *Night of the Dead* as a national representation of *mexicanidad* beginning in the 1920s, and by the 1940s, it had become associated with iconic Mexicanness.[114] Certainly, Sokolow was influenced by women she witnessed on cathedral steps in ritual advances on their knees. But the prominence of 1940s *Night of the Dead* public performances when Sokolow developed *Retablo* is significant when we consider how it was both a portrait of *mexicanidad* and a dance of remembrance since she performed it alongside her Holocaust memorial *Kaddish*.

In *Retablo* Sokolow underscored poor women's struggles to revolutionary ends, which many Mexican revolutionary artists, like photographer Tina Modotti, foregrounded in their work as Sokolow had in her proletarian dances. Other moments of "Señora" portray what Sokolow interpreted as the downtrodden aspects of poor women's lives by performing with a melancholy focus and defeated posture. In Figure 3.6, Sokolow props herself up against a wall as her *rebozo* falls over her shoulders. She rests her hands on her thighs and looks indirectly at the floor with drooping eyelids, as if she is looking inward rather than outward. In another photograph that captures Sokolow in three-quarter profile from her right, the *rebozo* engulfs her; she has pulled it over her head and wrapped herself in it.[115] Only her face and her hands clasping the shawl emerge from under the fabric. She looks quietly toward the floor beneath her lowered eyelids. In these moments, Sokolow embodied the despair she inferred in these women's lives.[116]

Critics did not write about the plight of this woman, but their reviews reflected the shift to a humble, more introverted mood in the second half of the dance. Although many hint toward the epidermal and continental darkness of the indigenous woman, in contrast to the white purity of the Madonna, Lloyd stated directly that "Señora" presented "dark, impassioned contrast to the serene luster of 'Our Lady.'"[117] Lloyd's comment sets up a dichotomy between light and dark, European (white) and indigenous (nonwhite), have and have-not, restrained and boisterous. Although most reviews of this piece discuss its calm mood, Vitak wrote in *Dance News*, "the dance is performed with an understanding that embodies the full religious fervor of the Mexican people."[118] It is possible that Vitak embellished with the word "fervor" for dramatic intensity in her review, feeling that Sokolow was dramatically successful with this solo. It does not appear that Sokolow was particularly fervent in this dance, and so this language, alongside Lloyd's reading of this solo as a "dark, impassioned contrast" to "Our Lady," projects primitivist

114. Ruth Hellier-Tinoco, *Embodying Mexico: Tourism, Nationalism & Performance* (New York: Oxford University Press, 2011), 1–29.
115. Printed in Giora Manor, "Creation of Peace," 18.
116. I thank Karen Eliot for this insight.
117. Lloyd, *Borzoi Book*, 222.
118. Vitak, "Anna Sokolow, May 12 at the YM&YWHA Dance Theatre, N.Y.," 6.

Figure 3.6: Anna Sokolow in " 'Señora, save him and I will adore you on my knees until my last days' " from *Mexican Retablo*. Photographer unknown. Courtesy of the Sokolow Dance Foundation.

fantasies onto Sokolow's performance of this penitence. Lloyd depicted Sokolow as "a shawled woman in an anguish of reverence before the image, imploring aid for one she loves."[119] As opposed to *El Penitente*, where Graham controlled the representational power, in "Señora" the critics negotiated the power balance with Sokolow. While she foregrounded the *pueblo* and projected empathy for the plight of lower-class women as she did so many times in the 1930s, the critics labeled her as Other, whereas they noted that Graham gave the illusion of the Other. Because they had been primed by Graham to look for transcendent representations of the Virgin, US critics likely did not see past Sokolow's specific presentation to her social statements.

Mexican Retablo and *Kaddish* presented essentialized spiritual portraits of women in Catholicism and Judaism to reinforce Sokolow's proletarian and anti-war themes. Sokolow's use of Mexican folk elements to approximate *mexicanidad* in *Retablo* engaged her in transnational revolutionary aesthetics. Along with *Don Lindo de Almería*, *Exile* (for both see Chapter 2), and *Kaddish*, *Retablo* surfaced

119. Lloyd, "Dance Recital Presented in Jordan Hall," 4.

the place of Jewishness within Mexican and US nationalisms. In *Kaddish*, Sokolow transgressed traditional Jewish gender roles to mobilize social politics about Holocaust mourning in an indictment more of God or the human collective than of the Nazis. Sokolow's embodiment of Catholic figures in *Retablo* resonated in her *Kaddish* ritual. Sokolow's complicated presentation in *Retablo* embodied Mexican *indigenismo*, except here the peasant stood for the *pueblo*'s plight instead of a mythic past that whitewashed her hardship.

Retablo introduced a productive tension for considering Catholic and Jewish syncretism in artistic representations. When asked in 1990 if she felt her work displayed Jewish identity, Sokolow responded, "I don't dare compare myself, but you take the paintings of great Jewish artists like Chagall. He has a painting of a crucifix, but what could be more Jewish than [that], so there."[120] Sokolow likely refers here to Marc Chagall's *White Crucifixion* (1938), in which Jesus of Nazareth, wearing the long beard of a Talmudic scholar and draped not in a loincloth, but in a *tallis* (Jewish prayer shawl) and turban, is crucified amid scenes of Jewish persecution.[121] On the left-hand side of the painting, the Red Army's pogrom burns a village as Jews escape in a small boat; on the right-hand side, flames engulf a German synagogue. An angel descending on the beam of light that divides the image and highlights the vertical line of the cross beckons to the dead floating at the top of the painting, while light from a menorah creates a halo under Jesus' feet. Jacob's Ladder leans against the cross and points up the light shaft to heaven. Above Jesus' head are the letters INRI: Jesus of Nazareth, King of the Jews. This image entwines the persecution of Jesus, Russian, and German Jews. According to art historian Ziva Amishai-Maisells, Chagall "emphasized Jesus' importance to both Christians and Jews, for the Jewish Jesus with his covered head and fringed garment is also a Christian."[122]

Like *White Crucifixion*, *Kaddish* and *Retablo* displayed intersecting Christian and Jewish embodiments. Chagall was known for his renderings of scenes and religious symbols that signify lived and invented European Jewish life through his dreamlike figures and thin washes of color. Because of these themes, and his form that portrays them, his paintings are associated with a visual Jewish aesthetic. Similarly, *Retablo* looked aesthetically similar to Sokolow's other Jewish solos in terms of its movement dynamics. Sokolow's Mexican supplicant did not make a statement about Jews, but the representation of that piety brought her closer to her own Jewishness. Making this dance may have contributed to Sokolow's deeper engagement with her heritage by exploring experience outside her own. Larry Warren identifies the following moment as an artistic turning point for Sokolow: "During dinner with José Bergamín in his home in Mexico City, she noticed a piously rendered painting of a

120. Anna Sokolow, quoted in *Jewish Women in Dance*.

121. http://www.artic.edu/aic/collections/artwork/59426. Accessed May 30, 2016.

122. Ziva Amishai-Maisels, "Chagall's *White Crucifixion*," *Art Institute of Chicago Museum Studies* 17, no. 2 (1991): 139. See also Marc Chagall, "Unity is the Soul of Culture," *Jewish Life* Supplement 2, no. 1 (1947): 3–5.

saint such as only a practicing Catholic would display. She gestured toward it and asked, 'Why?' His simple reply was, 'Why not?'"[123] In *Retablo, White Crucifixion*, and Bergamín's display of the saint, the lines blur between Judaism and Catholicism. US critics' reading of these dances' ethnic elements coincided with postwar religious pluralism, in which, despite increased anti-Semitism as Jews moved into white suburbs, the hyphenated word Judeo–Christian emerged as a way to connect these traditions into a perceived common American heritage even though Judaism and Christianity remained distinct.

Finding Jewishness within Catholic imagery further reflects Spanish and Mexican Jewish history. Many Jews converted to Catholicism during the Spanish Inquisition or in more recent generations, by force or for protection from anti-Semitic hierarchies, like those controlled by Franco and Hitler, in reaction to the anti-Semitism that surfaced in Cosmic Race ideology, or under generations of anti-Semitism in Mexico.[124] These *conversos* brought Jewish rituals into their Catholic worship. Sokolow later explored the tensions between Judaism and Catholicism in *conversos'* identity in *Los Conversos* (1981), an emotionally heavy group work featuring Sephardic music, a blending of Jewish and Catholic religious gestures, and a Star of David set piece that disappeared and reappeared through the dance[125] (Figure 3.7). The lines between Jewishness and Catholicism blended further in Mexico than they did in the United States during the time that Sokolow was there. *Kaddish* and *Retablo* reflect this intricate intimacy of identities.

WARTIME AND POSTWAR TRANSITIONS

Sokolow's mid-1940s shift in priorities reinforced her roles as teacher and social activist. Her Mexican engagements kept her away from New York for half of each year, and she welcomed the opportunity to withdraw from the New York scene because she felt like an outsider, as a result of critics' reviews of her work.[126] After her continental crisscrossing travels abated, Sokolow pursued solo work instead of forming her own company in New York.[127] Her solo dancing body was her dances' only constant between Mexico City and New York, given that she rarely performed in her group compositions during this time. This choice to focus on solo work was mainly for financial reasons, but during this time she also helped get the fledgling

123. Warren, *Rebellious Spirit*, 104.

124. See Cimet, *Ashkenazi Jews*, 1–26 (see Chap. 2, n3).

125. Anna Sokolow, *Los Conversos* [*The Converts*], performed by Juilliard Dance Ensemble in New and Repertory Dance Works, 1980–1981 Season, filmed by George Lamboy (New York: Juilliard Theater, April 7, 1981), JRDD, NYPL.

126. Anna Sokolow, interview by Katharine Wolfe, March 28, 1946, transcript, Box 12, Folder 6, Katharine Wolfe Papers 1912–1972, JRDD, NYPL.

127. Sokolow, interview, Wolfe.

Figure 3.7: The Juilliard Dance Ensemble in the premiere of Anna Sokolow's *Los Conversos* (music by Richard J. Neumann), April 3–6, 1981. Photo by Jane Rady, courtesy of the Juilliard Archives.

Negro Dance Company off the ground as one of its technique teachers and regis-suers.[128] Many dancers made similar choices to pursue solo work or projects rather than forming their own companies, much to the dismay of critics like Walter Terry, who lamented in 1946, "I would also like to see several of these young leaders join forces . . . and head companies of a scope somewhat like that of the ballet; then and only then, I believe, can the modern dance hope to rival, financially and theatrically, the established ballet."[129] Sokolow's choice to not establish a company impeded her work's prominence in New York, for which she yearned, but her influence went beyond choreographic fame into disseminating her political choreographic ideals through her students.

Sokolow's participation in populist causes as well as Communist events through the anticommunist 1940s reinforces the coalitions she built for chore-ography as social action. Sokolow was a featured artist, along with Paul Robeson, in a "Democracy in Battle: The Jews in Defense of America" pageant at the IWO Annual Fiesta on March 29, 1942, which boasted the theme: "Reflecting the unity of the Jewish, Negro, and other peoples in the fight for freedom and the building

128. "Broadway To See Dance at Its Best with Stars Galore," *The Chicago Defender*, December 5, 1942, 22, PQHN.
129. Walter Terry, "The 'New' Modern Dance," *Dance Magazine* (August 1946): 31.

of America."[130] She choreographed more Lenin meetings, logging one in Hartford, Connecticut, in 1943 and one at Madison Square Garden in 1947,[131] and contributed to the American Continental Congress for World Peace in Mexico City in September 1949. This event was part of a series of conferences that HUAC labeled the Communist Peace Offensive. Along with Sokolow, conference attendees, sponsors, and speakers included Mexican muralists Rivera and Siquieros, American choreographer Katherine Dunham, American playwright Clifford Odets, American novelist Howard Fast, American ethnomusicologist Allan Lomax, Russian-born American muralist Refregier, former Mexican president Cárdenas, and American entertainers Robeson and Charlie Chaplin.[132] One Congress attendee reported that it was the first hemispheric congress convened by the people instead of by diplomats, providing an opportunity to unite North and South American activists for world peace.[133] The goals and sentiments of this event aligned with many of Sokolow's ideals, and her close friends and compatriots attended or had roles in producing the conference. In collaboration with other Taller de la Gráfica Popular artists, for example, Sokolow's former lover Nacho Aguirre premiered a hand-drawn fifty-nine-frame filmstrip titled *Who Wants War, Who Wants Peace*. Its images ranged from satires of power and graft to metaphorical renderings of the people's strength that would lead to peace.[134] This event occurred while Sokolow split her time between New York and Mexico City and provided a political artistic event the likes of which no longer existed in New York.

Regrouping *Kaddish* and *Retablo* together again under the ethnic dance label, Hering invited Sokolow to perform in the April 17, 1952 "Modern Dance in Ethnic Style" concert that she curated at the Museum of Natural History as part of the Around the World in Dance and Song series that Hazel Lockwood Muller organized from 1943 to 1952. The purpose of this concert series was to introduce audiences to non-Western dance and music forms to contribute to cross-cultural understanding, yet, as Kowal has shown, this program exoticized these forms in the name of education.[135] Terming it an "unusual program," the press release for Hering's concert announced, "The relation of ethnic dance to the modern dance idiom will be interpreted by a distinguished group of dancers. [. . .Sokolow] will perform her well-known Mexican 'Retablo' and two dances of Hebraic origin, 'Kaddish' and

130. Advertisement, "Annual Fiesta of the International Workers Order," *New York Amsterdam News*, March 28, 1942, 17, PQHN.

131. "Minor at Lenin Rally in Hartford," 4 (see Preface, n12); and Summary of File References, May 7, 1951, Main File No 100-103377, Subject: Anna Sokolow, FOIPA No. 1138496-000.

132. HUAC, *Report on the Communist "Peace" Offensive*, 22–23 (see Preface, n12); and Brown, "What I Saw in Mexico," 8 (see Preface, n12).

133. Brown, "What I Saw in Mexico," 10.

134. "*Who Wants War, Who Wants Peace*: Drawings from a Film Strip by Artists of the Taller de Gráfica Popular, Mexico City," *Masses and Mainstream* 2, no. 11 (1949): 24–27.

135. Hazel Lockwood Muller, "Hazel Lockwood Muller," Box 2, Folder 12, Hazel Lockwood Muller Papers, JRDD, NYPL. For a full discussion of this performance series, see Kowal, "Choreographing Interculturalism," 454–479.

'The Bride.'"[136] Hering invited Sokolow to participate in this program because she wanted to see Sokolow perform again, because by that time Sokolow had retired from the stage.[137] Hering's dance writing reflects Sokolow's gradual absence. In her 1940s reviews Hering focused on Sokolow's performance qualities, and her reviews from the 1950s and early 1960s highlighted Sokolow's choreographic structures.[138] Ocko's 1948 review of these works gives a sense for what Hering missed: "Sokolow's power of dramatic evocation is astonishing ... She can shift from the passionate and large dimensioned 'Lament' to the brittle fragility of 'Our Lady' or 'The Bride' with no loss of emotional depth. She can be brutal and yet sympathetic."[139]

Hering chose *Kaddish, The Bride,* and *Retablo* for the 1952 performance because she felt they specifically addressed "ethnic" material.[140] It bears mention that the other works on this program reflected constructions of working-class Americana (Jane Dudley's *Reel* and *Harmonica Breakdown*), African American experience and urban settings (Donald McKayle's *Games*), and the Mexican-influenced American Southwest (Graham's *El Penitente* with the Jewish Pearl Lang dancing Graham's role).[141] This program offers a reminder that though Jews and other American non-whites assimilated after World War II, the onstage representation of these traditions remained marked within otherwise universalist modernist discourses.

ANNA SOKOLOW DID NOT TRAVEL WELL

The ramifications of a US-imposed postwar alignment with abstraction so as not to attract attention during the Second Red Scare changed Sokolow's relationship with Mexican dance. The discursive tension that did not allow folkloric themes to be coterminous with universal art came to a head in the 1950s when the Mexican dance community found itself in an identity crisis that stemmed from a dismissal of *mexicanidad* in favor of universal form.[142] Waldeen accused Sokolow, as a respected

136. The American Museum of Natural History, *Outstanding Modern Dancers Relate Modern Dance to Ethnic Forms in American Museum Presentation*, April 13, 1952, Anna Sokolow Clippings, JRDD, NYPL. Publicity materials advertised *Kaddish*, but reviews of the performance do not mention it. Schulman, "Modern Dance in Ethnic Style," 75–76. This concert was not reviewed in *Dance Magazine* or *Dance News*.

137. Hering, discussion.

138. Hering, "Anna Sokolow: YM &YWHA February 1, 1948," 41–42; Doris Hering, "An Evening of Dance Works by Anna Sokolow: 92nd Street 'Y' February 24 and 28, 1955," *Dance Magazine* (April 1955): 77; and Doris Hering, "The Freda Miller Memorial Concert, 92nd Street 'Y,' May 8, 1961," *Dance Magazine* (July 1961): 15.

139. Ocko, "Dance: Anna Sokolow," 1948, 96.

140. Hering, discussion.

141. American Museum of Natural History, *Outstanding Modern Dancers Relate Modern Dance to Ethnic Forms in American Museum Presentation*.

142. Raúl Flores Guerrero, "La crisis de la danza Mexicana," Supplement, "México en la Cultura," *Novedades* (México), March 27, 1955. Reprinted in *La danza moderna mexicana 1953–1959: Antología hemerográfica*, eds. Lin Durán and Margarita Tortajada Quiroz (México: INBA, 1990), 123–129.

teacher in Mexico, of exacerbating this crisis when she spoke at two Mexican dance conferences and delivered comments that Waldeen summarized as a racist, antinationalist series of attacks against patriotism in Mexican art, and specifically against Mexican dance for "being Mexican." This discussion was heated at a time when Sokolow toured *Poem* (1956), a controversial dance about explicit sexuality, to Mexico. Waldeen was concerned that Sokolow's respected opinions could destroy Mexican modern dance as she knew it.[143]

At a roundtable discussion at the second dance conference at the Casa de Arquitecto Avenida in Veracruz in June 1956 among Sokolow, artist and INBA dance director Miguel Covarrubias, Mexican dance historian Raquel Tibol, dancers Magda Montoya and Xavier Francis, muralist David Alfaro Siqueiros, and former Sokolovas Elena Noriega, Rosa Reyna, and Josefina Lavalle, Sokolow emphasized her beliefs that because Mexican dance was too concerned with nationalism, patriotism, and marking itself with indigenous and folkloric elements, it lacked individualism and potential for growth. Among the backlash to Sokolow's remarks, Tibol asserted that indeed, in Mexican art the form came from *indigenismo* with impulse for social action. Covarrubias suggested that Sokolow's intent in transcending nationality and patriotism was to not use those themes superficially.[144] These arguments over who decides what art counts as universal reflects US critics' power within a divide in a mid-twentieth-century struggle for hemispheric artistic legitimacy. The argument Sokolow perpetuated, that the form must transcend the content, is the same one that she found herself entangled in between American and Mexican critical discourses during her first years in Mexico City from 1939 to 1942 and that haunted her relationship with Mexican concert dance.

Although the 1956 Veracruz dance conference ended inconclusively, it sealed Sokolow's midcentury historical reputation. Waldeen asserted that Sokolow imposed on the panel the so-called decadent aesthetic theory of American modern dance,[145] the same criticism Soviet audiences leveled at Sokolow twenty years prior. Despite this conflict, in 1988 Anna Sokolow was one of nine awardees of the Mexican government's *El Águila Azteca* [The Aztec Eagle Honor, or Order of the Aztec Eagle]. This *Ecomienda* award acknowledges foreign nationals for lifetime contributions to Mexico's art and culture.[146] This honor's significance goes beyond

143. Waldeen Falkenstein, "Dejaran Morir la danca mexicana?" reprinted in Luna Arroyo, *Ana Merida*, 158, 160 (see Chap. 2, n32).

144. This information is summarized from the transcript of this conference session, labeled "2nd. Conference given by Anna Sokolow," parts of which were translated by a translator hired by Larry Warren whose name is hand-written and illegible in the document. Larry Warren Collection on Anna Sokolow and Lester Horton, MD, LOC.

145. Falkenstein, "Dejaran Morir la danca mexicana?," 158. "Durante su estancia en México, la señora Sokolow logró infiltrar en algunos de los miembros del Ballet, la decadente teoría estética de la escuela de danza moderna que ella representa."

146. Sokolow's fellow honorees included Friedrich Katz, an American-born historian of the Mexican Revolution; José María Fernández, an Argentine-born dramaturg and director who worked in Mexico beginning in the 1950s; and Erika Billeter, a German-born art historian

its recognition of Sokolow's fifty years choreographing and teaching in Mexico. *El Águila Azteca* deepened Sokolow's legendary status within the American and Mexican dance communities. The influence of Mexican art and culture on Sokolow was as reciprocally significant as her contributions that the *Ecomienda* recognized. In her struggle to retain transnational artistic legitimacy, Sokolow's negotiations to make work that satisfied her own desires challenged her ability to keep her politics and aesthetics legible to various audiences.

Sokolow's relationship with INBA and the Mexican dance community continued through periods of strain. In 1961, Sokolow felt ostracized by INBA in favor of her former Sokolova Ana Mérida. After a routine six-month INBA residency, Sokolow was left out of publicity materials and found herself in Mérida's shadow. In a feature story titled "Disillusioned by the Intrigue in the Artistic Field, Ana Leaves," Sokolow told the newspaper *Extra*, "I can't help but recognize that the attitude of the members of the Dance Academy has hurt me, and they have not known how to recognize the efforts that are being made to elevate Mexican dance from the state in which it has found itself for many years."[147] In a combination of retaliation for a bruised ego and perpetuating the attitude that embroiled Sokolow in a high–low, modernist–indigenous debate in Mexican dance, Sokolow's comments show how her attitude diverged from that of her earlier years of excited artistic collaboration and relatively favorable reception in Mexico City.[148]

Sokolow's insistence on universalism at the Veracruz conference is more a reflection of her reaction to the Second Red Scare, when the FBI followed her closely, than any decoupling of form from revolutionary content she upheld. In an unfortunate turn of events, Sokolow alienated a dance community that fed her deeply. She tried to protect herself when her government surveyed her for the revolutionary ideals that profoundly fostered her art. This surveillance dictated caution in Sokolow's verbal public statements. Sokolow's new acceptance by the 1950s American critical establishment into dance universalism, paired with the postwar assimilation of Sokolow's generation of American Jews into the societal mainstream, enabled her to continue choreographing revolutionary statements in the guise of abstract modernism.

working in Switzerland who brought widespread recognition to Mexican artists. George R. McMurray, "The Hispanic and Luso-Brazilian World," *Hispania* 72, no. 2 (1989): 336; Warren, *Rebellious Spirit*, 294; and Irene Herner, "Erika Billeter y el Arte Mexicano en Europa," January 3, 1993. *Nexos en Línea*, http://www.nexos.com.mx/?P=leerarticulo&Article=447177

147. Augustin Salmon, Jr., "Deceptionada de la Intriga en el Campo Artístico se va Ana," *Extra*, November 13, 1961, CENIDID, CENART, trans. Roland Wu: "no dejó de reconocer que me ha dolido la actitud de los componetes de la Academia de la Danza que no han sabido reconocer esfuerzos que se hacen por sacar a la danza mexicana del estado en que se encuentra desde hace muchos años."

148. In the 1970s, Sokolow found a home with Mexico City's Ballet Independiente, to whom she entrusted many of her dances and from whom she received continuing support.

CHAPTER 4

White Rooms, Red Scare

Sokolow Defines America

In the soul-draining desolation of *Lyric Suite* (1953), the existential angst of *Rooms* (1954), and the adolescent disillusionment of the *Opus* series (1958–1965), Sokolow's choreography disrupted 1950s quietism like sandpaper against a smooth surface. Instead of challenging the status quo, her dances made people uncomfortable by putting unspoken conditions on display. Amid the Communist-baiting entanglements of McCarthyism during the 1940s–1950s Second Red Scare climate of fear that disenfranchised thousands of people in the name of national security, being American meant assimilating into an anticommunist patriotism. Sokolow's revolutionary modernism was born in a 1930s American Communist moment conversely deemed un-American in the 1950s. Critics championed the modernism in Sokolow's postwar dances and heralded her as an American choreographer of postwar alienation, though some of them withheld praise during McCarthyism.[1] Americans privately reeled from World War II's psychological effects that few acknowledged publicly in the name of patriotism and the affluent, homogenizing social climate of normalcy. To navigate, Sokolow did not change what she said, but how she said it.

Domestic changes in American dance modernism that redefined postwar norms, coupled with US foreign policies that dictated the aesthetic properties of art suitable for export, inscribed Sokolow's choreography within a new set of compositional expectations. In this book I have argued that Sokolow's technical alignment with Martha Graham's vocabulary and Sokolow's own choreographic tendencies to present revolutionary content through bourgeois form marked her

---

1. Zelda Blackman to Larry Warren, Summer 1982, Larry Warren Collection on Anna Sokolow and Lester Horton, MD, LOC.

work as American, especially when she traveled abroad. Three anticommunist factors changed her domestic and international postwar reception. First, in 1946, as the US Congress reinstated HUAC, dance critic Gertrude Lippincott wrote a *Dance Observer* editorial in which she told dancers to avoid turning choreography into political propaganda by eschewing mass cultural social themes and embracing the lone artist's abstract expressionism.[2] Gay Morris noted that Lippincott's assertions were controversial but "typified the thinking that would come to dominate during the postwar period."[3] Second, the 1954 organization of the American National Theater and Academy (ANTA), an arm of President Dwight Eisenhower's (1953–1961) President's Emergency Fund for International Affairs established to send American performers abroad to prevent the spread of Communist influence by winning hearts and minds,[4] established what was suitable for American export. Through ANTA, the government defined what was aesthetically American on the international stage. The universal figuring of midcentury American dance modernism, dance historian Clare Croft argued, fit with US State Department goals to present art that was at once recognizably American and a blank slate into which audiences across the globe could emotionally insert themselves.[5] Third, State Department programs disengaged with racial tensions that marked the beginning of the Civil Rights Movement and instead framed jazz and the African American experience as synonymous with midcentury American modernism.[6] In ANTA's calculation to export jazz as American through artists like trumpeter Louis Armstrong, according to historian Penny von Eschen, US officials embraced jazz as "a uniquely American art form" that presented racial equality abroad during a time of domestic civil rights upheaval.[7] The postwar circulation of Sokolow's choreography suggests her subversion of postwar anticommunist limits set by the ANTA Dance Panel's critics and choreographers who determined what made American dance American.

To understand how Sokolow's dances refused postwar American universalism even as they appeared to uphold it, implications for communism, Jewishness, blackness, and queerness must be considered together. In this chapter I argue that Sokolow's jazz-driven movements appeared to reference nothing outside themselves as they assimilated nonnormative (and suspect) subject positions of Jewish, gay, and communist experiences into an Americanness that critics and audiences perceived as universal. Sokolow's compositional elements that marked Cold War art as American drew language in reviews that reinforced her Jewish generation's

2. Morris, *Game for Dancers*, 5–8 (see Introduction, n8), and Graff, *Stepping Left*, 167 (see Preface, n2).

3. Morris, *Game for Dancers*, 5.

4. See Naima Prevots, *Dance for Export: Cultural Diplomacy and the Cold War* (Middletown, CT: Wesleyan University Press, 1998), 30.

5. Croft, *Dancers as Diplomats*, 66–74 (see Introduction, n65).

6. See Croft, *Dancers as Diplomats*, 66–104.

7. Penny M. von Eschen, *Satchmo Blows Up the World: Jazz Ambassadors Play the Cold War* (Cambridge, MA: Harvard University Press, 2004), 6.

postwar assimilation into whiteness. I discuss the dances *Lyric Suite, Rooms,* and the *Opus* series to demonstrate how their jazz foundations engendered their Americanization by simultaneously masking and enabling Sokolow's revolutionary modernism.

Sokolow's blending of Jewish and Africanist compositional elements embodied an antisegregation worldview upheld by communist ideology and the IWO, and recalled 1930s–1940s Black–Jewish Communist coalitions in which Sokolow had participated. Her 1950s dances' subjects of urban discontent, jazz scores, and Africanist movement elements of syncopation, intensity through repetition, high-affect juxtaposition, and the "aesthetic of the cool" with hot energy underneath a cool composure,[8] reinforced her Americanization. She first composed with jazz in the 1930s in works such as *Ballad in a Popular Style* (1936), at which time the Popular Front considered jazz the new American folk.[9] In the 1950s, Sokolow used jazz as a revolutionary tool to portray the grit, pain, and countercultural youth rebellion of a nation reconciling the postwar period's competing factors. Jazz-as-American commentary in dance criticism furthered Sokolow's assimilation. Selma Jeanne Cohen expressed this sentiment when she wrote in a review of *Session for Eight* (1959), "Miss Sokolow continues her jazz studies as the true expression of our age."[10] Postwar acculturation engendered what Dixon Gottschild termed "the 'whitenizing' of the Africanist aesthetic," wherein white culture incorporates Africanist elements and dispossesses them of their roots.[11] Arguably, Lippincott's call to efface social justice from choreography in the name of apoliticalization similarly evacuated Jewishness from postwar abstraction. Apoliticization equaled whitening, so despite Sokolow's dances' Jewishness in their open endings with no concrete answers, her alignment with abstracted jazz reinforced her own Caucasian whiteness during Jews' public retreats from communism.

Jewish assimilation fostered Sokolow's political navigation of the postwar period. The stakes for Sokolow to look American and evade blacklisting (and its inherent immobility) accompanied her assimilation. During the Red Scare, as historian Rona Sheramy has shown, American Jews dissociated themselves from their communist pasts in efforts to show their patriotism and deflect anti-Semitism.[12] They demonstrated how Jewish tenets aligned with American democracy, and, especially during the Julius and Ethel Rosenberg espionage trial, Sheramy noted,

8. Kariamu Welsh Asante, "Commonalities in African Dance: An Aesthetic Foundation," in *African Culture: The Rhythms of Unity*, eds. Molefi Kete Asante and Kariamu Welsh Asante (Trenton, NJ: Africa World Press, 1990), 71–82; and Dixon Gottschild, *Digging*, 12–18 (see Chap. 1, n97).

9. Denning, *Cultural Front*, 284, 320 (see Introduction, n54); and Kriegsman, *Bennington Years*, 99 (see Chap. 1, n94).

10. Selma Jeanne Cohen, "Anna Sokolow Dance Company, York Playhouse; Dec. 26–Jan. 3," *Dance Magazine* (February 1959): 28.

11. Dixon Gottschild, *Digging*, 31.

12. Sheramy, " 'Resistance and War,' " 301 (see Introduction, n6).

Jews "assert[ed] their distance from communism and their loyalty to the United States."[13] Sokolow similarly verified her alignment with American sentiment in her dances that featured alienation through jazz music and compositional structures. This alienation caused by social scrutiny and strategies to avoid persecution were queer as well as Jewish and communist.

The joint threats of the Red Scare and Lavender Scare, which targeted homosexuals in government offices, yoked anti-Semitism with homophobia and hit the dance community especially hard. Postwar critics deflected anticommunist suspicions of the significant numbers of gays, lesbians, Communists, and sympathizers in the concert dance ranks. This support included Margaret Lloyd's assertion in her 1949 *Borzoi Book of Modern Dance* that though there were once left-wingers, "There are no reds in modern dance today."[14] John Martin commented in 1954 about *Lyric Suite*, "Miss Sokolow has happily attempted to read no literary program into it, but has choreographed the dramatic content of the music itself, which is quite enough, indeed."[15] Even though critics shielded dancers with their writing, the climate's infiltrating fear caused dancers, especially if they were gay, to cover their identities. The dance world protected the "open secret" of homosexuality in its ranks, "while," as Susan Manning notes, "granting gay men and lesbians full citizenship and often leadership within the profession."[16] Critics could not protect dancers from the political repercussions of all their secrets, but notably, they tried. When choreographers coded their dances with ostracization themes like the Salem witch trials during McCarthyism, critics either discussed the narratives literally or ignored euphemism in their reviews.[17] When Sokolow choreographed S. Ansky's Yiddish play *The Dybbuk* in New York in 1951, her role of Leah, the central character whose body becomes controlled by the restless spirit of her star-crossed lover, was, according to Larry Warren, "perhaps as a small antidote to the [McCarthy] environment [. . .since it] dealt with possession and exorcism."[18] Beyond *The Dybbuk*, Sokolow did not make metaphorically anti-McCarthyist work. Instead, the thematic alienation of *Lyric Suite*, *Rooms*, and *Opus* embodied criticisms of anticommunism, anti-Semitism, racism, and homophobia.

Critics' reviews of what Sokolow's movement figured but not what it signified steered her works from public suspicion, but did not prevent the government from tracking her actions. Historian Ellen Schrecker noted that McCarthyism changed what was acceptable in American social discourse: "It used all the power of the state to turn dissent into disloyalty and, in the process, drastically narrowed the

13. Ibid., 303–305.
14. Lloyd, *Borzoi Book*, 173 (see Chap. 1, n186).
15. John Martin, "The Dance: High Spots—Daniel Nagrin and Others in Recent Series," *New York Times*, April 11, 1954, X6, 92Y.
16. Manning, *Modern Dance, Negro Dance*, 181 (see Preface, n14).
17. Morris, *Game for Dancers*, 32–33.
18. Warren, *Rebellious Spirit*, 125 (see Preface, n2).

spectrum of acceptable political debate."[19] Sokolow made her opposition plain by flashing social unrest back at her audiences. The dance establishment did not trade Sokolow's dissent for disloyalty, but the US government did. Sokolow was never called to testify before HUAC, but documents in her FBI file show that the FBI and CIA made it difficult for her to travel freely. The switchboard operator in her apartment building informed the FBI daily on her comings and goings.[20] The US Passport Office routinely denied her travel requests to Israel and Europe between 1953 and 1955,[21] which Sokolow appealed. There is no way to determine who knew how closely the FBI followed Sokolow. Critics' upholding of Sokolow's work defined her as American amid government scrutiny of her perceived un-American activity.

As the US government suppressed Sokolow's personal liberties among those of so many others, it advertised a narrowly scripted brand of American freedom that claimed to protect citizens from foreign (communist) infiltration. The 1947 Truman Doctrine outlined Cold War American rhetoric as a worldwide struggle for American democracy to prevail over communism.[22] In his examination of freedom propagation through US history, historian Eric Foner noted, "during the Cold War, individual rights [were] seriously curtailed—often in the name of freedom."[23] Politicians continued this rhetoric to suppress citizens' civil and reproductive rights by claiming that such curtailment of liberties would keep the country safe. Foner suggested that postwar hysteria was rooted in the conservative Right's desire to regain power after twenty years of Democratic leadership. A 1949 Herblock political cartoon lampoons this sentiment. In it, a crazed-looking man, labeled "hysteria," screams "Fire!" as he scrambles up a ladder, carrying an overflowing water bucket toward the flame in the Statue of Liberty's torch.[24] State Department freedom values manifested in dance most clearly through the State Department's touring of Graham's choreography starting in 1955, which established modern dance whiteness through chronological narratives. As Manning, Jacqueline Shea Murphy, and Croft have shown, Graham's Americana and Greek mythology work figured a white universal subject by invisibilizing nonwhite elements within her dances' narrative-driven abstraction, to the point that bodies of color could be perceived as universal

19. Schrecker, *Many Are the Crimes*, xii (see Preface, n10).

20. Unclassified Office Memorandum, United States Government, From SA [Secret Agent] JP McCormick Jr 424 to SA C New York, 9/8/59, FOIPA No. 1138496-000.

21. Letter (with affidavit), To J. Edgar Hoover, Director, FBI, to Mr. Dennis A. Flinn, Director, Office of Security, Subject: Anna Sokolow, Born February 9, 1910, Hartford, Connecticut, June 3, 1955; Case File, Anna Sokolow, 9/30/55 with attached affidavit; and Passport review, 12/10/59 from FBI Director (100-379046) to SAC, WFO (100-24317), FOIPA No. 1138496-000.

22. Eric Foner, *The Story of American Freedom* (New York: W. W. Norton & Company, 1998), 252–253.

23. Ibid., xvii.

24. Herbert Block, "Fire!" in *The Herbert Block Book* (New York: Beacon Press, 1952), reprinted in Foner, *American Freedom*, 248.

in her choreography.[25] Aligning with State Department desires to export an idealized version of American democracy, Croft asserted that Graham aesthetically "equated whiteness, universality, and American freedom."[26] Narrative was good for the idea of American freedom but bad for the avant-garde, who eschewed capitalism by shrouding leftist tenets in nonnarrative abstraction that signified whiteness.[27] Within American freedom rhetoric, dance that presented a closed system of clear narrative was preferable to indeterminate dances that encouraged audiences to think for themselves. As Morris noted in Merce Cunningham's choreography that refused narrative through its compositional chance procedures of randomly shuffled movement phrases, "Freedom of interpretation empowered the spectator at a time when there was general social concern for decreasing individual freedom in America."[28] In the wake of Eisenhower's 1953 inauguration speech filled with American freedom ideology and the 1954 formation of the Dance Panel to export this freedom through American bodies,[29] Sokolow's dances purveyed whiteness and heteronormativity as they subsumed Africanisms, Jewishness, and queerness to stoke despair whitewashed by stifling freedom rhetoric.

To situate Sokolow among these developments, I begin this chapter with Sokolow's work on New York's Chanukah pageants for the Israeli Bond Corporation to underscore that her political Jewish actions concurrent with her modernist assimilation aligned with a majority of New York Jews of her generation. Her new association with Israel through choreographing Chanukah festival pageants for Israeli bonds and working in Israel paralleled her Mexican ties for retaining a position in international communist contexts. I then progress chronologically through the 1950s to show the arc of Sokolow's work from *Lyric Suite*'s quietism to *Opus*'s rebellion as 1950s normalcy dissolved into early 1960s questioning. With these dances, Sokolow reinserted herself into American dance after her 1940s Jewish-themed work and trips to Mexico had marginalized her. *Rooms* is the heart of this discussion. Its circulation among dance companies inside and outside the United States as the FBI followed Sokolow and the Dance Panel refused to export her dances helps address what is American about Sokolow's work.

"PARTY" PAGEANTRY FOR ISRAEL

Sokolow's involvement in Chanukah festivals to raise money for Israeli bonds provides insight into the specific negotiations of a subset of American Jews.

25. Manning, *Modern Dance, Negro Dance*, 118, 188, 141–142; Shea Murphy, *The People Have Never Stopped Dancing*, 148–168 (see Chap. 3, n104); and Croft, *Dancers as Diplomats*, 111–112.
26. Croft, *Dancers as Diplomats*, 107.
27. Morris, *Game for Dancers*, 18–20; and Manning, *Modern Dance, Negro Dance*, 208.
28. Morris, *Game for Dancers*, 174.
29. Croft, *Dancers as Diplomats*, 108–109.

The 1948 establishment of the State of Israel caused a 1940s–1950s surge in Zionism, and Sokolow, along with Sophie Maslow and other Jewish dancers, choreographed these concerts.[30] Zionism was a political movement for Jewish sovereignty born in Central and Eastern Europe in the wake of late nineteenth-century anti-Semitism and government-sanctioned pogroms against Jewish communities. As historian Emily Katz has argued, American Jews were not unified or consistent in their familiarity with the new State of Israel. The postwar assimilation of second- and third-generation American Jews resulted from their generational distance from their immigrant forebears, and they fully considered the United States home. Participating in Israeli cultural events, like bond pageants or Israeli folk dances, was a way for American Jews to assert their singular (Jewish) Americanness.[31] Financially supporting Israel was a politically Jewish action. Audience members asserted their upward mobility by buying the bonds, starting at $100, that gained them admission to the pageants.[32] Sokolow contributed by choreographing. Rebecca Rossen has demonstrated the central, though underacknowledged at the time, role that modern dance played during these festivals from 1951 to 1970 that united American Zionism, biblical epic pageantry, and modern dance.[33] These pageants' scheduling around Chanukah is significant in light of Jews' postwar assimilation. Chanukah is not traditionally a major Jewish holiday, but within Jews' American acculturation and Chanukah's timing near Christmas, Chanukah gained secular importance as a December Jewish holiday in the United States.[34]

The blending of American, Jewish, and Israeli nationalism forged an American Jewish connection to Israel and reinforced that Zionism and monetary support for Israel were acceptable, even necessary, ways for Jews to be American. Chanukah festivals were similar in scope to the Communist Party's Lenin meetings that Sokolow choreographed in the 1930s to 1940s. They occurred in the same venue of Madison Square Garden with programs including political speeches and theatrical pageants, and likely had the same people in the audience, now twenty years older with a new way of demonstrating their political affiliations. This time, they distanced themselves from communism and asserted their philanthropic power to build Israel with international monies. Programs included singing American and Israeli national anthems, blessing Chanukah candles, and salutations from the chairmen of the Chanukah Festival Committee, the Greater New York Committee for Israel Bonds, and Israel's Minister of Finance. Maslow choreographed most of the pageants, but

30. Graff, *Stepping Left*, 173 and Louise Guthman (lighting designer) in discussion with the author, February 26, 2009, Columbus, OH.

31. Emily Alice Katz, *Bringing Zion Home: Israel in American Jewish Culture, 1948–1967* (Albany: State University of New York Press, 2015), 7–9, 18.

32. Rossen, *Dancing Jewish*, 204 (see Introduction, n26).

33. Ibid., 203–223.

34. Ibid., 208–209.

Sokolow's 1953–1954 participation shows her standing among the Israel Bond Corporation and the New York Jewish community.

For Sokolow and her fellow choreographer Jerome Robbins, Israel offered a Jewish socialist political environment and escape from New York. Robbins and Sokolow had been close friends since the late 1940s and shared artistic and political backgrounds.[35] Sokolow began working in Israel in 1953 on Robbins's suggestion. Unlike Sokolow, Robbins was subpoenaed by HUAC. In his May 1953 testimony, Robbins said that he joined the Communist Political Association in 1943 in a show of solidarity as a Jew and an artist. He said the Communist Party "was fighting Fascism, and Fascism and anti-Semitism were synonymous to me. It also gave one the feeling that the artist under Communism was a very free and secure person economically."[36] During his hearing Robbins infamously outed critic Edna Ocko and other dance community members as Communist so that his own homosexual, Jewish, Communist positions would not end his career,[37] but he did not name Sokolow in his testimony.[38] Sokolow was abroad during most of 1953's HUAC hearings, as she made *Lyric Suite* in Mexico and worked with the Inbal Dance Theater in Israel.

Sokolow choreographed the Israel pageants after her first trip there. In so doing, she remade Communist pageantry in the name of socialist Zionism under American Jewish philanthropic auspices and with European–American capitalist investment in Israel. For *City of the Ages*, the October 20, 1953 program, Sokolow's dance drama of the same name celebrated "3000 Years of Jerusalem" and pitted hordes of Israelites against Romans under King David's leadership.[39] *City of Ages* reinforced Zionist claims to Israel by connecting a mythical 3,000 years of Jewish history in that place to the present day, while reinforcing the strength of Jews victorious against oppressors. The Chanukah story of the Maccabees' unlikely victory resonated against the contemporary specters of the Holocaust and the 1948 Arab–Israeli War/Israeli War for Independence in the recent past. The December 23, 1954 program *Chanukah Festival for Israel* featured performances by Israeli violinist Isaac Stern conducted by American Jewish composer Leonard Bernstein, and culminated in "The Great Dreamer," a dance drama about the founding of the State of Israel performed by Sokolow's company and

35. Jerome Robbins, draft of "An Appreciation" for *Anna Sokolow: The Rebellious Spirit* by Larry Warren, June 28, 1989, Larry Warren Collection on Anna Sokolow and Lester Horton, MD, LOC.

36. Quoted in Eric Bentley, *Thirty Years of Treason: Excerpts from Hearings before the House Committee on Un-American Activities, 1938–1968* (New York: Viking, 1971), 630.

37. Deborah Jowitt, *Jerome Robbins: His Life, His Theater, His Dance* (New York: Simon & Schuster, 2004), 228–231.

38. Jowitt, *Jerome Robbins*, 228–231; Amanda Vaill, *Somewhere: The Life of Jerome Robbins* (New York: Broadway Books, 2006), 172–173; and Bentley, *Thirty Years*.

39. Program, *City of the Ages presented by State of Israel Bonds*, October 20, 1953, Larry Warren Collection on Anna Sokolow and Lester Horton, MD, LOC.

members of the New Dance Group.[40] The epic scale of these pageants, like the mythology driving the universalism in Graham's works, in *mestizaje*, and in the ideology of the New Jew that I discuss in Chapter 5, purveyed whiteness through archetypal Jewish narrative. Pageants like these contributed to the Zionism that united the Jewish Diasporic community in the 1950s.[41] Sokolow did not make *aliyah* (a permanent move to Israel from the Diaspora), but she was vocal about Israel's influence on her Jewish identity, noting in 1979, "It makes me feel deeply who I am."[42] Sokolow's comment connecting her to the Jewish and socialist locale of Israel reasserted her Jewish communism within the guise of acceptable, assimilated Jewish Americanism.

JEWISHNESS, WHITENESS, AND ASSIMILATION

Lyric Suite reflected postwar Jewish assimilation through abstraction that read as whiteness. Mexican dancer Guillermo Keys commissioned Sokolow to create the dance in August 1953, as part of a late-1940s-initiated effort from INBA Dance Department head Miguel Covarrubias to revive Paloma Azul-era collaborative performance.[43] The New Dance Group invited Sokolow to present *Lyric Suite*, with New Dance Group dancers, on their April 4, 1954 concert at the 92nd Street Y.[44] Coming at the height of the Red Scare, *Lyric Suite*'s generalized poetics about postwar unrest brought Sokolow into high modernism. US postwar sentiment in general and among the dance community in particular considered Depression-era politics and leftist dance as youthful frivolities compared with the seriousness of McCarthyism and a generalized interest in humanism.[45] Cold War rhetoric infantilized and criminalized 1930s actions, and Sokolow's abandonment of proletarian aesthetic practices aided her acculturation.

Lyric Suite's existentially distressing vignettes registered a stylistic shift in Sokolow's career[46] and introduced the choreographic aesthetic for which she became known. The piece initiated what she called lyric theater, a blend of dancing, acting, poetry, and music stripped of its reliance on scenic elements. Sokolow told the Israeli newspaper *Ha'aretz* in 1964 about her ideal form: "I am asking for

---

40. Program, *Chanukah Festival for Israel presented by the State of Israel Bonds*, December 23, 1954, Larry Warren Collection on Anna Sokolow and Lester Horton, MD, LOC.

41. Wenger, *New York Jews and the Great Depression*, 194 (see Introduction, n14).

42. Helen V. Atlas, "Anna Sokolow's Work With Israeli Dancers," *Dance News* (January 1979): 9.

43. Warren, *Rebellious Spirit*, 143–144.

44. Program, *The Dance Center of the YM-YWHA presents the New Dance Group in its Second Annual Concert Series*, April 4, 1954, 92Y.

45. Halberstam, *The Fifties* (New York: Fawcett Columbine, 1993), 330; and Manning, *Ecstasy*, 266 (see Introduction, n27).

46. Warren, *Rebellious Spirit*, 147.

a new theatricality—a theatricality of bare movement."[47] Sokolow formed two companies, one in Tel Aviv and one in New York, under the name Lyric Theatre, and Jim May's Sokolow Theatre/Dance Ensemble takes Sokolow's lyric theater as an aesthetic and methodological point of departure. Moreover, *Lyric Suite* was Sokolow's first dance in which she did not perform. She last performed on stage in Doris Hering's 1952 Modern Dance in Ethnic Style concert at the Museum of Natural History (see Chapter 3), and on film in Shirley Clarke's *Bullfight* in 1955 (see Chapter 2). With *Lyric Suite*, Sokolow's choreographic career and the aesthetic look of her dances changed. She relied on dancers to generate movement through reacting to her verbal cues, and she began using the suite form, a series of individual vignettes, which became a defining characteristic of her work. Both shifts tie to whitening aesthetics reliant on generalization: in the former, by gathering dancers' movement contributions into a collective whole, and in the latter, by enabling meaning to emerge through layers of movement portraits that overrode specificity.

Lyric Suite, an emotional portrait named for its Alban Berg score *Lyric Suite for String Quartet* (1925–1926), contains six nonnarrative sections connected by despair.[48] Naming the dance with the music's title reinforced that the piece referenced nothing outside itself that could mark Sokolow or the dance with suspicion. Berg's score reportedly contained handwritten notes to a woman he loved in secret and compositional structures based on combining their initials together.[49] Angst lurked beneath the surface of Berg's music and Sokolow's choreography, producing tensions that reflected a society suppressing its apprehension. As critic Anna Kisselgoff noted in 1969, the dance portrayed "intermittent images of frustration and its thread of anxiety (beneath the surface when not on the surface)."[50] Berg's score features unsatisfied strings, sometimes screaming, sometimes plucking and perturbed, and sometimes low and languid. Sokolow's movement vocabulary includes arched backs, twisting abdominal spirals, reaching arms, predictable weight shifts, dropping body parts onto the floor, and rounded shapes resonant with the codified modern dance vocabularies of midcentury dance modernist whiteness.

It was important for Sokolow to appear white amid widespread anti-Semitism, anti-leftism, heteronormativity, and forced normalcy, but her movement was never

47. Anna Sokolow, quoted in Michael Ohad, "Anna does not want success," *Ha'aretz*, September 18, 1964, n.p., DLI, trans. Stav Ziv. Louis Horst also used this term, noting Sokolow's December 18, 1954 presentation of *Lyric Suite* and *L'Histoire du Soldat* was a "program of lyric theatre." Horst, "Modern Music, Drama and Dance," *Dance Observer* (February 1955): 25.

48. *Lyric Suite*, VHS, performed by Ohio State University, directed and introduced by John Giffin (n.d.), DNBX; "Largo desolato" on *The New Dance Group Gala Concert*, VHS, directed by Johannes Holub (American Dance Guild, 1994); and *Lyric Suite*, VHS, produced by Sal Speizia and Judith Mann (YMHA Kaufman Auditorium, 1974), JRDD, NYPL.

49. Douglas Jarman, *The Music of Alban Berg* (1979; Berkeley: University of California Press, 1985), 228.

50. Anna Kisselgoff, "2D Park Program by Utah Dancers," *The New York Times*, September 11, 1969, 53, Larry Warren Collection on Anna Sokolow and Lester Horton, MD, LOC.

only about itself. Critic Deborah Jowitt wrote in 1988, "Sokolow's lyricism is neither sweet nor easy; it involves passion, ecstasy, yearning meant to look almost
too intense for the dancers to bear."[51] Critics celebrated Sokolow as a choreographer who had arrived, that is, as one who transcended ethnic markers. A comment
Sokolow made in 1975 shows her shift to framing her own work in universal terms
of humanism instead of social agendas. She said *Lyric Suite* "was one of the first
things [she] did that didn't have a social theme. It was about humanity, rather than
just social [original emphasis]."[52] This ability to claim humanism (whiteness) over
social themes (Jewish proletarianism) indicates American Jewish postwar assimilation. As I discussed in this book's Introduction, postwar Jewish acculturation
related to social mobility. In the 1950s–1960s, upwardly mobile Jews moved out
of urban Jewish enclaves into mostly white suburbs. There, they contended with
tempered anti-Semitism as they chose, as theater historian Alisa Solomon asserts,
between "*shul* or swimming pool," or between spending their Shabbat (Saturday,
Jewish Sabbath) in synagogue or being part of their mixed suburban community.[53]
Their presence in secular spaces during a weekly moment previously reserved for
religious observance marked a shift in how Jews asserted their Americanness. In
addition to a generalized postwar malaise resulting from the pressures of normalcy,
Jews in the suburbs fought tensions between upholding Jewish traditions and
blending in to their surroundings. This era also saw the mainstream popularization
and mixing of *klezmer* (Eastern European Jewish music) songs like "Hava Nagila"
with Christian elements. One rendition of "Hava Nagila," for example, was parodied to "Have a Nice Christmas."[54] Sokolow's choreographic acculturation in *Lyric
Suite*'s strains reflected tensions in Jews' assimilation.

   Lyric Suite's first two solos portray individuals struggling against undefined
forces as their form-for-form's-sake movements suggest an all-encompassing quality that film theorist Richard Dyer identified as whiteness: "This property of whiteness, to be everything and nothing, is the source of its representational power."[55]
Sokolow extended this representation by inserting *Lyric Suite* into the twentieth-
century Euro–American canon, dedicating the first solo, "Allegreto jioviale," to
Vaslav Nijinsky, and the second, "Adante amoroso," to Isadora Duncan.[56] The
"Allegreto jioviale" dancer slowly articulates his feet through labored prances, lunging and changing his facing before pivoting through a swift backward turn on two
feet to suddenly face the front. He tilts his body to the left, extending his arms as he

   51. Deborah Jowitt, "Innocence: True and Feigned," *The Village Voice*, February 23, 1988, 81.
   52. Anna Sokolow, quoted in Anna Kisselgoff, "In Anna Sokolow's Dance, Her Beliefs," 46
(see Introduction, n36).
   53. Solomon, "Balancing Act," 25 (see Introduction, n70).
   54. *Hava Nagila: The Movie*, DVD, directed by Roberta Grossman (Los Angeles: Katahdin
Productions, 2012).
   55. Richard Dyer, "White," in *The Matter of Images: Essays on Representations*, 2nd ed. (London
and New York: Routledge, 2000), 127.
   56. Warren, *Rebellious Spirit*, 363.

rises onto the balls of his feet; his left leg slips into a bent *arabesque* line behind him as his torso tips forward. In a sudden, arresting instant he cuts his torso into a high arch and lengthens his arms out to his sides, as if he has given up while floating in water. Employing similar torso shapes in "Adante amoroso," the soloist runs across the space with her arms outstretched and sternum skyward through pathways that take her into half turns. Later, her arms form a classical position, with the right arm curved overhead and the left arm to the side. In anguish, she leans from side to side and turns in a tilted position. This section ends with the soloist's melting collapse, followed by a quick body flip into a supine position with her upper torso stretched into an arch against the floor. Following lyric theater, the environs are bare. Beyond the scenery-lacking stage, the recurring movements of back arches that expose the vulnerable lines of the dancers' necks strip them emotionally to the bone. These solos' lack of signifiers created movement that referenced nothing outside itself.

The central duet of *Lyric Suite*, "Largo desolato," a pained love duet between a man and woman based on the story of Tristan and Isolde,[57] reinforces postwar heteronormativity despite the strain in its coupling. Kisselgoff noted of a 1990s Juilliard performance that the dancers in this duet "gave a fine account of a love that deepens, not without shadows."[58] There is strife here, and desperation between the dancers. They reach, they yearn; they make contact but they do not connect. At the beginning of the duet, both dancers face upstage so the audience can only see their backs. They each extend an arm across the other's back, forming a thin rail of support over which they both lean, then fall and roll away from each other. They gather themselves, seated at opposite sides of the space, with their splayed legs forming a wide base at opposing angles. With their arms extended toward each other they drag themselves across the floor, gradually locomoting together until they meet at center stage where they clasp each other's wrists, joining their arms into one large circle. They create a shifting shape that is round on the top and angular on the bottom, with opposing pulls through their bodies. They push against each other to bring this symmetrical shape to standing.[59] The dancers rely on each other even as they struggle.

The ensuing moments of this duet uphold normative sexuality that reinforced postwar whiteness. The woman sits on the floor with the man's head on her lap. On a pelvic impulse, she brings her arms up to a V shape and dips her sternum backward, as his leg extends toward the ceiling. It is a pained, shared ecstasy. The couple appears to achieve simultaneous orgasm, an action cultural theorist Julian Carter identifies as part of early twentieth-century white heterosexual normality

---

57. Michael Kelly Bruce (dancer, choreographer) in discussion with the author, April 21, 2010, Columbus, OH.

58. Anna Kisselgoff, "The Young and Unknown Show What They Can Do," *New York Times*, November 12, 1990, C14, DNB.

59. "Jim May and Lorry May in Anna Sokolow's *Lyric Suite*, http://jwa.org/media/jim-may-and-lorry-may-in-sokolows-lyric-suite. Accessed July 30, 2016.

that reflects control and restraint to form a perfect union.[60] As sex was part of modern marriage, to uphold and reproduce whiteness in the early twentieth century, Carter asserts, simultaneous orgasm guaranteed a eugenically sound next generation.[61] As historian Matthew Frye Jacobson argued, moreover, sexuality and acculturation for Jews and other nonwhite racial groups went hand-in-hand: It "is one site at which all the economic advantages, political privileges, and social benefits inhering in a cultural invention like *Caucasian* converge and reside [original emphasis]."[62] At the end of the duet, the dancers gaze pleasantly into each other's eyes as they exit over runs and small punctuated leaps, connected at the shoulders through their outstretched arms. With different casts, this duet expressed connection or conveyed a pained distance, but retained a normative sexuality that reinforced acculturation. Although Jim and Lorry May united through this duet in a 1994 recording, critic Robert Sabin noted in 1954 that "the tender duet between Eve Beck and Jeff Duncan blended in mood and rhythmic impulse with the Largo Desolato," and critic Jean Battey found Ze'eva Cohen and David Jon Krohn's 1968 performance reinforcing alienation, as "nowhere in the program did she [Sokolow] make us feel the pull of two people in touch with each other."[63] Sokolow challenged heteronormativity by presenting friction and simultaneity in sexual pleasure.

"Adagio apassionato," the women's quartet that constitutes *Lyric Suite*'s final section, disrupts the dance's normativity. The section begins as the dancers perform a series of long leg extensions and torso tilts into bent *arabesque* lines. Toward the end, the dancers circle their legs along the floor and drop their weight into lunging undercurves, moving through sideways triply metered steps with their arms extended to the side. Their palms vulnerably face forward as they change positions in space. Sokolow leaves the ending unresolved as the dancers gradually fade into the darkness, hanging questions on the last screech of the score's strings. Sokolow defined the dance with these women's pain by ending it with them and refusing clean narrative, even if the easy coupling in "Largo desolato" left a lasting impression with critics.

Critical acclaim for this dance, from Horst and other establishment critics, relaunched Sokolow's American popularity after her time abroad and wrote her into a dominant modern dance narrative. Horst praised "the conception and beauty of its choreography,"[64] and Martin emphasized the dance had "the kind of magic that distinguishes a work of art from a journeyman job [. . .it] will stand considerable

---

60. Carter, *Heart of Whiteness*, 98–101 (see Chap. 3, n92).

61. Ibid., 117.

62. Jacobson, *Whiteness of a Different Color*, 3 (see Introduction, n70).

63. Robert Sabin, "Modern Music and Dance, 92nd Street YMHA, Dec. 18," *Musical America*, January 1, 1955, Anna Sokolow Clippings, JRDD, NYPL; and Jean Battey, "Sokolow Works Unrelenting," *Washington Post*, February 17, 1968, Alan M. and Sali Ann Kriegsman Collection, MD, LOC.

64. Louis Horst, "Reviews of the Month: Modern Music, Drama and Dance," *Dance Observer* (February 1955): 25.

re-seeing."[65] Five years after it premiered, Cohen linked *Lyric Suite* to high modernist ideals: "*Lyric Suite* has proved more timeless than anything else, and purest in its six emotional vignettes, ranging from torment to ecstatic love."[66] Comments relating to the work's timelessness connect it to universalism and lack suggestions that its vignettes portray anything dangerous. When *Lyric Suite* and *Rooms* appeared on the same program, critics considered them complements in composition, theme, and movement choices.[67] Whereas *Lyric Suite's* classical lines and understated angst aligned Sokolow with the aesthetic values of high modernism, *Rooms* struck a deeper postwar nerve. In it, subsurface tensions festered.

QUEER SPACES AND THE COLD WAR

Rooms' themes of postwar alienation and isolation manifested Jewishness, blackness, and working-class despair as they surfaced sexuality that flew in the face of 1950s conservatism. The piece's alignment with dance modernism allowed it to defy race, class, or gendered specificity, yet the subject reflected Jewish American culture, the compositional elements relied on jazz, and the structure absorbed queer lives. For many people, *Rooms is* New York.[68] "New York," specifically Sokolow's childhood Lower East Side tenements on which she based the work, is a Jewish space. Although Sokolow built *Rooms* around the Jewish working class in tenement houses, she used the scenario as a metaphor to reflect what Morris notes was a national feeling of unease, and what Rebekah Kowal identified as a reaction to the rapidly expanding built environment.[69] As Jews acculturated into the suburbs and gay people retreated into the closet, the white heteronormative critical establishment likely did not recognize the dance's Jewish roots or the nonconforming sexualities its inhabitants portrayed, and identified alienation in relation to generalized postwar sentiment. Instead of rejecting it as deviant, critics' embrace of *Rooms* as dark but universal accepted working-class leftist, Jewish, and queer spaces into mainstream representation and enabled the dance's inhabitants to define the society that otherwise excluded them. Sokolow embedded *Rooms'* codes within recognizable cultural narratives.

Because Sokolow did not define how spectators should watch this dance, breaking down midcentury dance modernism's embedded white heteronormative

---

65. Martin, "The Dance: High Spots," X6.

66. Cohen, "Anna Sokolow Dance Company, York Playhouse; Dec. 26–Jan. 3," 28.

67. George Beiswanger, "New London: Residues and Reflections," *Dance Observer* (February 1957): 21–23; Selma Jeanne Cohen, "Anna Sokolow Dance Company, York Playhouse; Dec. 26–Jan. 3"; and Louis Horst, "Reviews of the Month: Anna Sokolow and Company, Y.M.-Y.W.H.A. February 24 & 28, 1955," *Dance Observer* (April 1955): 51.

68. Deborah Zall (dancer, teacher) in discussion with the author, June 28, 2010, New York City.

69. Morris, *A Game for Dancers*, 88; and Kowal, *How To Do Things with Dance*, 87, 105–115 (see Introduction, n8).

assumptions enables its universalism to be composed of the elements it appears to refuse. I engage here dance theorist Jane Desmond's model that upsets concert dance's heteronormative assumptions and yields a queer framework that complicates gendered significations beyond a one-to-one relationship of desire.[70] The possibility that homosexuality undergirds *Rooms* struck me as I read the dance from Labanotation score. Ray Cook, whose membership in Sokolow's company during the 1960s gave him kinesthetic insight into the inner workings of her dances, notated many of her works. His scores include written motivational instructions for performing the movement. These kinds of notes in his *Rooms* score of the woman's solo "Escape" suggest queer underpinnings: "Running to your lover. She is so lovely" followed by "Your lover is flying in at the window."[71] In the 1970s, moreover, Sokolow said this soloist "thinks she is Greta Garbo waiting for a lover to come in."[72] This image of Garbo, the iconic actress and lesbian idol who is believed to have had relationships with women as well as with men, suggests the soloist may await a female lover.[73] Cook later insisted "She is so lovely" was a mistake,[74] but this phrasing caused me to rethink how I considered *Rooms*.[75] The more I thought about *Rooms*' vignettes among a consideration of alienation and the Lavender Scare, the more it became clear that *Rooms* enabled gay people and Jews to define the mainstream as social stigmas marginalized them from it.

Focused around eight dancers in eight chairs that represent apartments in a tenement building, *Rooms* presents nine vignettes of loneliness and unfulfilled desire.[76]

70. Jane C. Desmond, "Making the Invisible Visible: Staging Sexualities through Dance," in *Dancing Desires: Choreographing Sexualities On & Off the Stage*, ed. Desmond (Madison: The University of Wisconsin Press, 2001), 11.

71. Anna Sokolow, *Rooms*, notated by Ray Cook, 1967–1975 and 1983 (New York: Dance Notation Bureau, 1980; repr., 2003), 50.

72. Anna Sokolow, quoted in Warren, *Rebellious Spirit*, 150. José Luis Reynoso averred that, because of the lack of a physical lover, the "Escape" soloist could desire a man or a woman. Reynoso, "Some Constitutive Processes in Shifting Feminist Subjectivities: Anna Sokolow in the First Half of the Twentieth Century" (paper presented at "Dance Studies and Global Feminisms," Annual Meeting of Congress on Research in Dance, Hollins University, Roanoke, VA, November 14, 2008).

73. See Rodger Streitmatter, *Outlaw Marriages: The Hidden Histories of Fifteen Extraordinary Same-Sex Couples* (Boston: Beacon Press, 2012), 87–97.

74. Ray Cook in discussion with the author, July 2, 2011, Poughkeepsie, NY.

75. To queerly read *Rooms* I invoke Stacy Wolf's "lesbian" spectatorship in "'Never Gonna Be a Man/Catch Me if You Can/I Won't Grow Up': A Lesbian Account of Mary Martin's Peter Pan," *Theatre Journal* 49, no. 4 (1997): 493–509; and Sara Ahmed, *Queer Phenomenology: Orientations, Objects, Others* (Durham: Duke University Press, 2006).

76. Anna Sokolow, *Rooms*, WNET/New York, directed by Jac Venza and performed by Anna Sokolow Dance Company (1966), SDF; Anna Sokolow, *Rooms*, VHS, performed by Contemporary Dance System (1975), DNBX; Anna Sokolow, *Rooms*, VHS, performed by Juilliard Dance Ensemble (1976–1977), DLI; Anna Sokolow, *Rooms*, performed by José Limón Dance Company, *Anna Sokolow's Rooms: The Centennial Celebration*, presented by José Limón Dance Foundation, Inc., February 9, 2010, Baryshnikov Arts Center, New York City; Reedies Read *Rooms*, performed by Reed College Dance Department, October 28–29 and November 4–5, 2011, Reed College, Portland, OR; *Dancing History: Anna Sokolow's Rooms*,

Sokolow shaped this piece with students at New York's Actors' Studio, where she worked with director Elia Kazan and actor John White (her lover at the time, also known as Johnny Sylvester), premiered it in Mexico City in 1954, and presented it at the 92nd Street Y on February 24, 1955. *Rooms* includes "Alone," "The Dream," "Escape," "Going," "Desire," "Panic," "Daydream," "The End?," and an "Alone" reprise. The dance's casting was tied to performers' expressed gender, and the dancers' perceived genders signify larger themes related to their onstage power. Only in contemporary reconstructions does a woman perform a man's role, for example, because of casting needs. I situate analyses of *Rooms*' solos "Going" and "The End?" that resonate with narratives of closeting, and the explicit portrayal of sexual longing in the sections "Escape," "Desire," and "Panic" within *Rooms*' historical context, to demonstrate how these vignettes embody gender discourse and challenge Cold War rhetoric. The climate of fear implicated gay people in addition to Jews and suspected Communists,[77] and so Sokolow's repositioning of bodies, desire, and alienated angst in *Rooms* defied Cold War surveillance.

Rooms' vignettes present raw, unromantic, painfully sensual portraits of urbanites' psychological isolation. Kenyon Hopkins' experimental jazz score for a five-piece band, at times driving, at times dissonant, reinforces postwar unease and typifies the dance's modernity. In Hopkins's jazz music Sokolow found what she considered truth, as well as echoes of the pace of modernity and the reflection of the metropolis.[78] She used what she saw as irony in the music's syncopations to present the grit, not the glitz, of New York.[79] The movement in *Rooms*, as in many of Sokolow's works, is in dialogue with the musical score, but it does not always match the score's timing beat for beat. The driving overture at the beginning of the dance is halted by the silence of the dancers sitting on their chairs, eerily staring out into the audience. This juxtaposition matched Sokolow's intention. She remembered, "the curtain went up and there was this terrible shock because there the dancers sat, and they sat, and they sat. . . Then people began to realize that this was the first time jazz had been used seriously."[80] The music's dissonance and the

performed by Stanford University Dance Division, February 9, 2012, Stanford University, Stanford, CA; and *Rooms*, notated by Cook.

77. See David K. Johnson, *The Lavender Scare: The Cold War Persecution of Gays and Lesbians in the Federal Government* (Chicago and London: The University of Chicago Press, 2004), John D'Emilio, *Sexual Politics, Sexual Communities: The Making of a Homosexual Minority in the United States, 1940–1970*, 2nd ed. (1983; repr., Chicago: University of Chicago Press, 1998), and Nan Alamilla Boyd, *Wide Open Town: A History of Queer San Francisco to 1965* (Berkeley: University of California Press, 2003); Ellen Schrecker, *The Age of McCarthyism: A Brief History with Documents*, 2nd ed. (Boston: Bedford/St. Martin's, 2002), Halberstam, *The Fifties*, and Haynes Johnson, *The Age of Anxiety: McCarthyism to Terrorism* (Orlando: Harcourt, Inc., 2006).

78. Sokolow, quoted in Battey, "The Dance—Choreographer Works Slippers Off Dancers" (see Chap. 1, n53).

79. Ibid.

80. Sokolow, quoted in "Talking to Dance and Dancers: Anna Sokolow," 19 (see Introduction, n72).

movement's psychological turmoil embody alienation. For Sokolow, the dance "reflects," she said, "the tiny, awful loneliness of people shut up in their rooms in a place like New York."[81] This loneliness presents the vulnerability of people on society's margins.

Rooms' alienation sentiment spoke to the changing US public as the dance reflected tensions under society's affluent surface. Conservatism squelched dissent as the Red Scare progressed and the Cold War stirred anxieties of nuclear attack; racial tensions ensued with 1954 Civil Rights legislation *Brown v. Board of Education*; and returning WWII soldiers silently reconciled battlefield horrors as they acclimated to a conformist workplace and the social pressures of normalcy.[82] As novelist Jonathan Franzen noted about Sloan Wilson's 1955 novel *The Man in the Gray Flannel Suit,* which narrated one man's private postwar psychological vulnerability, the spirit of the 1950s encapsulated "the uneasy conformity, the flight from conflict, the political quietism, the cult of the nuclear family, the embrace of class privileges."[83] As pervasive sentiment cut across class and racial lines, critics embraced *Rooms* as having universal appeal. *Rooms* demonstrated journalist David Halberstam's assertion that alienation "could be just as powerful in a comfortable white-collar existence as it was in a harsh working class one."[84] Whether lonely or simply alone, *Rooms* characterized midcentury New York.

Due to Sokolow's shift in her choreographic process to rely on the Stanislavsky Method to build nonlinear narratives based on character studies for which performers drew on their own lives,[85] her dancers' actual experiences—homosexual and heterosexual—contributed to the work's creation. Sokolow asked questions in rehearsal such as, "How does it feel to be near someone who is not there?" to generate movement material.[86] Thematic movements include dancers sliding the soles of their feet along the floor and digging in their heels, vulnerable staggered leg shapes accompanied by arched backs, and vibrating fingers that convey nervous tension. Abdominal contractions from the Graham lexicon become chasms of sensuous longing. A recurring movement of dancers sliding the soles of their feet along the floor by digging in their heels, with a resilient lurch of the pelvis at the end of each slide, expels sexual discontent with feeling swallowed by a large city. Although they were not credited as such at the time, the dancers' individual experiences became part of the larger work. Later in life Sokolow claimed that the eight dancers

81. Sokolow, quoted in Doris Hering, "My Roots are Here," *Dance Magazine* (June 1955): 36.
82. See Sloan Wilson, *The Man in the Gray Flannel Suit* (1955; repr. New York: Thunder's Mouth Press, 2002); and Michael C. C. Adams, *The Best War Ever: America and World War II* (Baltimore and London: The Johns Hopkins University Press, 1994).
83. Jonathan Franzen, introduction to Wilson, *The Man in the Gray Flannel Suit*, viii.
84. Halberstam, *The Fifties*, 528.
85. Warren, *Rebellious Spirit*, 116, 119–120.
86. Anna Sokolow, quoted in Warren, *Rebellious Spirit*, 119.

represented facets of herself,[87] yet the onstage personalities presented a wider range of knowledge based on what dancers brought to the piece.

By staging queer desire in a closeted society, Sokolow wrote gay people into the Cold War's dominant narrative by exposing the plight of all who drowned in wells of loneliness. *Rooms'* vignettes represent people's fantasies, which differ starkly from their realities outside their apartments.[88] In pre-Stonewall New York, social codes and law enforcement policed gay people's bodies. Gay men and lesbians exchanged public desire in nuanced cues, building sexual tension that they could later commence in private spaces or generating longing that they could not satisfy by themselves. Taken with *Rooms'* "Desire" section, wherein one man's chair turned toward another's quietly denotes homosexual desire, the sapphically cryptic pieces of information in "Escape" reveal implicit gay, lesbian, and nonheteronormative themes in *Rooms*. The dance's inhabitants' discontent stems from sexual dissatisfaction and an inability to connect with other people. The sexuality *Rooms* expresses is of frustrated, unfulfilled yet visceral sex, with many bodies splayed across chairs, in contrast to the simultaneous orgasmic connection of *Lyric Suite*. *Dance Observer* critic George Beiswanger wrote of the sexuality in *Rooms*, in comparison with *Lyric Suite*, "The inhabitants are no longer in the garden of Eden ... for they lust alone. We moderns no longer talk of lechery, but it has not been abolished by naming it sex."[89] As music theorist Nadine Hubbs noted in her study of gay modernist composers whose music defined midcentury American nationalism, "for pre-Stonewall homosexual subjects to defy the dominant culture's paramount message to them—that they should not exist—was the most crucial form of queer social resistance."[90] Queerness is part of, not outside of, the generalized experience that Sokolow portrayed in this dance, as McCarthyism was a significant catalyst for the 1969 Stonewall riots that initiated the gay liberation movement in New York. By creating spaces of absent lovers who may or may not be of the same or opposite gender, *Rooms* is a site of social resistance because its characters exist and are not necessarily marked as queer.

Sokolow subverted contemporary expectations for gendered and sexualized bodies onstage. She was known to date men, but was part of broader coalitions for the gay community as her inclusion of openly gay company members in the 1950s,[91] and the location of her last apartment at One Christopher Street, two blocks down from the Stonewall Inn in the heart of Manhattan's historic gay neighborhood,

87. Warren, *Rebellious Spirit*, 253.

88. Jack Moore, interview by Larry Warren, April 11, 1987, transcript, 3, Larry Warren Collection on Anna Sokolow and Lester Horton, MD, LOC.

89. Beiswanger, "New London: Residues and Reflections," 22.

90. Nadine Hubbs, *The Queer Composition of America's Sound: Gay Modernists, American Music, and National Identity* (Berkeley: University of California Press, 2004), 94.

91. Warren, *Rebellious Spirit*, 158.

attest.[92] Moreover, *Rooms* encompassed a larger upset of normative gender expectations based on Sokolow's life choices and dances that do just that: She never married her romantic partners, and she performed solos, such as *Case History*, *Bullfighter*, and *Kaddish*, wherein she took on the power of men's roles and significations that challenged onstage gender hierarchies. *Rooms'* positioning of its spectator as voyeur, through audience members peering into the private, vulnerable spaces of the characters' apartments, invites a queer reading wherein queer signifies the subversion of gender conventions. I take gender theorist Teresa de Lauretis's tack of "queer" as a marker of critical distance to highlight nonheteronormative women's experience in *Rooms'* vignettes, from women in charge of their own sexuality to making visible lesbian and gay male spaces, and dance theorist Suzanne Juhasz's use of "queer" as a verb that subverts gender conventions.[93] For example, the "Escape" soloist, donning an evening gown with her long hair flowing, is frankly forthright in her intimate cravings. As an empowered subject instead of a passive object, her sexuality overturns gender hierarchies: She is in control of her interaction with her absent lovers instead of allowing them to define her, regardless of the absent lover's gender. Although queer discourses often privilege male experience,[94] and *Rooms'* overt presentation of male homosexual desire versus covert lesbian desire reinforces lesbian invisibility, the centrality of women's experience to Sokolow's dance opens a space for all kinds of female desire wherein invisible queer(ed) women's spaces become visible. Thus *Rooms* presents different queer potentialities: first, a challenge to patriarchal, normative gender and sexuality conventions; and second, representations of gay and lesbian experience against the postwar climate of fear. Through modernist universalism, Sokolow negotiated a way to stay ideologically safe while managing to profoundly disturb her viewers through *Rooms'* upending gendered and modernist conventions.

Rooms' social statements stand out against other postwar choreography, such as that of Alwin Nikolais and Merce Cunningham, gay choreographers who arguably deflected spectators' interests in their personal lives with objective, abstracted choreography that denied fleshy coupling of any kind.[95] Similarly to the composition

92. Sokolow continued this queer solidarity choreographically in *And the Disciples Departed* (1967), a work for Boston's WBZ-TV that accused idle standersby in the rape and murder of bar manager Kitty Genovese outside the apartment she shared with her girlfriend. SDF.

93. Teresa de Lauretis, "Queer Theory: Lesbian and Gay Sexualities—An Introduction," *differences: A Journal of Feminist Cultural Studies* 3, no. 2 (1991): iv, and Suzanne Juhasz, "Queer Swans: Those Fabulous Avians in the *Swan Lakes* of Les Ballets Trockadero and Matthew Bourne," *Dance Chronicle* 31, no. 1 (2008): 58–59.

94. See Judith Butler, *Gender Trouble: Feminism and the Subversion of Identity* (1990; repr. New York and London: Routledge, 2006), ibid., *Bodies that Matter* (see Introduction, n15), Desmond, "Making the Invisible Visible," 3–32, George Chauncey, *Gay New York: Gender, Urban Culture, and the Making of the Gay Male World 1890–1940* (New York: BasicBooks, 1994), Lisa Duggan, *Sapphic Slashers: Sex, Violence, and American Modernity* (Durham: Duke University Press, 2000), and de Lauretis, "Queer Theory," iii–xviii.

95. See Susan Leigh Foster, "Closets Full of Dances: Modern Dance's Performance of Masculinity and Sexuality," in *Dancing Desires*, ed. Desmond, 147–207, Manning, *Modern*

of Nikolais's and Cunningham's companies, Sokolow employed dancers who were highly trained, mostly in the Graham technique she taught coupled with elements of the Stanislavsky Method. Dissimilarly to Nikolais's and Cunningham's choreography, Sokolow drew *Rooms'* movements from quotidian gestures and behaviors. This artistic choice cemented the dance in a gritty present that Kowal points to as something that makes Sokolow's "ordinary" actions extraordinary through the realistic struggles they convey instead of epic archetypes.[96] As Sokolow challenged modern dance conventions in *Rooms*, reading *Rooms* queerly pushes against the grain not only of the work's presumed heteronormativity, but also against the hegemony of universality in postwar modern dance.[97]

Even though *Rooms* put forth a spectrum of sexual desire that was otherwise marginalized, critics' laudations after the US premiere suggest they supported its cry against an oppressive society in which repressed desire was an unmentionable part. Critics spoke in generalized terms about the dance's theme of sexual loneliness and its overall darkness. In *Dance Observer*, Beiswanger described the work as a contemporary hell, and in the *New York Times* Martin asserted that *Rooms'* "ultimate aim seems to be to induce you to jump as inconspicuously as possible into the nearest river," yet Hering noted in *Dance Magazine* that "underlying its bleakest moments is the current of human generosity."[98] Sokolow portrayed a dismal experience, but the piece retains elements of agency. Assessing the critics' reaction at the premiere, Morris connects this public embrace of *Rooms* with the dance's understood universality: "Audiences perceived in its alienation an essential element of modernity. As such, *Rooms* proved to be one of the rare instances in the 1950s when a dance of devastating critique was acknowledged as successful, even if its full implications were deflected."[99] One of these averted implications is that *Rooms* veiled individual identities within the climate of fear.

Rooms' inhabitants' anxiety embodies the Lavender Scare, which began in 1947 in what historian David K. Johnson defined as a systematic firing of suspected homosexuals from the State Department and subsequent witch hunt of gay men and lesbians inside Washington, DC—all done in the name of national security. Similar to Jews with assumed or documented Communist pasts, gay people became scapegoats through the rhetoric of mapping Communism through their bodies. The Lavender Scare's discourse was that gay people were

---

Dance, Negro Dance, and Rebekah Kowal, "Being Motion: Alwin Nikolais' Queer Objectivity," in *The Returns of Alwin Nikolais: Bodies, Boundaries, and the Dance Canon*, ed. Claudia Gitelman and Randy Martin (Middletown, CT: Wesleyan University Press, 2007), 82–106.

96. Kowal, *How To Do Things with Dance*, 86–87.

97. Thank you to Clare Croft for helping me articulate this idea.

98. Beiswanger, "New London: Residues and Reflections," 21, John Martin, "Dance: Study in Despair," *New York Times*, May 17, 1955, 26, Anna Sokolow Clippings, JRDD, NYPL, and Doris Hering, "An Evening of Dance Works by Anna Sokolow: 92nd Street 'Y' February 24 and 28, 1955," *Dance Magazine* (April 1955): 75.

99. Morris, *A Game for Dancers*, 105.

morally and ideologically weak and penetrable and posed the risk of leaking state secrets, and thus, as Johnson notes, they "needed to be systematically removed from the federal government."[100] Government hearings pitted gay men and lesbians against one another with pressure to name names in proceedings that mirrored hearings of suspected Communists. Gay people were no safer within the gay community than in mainstream society.[101] Historian John D'Emilio avers the conspiracy associated with gays and lesbians stems from the fear that because homosexuality is not necessarily marked on the body, gays and lesbians could invisibly infiltrate public institutions; within the discourse, no one was safe from gay people's stealthy, morally weak, highly sexualized bodies. Since the 1948 Kinsey Report noted that a large percentage of American men were likely homosexual, and a large percentage of government workers fired in the 1950s on moral grounds were assumed homosexual, the penetrable homosexual body vulnerable to the Communist threat could contaminate society.[102] In *Rooms*, men and women are equally vulnerable, an emotional state that opposed a Cold War policy of impenetrability.[103]

The voyeurism embedded in *Rooms* reproduces this government surveillance and anxiety within the space of the performance.[104] *Rooms'* solos "Going" (the fourth vignette) and "The End?" (the penultimate section) present ostracized individuals pressured to the end of their wits. Many gay people killed themselves during the Lavender Scare, when more homosexuals than Communists lost their government jobs.[105] The quiet suffering of gay men and lesbians closeted during the 1950s suffocating climate of fear resonates in the feelings of isolated individuals Sokolow evoked with these solos. Through the midcentury dance universality of this work, these characters' onstage fears reflect everyone's anxieties. Thinking about Cold War gay suicides through dance instead of empirical evidence or historical anecdote allows for kinesthetic empathy with the honest bodies onstage that implicates viewers in these characters' social and physical suicides. By distressing audiences to rethink their own place in society, *Rooms* continued Sokolow's quest to enact social change through dance.

In "Going," a man fights—and loses to—a society in which he can never relax. He moves as if he does not have enough air to breathe. Jack Moore remembered that Sokolow coached him to perform the role as a prize fighter who could not win against the world.[106] In 1955 critic Walter Terry asserted the need for escapism when he wrote in the *New York Herald Tribune* that the dancer "soon becomes 'real gone' as

100. Johnson, *Lavender Scare*, 9.
101. Ibid., 147–163.
102. D'Emilio, *Sexual Politics, Sexual Communities*, 40–53.
103. See Croft, *Dancers as Diplomats*, 118.
104. I thank Takiyah Nur Amin for this observation.
105. Johnson, *Lavender Scare*, 158–160.
106. Moore, interview, 3.

Figure 4.1: Jack Moore in "Going" from *Rooms*, 1966. Photo by Edward Effron. Larry Warren Collection on Anna Sokolow and Lester Horton, Box 1, Music Division, Library of Congress, Washington, DC.

he submits to hypnotic, self-mesmerizing rhythms of jazz."[107] Here, the music's syncopations represent restless unease. Cook's motivational notes in the Labanotation score assert, "The more gone he is, the sadder it is."[108] The music, which until this section consisted of a lonely trumpet against pounding drums of varying intensity, shifts to an orchestration reminiscent of big band swing with a quickly syncopating snare drum. The dancer retains a nervous resiliency in his joints and defiantly claps his hands as if to snap us all out of his nightmare. He perches, twitters uneasily, quickly crosses and uncrosses his legs, twists his ankles and knees along jagged pathways performing the "shorty George," and boxes an invisible opponent. After briefly partnering the chair, he walks forward, crouched over, and snaps his fingers on the downbeat similarly to the opening of Robbins's *West Side Story*. He cantilevers his body forward, swiftly kicks his legs alternately behind his body, and rhythmically squeezes his palms open and closed (Figure 4.1). He slides across the floor, seeking places to hide. He is cornered; he never relaxes. He is alone in his room or hiding in an alley. Is he plotting something? Do his movements reveal feelings that belie his normative baseball jacket? Even at the end, when he sits on the floor and drops his arms more in exhaustion than relief, he remains tense.[109] The character's need to "become gone"

107. Walter Terry, "American Dance," *New York Herald Tribune*, May 16, 1955, n.p., Lester Sweyd Collection, Anna Sokolow Clippings, JRDD, NYPL.

108. *Rooms*, notated by Cook, 66.

109. In February 2012, Nia-Amina Minor performed "Going" in a Stanford University performance of *Rooms* staged by Lorry May. May chose Minor for the vignette because she had the

and lose himself in the privacy of his apartment through music, drugs, or alcohol displays his buckling under social pressures.

With similar feelings of desperation, in "The End?" a woman on the rooftop is driven to suicide with abrupt, aggressive, and self-destructive movement. Her vibratory fingers evoke the senseless chatter of a world closing in on her. She pulls and tears at her own face, chokes herself, thrusts her torso forward and back, and blindly throws herself forward over her chair. In the stark musical score a snare drum rasps sharply, but intermittently, and a trumpet screams, scolding yet foreshadowing. The soloist's pain manifests in deep dips of her head backward that expose the vulnerable angles of her neck. In a moment of silence, the dancer reaches skyward before falling in a heap on the ground with a sickening empty thud—twice. The last moment is eerily tranquil: The dancer, having gingerly climbed up onto the chair as if on a ledge, serenely moves her arms up and down, navigating an otherworldly ether. This upsetting but oddly peaceful image makes this woman's suffering visible while engaging the audience as witnesses to her death (Figure 4.2).

The heart of *Rooms* beats in the fierce longing of rhythmic heel slides in the central section "Desire," with unanswered, aching twists through the spine extending arms grappling for someone to love them and heads dropped so far backward that the people seem absent from their own agony (Figure 4.3). In this vignette's explicit sexual desperation—"God damn it, why doesn't someone make love to me?" a motivational note in the Labanotation score cries—a mix of gendered couplings and overt sexual displays disrupts postwar dominant narratives of love and kinship.[110] In *Rooms*, women desire as much as men; both are lonely, and neither seem particularly available. "Desire" features three men and three women seated in facing rows of chairs sharply angled through the middle of the stage. They perform myriad presentations of overt, masturbatory sexual cravings. 1950s discourses of normative sexuality dictated gender roles for women to be driven by their emotions, dependent on men, and sexually available but not sexually aggressive, and for men to be rational and emotionally aloof, which displayed social strength.[111] "Desire" portrays just the opposite. Through full-body pleadings and pulsing leg gestures that originate in the groin and desperately dig the heel into the floor, all with a gaze that is more self-deprecating than aggressively sexual, Sokolow staged raw, unromantic sexuality during an era that tempered women's public presentation of sensuality.

---

requisite technical abilities. The solo still appeared queer. Minor blended seamlessly into the role, yet her use of strong weight, syncopated urgency, and her ability to take up a lot of space, paired with the baseball jacket, appeared masculine in contrast to her biologically presenting woman-ness. When I spoke to Minor backstage, she was surprised to learn that a man traditionally performed the solo; that detail did not surface when she learned it. She, it seemed, embodied "Going" as an early twenty-first-century woman influenced by second-wave feminism and post-feminism's "girl power." Or she assimilated movement made for someone else into her body in a short rehearsal period, disconnected from its historical significance.

110. *Rooms*, notated by Cook, 84.
111. Kowal, "Being Motion," 98.

Figure 4.2: Ze'eva Cohen in "The End?" from *Rooms*. Photo by Mula Eshet. Courtesy of Ze'eva Cohen.

Figure 4.3: "Desire" section of *Rooms* (choreographed by Anna Sokolow, Lyric Theatre premiere, 1963). Photographer unknown. From the Collection of the Israeli Dance Archive at the Beit Ariela Library, Tel-Aviv. Dancers: Moshe Romano, Avraham Tzuri, Yanun Neeman, Dahlia Harlap, Liora Hackmey, and Ze'eva Cohen.

Sokolow reorganized gendered modern dance conventions beyond her upending of the sexual longing people could express onstage. "Desire" counters theatrical heterosexual coupling in Martha Graham's and José Limón's mythically abstract archetypal narratives that covered over queer subjectivities.[112] By fitting dancers into clearly delineated heterosexual romantic roles, Graham's and Limón's dances portrayed a heteronormative status quo even if the dancers performing these roles were gay. With its raw desire and its portrayal of, according to Kowal, "typical people in recognizable situations," *Rooms* contrasts Graham's and Limón's chaste, abstracted epic choreographies.[113] Offering an alternative to heteronormative mythic narrative, *Rooms* upset midcentury modernism beyond its nonconforming sexuality. It featured nonsequential vignettes built on character studies instead of an archetypal chronology, movements built from everyday postures and gestures instead of an abstracted movement vocabulary, and a portrayal of the people next door instead of a satisfying and exotic mythic journey. *Rooms'* characters, as well as the audience, want an escape.

"Desire" highlights queer, more than normative, yearning. This begins, but does not end, with the facing of the man in the middle toward the downstage man instead of the woman opposite him to imply homosexual longing.[114] His craving sets the tone for the section: With a piercing gaze at the downstage man, he first slides his heels in silence and the others join when the music begins. Although, according to Ze'eva Cohen, who performed *Rooms* during the 1960s, Sokolow never discussed this moment of homosexual desire with the cast, it seems to be an open secret among dancers who know this work.[115] A handful of gay men I have encountered who performed *Rooms* under Sokolow's direction report being cast in this role. Whether these men's experiences reflect a necessity for blurring the boundaries between art and life for a gay man to perform this role or whether it is coincidence remains unclear. Regardless of Sokolow's intent or the rehearsal room culture, this moment invites queer spectatorship by explicitly staging homosexual desire, as opposed to the implicit homosexuality in the dance's other vignettes.

Additional gay-coded movements in "Desire" disrupt heteronormative assumptions more deeply than the man with the turned chair. As the dancers lie supine in heterosexual pairs, two women end up next to each other. The performers blindly reach for each other in space, sensuously undulate as they rise and return to the floor, and hug their knees in vulnerable frustration. Failing contact, they rock back and forth, cupping their bodies in long contractions. The most upstage woman couples, pausing, with the woman of the middle pair who also swings with the man to her downstage side. Although this moment could be interpreted as lonely people experiencing universal longing, the significance of the gendered casting of

112. See Manning, *Modern Dance, Negro Dance*, 183–184.
113. Kowal, *How To Do Things with Dance*, 116.
114. Kowal, *How To Do Things with Dance*, 108, and Reynoso, "Constitutive Processes."
115. Ze'eva Cohen in telephone conversation with the author, February 5, 2012.

this dances' roles, the silence of these two women connecting, and the fact that a viewer could miss this brief moment amid the activity, renders this lesbian desire barely visible. When the dancers reprise the heel slides, all but the original "gay" man pause, foregrounding his yearning against the rest.

Even though the spectator observes people in their apartments, these people look inward on themselves and prevent a pleasurable return of the voyeuristic gaze. Critic Clive Barnes noted as much when he wrote in 1967, "The voyeur's eye view that Miss Sokolow offers us is not elevating but is salutary. No one could ever enjoy 'Rooms,' but they might be all the better for being horrified by it."[116] This looking produces a subjectivity for *Rooms'* inhabitants in which they expose, yet deflect the gaze of, their vulnerability. In the harrowing final image of "Desire," the dancers stand on their chairs with hollowed-out chests, hunched shoulders, limbs succumbing to gravity, and bodies rotating as if swaying in a gentle breeze. They appear to have hanged themselves to escape their pained and unquenchable needs. This shared fate envelops the dancers' differentiated desires into similar marginalization.

This "Desire" section on which the full work pivots destabilizes the heteronormativity of postwar alienation instead of reinforcing it. To wit, an absent lover does not have to be assumed to be of opposite gender to the desirer. In questioning a causal relationship between gender and sexuality in terms of identification and desire, Judith Butler asserted, "The heterosexual logic that requires that identification and desire be mutually exclusive is one of the most reductive of heterosexism's psychological instruments: if one identifies *as* a given gender, one must desire a different gender [original emphasis]."[117] The universality associated with *Rooms* manifests Butler's assertion. With the exception of the man in the turned chair, the dancers are assumed to desire members of the opposite gender, because their lovers are absent. Spectators have traditionally considered this man gay because the man he reaches toward is present to confirm his yearning. Yet an absent lover can denote queer desire. Dance theorist Valerie Briginshaw argues that because dances with lesbian content exist outside heterosexual binary assumptions of self and other, a space created by an absent lover is a reciprocal partner in the desire that renders this desire productive instead of a lack.[118] She asserts: "space, desire and bodies need to be rethought as reciprocally productive, that is they continually produce and are produced by each other."[119] This productivity supports Terry's 1955 assertion that *Rooms* is about aloneness (a filling of the space) instead of loneliness (a spatial lack). He described *Rooms'* sections as "examples of aloneness," so that not all who are alone are necessarily lonely.[120]

116. Clive Barnes, "Dance: Sokolow 'Rooms,'" *New York Times*, September 8, 1967, n.p., Alan M. and Sali Ann Kriegsman Collection, MD, LOC.

117. Butler, *Bodies That Matter*, 239.

118. Valerie A. Briginshaw, *Dance, Space and Subjectivity* (Hampshire and New York: Palgrave, 2001), 77–78.

119. Briginshaw, *Dance, Space and Subjectivity*, 78.

120. Terry, "American Dance."

The solos "Escape" and "Panic" reframe heteronormative expectations about desire through ambiguous or absent lovers. Both feature one chair set apart from four. The empty chairs of "Escape" offer space for queer reception through their coproduction of desire, whereas the defined presence of the people in "Panic" suggest many relationships. Whereas in "Escape" the empty chairs hold what is in the dancer's imagination, in "Panic" four people fill the chairs, each staring placidly into space. In "Escape" the single chair is the space of reality and the four chairs are fantasy; in "Panic," the single chair offers solace and the four chairs present inescapable reality. In "Escape," the woman's illusion, or the reality that she cannot have it, disappoints her; in "Panic," a world full of people with whom the man cannot communicate chokes his fantasies.

As "Desire" portrays gay men's yearning, "Escape" facilitates lesbian desire. A queer reading of "Escape" upsets the assumption that a woman desires a man unless she engages with a woman. Performers associated with "Escape" have assumed otherwise, and the solo retains its heteronormativity in the way coaches pass it down. Many pieces of evidence report that the "Escape" soloist desires men. The notation score notes her interest in men, and Cohen remembered that in her performance of the fantasy she was glamorous and desired by many men.[121] In a 2011 coaching session, Suellen Haag took into account the fact that the all-women cast might themselves imagine variously gendered lovers, yet it was clear from her coaching that the prescribed gender of the absent lover was male.[122] From Butler's and Briginshaw's assertions, the flexibility for the dancer to imagine any form of lover extends to the spectator.

This woman's performance does not suggest her lover's gender, but what is more subversive about this solo than whom the soloist desires is the power and control that she possesses over her own sensuality. In the opening of a dimly lit scene set by a melodic exchange between piano and trumpet, the "Escape" performer passionately runs among a handful of empty chairs and visits an imaginary lover in each one. Losing herself in her fantasy, she grabs hold of her skirt as if tearing off her dress and pulsates her hips while her fingers rain down her sides. As Cohen recalled, she is loved in the way that she wants to be loved and desired in the way that she wants to be desired.[123] Briginshaw notes in lesbian-defined concert dance spaces, women as both subject and object control the voyeuristic gaze.[124] This solo's raw moments of pleasure and pain, paired with a sexually empowered woman with her unidentified lover, create a queer space of sexual strength. Seeking a warm body to quench her desire, the woman approaches an empty chair from behind; with a turning flourish she satisfyingly flops into it as she broadly fans one leg open and lands her wide-flung

121. Cohen, conversation, February 5, 2012.
122. Haag coached my Reed College students in "Escape" and "The End?," which they staged from Labanotation score.
123. Cohen, conversation, February 5, 2012.
124. Briginshaw, *Dance, Space and Subjectivity*, 92–94.

heel with a heavy thud. Digging the ball of her foot into the floor with repetitive friction that resonates in a rocking motion deep within her pelvis, she emits palpable sexual tension in a moment of rapture. In the solo's climax, the performer creates a bed by rearranging two chairs to face each other, where she shares a rocking embrace with the chair's invisible inhabitant. Supine, she traces wide arcs with an extended bare leg as her dress falls open, losing herself in fulfilling intimacy before she realizes that she is alone, and she thrusts the chairs aside. The soloist cannot sustain her fantasy of freely loving and being loved in return. Lacking the satisfaction of fleshy comfort with a tangible lover, the woman leaves her fantasy and returns to grip the back of a single chair, where she stands staring into empty space, as if into a mirror or out a window onto the stifling street. The woman's disillusionment when she faces reality may be of a lover scorned, and it may also reflect her resentment of not being able to have such a relationship, with another woman, in public.

Unlike the empowered spaces and absent lovers of "Escape," the people in "Panic" define the space with their presence. The movement and soundscore for this section are stark and desperate. In his personal hell, the "Panic" soloist runs frantically among the people in the chairs, at once afraid that they will see him and frustrated that they do not. He takes solace in his set-apart chair, onto which he grasps as he kicks his legs like an ensnared rodent, before hiding his face behind his hands. Who are these people, and why does the soloist feel trapped? Are they lovers, friends, a wife or family who would not understand? After the soloist spins in painfully tiny circles, falling and repeatedly banging his head against the floor, the people in the chairs leave one by one. This deep-seated panic has dire consequences. Literally alone onstage at the end of the section, the soloist covers his face in anguish. Did his honesty drive everyone he loved away? Or did they refuse to see him for who he really is? With labored breathing, he bolts across the stage and grabs onto an empty chair, which previously held the man who was the last to leave. The lingering of this now-absent man suggests that he was the most significant person for the "Panic" soloist; he takes on the role of the desired man in "Desire." Was he a closeted lover? His new absence suggests that he slipped through the soloist's fingers. The soloist's desperate grabs for the empty chair vacated by a physical (instead of imaginary) man suggest that perhaps his panic is not just the pressure of postwar unease, but is also the fear of being outed, of losing the ones he loves, or the pain of being unable to honestly converse with the people around him.

Quite possibly, the people in *Rooms* and especially the soloist in "Panic" no longer felt welcome within their own community. The tangible fear in "Panic" reflected resulting behavior from the Lavender Scare's queer surveillance. Stigmatized public presence of homosexuals as sexual perverts featured prominently in newspaper articles during this time, and writers coded the language in these discussions for 1950s readers.[125] This environment catalyzed the homophile movement, which,

125. Johnson, *Lavender Scare*, 5–7.

as precursor to the gay liberation movement, worked to combat discrimination against gays and lesbians.[126] Groups like the Mattachine Society and the Daughters of Bilitis formed with the goals of creating a sense of gay pride within a national subculture. By bringing gay activism into the public sphere, these groups upset the divide between the underground (and subject to frequent police raids) spaces of gay subculture in bars, drag clubs, and private parties, and the homophobic mainstream. Mid-1950s tensions increased between the young activist movement and the long-standing gay bar culture, as the homophile groups further aligned themselves with mainstream US values by insisting their members dress and act like members of the heteronormative white middle class.[127] The shifting spaces of this gay community, with assimilationist actions necessary for political change that further marginalized nonconforming gender expression, paired with homophobic and racist rhetoric, intensified social pressures for those people, as in *Rooms*, who felt doubly alienated.

These anxieties came to a head in "Panic," where Sokolow reproduced the frenzied, irrational-feeling fear of being caught. For Beiswanger, "Panic" is unbearable. He exclaimed in 1957, "Dante perceived no hell, as *Rooms* does, in 'Panic,' the bottomless pit of total insecurity and its terror into which the 'untouchable' are callously thrust. Dante envisioned the love-lost but not the unloved."[128] *Rooms*' queer spaces surface in Beiswanger's review. Jews and gay people were among the US's "untouchables" in the 1950s, and significantly, many men who performed this solo, including Alvin Ailey, Jeff Duncan, and Paul Sanasardo, were gay. The social undercurrent generated by the homophile movement's work to cultivate a national subculture, along with and by means of Sokolow's choreographic practice of drawing from the dancers' own experiences to create their characters, entered *Rooms*. "Panic" thus lives up to its name.

In challenging Cold War social hierarchies, *Rooms* revealed the insecurity of living under tight social and government surveillance wherein nonnormative actions and associations had dire consequences. Juhasz has noted about British choreographer Matthew Bourne's 1995 queer reenvisioning of *Swan Lake*, wherein the swan *corps* of men function as a metaphor for a yearning to feel safe within one's identity, "[that] the viewer is compelled to struggle over the real/not real issue clearly mimics the situation of queer spaces in everyday life."[129] Bourne's swans provide an imaginary haven with dangerous real-world implications that end in the protagonist's death; similarly, the socially constructed closet of queer life offers a kind of security by masking queer identity and actions from those outside the queer community. Amid widespread anti-Semitism, this closeting resonated as whiteness for assimilated Jews. *Rooms* presented imagery combining reality and fantasy, and

---

126. D'Emilio, *Sexual Politics, Sexual Communities*, 2–3.
127. Boyd, *Wide Open Town*, 179.
128. Beiswanger, "New London: Residues and Reflections," 22.
129. Juhasz, "Queer Swans," 71.

outwardly manifesting characters' inner fears. There is not one way to perform any of Sokolow's dances in terms of motivation. Ze'eva Cohen imagined men in the "Escape" chairs, but another dancer could imagine women. Similarly, not all dancers who performed "Panic" were gay. The perceived universalism in the movement enabled audience members who were not alienated by the work to imagine themselves in it, whether they felt the clammy fear of "Panic" or awaited their "Escape" woman to come home. *Rooms'* spaces spited the red and lavender fear mongering by enveloping the Cold War's "untouchables" into a universalized experience. As *Rooms* embodied Cold War sentiments with movement that was explicit but nevertheless about itself, so too did *Rooms'* queer outsiders define the mainstream.

Eight months after *Rooms'* New York premiere, Sokolow tasted the consequences of surveillance. On November 1, 1955, two FBI agents interviewed her at her apartment. They pumped her for information about the organizations she supported in the 1930s–1940s, most of which, like the Joint Anti-Fascist Refugee Committee, the Negro Cultural Committee, the American League for Peace and Democracy, the Theatre Arts Committee, and the School of Jewish Studies, were what the FBI called "pursuant to Executive Order 10450," which means the US government identified them as Communist and a national security threat.[130] The agents interrogated Sokolow about her membership in the Jewish People's Fraternal Order and her involvement in Communist Party pageants, to which Sokolow responded that she took the work because she was an artist and needed to make a living. The agent reported to the FBI that Sokolow said she was an American patriot and would support the United States in the event of war with the Soviet Union, but she refused to disclose Communist Party members' names on principle of not outing friends. Sokolow expressed that she found it prudent to sever Communist ties in 1949 so that they would not impede her career. The agent seemed satisfied that Sokolow did not pose a threat to national security and recommended that the FBI close Sokolow's case. The FBI reopened and reclosed Sokolow's case, and reissued and refiled her Communist Index Card, many times between 1955 and 1968, mostly because of new reports of her 1930s–1940s activities and her subscription to *Jewish Life*, a progressive magazine published by the *Freiheit* corporation.[131] In the following years, the dancers in Sokolow's *Opus* series portrayed jaded teenagers. They could just as easily have been a mass of angry Sokolows flipping off the FBI.

JAZZ, REBELLION, AND AMERICAN COUNTERCULTURE

Sokolow's social commentary in the *Opus* series is as biting as the pithiest of political cartoons. She incorporated Teo Macero's jazz scores as an embodiment of youth

130. http://www.archives.gov/federal-register/codification/executive-order/10450.html. Accessed September 15, 2015.
131. FOIPA No. 1138496-000.

unrest and countercultural rebellion. These dances, *Session for Six* (1958), *Opus '58* (1958), *Opus Jazz 1958* (1958), *Session for Eight* (1959), *Opus '60* (1960), *Opus '62* (1962), *Opus '63* (1963), and *Opus '65* (1965), contain similar movement and thematic material with slight variations. Based on videos, reviews, photographs, and Labanotation scores of versions of these dances, the movement features resiliently weighted accents, snippets from popular social dance, melodramatic dropping of body parts onto the floor, and gut urgency similar to the "Cool" episode from Robbins's *West Side Story* (1957).[132] *Opus* launched Sokolow's popularity as the voice of first the beatnik, then the hippie, counterculture. In the late 1960s, Sokolow's jazz-as-counterculture took the shape of protests against the war in Vietnam, in her *Time+* series, and in her choreography for the musical *Hair* beginning in 1966. She did not subscribe to her own generation's Americana, and instead made dances that epitomized postwar youth counterculture. Her 1930s proletarian and antiwar statements gelled with similar countercultural sentiments of the 1950s–1960s, as young adults became disillusioned with postwar affluence. By giving the American counterculture voice, Sokolow reinforced her own acculturation into US society.

Sokolow's *Opus* works feature twisting, bopping teenagers over a more sinister countercultural critique of a "social manifesto," as Barnes observed in 1969.[133] A program note accompanying an Israeli performance of *Opus Jazz 1958* explained, "this work seeks to express the undercurrents and the tensions, the rhythms and tempos, the agonies and the aspirations of today's people, as sung by the composer in his haunting jazz melodies."[134] As a lyric theater work, Sokolow stripped the dance of external theatrical elements. With the exception of a teased wig in *Opus '63* and *'65*, the costumes consisted of leotards, tights, and t-shirts, and the stage was bare; in some productions, Sokolow removed the proscenium's drapery and the dancers performed against the theater's brick wall.[135] Macero's scores feature rumbling drums underneath crying horns; there are reverberations and pauses, slow builds and trembles with clashing punctuations. Saxophones and trumpets alternate between playing off one another in unpredictable syncopation followed by tighter chords. Sometimes the trumpet screams; at points the metallic clashing sounds like pots and pans dropping onto and rolling across the floor.

132. Anna Sokolow, *Opus '63*, performed by Juilliard Dance Ensemble (1963), Larry Warren Collection on Anna Sokolow and Lester Horton, MD, LOC; Anna Sokolow, *Session for Six*, performed by Juilliard Dance Ensemble (1964), JRDD, NYPL; *Opus '65* on *USA: Dance: Robert Joffrey Ballet*, directed by Karl Genus, National Educational Television, 1965, DLI; and *Opus '63*, notated by Ray Cook and Martha Clarke, n.d., unchecked work-in-progress copy, DNBX.

133. Clive Barnes, "The Dance: 'Opus '65,'" *New York Times*, March 2, 1969, Larry Warren Collection on Anna Sokolow and Lester Horton, MD, LOC.

134. Program, *Suite for Violin, Clarinet and Piano, Opus Jazz 1958, and L'histoire du Soldat*, Programs folder, Anna Sokolow's Lyric Theatre Collection, DLI.

135. Ralph Hicklin, "Joffrey Ballet is Stunning in Anna Sokolow's terrifying 'Opus '65,'" *Globe and Mail*, February 23, 1967, Larry Warren Collection on Anna Sokolow and Lester Horton, MD, LOC.

One section of this series features a wriggling clump of four men and one woman (in the teased wig), who, in a desire for some kind of entertainment and intimacy, wind up collapsing. The dancers break out into the Twist, wringing as many body parts as they can against as many others as possible in the time allotted, punctuating this frenzy with short pops of jitterbug. They mangle into a tight clump, where one man lasciviously grabs the woman's buttocks, another her ankles, and they hoist her skyward; she ends up horizontal in the air and the men are in a line, holding her up. She contracts her body through a pleading that brings her up to sitting, perched on their hands, with one man supporting her seat and another under her flexed ankles. She takes a large, exaggerated full-body yawn before luxuriating backward over the men's supporting hands. The men toss her skyward three times before she slides off their grips and down one of the men's turned backs, feet first onto the floor. She falls backward into the line of men, causing a slow-motion domino effect. They collapse in a pile with the woman on top. While her movement of shaking her head back and forth is most prominent, they all shake and rotate what they can under the strain of the pile. The weight of their adolescent ennui is too much for them.

As in *Rooms*, the jazz music functions as a vehicle for the dance to become an unsung spokesman of the times. It fashions depth, grit, and foreshadowing something undefined yet urgent, impending, and dark. To this end, Hering noted, "The exuberance of young people often has a faint undertone of uneasiness."[136] The dancers temper this uneasiness beneath their "mask of the cool," tamping this nervous energy underneath adolescent composure.[137] Quick, steadily held changes in focus punctuate small, inconsequential movements throughout the dance's four sections. Dancers throw their upper bodies around while their feet skitter out complex series of syncopated beats. They walk on their hams; they lie on their bellies and stare at the audience (Figure 4.4). Sections of emotional, weighty seriousness in the movement and music interrupt carefree moments. One dancer offers her hand to another, as if to say, "Gimme some skin."[138] Transitions between sections are nonexistent or consist simply of purposefully walking offstage or to a new spot onstage. In heterosexual pairings, dancers intricately entwine and manipulate their bodies with and against one another into angular shapes and sudden drops and torques. Although there are moments of emotional lightness, a descending cloud of doom overshadows this piece. In some iterations, the dancers yell expletives at audience members and tell them to fuck off[139] and then "jump into the figurative equivalent

---

136. Doris Hering, "Juilliard Dance Ensemble, Juilliard Concert Hall, April 14, 1964," *Dance Magazine* (June 1964): 33.

137. See Dixon Gottschild, *Digging*, 16–17.

138. Labanotation excerpt from Opening Section of *Session for Six*, in *Elementary Reading Studies*, collected and edited by Peggy Hackney, Sarah Manno, and Muriel Topaz (New York: The Dance Notation Bureau, 1970), Lesson IX, 12.

139. John Giffin (dancer, choreographer), in discussion with the author, April 20, 2010, Columbus, OH.

Figure 4.4: Lyric Theatre (Israel) in rehearsal for *Opus '63*. Photograph by Zvi Glaser. Courtesy of Ze'eva Cohen. Dancers, left to right: Johanna Peled, Galia Gat, Yanun Neeman, Rina Schenfeld, Moshe Romano, Ze'eva Cohen, Leora Hackmey, Ehud Ben David, Rina Shacham, and Avraham Tzuri.

of an abyss—the orchestra pit."[140] In *Opus*, the younger generation's soothsayers purvey the only warnings the older generations will get.

The similarities of Sokolow's *Opus* series to Robbins's choreography in *West Side Story* and *New York Export Opus Jazz* (1958) show the choreographers' reciprocal artistic influences as they lay bare government-level inequities. *Opus* was perhaps the most difficult for Sokolow regarding her relationship with Robbins and her struggles with the US State Department. In 1958, the ANTA Dance Panel chose Robbins's company Ballets: USA and *NY Export* to tour Europe, instead of Sokolow.[141] The Dance Panel refused to present Sokolow despite Robbins's glowing letter of recommendation.[142] Sokolow's acculturation at home was not enough to send her abroad. In March 1958, the Dance Panel deemed Sokolow's work unfit to be presented abroad because it "would escape foreign audiences."[143] By 1958,

---

140. Anna Kisselgoff, "'Opus '65,' a Dance to the Loss of Innocence," *New York Times*, October 8, 1976, Alan M. and Sali Ann Kriegsman Collection, MD, LOC.

141. Jowitt, *Jerome Robbins*, 296–300.

142. Jerome Robbins to Robert Schnitzer (ANTA), March 5, 1958, Box 530, Folder 2, Jerome Robbins Papers, JRDD, NYPL.

143. ANTA Dance Panel minutes, March 20, 1958, quoted in Croft, *Dancers as Diplomats*, 113. See also Prevots, *Dance for Export*, 62.

audiences in Mexico, Israel, Switzerland, and Canada had warmly received her work for nearly twenty years. In future years, Sokolow successfully toured Europe and was awarded a teaching Fulbright to Japan in 1966. The Ailey and Joffrey companies toured her work in their repertory, and in 1962 Juilliard took her *Session '58* on its South American tour.[144] Although ANTA cited *Rooms* as the impenetrable work,[145] in 1958 Robbins's *NY Export* was nearly identical to Sokolow's *Opus* series that she was then touring. Deborah Jowitt averred that Robbins included an homage to Sokolow in the way the dancers rushed toward the audience and "stopped dead at the edge of the pit, as if some hostile force were emanating from the audience, then backed up slowly, staring" at the beginning of *NY Export* that mirrored *Session '58*.[146] Despite Sokolow's dances' jazz-as-American packaging, their anticapitalist irony and open-endedness did not support State Department priorities.

The details of Sokolow's FBI file had no bearing on ANTA's rejection of her work. The Dance Panel would not have seen Sokolow's file before considering her work, but if the panel recommended Sokolow for presentation, the State Department would have reviewed the file.[147] In the 1950s to early 1960s, Sokolow traveled to Israel under America–Israel Cultural Foundation (AICF) auspices instead of with the State Department. Even though the FBI considered Israel a Communist location, the FBI did not deem the AICF a Communist organization, and so the FBI considered her travels to Israel with the AICF acceptable.[148] As in Mexico in the 1940s, Sokolow could live out her communist values in Israel in a way she could not do in the United States. The State Department did not export Sokolow's dances as examples of American art, but her choreography was American enough to solidify her place in American dance modernism.

144. Martha Hill to Anna Sokolow, June 20, 1962, Box 1, Folder 15, Sokolow, Anna: Correspondence, newsclippings, programs, etc., 1934–1936, 1955–1969, Juillliard.

145. Kowal, *How To Do Things with Dance*, 49.

146. Jowitt, *Jerome Robbins*, 301.

147. I thank Clare Croft for this clarification.

148. Memo to Director, FBI (100-379046) to SAC, New York (100-103377) Re Anna Sokolow SM–C (00: New York), 10/11/61, FOIPA No. 1138496-000.

CHAPTER 5

Modernist Forms in a Jewish State

Under Anna Sokolow's discerning eye, members of Israel's Inbal Yemenite Dance Group perform in a 1954 lecture–demonstration in Tel Aviv for visiting members of the American Fund for Israeli Institutions (AFII), the organization that funded Sokolow's work in Israel. Dressed in dark shorts that hit midthigh, white t-shirts (women) or bare torsos (men), the dancers thrust their fingertips skyward in a movement that drops their heads back into a cascading arc as their bared abdominals reveal their muscular effort and their legs, trained into parallel positions, root themselves into the floor. Figure 5.1 captures Sokolow's influence in Israel: An American Jewish choreographer backed by North American funding retrains dancers in American modern dance during a time when American political influence ascended in Israel.

Sokolow worked in Israel when American dance modernism solidified with transcendent themes portrayed through abstracted movements and codified vocabularies in the shadow of the Second Red Scare. She first went to Tel Aviv in 1953 with the AFII (which became the America–Israel Cultural Foundation, or AICF, in 1956) on the recommendation of Jerome Robbins, to train Inbal (later known as the Inbal Dance Theater) primarily in Martha Graham technique in preparation for international touring under the aegis of American Jewish impresario Sol Hurok. The 1953 trip birthed a fruitful artistic collaboration for Sokolow, a long friendship with Inbal's artistic director Sara Levi-Tanai, and a spiritual connection to Israel. By now Sokolow had gained international recognition as a prominent contemporary choreographer, but she struggled personally with longings for permanence and a sense of place. Her 1950s work with Inbal aligned in time with her US premieres of *Lyric Suite, Rooms,* and *Opus,* and her continued exchanges in Mexico. Her mobility among the three countries furthered revolutionary spectatorship among new postwar alliances. Sokolow presented her own choreography with the collective Bimat Makhol [Stage for Dance] in Tel Aviv in the late 1950s before premiering her Lyric

Figure 5.1: Anna Sokolow leads Inbal Yemenite Dance Group during a 1954 lecture–demonstration in Tel Aviv for an audience including members of the American Fund for Israeli Institutions. Photographer unknown. Courtesy of Inbal Dance Theatre and The Israeli Dance Archive at Beit Ariela, Tel-Aviv.

Theatre in 1962.[1] In 1964, Jewish dance patron Baroness Bethsabée de Rothschild, daughter of French philanthropist Baron Edmond de Rothschild who was a patron of Jewish settlements in late-nineteenth-century Palestine,[2] founded the Batsheva Dance Company as a foothold for Graham in Israel. Offering the year-round contract and living wage that the Lyric Theatre did not, Batsheva effectively closed Lyric Theatre. The AICF supported Sokolow as a guest choreographer with the Batsheva and Bat-Dor Dance Companies after the Lyric Theatre folded. Sokolow's 1950s–1960s presence in Israel and her 1964 eclipse by de Rothschild's targeted funding exemplify Euro–American cultural and political prominence in Israel.

Sokolow's choreography and teaching were integral to the midcentury international circulation of Jewish American influence in Israel. A feeling of Zionism-as-Jewish-nationalism resonated in the United States, as exemplified in the era's Chanukah pageants for Israeli bonds (see Chapter 4). Sokolow's Israeli work was

---

1. Henia Rottenberg, "Anna Sokolow: A Seminal Force in the Development of Theatrical Dance in Israel," *Dance Chronicle* 36 (2013): 44, and Ze'eva Cohen in conversation with the author, New York City, February 11, 2010; and Sorrell, "We Work Toward Freedom," 73 (see Introduction, n89).

2. Warren, *Rebellious Spirit*, 198 (see Preface, n2); and Ben Halpern and Jehuda Reinharz, *Zionism and the Creation of a New Society* (New York: Oxford University Press, 1998), 76–89.

swept up in Cold War currents that privileged American cultural values, new political and military alignments between the Israeli and American governments in the wake of Allied victories over the Axis powers in World War II, and American Jews' excitement to engage with Israel in the wake of the Holocaust. In the 1950s, the United States had the largest Jewish population in the world, and, according to historian S. Ilan Troen, "America replaced Europe as the society against which Israel measured itself and on which, in many ways, it consciously tried to model itself."[3] Many American Jewish Zionist World War II veterans took advantage of the GI Bill's lack of geographic restrictions and went to Hebrew University in Jerusalem,[4] populating Israeli higher education with American students by American government funds. Sokolow's first decade there coincided with this shift in cultural power from European to American influence, which brought a preference for American modern dance over the German expressive dance central to Israeli contemporary dance since the 1920s. The prominent work of the AICF, which has pumped private American and Canadian monies into building arts and cultural institutions in Israel since 1939,[5] exemplified American influence and was instrumental in supporting Sokolow's 1950s–1960s Israeli endeavors. The work of the AICF, along with other American Jewish philanthropic and cultural enterprises, was, as Emily Katz noted, "instrumental...to Israel's emergence on the world stage as a full-fledged nation."[6] As such, Sokolow's work was part of North American efforts to build Israel's cultural infrastructure. This influence was corporeal as well as diplomatic. Sokolow trained Israeli dancers in Graham technique and American choreographic structures that, like all physical practices, shaped their physiques. As these dancers acted in society through the physical values she imbued in them, they brought American physicality into everyday Israeliness. This phenomenon exchanged the permeability of honest bodies onstage into physical culture.

Israel, too, shaped Sokolow. The Israeli form of socialism undergirding institutions like communal agricultural collectives called *kibbutzim* that were established

3. S. Ilan Troen, "The Construction of a Secular Jewish Identity: European and American Influences in Israeli Education," in *Divergent Jewish Cultures*, eds. Moore and Troen, 42 (see Introduction, n69).

4. Deborah Dash Moore, *GI Jews: How World War II Changed a Generation* (Cambridge, MA: Harvard University Press, 2004), 116, 261.

5. Program, *S. Hurok Under the Auspices of the America-Israel Cultural Foundation presents Inbal Dance Theatre of Israel*, Boston Wilbur Theater, February 17, 1958, Coburn Dance Program Collection, MD, LOC; and "Our Impact on Israeli Culture," America-Israel Cultural Foundation, accessed August 17, 2014, http://www.aicf.org/about. Since 1984 the AICF's Shades of Dance Festival has established which Israeli choreographers receive national funding through its choreography competition. Deborah Friedes Galili, "Reframing the Recent Past: Issues of Reconstruction in Israeli Contemporary Dance," in *Dance on Its Own Terms*, eds. Bales and Eliot, 65 (see Introduction, n27). See also Edward A. Norman, "Israel—USA Cultural Links: Spirit of Creation, Cultural Exchanges," magazine of American Fund for Israel Institutions, no date, 60, Inbal 111.4, written items through 1966, DLI.

6. Katz, *Bringing Zion Home*, 6 (see Chap. 4, n31).

in the 1910s, and the development of the modern welfare state, enriched the revolutionary modernism of Sokolow's choreography. As did her 1940s experiences in Mexico, Sokolow's time in Israel provided her a socialist society within which she could form her communist coalitions in a way she could no longer do in New York.[7] The Israeli dancers with whom Sokolow worked, moreover, infused her repertory with what I am calling "*sabra* physicality." The Ashkenazi-influenced cultural term *sabra* refers to a person born or acculturated in Palestine or Israel, considered tough on the outside and sensitive on the inside. Its name comes from the *tzabar*, or *sabra*, plant, a cactus that bears prickly fruit with a sweet center.[8] The *sabra*'s emotional and embodied toughness is based on ideology associated with the New Jew archetype that dates to the early twentieth century.[9] It featured a connected-to-the-land, tough Jew who severed ties with European memories and, with them, stereotypically perceived European Jewish weakness, replacing images of men pale from studying with archetypes of men and women healthily suntanned from tilling *kibbutz* soil. Although New Jew ideology fashioned strong bodies for a sovereign Jewish nation, it covered denial of Jewish suffering and negotiation of ongoing regional conflict under a hardened emotional exterior. *Sabra* physicality combines an assertive way of being with an unapologetically direct yet vulnerable performance presence. It is integral to Sokolow's dances.[10]

In this chapter, I contextualize Jewish nationalist ideologies using Sokolow's work to show how the midcentury relationship between Israel and the United States played out in Sokolow's dances and through the bodies of the Israeli dancers she trained. I argue that in the midst of the AFII/AICF's construction of Israeli arts and cultural organizations in the US image as American interests and cultural influence proliferated in Israel, Sokolow's work and its reception reveal how American modern dance indexed the multiple migrations, diasporas, and state and capital interests at play through Israeli bodies. As Nina Spiegel has argued, dance and physical culture fostered Hebrew nationalism in British Mandate Palestine (1917–1948).[11] Remaking Jewishness in the Holocaust's aftermath, moreover, depended on healthy Jewish bodies taking up space. Israeli dancers' physicality, resilience, and intensity similarly defined this embodiment in Sokolow's postwar dances in Israel and the United States.

7. See Rottenberg, "Anna Sokolow," 39.

8. Roginsky, "Orientalism, the Body, and Cultural Politics in Israel: Sara Levi Tanai and the Inbal Dance Theater," *NASHIM: A Journal of Jewish Women's Studies and Gender Issues* 11 (2006): 182; Spiegel, *Embodying Hebrew Culture*, 179 (see Preface, n9); and Oz Almog, *The Sabra: The Creation of the New Jew*, trans. Haim Watzman (Berkeley: University of California Press, 2000), 1–16. Almog notes that the Yom Kippur War (1973) changed the cultural view of the sabra archetype from one of heroic indefatigability to one susceptible to vulnerability.

9. Spiegel, *Embodying Hebrew Culture*, 8–11.

10. Gaby Aldor elaborates how these movement qualities, heightened by the political situation in the 1980s–1990s and a sense of borderlessness, are further intensified in Israeli contemporary dance. Aldor, "The Borders of Contemporary Israeli Dance: 'Invisible Unless in Final Pain,'" *Dance Research Journal* 35, no. 1 (2003): 81–88.

11. Spiegel, *Embodying Hebrew Culture*.

I show how Sokolow's work in Israel distinguishes how Jews in the United States and Israel defined what it meant to be Jewish in the aftermath of World War II at the same time that American and Israeli institutions became invested in each other through cultural exchange. I first define how Hebrew (1880s–1948) and Israeli (post-1948) nationalist agendas framed Sokolow's work with Inbal, then discuss Sokolow's dances *Opus '63* (1963), *Forms* (1964), and *Odes* (1964) with Lyric Theatre, and finally explain how divergent approaches to Jewish peoplehood manifest in reception of Sokolow's Holocaust indictment *Dreams* (1961) in Israel and the United States.

Sokolow's work and teaching in Israel expand what counts as American modern dance. Israeli dancers trained primarily in *Ausdruckstanz* (expressive dance from Germany's and Austria's *Neue Tanz* or *Freitanz* early twentieth-century movement) but also Yemenite dance changed her performance qualities with their bodily histories and redefined midcentury American modern dance in international contexts. Based in teachings of Rudolf Laban and Mary Wigman, *Ausdruckstanz* focused on improvisation, a dancer's relationship to space, the outward expression of inner emotional and psychological states, and creating harmony through movement choirs. Prior to World War II, it was an ideologically good match for socialist Zionism because of its egalitarianism, and for New Jew ideology, because both imagined building a new society through a cultivated body and a split from the past.[12] As a result, German and Austrian immigrants and refugees trained in this form brought it with them to Mandate Palestine in the early twentieth century, and Jewish dancers born in Palestine went to Germany to study and brought the training back with them. In 1924 choreographer Margalit Ornstein opened the first dance studio in Tel Aviv, based in German expressive dance, and the first National Dance Competition for theatrical dance occurred in 1937.[13] By the time Sokolow arrived, Western theatrical dance was well established in Israel.

As the United States replaced Europe as Israel's cultural model, American modern dance influences, from Sokolow and from Martha Graham, supplanted German expressive dance. Laban's and Wigman's associations with Nazism, and Laban's desires for *Ausdruckstanz* to represent German racial superiority untainted by foreign (Jewish) influence were undesirable in Israel.[14] The AFII/ AICF funding of American modern dance catalyzed the shift from European to American influence in Israeli dance.[15] This American training came first through Graham dancers, including Sokolow and Rena Gluck, and then through de

---

12. Aldor, "Borders," 82.

13. Spiegel, *Embodying Hebrew Culture*, 97–131.

14. Marion Kant, "German Dance and Modernity: Don't Mention the Nazis," in *Rethinking Dance History: A Reader*, ed. Alexandra Carter (London: Routledge, 2004), 112–115. See also Karina and Kant, *Hitler's Dancers* (see Chap. 1, n162); and Manning, *Ecstasy*, 164 (see Introduction, n27).

15. Building on the work of Judith Brin Ingber and Ruth Eshel, Rottenberg argues that Jerome Robbins's choice of Sokolow to train Inbal was the catalyst for the European-to-American shift. Rottenberg, "Anna Sokolow," 41.

Rothschild's founding of Batsheva with Graham as artistic director. The codified Graham technique Sokolow taught contrasted the egalitarianism that German expressive dance espoused. Although Sokolow had dismantled Graham's star system in her choreography since the 1930s and used bourgeois tools for proletarian work, the Graham technique nonetheless trains the body into grounded, assertive postures. Sokolow's training empowered dancers through her insistence on their deep emotional commitment to the material and further provided an unapologetic toughness that fit with New Jew ideology. Through her work with Inbal and Lyric Theatre, Sokolow brought revolutionary modernism into the revenue-generating engine to build Israeli cultural organizations with American funds, and reconciled hierarchical American modern dance within egalitarian Israeli socialist Zionism.

EAST AND WEST, INBAL DANCE THEATER AND SOKOLOW

In the 1950s, Sokolow's Jewish leftism marked her as Other in the United States but put her in a position of cultural power within Israeli society under the Ashkenazi-led socialist government structure. There, she was imbricated in the Israeli nationalist project of building a Middle Eastern Israeli state with Western cultural values. This was most pronounced in her work with Inbal Dance Theater, where she taught Graham technique to a company comprising mostly Yemenite Jewish immigrants. Sokolow's work with Inbal was entangled in Israeli cultural tensions negotiating Jewish traditions from the Middle East, Africa, Asia, and Eastern, Central, and Western Europe that tilted European when it came to cultural and political power. These tensions stemmed from a dominant population of Ashkenazi Jews who colonized the region and held positions of power in the Israeli government despite a non-Ashkenazi majority of Israel's population. European influence also undergirded the state education system, wherein Israel's Ministry of Education's curriculum based on Western European models and literatures indoctrinated Israeli children into a Jewish European way of life.[16] The following Israeli joke that *Jewish Life* ran in 1955 provides a cultural critique of this dominance:

> One Israeli asks another: "What is the difference between the great Hebrew poet of the Middle Ages in Spain, Yehuda Halevy, and the present leaders of Israel?" Comes the answer: "The difference is simple. Halevy said, 'I live in the West but my heart is in the East.' But Sharett and Ben Gurion proclaim, 'We live in the East but our hearts are in the West.' This is so true it's not funny."[17]

16. Troen, "Construction," 29–30, 35.
17. "It Happened in Israel," *Jewish Life* (December 1955): 20–21.

David Ben-Gurion and Moshe Sharett, the first and second prime ministers of Israel from 1948–1953 and 1953–1955, respectively (followed by Ben-Gurion's reprise in 1955–1963), were Eastern European–born Zionist leaders. The joke lambasts Israel's priorities by contrasting Halevy's pre-Zionist romantic yearning to be in the Middle Eastern Jewish spiritual homeland with a reality that contemporary leaders built a Middle Eastern Jewish state in Europe's image instead of reimagining Jewish sovereignty in a shared Middle Eastern locale. Israel's theatrical dance scene participated in this vision of building a spiritual home in the East with the tools of the West: Choreographers, the majority of whom were Ashkenazi, built the theatrical dance community with German expressive dance, alongside a smaller but significant ballet scene from Russian Jewish immigrants. Sokolow's introduction continued this influence as Israel shifted from using Western and Central Europe to the United States as a cultural barometer. The discourses that fueled the AFII/AICF's support and embrace of Sokolow, and that of universal art with which Sokolow aligned herself, reinforced the Eurocentric dominance built into Israel's cultivated cultural ethos.

The cultural theory of socialist Zionism further charged the environment that fostered Sokolow's work. It was central to Hebrew nationalism in Palestine during the British Mandate period and continued into Israeli statehood. Zionist ideology splintered among many factions for varying political initiatives over the course of the twentieth century. All Zionisms share a desire for Jewish sovereignty, and many include a physical, if not spiritual, connection to the land of the biblical and contemporary geographical region of Israel.[18] Multiple Zionisms reflected changing political ideologies. My discussion focuses on socialist Zionism, which undergirded the ideology of the New Jew and Hebrew nationalism. It was the dominant ideology during Sokolow's time in Israel. Socialist Zionism called for an equal, unified society that valued the collective over the individual, the romanticized rural landscape over the city, and a people-focused rather than god-focused understanding of Jewish life.[19] Socialist Zionist ideology offered Sokolow an egalitarian atmosphere that the Second Red Scare in the United States curbed in the 1950s. During the time that Sokolow worked with Inbal, Levi-Tanai and the dancers called each other *chaverim*, or comrades. *Kibbutzniks*, the workers and inhabitants of socialist-based *kibbutzim*, also referred to each other as *chaverim*.[20] As the notion of workers as

18. See, among others, Spiegel, *Embodying Hebrew Culture*; Halpern and Reinharz, *Zionism and the Creation of a New Society*; Noam Pianko, *Zionism and the Roads Not Taken: Rawidowicz, Kaplan, Kohn* (Bloomington: Indiana University Press, 2010); Eran Kaplan and Derek J. Penslar, eds., *The Origins of Israel, 1882–1948: A Documentary History* (Madison: The University of Wisconsin Press, 2011); and Avraham Sela, "The 'Wailing Wall' Riots (1929) as a Watershed in the Palestine Conflict," *The Muslim World* 84, no. 2 (1994): 60–94.

19. Spiegel, *Embodying Hebrew Culture*, 13–18.

20. Sara Levi-Tanai with Judith Brin Ingber, "From Street Urchin to International Acclaim: A Personal Testimony," in *Seeing Israeli and Jewish Dance*, ed. Ingber, 26–27 (see Introduction, n71).

comrades became suspect in the United States, Israel supported Sokolow's revolutionary values as had Mexico a decade before.

Socialist Zionism redefined Jewish physical culture through the New Jew archetype that grounded Israeli's dancers' *sabra* physicality. Despite Ashkenazi cultural dominance, the New Jew archetype refused European cultural markers. This invention included speaking Hebrew instead of Yiddish, basing customs on Middle Eastern instead of European traditions, and associating Jews with the *kibbutz* instead of the *shtetl* (European Jewish ghetto). New Jew ideology aligned with "muscular Judaism," an international physical culture movement intended to disassociate Jews from effeminacy and softness[21] by changing the view of Jewish men from weak and pale to strong and vibrant, and, later, instituting mandatory military service that centered masculinity in Israeli society.[22] The New Jew was secular instead of religious, placed human action instead of divine intervention at the center of Israeliness, and treated the Bible as a humanist historical document instead of as a sacred text.[23] By the 1950s, this cultural ideology became politically and financially bolstered by US entities.

Sokolow's work with Inbal shows how New Jew ideology exacerbated conflicts between Ashkenazi and Mizrahi Jewish ethnicities through dance.[24] The New Jew provided a narrow definition for Hebrew and Israeli embodied nationalism based in Eurocentric cultural values. Buried within a sense of "togetherness," as Spiegel highlights the ideological and aesthetic confluence of values in which everyone supported their fellow Jew,[25] was an Orientalist association that Mizrahi Jews from the Middle East, North Africa, and Asia were simultaneously considered authentically Israeli and seen as Other because of their geographic origins. Thus Israel's Yemenite Jewish community was considered to have more authentic ties to the biblical land of Israel than European Jews because of their origins in Yemen. At the same time, Ashkenazi Jews treated Yemenites as subordinate, and even exotic, because of their

21. Foulkes, "Angels 'Rewolt!'" 236 (see Introduction, n58).

22. See Galia Golan, "Militarization and Gender: The Israeli Experience," *Women's Studies International Forum* 20, nos. 5/6 (1997): 581–586; and Hanna Herzog, "Homefront and Battlefront: The Status of Jewish and Palestinian Women in Israel," in *Israeli Women's Studies: A Reader*, ed. Esther Fuchs (New Brunswick: Rutgers University Press, 2005), 208–228.

23. Troen, "Construction," 31–33.

24. Ashkenazi Jews developed Mizrahi as a blanket term for Jews from the Middle East, North Africa, Asia, and other Arabic points of origin. It is a politicized label that denotes Otherness and marginalization. I acknowledge this term's problematic nature as well as the tension that there is currently no term to replace it. When possible, I instead identify these Jews' points of origin. I thank Nina Spiegel for this articulation. See Ella Shohat, "The Invention of the Mizrahim," *Journal of Palestine Studies* 29, no. 1 (199): 5–20. Mizrahi Jews came together in a shared group consciousness across their language barriers and different countries of origin to unite against Ashkenazi oppressors during the Mizrahi civil rights struggle from the 1940s to 1960s. Bryan K. Roby, *The Mizrahi Era of Rebellion: Israel's Forgotten Civil Rights Struggle, 1948–1966* (Syracuse: Syracuse University Press, 2015), 7.

25. Spiegel, *Embodying Hebrew Culture*, 18.

Arabic roots.[26] Inbal's perceived exoticism revealed tensions in Israeli society that Spiegel identifies that began in Mandate Palestine and came forth in dance. Two of these are between the ancient and the modern, with invented traditions connecting biblical stories to contemporary life, and between East and West, as Jews from Eastern and Western Europe, the Mediterranean, North Africa, the Middle East, and Asia tried to live in cultural harmony.[27] The 1950s–1970s Israeli cultural climate under the *mizug hagaluyot* [melting pot] state policy that sanctioned assimilation into an Ashkenazic ideal marginalized Yemenites and other Jews of color, while the Israeli government appropriated their traditions into a homogenous culture of what it meant to be Israeli.[28] The melting-pot ideology became a modernizing and whitening process for Mizrahim, who the Ashkenazi-controlled state considered uncouth and predisposed to crime.[29] This mythical heightening of an oppressed ethnic group within a Europeanist frame—the belief that Jews of Middle Eastern, North African, and Asian origin were authentically Israeli—recalls Mexico's cultural theory of *mestizaje*: celebrating indigenous elements by usurping them into Europeanist forms while suppressing contemporary indigenous people.[30] Because of Inbal's Arabic themes and movement, Levi-Tanai could not shed folk labels, which were synonymous with undervalued cultures and so-called low art—similar to Sokolow's experience with American critical response to her Mexican-folkore-themed dances. Levi-Tanai's connections to Ashkenazi political figures did not help to smooth this East–West tension or enable Inbal to be fully considered as high art.[31]

Inbal's staging incorporating Yemenite traditions into a European performance frame fit the American view of what Israel should be. Levi-Tanai founded Inbal in 1949 after massive Yemeni immigration during an Israeli governmental airlift of Jewish Yemeni refugees. Levi-Tanai based her choreography on biblical women figures, Yemenite Jewish women's rituals, and Talmudic prayer traditions.[32] Combining polycentric movement endemic to African and Middle Eastern forms with an elongated torso from the European tradition, her choreography presented Yemenite culture while remaining legible to audiences trained in European aesthetics. Levi-Tanai's choreography featured textured tableaux with movements that began as representational mimesis and became abstract shapes. Inbal men, along with the women, danced strongly and lithely as embodiments of

26. Ze'eva Cohen, discussion, 2009 (see Introduction, n85); Judith Brin Ingber in telephone conversation with the author, March 7, 2010. See also Roby, *Mizrahi Era*; and Esther Meir-Glitzenstein, "Operation Magic Carpet: Constructing the Myth of the Magical Immigration of Yemenite Jews to Israel," *Israel Studies* 16, no. 3 (2011): 149–173.

27. Spiegel, *Embodying Hebrew Culture*, 11–17.

28. Roginsky, "Orientalism," 188; and Roby, *Mizrahi Era*, 7–8.

29. Roby, *Mizrahi Era*, 1–7.

30. See Earle, *The Return of the Native* (see Chap. 2, n12).

31. Roginsky, "Orientalism," 166.

32. See Levi-Tanai with Ingber, "From Street Urchin to International Acclaim," 25–42; and Roginsky, "Orientalism," 168–171, 175.

the *sabra* figure. Inbal's costumes recalled traditional Jewish Yemenite dress, with tall winding headdresses, wide striped tunics, and metallic filigree jewelry. Inbal's aesthetic characteristics played to melting-pot acculturation and to Mizrahi self-determination during Israel's policies to assimilate Arab Jews. To this end historian Bryan K. Roby asserted, "During the state's first decades, Mizrahim continued to assert their Middle Eastern identity through cultural production such as literature, plays, and religious festivals derived from their countries of origin. This rejection of Eurocentric notions of modernity was in itself an act of resistance."[33] By staging Yemenite performances, Levi-Tanai asserted her Mizrahi identity as part of the collective. But as a Palestinian-born, Ashkenazi-raised and *Ausdruckstanz*-trained Yemenite Jew, her framing of Yemenite forms through a European theatrical frame attempted melting-pot ideology. Sokolow's training was integral to this process.

Sokolow's work provided Inbal a similar kind of international vetting as had her engagement with Mexico City's Bellas Artes students in the 1930s to 1940s (see Chapter 2). Similarly to the training at Bellas Artes, Sokolow trained Inbal dancers in Graham technique and presented technical demonstrations for funders and government officials. In Israel, these consumers were largely members of the AFII and AICF. Similar to her work in Mexico, Sokolow's training enabled dancers of color to embody an internationally prominent concert form to read as professional to a Eurocentric presenting eye. In contrast to her work at Bellas Artes, Sokolow's work in Israel was funded by private American organizations invested in building the state instead of support from the host government.

Rebuilding Israeli culture in an American image required melding new bodies of imagined indigenous Israeli ethnicity in American modern dance technique. To do this, in the early 1950s, the AFII enlisted Robbins to scout out a dance company to represent Israel internationally. He targeted Inbal and recommended the AFII hire Sokolow to train them.[34] The sentiment at the time that Inbal's improvisatory training and Yemenite movement vocabulary were not good enough to be considered on a national, much less international, stage reflected the Israeli state's refusal to recognize African and Asian Jewish immigrants as equal partners to Eastern European and German Jewish immigrants in nation-building.[35] Narratives by and about Inbal in the 1950s that uphold Sokolow as a great American whose Western teaching made Inbal a more professional and modern company suggest that Sokolow's imbuing Inbal's bodies with American training made them suitable participants in the Israeli nationalist project (Figures 5.2 and 5.3). The professionalism associated with midcentury American dance modernism included training in a defined technique, the ability to string movements together into phrases performed

---

33. Roby, *Mizrahi Era*, 8.

34. Aviva Davidson (executive director of Dancing in the Streets and daughter of Judith Gottlieb, secretary-general of America–Israel Cultural Foundation in Tel Aviv) in discussion with the author, June 29, 2010, New York City; and Rottenberg, "Anna Sokolow," 43.

35. Roby, *Mizrahi Era*, 6–7.

Figure 5.2: Sokolow teaches Graham technique to Inbal Dance Theater. Margalit Oved is front left. Photograph by Ephraim Erde. Larry Warren Collection on Anna Sokolow and Lester Horton, Box 1, Music Division, Library of Congress, Washington, DC.

consistently each time, bodies with defined muscles that suggested a high level of specific and rigorous physical training, and staging that valued an endstage proscenium configuration. This was in opposition to dance forms like those of Africanist or Middle Eastern origin, or even of *Ausdruckstanz*, with improvisation as a keystone of the form and performances that enabled many points of focus for an audience, rather than the one front-facing side a Western proscenium stage required. Once Sokolow trained Inbal for a few years with AFII/AICF support, bolstered by teaching assistance from Laban-trained Yehudit Ornstein (Margalit's daughter),[36] Inbal had the chops to compete with *Ausdruckstanz*-trained dancers in the Israeli theatrical dance community and to be exported on international tours.[37] Sokolow enabled the AFII to achieve its goal of touring Inbal to Europe and the United States under Hurok's auspices. Inbal's dancing reinforced a Euro–American desire to imagine Israel composed of an indigenous Jewishness performed by bodies of

36. Rottenberg, "Anna Sokolow," 42.
37. Ingber, conversation.

Figure 5.3: Sokolow teaching Meir Ovadia and unidentified dancer, Inbal Dance Theater. Photograph by Mirlin-Yaron. Larry Warren Collection on Anna Sokolow and Lester Horton, Box 1, Music Division, Library of Congress, Washington, DC.

color in an indeterminate Middle Eastern locale instead of a Western nation defined through German ideals outdated through Nazi associations.

Although she later spoke out against the Israeli government's marginalization of Yemenite art and culture, Levi-Tanai was one of the first progenitors of the myth that Sokolow raised her company from their "Oriental" (her words) origins to meld themselves into a Western aesthetic. Addressing the studio audience of AFII members gathered for Sokolow's 1954 technical demonstration that opened this chapter, Levi-Tanai said that her company members "have finally reached the stage of concentration, discipline and of responsibility towards their art. Their bodies are disciplined, their efforts are focused on a definite goal." She continued, "Anna, in her day-to-day work, has harnessed our wild talent and has compelled us to march bodily in the path of art."[38] Levi-Tanai's propaganda continued in print. In a 1955 letter to *Dance Magazine*, she specified how Sokolow's training upgraded Inbal's ethnic status: "It was interesting to observe our Eastern-looking boys and girls, accustomed to an oriental way of moving, suddenly learning to move in the style of the Western world. It seemed perfectly natural because Anna instinctively knew how long to teach us the new without destroying our own style."[39] With publicity like this, Levi-Tanai reinforced the dominant cultural view that Yemenites were both inferior to Western modes and somehow special in their wake.

Sokolow, too, upheld the association of folk elements with low art needing to be trained. She reported in 1955, "They [Inbal] have long emerged from the folk dance stage and have matured into a performing dance company of high quality. There is no question in my mind but that they would be a great success anywhere."[40] Folk elements no longer signified revolution in the United States, and Sokolow, who in 1956 would stir resentment at the Mexican dance conference in Veracruz because she would not accept Mexican modernism as being on a continuum embracing abstraction and autochthonous elements (see Chapter 3), similarly with Inbal considered the folk as something from which to mature instead of something that is in reciprocal dialogue with modernist form, or as she puts it here, high quality. Inbal seems to have achieved an American professional aesthetic look, though, because in October 1955, Sokolow wrote to Robbins how impressed she was with Inbal's growth in their technical and performance qualities, as well as with Levi-Tanai's improved choreographic prowess.[41]

The Israeli government appropriated Inbal's work without recognizing the company as a full art entity. According to cultural theorist Dina Roginsky, Yemenite traditions were vital to the invented traditions central to Israeliness: "[T]he Yemenite dances served Israeli culture as a symbolic declaration of the existence of a continuous Jewish tradition that had been kept alive for years and was revived in Israel."[42] Within these Orientalist parameters, AFII/AICF funding and Sokolow's teaching brought Inbal's imagined ancientness into the contemporaneity of modernist dance and the modern state of Israel, fulfilling New Jew and melting-pot ideologies. AFII/AICF propaganda and American critical response surrounding Sokolow's work with Inbal supported this East–West tension and upheld the United States as liberator—all by means of American funding.

38. Reprinted in an unknown AFII publication, ca. 1954 as Sara Levi-Tanai, "Anna Sokolow," 21. Sokolow Dance Foundation.

39. Sara Levi-Tanai, "A Letter to Dance Magazine About Inbal and Anna Sokolow," *Dance Magazine* (June 1955). Unpublished manuscript. SDF.

40. Anna Sokolow, quoted in "GENERAL: US Choreographer Lands Israel Dance Group," Jewish Agency's Digest, September 23, 1955, n.p., 111.4, Inbal Clippings through 1966, DLI.

41. Anna Sokolow to Jerome Robbins, October 16, 1955, Folder 2, Box 530, Jerome Robbins Papers, JRDD, NYPL.

42. Roginsky, "Orientalism," 188.

Through tours like Inbal's, the AFII reinforced cultural and economic links between Israel and the United States. To this end, AFII director Edward A. Norman wrote, "the basic democratic and pioneering traditions of America, revealed in its history, philosophy, art and culture, are a veritable treasure trove for the parallel traditions of Israel."[43] Norman connects the Americana mythological pioneering spirit to that of the *halutzim,* Jewish immigrants called pioneers who drained swamps or cultivated deserts in efforts to build *kibbutzim* in Palestine. The AFII charged Judith Gottlieb, its secretary-general in Israel, with developing cultural centers in rural areas like *kibbutzim* and in touring American donors around Israel to show them established cultural institutions like the philharmonic hall.[44] This propaganda spoke to Jews in the United States and Israel alike, though Norman intended these connections to attract American Jews to buy Israeli bonds and donate to the AFII.

Postwar American Jewish rhetoric that equated Zionism with Americanism by connecting essences of heroism to a pioneering spirit further increased American Jews' sense of connection to Israel.[45] By 1956, the AFII had pumped $10 million into artistic exchange programs and arts buildings in Israel.[46] A 1956 essay by Norman outlining the goals of the organization echoes 1950s American freedom discourses.[47] He articulates the benefit of US support for Israel including a democratic way of life bolstered by strong artistic and cultural institutions leading to a sense of freedom and power. In return, he says, Israel can give the United States what he calls "the cultural heritage of thousands of years" as the contemporary geography of biblical lands.[48] The rhetoric of freedom and democracy normalized the socialism of Israel's welfare state and established it as the cradle of Christianity in the midst of McCarthyism and a public prominence of Christian religious values in the 1950s United States. The Merry-Go-Rounders, a 92nd Street Y resident dance company for children's performances, brought the democracy message to Jewish children in New York through dance when they presented Israel as a cultural democracy as part of their educational programming.[49] In the McCarthyist 1950s it was important for American Jews, who actively distanced themselves from their 1930s communist pasts as a way to assert their Americanness, to imagine a democratic instead of socialist Israel.[50]

The Israeli–American institutional cultural exchange to get each country invested in the other relied on American Jewish interest in Israel: on emotions tied to Zionism and a desire to connect with the exotic brethren who resided there.

43. Edward A. Norman, "Israel—USA Cultural Links."
44. Davidson, discussion.
45. Sheramy, " 'Resistance and War,' " 289–290, 301 (see Introduction, n6).
46. Edward A. Norman, "Israel—USA Cultural Links."
47. See Foner, *American Freedom* (see Chap. 4, n22).
48. Edward A. Norman, "Israel—USA Cultural Links."
49. Jackson, *Converging Movements,* 115 (see Introduction, n58).
50. See Sheramy, " 'Resistance and War,' " 302–303.

Sokolow's work, first with Inbal and later with Lyric Theatre, became part of the AFII/AICF's new vision in 1956 to go beyond supporting Israeli institutions to developing new ones. This shift occurred when Samuel Rubin assumed the AFII leadership after Norman's death in 1956 as the organization changed its name to the AICF. Rubin's five-year plan included "Tours of the Israeli Philharmonic Orchestra, Inbal Dance Troupe, the Pantomime Troupe of the Chamber Theatre, Choirs, art festivals and exhibitions."[51] He planned to connect AICF efforts with the US State Department cultural exchange program, so that "the fund might enlist support for projects launched in Israel revolving about American orchestras, ballets and other cultural avenues embracing American citizens."[52] Sokolow's 1961 proposal for founding a dance company in Israel to perform her work aligned with Rubin's goals.[53] Despite its short existence and lack of touring outside Israel, Sokolow's Lyric Theatre fulfilled Rubin's desire to plant American art institutions in Israeli soil. As a company comprising Israeli dancers from diverse cultural backgrounds, Lyric Theatre embodied Israeli melting-pot ideology by training these dancers in Sokolow's revolutionary modernist, but indisputably American, aesthetic. Even during the Grahamification of Israeli modern dance, Lyric Theatre notably provided deep theatrical grit that the Batsheva Dance Company's Graham repertory did not match. The *sabra* physicality on which Sokolow capitalized from her company members rubbed too uncomfortably against the alienating abstraction in her choreography for audiences' responses to recognize Rubin's plans. Instead, the tensions surrounding her Lyric Theatre represented political schisms in the wake of the AICF's artistic colonialism.

LYRIC THEATRE

Lyric Theatre laid bare tensions of East–West (here, Israel–United States) and local and international funding by training Israeli dancers in Sokolow's American repertory. The company toured Israeli cities and *kibbutzim* to mixed reviews, worked for six to eight months each year, often rehearsed and performed in Sokolow's absence, and earned a stipend that did not add up to a living wage.[54] The Lyric Theatre

51. Joseph Gale, "Israel Institutions Fund Here May Be Completely Changed, Including The Group's Name," *National Jewish Post* (Indianapolis), June 29, 1956, n.p., 111.4 Inbal Clippings through 1966, DLI.

52. Gale, "Israel Institutions Fund Here May Be Completely Changed."

53. Anna Sokolow, "Suggestions for a New Dance Theatre in Israel," proposal to AICF, July 6, 1961, typescript, SDF.

54. Sokolow's Lyric Theatre was the first Israeli dance company to pay dancers a salary, even though it was small. See Rottenberg, "Anna Sokolow," 52. Sokolow's budget for the Lyric Theatre's first season proposed paying dancers a salary of 150 shekels each for a period of six months, which was approximately $69.44 ($559.36 adjusted for inflation at this book's publication). For comparison, she budgeted 600 shekels, or $277.78 ($2,237.60 with inflation), for six months' studio rental. Sokolow, "Suggestions."

mostly performed Sokolow's existing repertory, like *Rooms, Dreams* (1961), *Opus,* and *Forms* (1964), and toured new pieces like *Odes* (1964). For each of the Lyric Theatre seasons, Sokolow regrouped her company based on available dancers, and, due to dancers' unpredictable employment and studies abroad, Sokolow often frantically gathered her group for the season.[55] American organizations funded Lyric Theatre, and so American influence pervaded the Israeli theatrical dance scene through Sokolow's work.

From 1962 to 1964, Israeli critical response to Sokolow's Lyric Theatre prized dramatic content over abstraction.[56] Sokolow's *Dreams,* her 1961 Holocaust indictment that I discuss in the next section, attracted critical acclaim from Israeli audiences. During a time of Israeli excitement about American dance, however, Israeli critics panned her abstract dances on the same programs, such as *Opus '63, Forms,* or *Odes,* that US critics considered quintessentially American because of their themes of urban alienation and disaffected youth and their compositional elements based in abstraction and jazz forms. Response to Sokolow's dissemination of Graham-based technique during the era of Graham's Israeli rise, and to the Lyric Theatre, reveals tensions within Israeli modernism and the midcentury Israeli dance scene.

Sokolow engaged in choreographic projects in addition to her work with Inbal that led to her establishment of the Lyric Theatre. She first presented her choreography in Tel Aviv's Opera House with AICF support in 1959 when she staged *Poem* (1956) for Bimat Makhol, the dance collective run by Rina Shacham, Rena Gluck, and Naomi Aleskovsky from 1958 to 1960 in Tel Aviv. Shaham, along with Bimat Makhol dancers Ze'eva Cohen and Avraham Tzuri, became part of Lyric Theatre.[57] The company ran for three seasons from 1962 to 1964 funded by the AICF, the Lena Robbins Foundation, the Harkness Foundation, and Cleveland's Fiermont Synagogue, and the words she used to list her company members, *chaveri ha'lahakah,* denote a troupe of artists joined in comradeship.[58] The title Lyric Theatre shared its name with Sokolow's performance form that blended dancing and acting. To build the Lyric Theatre, Sokolow gathered dancers she knew from Inbal and Bimat Makhol, and through large master-classes-turned-auditions that she held in the gymnasium of a teacher's seminar building, the Inbal studios, and other places in Tel Aviv.[59] She based these classes on her variation of the Graham

55. Michael Ohad, "Anna does not want success" (see Chap. 4, n47).

56. See Ohad, "Anna does not want success." See also Warren, *Rebellious Spirit,* 133–141 and 191–200, and Rottenberg, "Anna Sokolow," 36–58.

57. Rottenberg, "Anna Sokolow," 44, and Ze'eva Cohen in conversation with the author, February 11, 2010, New York City. See also Ruth Eshel, *Dancing with the Dream: The Development of Artistic Dance in Israel 1920–1964* (Tel Aviv: Dance Library of Israel, 1991).

58. Anna Sokolow, quoted in Sorrell, "We Work Toward Freedom," 73; and Program, *Anna Sokolow's Lyric Theatre presents Programme B: Dreams, 4 Jazz Pieces, Opus '62,* Anna Sokolow's Lyric Theatre Programs 111.17.2.1, DLI.

59. Moshe Romano (Lyric Theatre dancer, Batsheva artistic director) in discussion with the author, November 6, 2009, Tel Aviv, Israel; Lea Avraham (dancer with Inbal and Batsheva

technique. Moshe Romano, a Lyric Theatre member who later danced with and directed Batsheva, remembered skipping a Saturday at the beach to take Sokolow's class, and he became hooked.[60]

Many Israeli dancers preferred elements of Sokolow's style based on the Graham technique but that diverged from Graham. Sokolow's training offered dancers a viscerality, a coming from the *kishkes*, that Graham's work lacked. When I spoke with some of these dancers in 2009–2010, they passionately remembered their respect for Sokolow's uncompromising demands and personality, their desire to rise to the standard she set, and their preference for her requirements that they relinquish sentimentality, pierce the heart of the matter by abandoning outer beauty for inner sincerity, and give more of themselves than they thought was possible. During one rehearsal in a hot, rundown studio next to a slaughterhouse in Tel Aviv, for example, the dancers complained of the overpowering smell coming from the raw meat next door. Sokolow scolded one woman, who sprayed the air with perfume, for her attempt to mask a bodily truth. "That's the smell of life!," Romano remembered Sokolow telling this dancer. "You cannot *spritz spritz* over life."[61] For Romano, Sokolow's work offered an emotional meatiness in contrast to the intellectualism of Graham's choreography. He preferred Sokolow's version of Graham's vocabulary, which he recalled with enthusiasm as an animalistic type of Graham class, that was instinctually strong.[62] Israeli critics and dancers appreciated Sokolow's unapologetic straightforwardness, raw movement aesthetic free of excess ornamentation, and dismissal of narcissistic beauty in her technique classes and choreography. *Sabra* physicality matched Sokolow's no-holds-barred, all-grit approach with tangible sexuality and no prettiness for its own sake. It aligned with the instability, fearlessness, immediacy, straightforwardness, and strength through vulnerability that dance historian Gaby Aldor (also Margalit Ornstein's granddaughter) argues make Israeli contemporary dance Israeli.[63]

The toughness and unapologetic vulnerability in Sokolow's training matched New Jew ideology. Sokolow commanded Lyric Theatre dancers to dig deep into their understanding of themselves to perform with sincerity and without mythology and to find what she called the truth in movement. Sokolow's training empowered dancers through her insistence on their deep emotional commitment to the material, which, as dance historian Henia Rottenberg notes, many Israeli dancers found liberating and exhilarating.[64] Lea Avraham, who danced in Inbal and Batsheva, remembered Sokolow's emphasis on engaging the abdominal core through a strong

companies), telephone conversation with the author, May 4, 2010; Cohen, discussion, February 2010; and Davidson, discussion.

60. Romano, discussion.
61. Ibid.
62. Ibid.
63. Aldor, "Borders," 81–96.
64. Rottenberg, "Anna Sokolow," 37.

upward thrust, paired with a lyricism that Graham lacked.[65] As part of the AICF's project to build Israeli cultural organizations with American funds, Sokolow's work uneasily reconciled hierarchical American modern dance within egalitarian Israeli socialist Zionism.

Israeli dancers who worked with Sokolow embraced the syncopation, atonality, juxtaposition, irony, and intensity in her training. Romano, Avraham, and Cohen were drawn to this way of working. They preferred its provocation, what Cohen called its texture and density, and the way it made them feel fully human when they were vulnerable or emotionally stripped raw.[66] A 1966 film of Sokolow coaching students at The Ohio State University in *Odes* (1964) gives a sense of the demands she made in the studio of her Lyric Theatre dancers. In addition to pushing the dancers to their physical and emotional limits—"More, more, MORE, MORE, faster, FASTER!" she yelled from her chair with measured precision—Sokolow focused on connecting emotions through physical actions. "All the things that you do are built on an inner rhythm," she tells the dancers. "It's not an intellectual rhythm. It comes from the emotions."[67] According to Vera "Vickie" Blaine, an Ohio State Department of Dance faculty member during this residency who performed in *Odes* under Sokolow's direction there, this rhythm comes from feelings and from a weighted sensing of the emotional imperatives of the work.[68] AFII Secretary-General Judith Gottlieb's daughter Aviva Davidson, a dancer and actor who took Sokolow's classes in Tel Aviv, associated a similar rhythmic accuracy with what Sokolow called truth.[69] Israeli dancer and choreographer Rina Schenfeld, too, foregrounded rhythm in her memory of Sokolow's rehearsal coaching, in which Sokolow focused on rhythmic accuracy and fluidity in connecting movements together.[70] Sokolow also trained the Lyric Theatre in ballet, for which she brought in teachers from Israel's Russian immigrant community.[71] Sokolow believed that contemporary dancers needed modern dance and ballet training to access their full range of movement and emotional capacity.

Sokolow's stature as an American choreographer enabled her to align herself with universality and transcend cultural specificity that Israeli critical discourses did not permit to German expressionist or Yemenite dancers. In a 1964 interview with the leftist Hebrew-language Israeli newspaper *Ha'aretz*, reporter Michael Ohad asked

65. Avraham, conversation.

66. Cohen, discussion, February, 2010; Romano, discussion; and Avraham, conversation.

67. *Anna Sokolow Directs* Odes: *Artist in Residence, Winter 1966*, directed by David L. Parker, produced by The Ohio State University Department of Photography and Cinema, Columbus, OH, 1972, DD, OSU.

68. Vera "Vickie" Blaine (dancer, choreographer), in discussion with the author, April 5, 2010, Columbus, OH.

69. Davidson, discussion.

70. Rina Schenfeld (dancer, choreographer), in discussion with the author, November 12, 2009, Tel Aviv, Israel.

71. Cohen, discussion, February 2010.

Sokolow about the connection between her dance and Israel. Her response, "No connection. My dance is not nationalistic," linked her to the transcendent aesthetic values of midcentury American dance modernism that denied specificity. Sokolow denied using folkloric source material as she continued: "It may be that they [other choreographers] need it [folklore]. I am not interested in it. My dance deals with the inner-conflicts of humans, and humans are everywhere. The folklore is good for the castles."[72] Ohad's question perhaps should have struck a chord with a Jewish choreographer who was vocal about the spiritual impact Israel had on her and who used folklore to revolutionary ends in Mexico, but Sokolow aligned herself with an unmarked universality that went unquestioned in Israel because of her Ashkenazi Americanness. Sokolow's further comment, "When I expressed this at a conference in Mexico they almost kicked me out of the country," was ostensibly intended to show that she stuck to her ideals that transcended the low-art associations with folk elements.[73] Instead it reinforced how Sokolow alienated the Israeli dance community as she had the Mexican dance community in the 1950s. Sokolow's Graham training and American movement registers aligned her with American abstraction that erased markers of race, ethnicity, and nonconforming gender presentation, even though her choreography contained these elements as part of her revolutionary modernism.

The funding politics surrounding Sokolow's formation of the Lyric Theatre as the first Israeli dance company based in American modern dance with substantial international support highlight divisions in the Israeli theatrical dance community. The 1960s registered the tide change that shifted the dominant theatrical movement influence from German (*Ausdruckstanz*) to American (Graham) dance forms, with AICF and other American funding earmarked for American choreographers setting up shop in Israel. Lyric Theatre demonstrates the overwhelming impact that an internationally funded choreographer can have on a struggling local dance scene. Nevertheless, Sokolow had trouble fitting in. In 1959 she wrote to Robbins that some Israeli dancers embraced her, but many others resented her.[74] Some members of the Israeli theatrical dance community welcomed Sokolow's work as an opportunity to expand the field. One critic wrote after the Lyric Theatre's debut: "[T]he hostile attitude some Israeli professionals displayed toward this beginning was fundamentally unfair. The dance field, like any other field in the arts, is not held permanently in certain hands and closed off to others."[75]

The majority of the Israeli theatrical dance community, led by Gertrud Kraus, Yardena Cohen, and Yehudit Orenstein, however, were irritated that Sokolow came

---

72. Ohad, "Anna does not want success."

73. Ibid.

74. Sokolow to Robbins, August 27, 1959, Jerome Robbins Personal Papers, Box 115, Folder 7, JRDD, NYPL.

75. No author, "A. Sokolow's Lyric Theatre," no source, 1962, n.p., Folder 111.17.2.4 Anna Sokolow's Lyric Theatre Clippings, DLI, trans. Stav Ziv.

to Israel with international funding and took all its dancers, especially when the *Jerusalem Post* ran a preview in June 1962, announcing Sokolow's formation of the Lyric Theatre that claimed Sokolow as an American savior of a company with no previous dance scene upon which to build. The author heralded Sokolow's arrival to a "lack of trained dancing talent in a country which has no. . .dance school to speak of."[76] Two aspects come into play here: one, a context-free building-up of Sokolow in the *Post*, an English-language daily Israeli newspaper that American donors to the AICF surely read; and two, a reinforcement of the midcentury American perception that improvisation-based forms like *Ausdruckstanz*, as opposed to codified forms like the Graham technique, produce dancers who appear untrained. Kraus, Israel's leading dancer since the 1930s, disdained Sokolow,[77] likely because of international interest in Sokolow's work in Israel when Kraus's *Ausdruckstanz* was in decline. Kraus wrote in response to this *Post* column on behalf of the Dancers Association in Israel: "We, the dancers, teachers and choreographers in Israel welcome any advance in the field of art or theatre in this country. [. . .However,] Miss Sokolow's group is composed of the product of those schools and institutes which your writer stated are non-existent."[78] Kraus argued that Sokolow drew from the many existing Israeli dance schools to fill her company, not without disruption from the schools' routines, and that her Lyric Theatre benefited from years of dance educational groundwork in Israel and international financial support to which local choreographers did not have access. Ornstein expressed similar frustration in her lukewarm review of Lyric Theatre's debut in *Ha'aretz*. Frustrated by a double standard in which funders supported Sokolow while dropping Israeli choreographers for similar compositional failures, Ornstein concluded: "And the lesson has to be: Every creator runs the risk of making mistakes. And if the rule applies to respected guests from abroad, then it certainly applies to us as well."[79] Ornstein refers here to Sokolow's *L'Histoire du Soldat* (1954), which received unanimously bad reviews due to what critics read as a weak integration of dancing and acting. Sokolow continued to receive funding and public support despite mixed reviews. This was a privilege, Ornstein implies, that Israeli choreographers did not enjoy.

Other works by Sokolow received mixed or no reviews, despite their manifestations of Americanness that appealed to Israeli audiences' tastes. Arguably the most American of Sokolow's 1960s dances because of their abstracted movement vocabularies, use of jazz as irony, and themes of countercultural *ennui*, Israeli critics rejected what they called Sokolow's inscrutable choreography in *Forms* and *Odes*

76. No author, "Curtain Raiser," *Jerusalem Post*, June 7, 1962, DLI.
77. No author, "Screen and Mask: The Argument Went Up in Smoke Before It Even Began," *Ma'ariv*, September 23, 1962, Folder 111.17.2.4 Anna Sokolow's Lyric Theatre Clippings, DLI, trans. Stav Ziv.
78. Gertrude Kraus, "Dance Schools—Editor," *The Jerusalem Post*, June 19, 1962, DLI.
79. Yehudit Ornstein, "Anna Sokolow's 'Lyric Theatre,'" *Ha'aretz*, no month [1962], n.p., Folder 111.17.2.4 Anna Sokolow's Lyric Theatre Clippings, DLI, trans. Stav Ziv.

amid public support for American dance. These dances were illegible to Israeli critics and received disparaging, if any, mention in reviews. Writing in the Hebrew-language paper *Yediot Aharonot*, Asher Nahor complained in 1962 that Sokolow "ignores the issue of its [the choreography's] understandability to the viewer." He further protested, "the viewer has to make an effort to decode Anna Sokolow's movement language."[80] Similarly, A. Ben Meir grumbled that these dances did not appear to communicate anything and left viewers to their own devices for interpreting the works, which drained enjoyment from the viewing experience.[81]

Forms demonstrated how Sokolow transposed, instead of translated, an American theme into an Israeli milieu. In the dance, performers clump together with angled limbs, bent knees, or arcing torsos that dot the physical landscape; they hoist each other skyward or climb over each other's backs. Dancers perch in various stages of moving in and out of a seated Graham fourth position, which demands their bent legs to splay on the floor; and they stand together en masse, blankly stare out into space, some with tedium, some with sarcasm, and some with anticipation. The dance responded to an uncertain and fear-ridden world, but Sokolow's specific motivational references to Central Park and American race tensions fell flat. Sokolow instructed the dancers, "imagine you are walking in Central Park and suddenly the park turns into a jungle. [. . .You are] Afraid to proceed, afraid to run back. You have a feeling that someone is following you, in a moment will put a knife in your back."[82] With a jazz score that evokes a dingy New York by Teo Macero, with whom Sokolow had collaborated in *Opus*, this piece bore the markings of the American-themed work of Sokolow and Robbins, even of Balanchine, but not of Graham, despite the movement base. The *Forms* set recalls Robbins's *West Side Story* in an urban wasteland with a pile of junk where two walls—one of tired, exposed brick and an industrial metal one covered in graffiti—intersect (Figure 5.4). *Forms'* thematic paranoia goes beyond *West Side Story's* musically smoothed-through racial tensions. In one *Forms* formation, dancers hug a bent elbow into their waist and spread their fingers wide into a relaxed but nonetheless recognizable "jazz hand." Another moment features Rina Shacham diving forward and catching herself with one hand as the opposite leg shoots into the air.[83] *Forms* was abstract, but it evoked racial tensions. Sokolow commented in rehearsal about a section of the dance, in which a hunter chases deer, "What do you say to this? The problem of struggle between the races in America today is a reality."[84] Her seemingly offhanded

80. Asher Nahor, "Anna Sokolow's Lyric Theatre—Second Program," *Yediot Aharonot* (October 14, 1962), n.p., Folder 111.17.2.4 Anna Sokolow's Lyric Theatre Clippings, DLI, trans. Stav Ziv.

81. A. Ben Meir, "On Stages and Exhibitions: The Lyric Theatre, Program B," no source, no date, no page, Larry Warren Collection on Anna Sokolow and Lester Horton, MD, LOC, trans. Jeremy Cosel.

82. Quoted in Ohad, "Anna does not want success."

83. Anna Sokolow's Lyric Theatre, Folder 111.17.2.3-111.17.2.6 Photographs, DLI.

84. Ohad, "Anna does not want success."

Figure 5.4: Lyric Theatre in *Forms*, 1964. Photograph by Yaacov Agor. Courtesy of The Israeli Dance Archive at Beit Ariela, Tel-Aviv. Dancers, left to right: Leora Hackmey, Avraham Tzuri, Avraham Manzur, Ofra Ben-Tzvi, Gideon Avrahami, and Yanun Neeman.

comment about the hunter and the hunted highlights American race relations at the height of the Civil Rights Movement, and the jazz elements of the dance embody Africanist presence. Notably, discrimination against Yemenite Jews continued in Israel, yet the discourse reflects American, not Israeli, ethnic conflict. Sokolow's comment came during the Mizrahi civil rights struggle that fought suppression under Israeli melting-pot policies. Police aggression against Mizrahi communities in transit camps and ghettos mirrored police raids and violence against African American neighborhoods.[85] In a reverse and tone-deaf maneuver from her problems translating her Mexican dances in New York and her own Jewish–Black coalition work, the American urban references Sokolow used to coach *Forms* did not easily land among Israeli performers.

Odes, conversely, engaged *sabra* physicality in bleaker themes while the Holocaust remained an unspeakable darkness beneath society's surface. Stark like *Forms*, but made and debuted in Israel, *Odes* demanded that dancers dig into the extremes of their bodies in terms of weight, timing, and depth of back arches.[86] Ohad reported seeing dancers in rehearsal "skip, struggle, [and] free fall."[87] Sokolow's grounding in Graham's vocabulary is evident here, as when floorbound dancers scoop their trunks into a full-body contraction called a pleading, with the tops of their heads bracing against the floor; they raise both arms to the ceiling in agony. At one point, the dancers stand, facing upstage; in less than a breath, their pelvises hit the floor and they raise their arms sideways to cover their bowed heads in silence. As quickly as they were down, they are up again. They skim a big toe along the floor as they plunge their torsos backward, so that they can see the audience upside-down, and raise their arms to a V above their sternums. They cover their faces with their hands, wiggling sequentially through their snaking spines as if they are in an animated Munch painting, before falling again to the floor. When Sokolow made the work in Israel, she engaged the music of Israeli composer Alexander Boskovich, but when she brought the work to the United States, she replaced the Boskovich score with one by French-born American composer Edgard Varèse.[88] The Varèse score features metallic wails, grinding machinery, and dissonant tones. In some ways, the movement has an internal rhythm independent of the music, but in others, the movement and music converse. This work features the angularity and bound flow, with muscles squeezed tight, endemic to Graham's technique and less common in Sokolow's work. Its dissonance ran counter to New Jew ideological values of harmony, and made space for pain amid abstraction that fed discussions about Sokolow's Holocaust work.

DIVERGING DISCOURSES: RESPONSES TO A DANCE ABOUT THE HOLOCAUST IN ISRAEL AND THE UNITED STATES

Critical reviews of Sokolow's work in Israel and the United States show how cultural context affects a work's reception and how Israeli and American milieus remained different although agencies like the AICF worked to establish continuity between

---

85. Roby, *Mizrahi Era*, 90–91.
86. *Anna Sokolow Directs* Odes.
87. Ohad, "Anna does not want success."
88. Warren, *Rebellious Spirit*, 200.

both communities. A conflict of specificity versus abstraction came forth in the critical reception of *Dreams*, which premiered in New York in 1961 and in Tel Aviv in 1962, that pitted the experiences of Jews living in a post-Holocaust, Israeli state against those in the US's pluralistic Judeo–Christian society. A harrowing thirty-minute dance about the Holocaust, *Dreams* represents concentration camp terrors through performers' bodies. Here, the healthy bodies of trained dancers become the decaying bodies of camp victims: A woman desperately climbs over a group of guards as if over barbed wire and silently screams; couples collapse under their own skeletal weight; and a group of people diminish as they succumb to a gas chamber even though they reach toward the heavens. One of the dancers haltingly recites the first words of Genesis that describe God's creation of the world; a drummer's frenetic tapping on every available surface produces frenzied sharp rhythms that echo machine gunfire; and chords of Bach fade in and out as Teo Macero's horns scream in a mangled storm.[89] *Dreams* is perhaps Sokolow's dance most changed by her work with Israeli dancers, primarily because of Sokolow's meeting and working with Holocaust survivors in Israel.[90] In *Dreams*, Sokolow implicated her audience members as witnesses to onstage atrocities, demanding they finish the dance with their actions outside the theater. By exposing the pain of the Holocaust and opposing postwar discourses that celebrated Jews' resilient spirits, Sokolow forced audiences to confront it as part of their collective history. In the United States, where the Jewish community grappled with the Holocaust in Jewish education during the 1960s, critics preferred abstraction; yet in Israel, where people did not discuss the Holocaust or publicly recognize Holocaust survivors until 1977, and Israeli choreographers did not address the Holocaust in dance until 1994,[91] critics' preference for specificity over abstraction of these themes reflected Israel's culture of unapologetic directness.

1960s critical receptions of *Dreams* in the United States and Israel reveal diverging sentiments about the *Shoah* [Holocaust] that reflect each culture's ways of reclaiming Jewishness. In the United States, artists, writers, and choreographers evoked images of a reimagined quaint *shtetl* life to remember European Jewry in the face of its destruction, or yoked heroism and Zionism in a continuing performance of Jewish vitality.[92] Part of American Jews' 1950s assimilation into a non-Jewish

89. *Anna Sokolow: Dreams*, directed by Roger Englander (New York: WNET/TV's Camera Three, 1979; *Dance in Video Volume 1*, Creative Arts TV, 2007), http://search.alexanderstreet.com/view/work/394454. Accessed August 1, 2016; and Anna Sokolow, *Dreams*, VHS, performed by Batsheva Dance Company, 1980, DLI.

90. *Anna Sokolow*, produced and directed by Marvin Diskin, Amphi Productions, 1990, JRDD, NYPL.

91. Gaby Aldor, "Naming It Jewish: The Dichotomy between Jewish and Israeli Dance," in *Seeing Israeli and Jewish Dance*, ed. Ingber, 381–382 (see Introduction, n71). See also Tom Segev, *The Seventh Million: The Israelis and the Holocaust*, trans. Haim Watzman (New York: Holt, 1991).

92. See Foulkes, "Angels 'Rewolt!' "; Jackson, *Converging Movements*; Kosstrin, "*Kaddish* at the Wall" (see Chap. 3, n26); and Rossen, *Dancing Jewish* (see Introduction, n26).

society included discussions about Jewish identity that enabled Jews to be equally American and Jewish. As Rona Sheramy demonstrated, American Jewish educators in the 1950s highlighted Jews as heroes in Holocaust stories in order to uplift children and make them proud of their Jewish identity.[93] In 1950s Israel, Holocaust wounds remained fresh but camp survivors went largely unacknowledged in society despite the Knesset's 1953 establishment of Israel's Holocaust memorial Yad Vashem in Jerusalem. Like Polish-Israeli writer Aharon Megged's short story "Yad Vashem" [The Name] (1955) that addressed the emotional ramifications of generationally-divided Israeli disagreements related to familial Holocaust memorialization, *Dreams* forced audiences to face the *Shoah*. In Israel and the United States, cultural discourses highlighted Jews' heroism instead of their victimhood through stories of ghetto uprisings and resistance heroes like Hannah Senesh, a Jewish Hungarian–Palestinian paratrooper who was executed in Hungary for espionage after returning there to aid Yugoslavian anti-Nazi forces during the war.[94] Alongside and despite these efforts, however, Holocaust survivors and their children experienced nightmares about concentration camps. Clive Barnes wrote in the *New York Times* in reaction to *Dreams* that Sokolow "has a very proper respect for Hell. . .that even Dante might envy."[95] Although *Dreams* portrays Jews fighting back, it shows pain in the camps as a way to address the realities of the recent past. Israeli critics more easily read the Holocaust imagery in *Dreams* than did New York's predominantly white, non-Jewish 1960s dance press corps, and Israelis were familiar with Andre Schwarz-Bart's historical novel *The Last of the Just* (1959), on which Sokolow based the dance, which US critics were not. Dance critics in both countries spoke of *Dreams'* onstage horrors, yet both critics' insistence that its movement abstraction contributed to these memories as nightmares instead of reality denied the ongoing effects of the Holocaust in both countries.

Despite Israel's modeling of cultural institutions on those in the United States, American Jewishness differed from Israeliness. Cultural aspects relating to Jews' expression of Jewishness that diverged in Israel and the United States further affected how critics and audiences received *Dreams* in each country. Aldor differentiated Diaspora Jewishness and Israeli Jewishness in relation to treatments of the past: Diaspora Jewishness accesses memory as a way to reembody a lost past and cement a sense of place in the face of uprootedness that was due to Diasporic dispersion, whereas Israeliness severed ties to the past to look forward and pursue the future and what is new.[96] *Dreams* cut across these

93. Sheramy, " 'Resistance and War,' " 297–298.

94. Judith Tydor Baumel, "Hannah Szenes (Senesh)," *Jewish Women: A Comprehensive Historical Encyclopedia*. March 1, 2009. Jewish Women's Archive. (Viewed on September 25, 2014) <http://jwa.org/encyclopedia/article/szenes-hannah>.

95. Clive Barnes, "Dance: Powerful 'Dreams: Anna Sokolow Shows Man, Unable to Communicate, Reduced to Fear," *New York Times*, no date, 1966, Alan M. and Sali Ann Kriegsman Collection, MD, LOC.

96. Aldor, "Naming," 377–379. See also Galili, "Reframing."

lines and complicated this reception in Israel. The piece engages memory by conjuring the ghosts of family members lost in the camps. It presented Israeli audiences with a contemporaneity that they refused to acknowledge to move forward: Many who survived the camps walked among them in society. Critics' responses in Israel and the United States regarding the specificity or abstraction of the work further reflected the divide between American Jewishness and Israeliness. Many American Jewish choreographers accessed a sense of universality through modern dance abstraction for their dances with Jewish themes.[97] In this way, suffering in dances like *Dreams* stands in for universal agony experienced by all people who face inhumane oppression. In Israel, according to Aldor, Jewish suffering, especially relating to the Holocaust, cannot be abstracted or universalized.[98] Sokolow's staging of Jewish torture in *Dreams*, in specific and generalized terms, attracted critical acclaim from Israeli audiences who did not consider her more abstract dances on the same programs, such as *Forms* or *Odes*, as effective as *Dreams*.

Although Graham's influence in Israel spread widely and quickly, American modern dance values of abstraction as they came through the Graham technique conflicted with Israeli dance preferences for specificity. In a 1982 comparison of contemporary dance in the United States and Israel, specifically the relationship of Graham to Levi-Tanai, Judith Brin Ingber concluded that most American dance focused on individualism and self-expression, with a lack of intimacy between the performers, specifically in Graham's *Appalachian Spring* (1944). Within the American progressive view that people can change their destiny, the work lacked the emotion and expressiveness that Ingber saw in Israeli choreography.[99] Graham's use of transcendent themes was a way to prevent direct self-expression considered indulgent in Protestantism.[100] The sin of self-indulgence was not an issue for Israeli dancers and audiences, who found Graham's abstraction overly intellectual. The pioneering associated with *halutzim* in Israeli cultural mythology resonated with aspects of an American pioneering spirit in Americana dances like *Appalachian Spring*, and the purpose of the New Jew was to create a new Jewish future. Yet for Israeli audiences battling the reality of the Holocaust beneath their tough exteriors, destiny was more complicated. Sokolow's movements, abstracted from gritty reality with vocabulary beyond her Graham base, embraced intimacy between

97. Naomi Jackson, "Searching for Moving Metaphors: Jewishness in American Modern and Postmodern Dance," in *Seeing Israeli and Jewish Dance*, ed. Ingber, 359–360 (see Introduction, n71). See also Daniel J. Elazar, "Changing Places, Changing Cultures: Divergent Jewish Political Cultures," in *Divergent Jewish Cultures*, eds. Moore and Troen, 319–331 (see Introduction, n69). Elazar argues that shared values of social justice and a balance between the universal and particular connect Jews in the United States and Israel.

98. Aldor, "Naming," 384.

99. Judith Brin Ingber, "What is American About American Modern Dance?" *Israel Dance* (1982): 5–8.

100. Jowitt, *Time and the Dancing Image*, 165 (see Chap. 1, n58).

performers and a deeply expressive self through performing sincerely, earnestly, and from the gut.

Dreams' detailed strife through technical and pedestrian movements resonated with audiences seeking universality and specificity. A woman in a white dress peering through a phalanx of guards opens the work.[101] (Figure 5.5) She climbs over their shoulders as if over rooftops;[102] she crumples to the floor; she widens her mouth into what Yehudit Ornstein described as a "mute cry of horror."[103] Each guard lifts an arm to the side and haltingly slams it into his thigh as the woman weaves through the pillars of their bodies. She knocks on the men's backs as if they are doors that could open and offer her a place to hide.[104] When coaching this work, Jim May told the dancer to imagine running from barking dogs; dancer Samantha Geracht, a second-generation Holocaust survivor, spoke of having to instead imagine herself in a busy grocery store when she performed this role because she found the overwhelming intensity of the scene too real.[105] Sokolow imagined that this woman, and also the three prostitutes who appear later in the dance, retained their inner purity despite the hell they experienced. Avraham remembered Sokolow telling her that the white dress represented an honesty that prevented the ugliness of the situation from touching her; she became the soul of the children who did not know what would happen to them in the death camps.[106] The prostitutes, wearing red dresses with their faces hiding behind their loose hair, also represented the innocence of children in the concentration camps. Israeli critics suggested that the red flowers tied to the dancers' wrists represented blossoming bloodstains, blood-filled wounds, or even crucifixion points, as if their souls, or even their wombs, bled.[107] Years later Sokolow explained about the three women: "The Nazis took these girls off and put them on the street and told them to smile and be sexy. So my conception was, on the outside they did that, but on the inside they were pure. That's why the music is Bach."[108] Inside this work's terror, Sokolow retained the rhetorical optimism and heroism that became part of 1960s American Jewish Holocaust discourse.

101. The piece was initially a small ensemble work for five dancers that reflected Sokolow's nightmares about her recent breakup with John White and began not with the scene of the woman and the guards, but with the duet that follows. Moore, interview, 12–13 (see Chap. 4, n88).

102. Sondra Horton Fraleigh, *Dance and the Lived Body: A Descriptive Aesthetics* (Pittsburgh: University of Pittsburgh Press, 1987), 226.

103. Ornstein, "Anna Sokolow's 'Lyric Theatre,'" [1962].

104. Avraham, conversation.

105. Samantha Geracht (dancer) in discussion with the author, October 26, 2009, New York City.

106. Avraham, conversation.

107. Ben Meir, "On Stages and Exhibitions: The Lyric Theatre, Program B"; Asher Nahor, "Anna Sokolow's Lyric Theatre—Second Program"; and Asher Nahor, "Anna Sokolow's 'The Lyric Theatre,' Program A: The Pairing Didn't Work," *Yediot Aharonot*, July 8, 1962, n.p., Folder 111.17.2.4 Anna Sokolow's Lyric Theatre Clippings, DLI, trans. Stav Ziv.

108. Anna Sokolow, quoted in "Learning from Performers: Anna Sokolow, Agassiz Theatre, October 31, 1986," cassette, Morse Music Collection, Lamont Library, Harvard University.

Figure 5.5: Hannah Kahn as the woman in white, *Dreams*. Photograph © Lois Greenfield. Jerome Robbins Dance Division, The New York Public Library for the Performing Arts.

Attitudes toward abstraction divided US and Israeli dance critics in their 1960s reactions to *Dreams*. Midcentury US critics upheld values of American modernism that privileged abstraction, whereas Israeli reception of *Dreams* emphasized how personal stories intensified the impact of cultural memory better than generalized statements about human suffering. Israeli critic Ilan Reichler articulated the importance of Sokolow's use of specificity instead of abstracted generalities: "She does not try to ponder and philosophize. . .as we sometimes see in Martha Graham's works, in which an abstract idea is translated into even more abstract movement. . . that ultimately leaves us. . .distanced a thousand kilometers from the stage."[109] A program note that appeared at the Israeli, but not the American, premiere of *Dreams* reinforces how Israeli audiences further received this specificity within the dance's framing. The note read, "In the dance, with its abstract illustrative measures, hints of realistic elements are integrated (such as the Nazi salute, the forest [likely a reference to the Babi Yar massacre], the wall, the shattering of the window glass [*Kristallnacht*] and the gratings [barbed wire]). One main symbolic element is the hair, which seemingly gets its own life."[110] This final image references Nazi use of prisoners' hair in death camps: Guards shorn women and men upon their arrival, and prisoners forced to remove corpses from the gas chambers removed any remaining hair, which was bought by private firms and made into rope, mattresses, and other products.[111] In the dance, this note points to the trio depicting young women forced into prostitution, whose long hair covers their faces for most of the vignette (Figure 5.6.) Even before the curtain rose in Tel Aviv, audiences had a visceral sense of what would unfold in the dance. Although the Batsheva Dance Company and its Graham repertory soon eclipsed the Lyric Theatre, Israeli audiences notably supported Sokolow's representation of the particular instead of the universal.

For Israeli audiences the specificity in *Dreams* came through personal histories and *The Last of the Just* narrative.[112] To read *Dreams* through *The Last of the Just* illuminates a dimensionality not just of the human toll of man's inhumanity to man, but also of the Holocaust's implications for Jewish lineages and traditions. Schwarz-Bart's novel, published in French in 1959, was translated into Hebrew in 1959 and English in 1960. It follows the genealogy of a family that Schwarz-Bart named "Lamed Vovniks" (righteous men) with the surname Levy (derived from the Jewish priestly line of Levites) through generations from twelfth-century England to World

---

109. Ilan Reichler, "On the Dreams—A. Sokolow's Company's Program B," no source, no date, Anna Sokolow's Lyric Theatre Clippings—Reviews, Articles, DLI, trans. Stav Ziv.

110. *Anna Sokolow's Lyric Theatre presents Programme B*, trans. Galit Golan.

111. United States Holocaust Memorial Museum, "At the Killing Centers," *The Holocaust: A Learning Site for Students*, http://www.ushmm.org/outreach/en/article.php?ModuleId=10007714. Accessed September 3, 2015.

112. André Schwarz-Bart, *The Last of the Just*, trans. Stephen Becker (1960; New York: Athaneum, 1973; Cambridge, MA: Bentley, 1981).

Figure 5.6: Women's trio from *Dreams*. Photograph © Lois Greenfield. Jerome Robbins Dance Division, The New York Public Library for the Performing Arts.

War II in Germany and France.[113] The book's conclusion presents an incredible sense of loss when the last scion, Ernie Levy, dies in a gas chamber—of generations

113. The Hebrew translation of the book uses *tzaddik* (righteous person). From the Hebrew letters *lamed* and *vav* that together signify thirty-six, the lamed-vav Talmudic (b.Sanhedrin 97b) and kabbalistic traditions believe that there are at least thirty-six anonymous righteous people, called hidden or secret saints, in every generation who can save the world. *Lamedvovniks* are Yiddish folkloric figures that continue this tradition. Schwarz-Bart based the Levy family on this tradition but assigned one known Lamed Vovnik per generation in the same familial line to question the existence of God in the Holocaust's aftermath. See Kathleen Gyssels, "*Le Dernier des Justes*—A Jewish Child's Apprenticeship of 'The Impossibility of Being a Jew,'" *European Judaism* 42, no. 1 (2009): 90–106; D. Mesher, "André Schwarz-Bart (1928 –)," in *Holocaust Literature: An Encyclopedia of Writers and Their Work*, ed. S. Lilian Kremer (London: Routledge,

Figure 5.7: Lyric Theatre rehearsing *Dreams*, 1963. Photograph by Zvi Glaser. Courtesy of Ze'eva Cohen.

gone, of a lineage extinguished. This texture gives each person in Sokolow's work at once a history and many histories. Throughout the dance, Sokolow builds empathy with the people onstage through movements from pedestrian vocabularies taken to extremes—running, screaming, retching, slamming into walls—paired with vulnerable chest arches. The thematic posture in Figure 5.7 returns throughout the piece: Limbs stick out at splayed angles, jugular exposed, faces contorted in agony. This specificity of pain, instead of abstracted representation, made *Dreams* feel cathartically familiar. To this end, Reichler noted, "You watch *Dreams* and a feeling develops as though you have opened a set of personal letters. . .that make the work honest, of value, and convincing."[114] The Israeli critics saw this, but the American critics did not. Critics' and audiences' varying abilities to read the dances' codes based on their level of familiarity with the Holocaust and Jewish experience reveals the multiple levels on which *Dreams* operates and accounts for how *Dreams'* impact diverged in Israel and the United States.

The dancers' bodies in *Dreams* depict people's experiences in the camps, signifying both the centrality of the Jewish body to anti-Semitic persecution and the physically strong archetype of the New Jew to combat the weakness associated with Eastern European Jewish physicality. The movement in *Dreams'* final section shows decrepit bodies against which New Jew ideology prevailed. With rags hanging off

2002), Credo Reference; and Geoffrey W. Dennis, *The Encyclopedia of Jewish Myth, Magic and Mysticism* (Woodbury, MN: Llewellyn, 2007), 149–150, 220.

114. Reichler, "On the Dreams—A. Sokolow's Company's Program B."

their bones, prisoners slap and scuff their feet against the concrete floor, sending resounding, hollow sounds through the space. After scattering, they lope from one foot to the other, torsos over, some heads looking to the side, all legs bending resiliently behind them. Suddenly, a dancer stops, slicing his right arm forward and high in front of his head; the others follow suit. One by one, they begin to retch, thrusting their torsos forward. They teeter violently back and forth, forcing out a deep, sharp exhalation of breath with each expulsion. The final thrust forces each dancer's torso into a backward curve over a base of widely spread feet. The performers' arms direct extended angles from their shoulder sockets, and their mouths gape against their exposed necks and the cries of the score's trumpets. This section renders a visceral malady through a scene that feels frighteningly real.

In Israel, *Dreams* posed redemption for bodies lost in the camps. Photographs of prisoners' skeletal physiques evidence how the Nazis dehumanized them through starvation and physical labor.[115] Ingber has shown how two groups of Jews in 1947, Yishuv dancers who performed Israeli folk dances for Holocaust survivors in a tour of European displaced-persons camps, did not recognize the other as Jews across their experiential divides, bringing the body differences of the *galut* [Diaspora; here, Europe] and the New Jew, and divergent experiences of Jews in Europe and Palestine during World War II, into stark relief.[116] In *Dreams*, Israeli bodies performed European bodies and reclaimed, or reembodied, those that perished. Cohen remembered that when she performed *Dreams*, she put herself into a hazy space of "nowhere" because of the work's dream aspect, and yet, the dance's grounded physicality made the situation unmistakably real.[117] In *The Last of the Just*, Ernie Levy survived years of anti-Semitic violence before the gas chamber, including being hit in the head with rocks, stripped naked in front of classmates, beat up, ignored by people he thought were friends, left for dead on the sidewalk, and surviving suicide attempts that permanently marked his body. In the gas chamber, he died unmarked in a body that no longer mattered with his arms wrapped around his beloved fiancée Golda. This bodily history and sense of generations destroyed were inscribed on Sokolow's dancers.

The final moments of *Dreams* display this moment, as the group's slow, measured steps backward denote their entry into the gas chamber. Coaching Indianapolis's Dance Kaleidoscope, Sokolow instructed the dancers that these walks are dignified.[118] The mass melts to the floor, pulsing, ending on their knees with their bent torsos spiraling over to one side, in what Sokolow imagined was the "rhythm of the

115. See, among others, the photographic collection on the United States Holocaust Memorial Museum website, http://www.ushmm.org. Accessed September 12, 2015.

116. Judith Brin Ingber, "Vilified or Glorified? Nazi Versus Zionist Views of the Jewish Body," in *Seeing Israeli and Jewish Dance*, ed. Ingber, 251–277 (see Introduction, n71). Yishuv refers to the Jewish community in Palestine before the 1948 establishment of the State of Israel.

117. Cohen, conversation, 2009.

118. *Anna Sokolow*, produced by Marvin Diskin (1990), JRDD, NYPL.

gas chamber."[119] Their heads stretch away from their hands as their outstretched palms reach toward the ceiling and the other hand covers their faces. Even though their bodies succumb to the gas, one arm reaches skyward in a determined triumph of spirit, a stable triumph in the face of instability, fear, and strife. What are these people's relationships to each other? Are they strangers? Siblings? Lovers? Does it matter? Or does the movement read as universal enough that we are simply horrified? Or sad? Or empowered to take up the mantel of Never Again? In a version of *Dreams* that Sokolow coached for Maryland Dance Theater, the child from an earlier section returns to observe this scene and folds into a child's-pose-type position as the adults yield to the gas.[120] The child observes the death, literally of her parents and metaphorically of generations.

Dreams appeared in Israel and the United States within Jewish social contexts that highlighted Jewish resistance during the Holocaust, but American critics' reviews of *Dreams'* early performances that do not mention the Holocaust invisibilize Jewish experience and uphold an American Cold War refusal to address political statements. This changed between the mid-1960s and 1990s when Sokolow named the dance's theme. *Dreams* embodies currents of valuing courage over victimization and of directly addressing the Holocaust, but Sokolow did not publicly label it as a Holocaust work until stating in her 1965 *Dance Magazine* essay "The Rebel and the Bourgeois" that *Dreams* was her "indictment of Nazi Germany."[121] She wrote, "When I started, I only had the idea of dreams, but they became nightmares, and then I saw they were related to the concentration camps."[122] Similarly, in 1995, Sokolow recalled that she made *Dreams* so that people "would never forget" what transpired during the Holocaust.[123] Prior to the political acceptability of indicting the Holocaust onstage, *Dreams* presented American audiences with indiscriminate horror.

1960s American reception showed *Dreams'* themes were not fully legible to American audiences. US critics reinforced Sokolow's modernist reputation and presented *Dreams* as another study in urban alienation, thematically following *Lyric Suite* and *Rooms*. Although critics Doris Hering and Marcia Marks acknowledged the darkness of the piece, they did not define it. Hering discussed it as a continuation of Sokolow's 1950s work in alienation, writing of its premiere, "As Miss Sokolow's *Rooms* represented a level deeper than her *Lyric Suite*, so did *Dreams* find a level deeper than *Rooms*. It was still another time in the heart's night."[124] Marks's

119. Ibid.

120. I thank Anne Warren for sharing this with me.

121. Anna Sokolow, "The Rebel and the Bourgeois," in *The Modern Dance: Seven Statements of Belief*, ed. Selma Jeanne Cohen (Middletown, CT: Wesleyan University Press, 1966), 36.

122. Ibid.

123. Henning Rübsam, "Anna Sokolow and *Dreams*," *Stern's Performing Arts Directory*, 1996, 14–15, Biographical File—Sokolow, Anna, Juilliard.

124. Hering, "The Freda Miller Memorial Concert, 92nd Street 'Y,' May 8, 1961," 15 (see Chap. 3, n138).

1964 review further relates more to urban alienation than to any Holocaust thematic material: "*Dreams* [was] Miss Sokolow's series of dreams disturbed, disrupted, distorted. Though a work of highly imaginative variety within its single
subject, it turned the two-part program into a stark and sinister event."[125] After
Sokolow named *Dreams* a Holocaust work, Barnes wrote, "Now in 'Dreams,' she
has taken her argument further to the point, where man, totally disassociated from
his environment, can no longer communicate with himself, and is the prey of bestial fears."[126] Although Barnes still compared *Dreams* to *Rooms*, his comment about
"bestial fears" veils a Holocaust reference. During this time *The Diary of Anne Frank*
(1952) and Elie Wiesel's *Night* trilogy (1960–1962) circulated.[127] These books
show the persistence of the human spirit despite the horrors of Nazi occupation and
the camps. Notably, *The Last of the Just*, which ends without a sense of hope, is not
widely read in the United States, and American critics did not mention Schwarz-
Bart as Israeli critics did. More than ten years later, *Dreams* was billed in the United
States as being inspired by *The Diary of Anne Frank* and *The Last of the Just*.[128] By
1975, when the Mary Anthony Dance Theatre performed *Dreams*, US audiences
considered it imbued with Holocaust imagery. According to Anthony, audiences
initially found *Dreams* inaccessible. People feared the Holocaust might recur, and
the piece made them uncomfortable.[129] US reactions to *Dreams* reflected a desire to
keep the Holocaust in the past.

Israeli accounts of *Dreams* from as early as 1962 identify the Holocaust references and symbolism in a way US critics did not or could not, while denying a
Holocaust reality. The most prominent reference is the barbed-wire fence that
many Israeli critics report lowering from the ceiling at the end of the dance that
most effectively framed the piece. Nahor situated Sokolow's realization of *The Last
of the Just* within popular opinion and noted, "the tortures of the Holocaust victims
are turned into abstract nightmares of sorts, which have no need to be grounded
in reality."[130] This sentiment, that the *Shoah* should only be the stuff of nightmares,
maps onto what historian Gulie Ne'eman Arad terms "disremembering": Israel's

125. Marcia Marks, "Anna Sokolow Dance Company, 92nd Street 'Y,' April 26, 1964," *Dance
Magazine* (June 1964): 67.

126. Barnes, "Dance: Powerful 'Dreams.'"

127. Anne Frank's father Otto Frank published *The Diary of Anne Frank* in Dutch as *The Secret
Annex* in 1947. It was translated into English as *Anne Frank: The Diary of a Young Girl* in 1952.
Wiesel published *Night* in Yiddish in 1955. It was published in English in 1960. Wiesel published *Dawn* and *Day* in English in 1961 and 1962, respectively. I use the English dates here to
show the time that they came into currency in the United States.

128. Press release, CBS Television Network Press Information, "Choreographer Anna
Sokolow's Work, on 'Camera Three,' Aug. 20," July 18, 1978, Box 142, Folder: Sokolow, Anna,
the Alan M. and Sali Ann Kriegsman Collection, MD, LOC; and Warren, *Rebellious Spirit*,
186–187.

129. Mary Anthony (dancer, choreographer) in discussion with the author, August 27, 2008,
New York City.

130. Nahor, "Anna Sokolow's Lyric Theatre—Second Program."

postwar cultural discourse that, in cutting Israel off from Europe to build a strong Jewish nation anew, denied the realities of Holocaust events.[131] Many critics identified *Dreams* as the strongest piece on the 1962 Lyric Theatre program and continued to support it through 1964. One highlighted the "sleepwalkerlike precision" with which the dancers executed their life and love among the horrors.[132] This performative quality manifests in the penultimate vignette of the dance, wherein two lovers, who could be Ernie and Golda, dance their last duet in blind sadness and seem to feel their lineage die with them. *Dreams'* Tel Aviv premiere came on the heels of the months-long 1961 trial, and June 1962 execution, of Gestapo officer Adolph Eichmann, which led to a national preoccupation with the *Shoah*.[133] Attention to Eichmann's trial crystallized late-1950s social sentiments connected to what historian Dalia Ofer identifies as a "Jewish consciousness," one part of which was "conceiving of the Holocaust as an episode that strengthens the bonds of a common Jewish identity, serving as a connecting link between various segments in Israeli society."[134] The Lyric Theatre toured Israel from 1962 to 1964, between the Eichmann trial and the 1967 Six-Day War, at which time the Israeli government used the *Shoah* as rationale for military action against its geographical neighbors.[135] Just prior to this foreign policy shift, from denying the Holocaust's place in society to promote New Jew ideology to using the Holocaust as rationale for expanding Israel's borders, *Dreams* invoked lost generations to interrogate history by stripping Holocaust memory raw to fight injustice.

Despite the connection between her choreographic imperatives and Israeli cultural values, Sokolow's routine absences from Israel and financial straits wreaked havoc on her work in Tel Aviv. The funding Sokolow received was not enough to keep the Lyric Theatre in upgraded studio spaces or, ultimately, to keep the company going. In retrospect, dancers like Romano were in high spirits about economic hardships. He likened dancing on pushed-together dining-room tables at *kibbutzim* to pioneering, saying how much he loved working for Sokolow and how dedicated he was to her work, and he implied that if the Lyric Theatre had sufficient funding, they could have rivaled large companies.[136] Sokolow's long absences each year exacerbated these problems. She struggled to secure annual funding for the Lyric Theatre and could not compete with de Rothschild's independent wealth. In 1964

131. Gulie Ne'eman Arad, "The Shoah as Israel's Political Trope," in *Divergent Jewish Cultures*, eds. Moore and Troen, 194 (see Introduction, n69).

132. "A. Sokolow's Lyric Theatre."

133. Arad, "The Shoah as Israel's Political Trope," 200; and United States Holocaust Memorial Museum, "Eichmann Trial," http://www.ushmm.org/wlc/en/article.php?ModuleId=10005179. Accessed September 12, 2015.

134. Dalia Ofer, "The Holocaust, the Creation of Israel, and the Shaping of Israeli Society," in *Shared Histories: A Palestinian-Israeli Dialogue*, eds. Paul Scham, Walid Salem, and Benjamin Pogrund (Walnut Creek, CA: Left Coast Press, 2005), 143.

135. Arad, "The Shoah as Israel's Political Trope," 201–204.

136. Romano, discussion.

Sokolow's dancers flocked to Batsheva's full employment and year-round contract, and Sokolow felt betrayed.[137] In *Dance Magazine*, Hering called Batsheva "*Sabra Graham*." She affirmed the midcentury belief that, despite transnational negotiations, dance modernism remained unchanged through Graham's codified technique: "Miss Graham's choreography *can* translate to dancers other than her own because as choreography it does have universality [original emphasis]."[138] Yet, when Batsheva first toured internationally, reviewers remarked on the dancers' boundless energy and emotional depth of performance,[139] all through Graham-trained bodies, as if even the restrictions of a codified technique could not bind the mythical ancient Israelite spirit from springing forth through contemporary abstraction.

Although Sokolow benefitted from her dancers' *sabra* physicality, she could not handle the emotional and security implications of war in the region. In the middle of a 1973 residency with Batsheva, for which Sokolow was engaged to stage a full evening of work, the Yom Kippur War broke out. Sokolow fled Israel and left her work unfinished. She lost respect from the company and American dancers living in Israel for not showing solidarity in a time of crisis.[140] Sokolow spent her career putting her body on the line and digging into the gritty trauma of reality but fled with her proverbial soapbox in her suitcase in the heat of this political upheaval. As Sokolow aged, she retreated into abstraction while trying to retain revolutionary credibility. This began with her failure in the experimental countercultural rock musical *Hair* (1967), which suggested the emerging generation was beginning to pass her over. Despite the 1973 War incident, Sokolow retained working and personal relationships in Israel through the rest of her life. She staged repertory for Batsheva and its sister company Bat-Dor through the 1980s and taught often at the Jerusalem Academy of Music and Dance. She choreographed stage productions for theaters in Tel Aviv and Jerusalem until 1989.[141] She continued to teach classes for Inbal and retained a close friendship with Levi-Tanai through the 1990s.

The AICF employed Sokolow to culturally shape Israel in an Americanized image, yet the reverse also occurred: Israeli influences on Sokolow changed American modernism during the Cold War. The commitment and attack that Israeli dancers brought to the movement through the unapologetic directness, visceral sexuality, outer toughness, and inner vulnerability of *sabra* physicality affected the performance quality of Sokolow's work. She furthermore sponsored Israeli dancers, like Cohen, at Juilliard and brought them into her New York company. This migration of people shows the mobility of cultural, political, and aesthetic values

137. Anna Sokolow to Abraham Zauri ("Tzuri"), December 16, 1963, and January 1, 1964, Correspondence file 111.17.2.5, Anna Sokolow's Lyric Theatre Collection, DLI; and Romano, discussion.

138. Doris Hering, "Sabra Graham," *Dance Magazine* (February 1971): 60.

139. *Let's Dance!*, directed by Gabriel Bibliowicz (Israel: Norma Productions, 2012).

140. Rottenberg, "Anna Sokolow," 53.

141. Ibid.

through honest bodies. From this international circulation, socialist Zionism reinforced the revolutionary modernism in Sokolow's choreography, which in turn reflected Jewishness as secular lived experience. Despite bringing Israeliness into American modern dance, Sokolow's choreography retained an abstracted look that felt familiar to American audiences. By canonizing Sokolow in the 1950s and 1960s, critics in the *New York Times* and *Dance Magazine* compressed her Jewish socialism into abstracted dances they deemed quintessentially American. Their comments normalized Sokolow's subversions as her communist, global-minded currents composed American modernism in dance through international corporeal discourses.

No Fists in the Air

Anna Sokolow and the Cold War

In the final section of Anna Sokolow's Vietnam protest dance *Time+* (1966), four camouflage-dressed soldiers emerge, kneeling, against a dark curtain. Their bare legs are bandaged at the knee. As they *bourrée* forward on their kneecaps, it is clear that they represent amputees, as if one of the Vietnam War's landmines blew off the bottom parts of their legs. Their tiny advances forward are inwardly rotated and pitiful. It is uncanny when the dancers rise to stand on their feet and reveal that their legs do not end at the knee. In that moment they become normative Everypeople instead of injured individuals. They cling to each other as they totter around the stage and suddenly reel back and fall into a heap as if they have just been shot. I can almost smell their flesh as it hangs off their bones. One arm reaches out despairingly—Can someone help? Will aid ever come?—and the dance ends.[1]

As 1960s leftist currents built on those of the 1930s, the packaging changed more than the message. As should be clear at the end of this book, *Time+* continued a long line of Sokolow's choreographies between the 1930s and 1990s that called for social justice through gut-twisting imagery. Historian Maurice Isserman notes that the main difference between the Communist Old Left that collapsed between 1956 and 1958 and the New Left that developed with the 1962 founding of Students for a Democratic Society was the New Left's dismissiveness of the Old Left's generation but not necessarily its values. Where the Old Left spent too much energy splintering factions along narrow ideological differences, he argues,

---

1. *Sokolow: Timely, Timeless—Time+*, DVD, reconstructed by Greg Drotar, Lenore Latimer, and Kathy Posin (Sokolow Dance Foundation, 2004), JRDD, NYPL.

the New Left did not work cohesively or systematically enough to sustain a deeply rooted social movement.[2] Sokolow and her work were caught between these shifting generations. She was an old communist who became known again as a voice of the counterculture through the ennui of her *Opus* series. Sokolow's choreography did not engage what performance theorist Jill Dolan calls utopian performatives, or moments in which onstage events propose a world better than the one in which we live.[3] Rather, by reflecting society as it was and staging society's deep social and emotional dregs, Sokolow created an onstage space in which to address those problems. The honest bodies in Sokolow's work produced critiques that propelled her activism to repair the world.

The dance and theater fields' consideration of Sokolow as the sardonic yet liberating voice of a new counterculture landed her a position as the first choreographer of *Hair: The American Tribal Love-Rock Musical* in 1966. Qualitatively different than the 1979 motion picture choreographed by Twyla Tharp that featured hippies moving in Tharp's characteristic resiliently weighted style with performers lolling through movements derived from social dances and the occasional lift with a leg virtuosically thrust skyward, the stage version of *Hair* (1967) that premiered at the experimental laboratory Public Theater in New York's East Village featured Sokolow's gritty use of jazz by stringy haired, disaffected teenagers. It recalled the end of *Opus*, where the dancers yelled expletives at the audience before rushing the orchestra pit. Much to Sokolow's dismay, producer Joseph Papp fired her after a series of events caused upheaval in the production. *Hair*'s performances bore clear markers of Sokolow's movement style even though Papp removed her name from publicity materials.[4] After this episode, Sokolow slipped into the depression that I mentioned in this book's Introduction.

Sokolow's experience in *Hair* reflected deep generational divides that surfaced during the 1960s tempestuous social changes. Could the Old Left's revolutionary modernism endure when the New Left rose? Sokolow kept current but fell prey to the New Left's desire for youth and leadership by red diaper babies instead of Reds. Yet communist discourse in her choreography still circulated within a new liberal context in the 1970s, as repertory companies performed her dances and university dance departments staged them from Labanotation score. This dissemination was important for Sokolow and the continued transmission of her work. She appreciated staging processes like those from Labanotation that enabled her dances to be performed in many places at the same time and that kept her established repertory

2. Maurice Isserman, *If I Had a Hammer: The Death of the Old Left and the Birth of the New Left* (1987; repr., Urbana: University of Illinois Press, 1993), 174–219.

3. Jill Dolan, *Utopia in Performance: Finding Hope at the Theater* (Ann Arbor: University of Michigan Press, 2005), 5.

4. Warren, *Rebellious Spirit*, 223–227 (see Preface, n2); and Eric Grode, "The Roots of 'Hair,'" *American Theatre* 28, no. 1 (2011): 115.

alive while freeing her to make new work.[5] As Isserman argued that the labors of the Old Left were integral to the successes of the New Left, so too was Sokolow's body of work an important nexus of social statements for ensuing generations of dancers, even as her popularity as a current choreographer declined.

As the 1960s gave way to the 1970s, many 1930s leftists denied their political associations after the hell of McCarthyism. Sokolow's own assimilation during the 1950s to 1960s diverted attention from her past and enabled political amnesia regarding her communist coalitions pre-McCarthy.[6] In a 1975 interview, Sokolow exemplified Isserman's characterization of the main difference between Old Left members being particular about the strands of the movement to which they belonged, as opposed to the New Left's general rallying around common social values. When questioned about her communist past, Sokolow expressed her affinity for the Communist Party's goals over its politics: "I believed in what the party could do. In principle, yes. Of course, later, it became shockingly disillusioning. But even then I never, for example, finished a dance with a fist up in the air, or took a red flag out and waved it. . . .I tried to show people the truth, then let them make up their own minds."[7] Although puncturing the air with a fist, like Miriam Blecher in *Awake* (1933), or weaving red fabric through a group of bodies, like Edith Segal in *The Belt Goes Red* (1930), denoted that a dance was for the revolutionary cause,[8] such a dance was not choreographically consistent with the marriage of form and content that modern and revolutionary dance critics valued in the 1930s. Sokolow even lectured to Soviet audiences in 1934 that simply waving a red flag does not make a revolutionary dance. At the time, she was disappointed to find that the Soviet Union had no revolutionary dance movement to rival the one in the United States, and moreover, despite communist themes in many Soviet productions, for Sokolow, Soviet ballet reeked of aristocratic hierarchy.[9] Unlike the American leftist dancers who liberally sprinkled skyward fists and flying flags in their choreography, Sokolow aligned herself with universalism by considering her work a personal reaction to the social situation, and not propaganda.[10] She never ended a dance with a fist in the air because she did not make mimetic dances. Sokolow's revolutionary

5. General letter from Anna Sokolow, February 6, 1976, Collection of Dance Notation Bureau (DNB); Anna Sokolow to Rhoda Grauer (National Endowment for the Arts), May 14, 1979, DNB; Anna Sokolow to Dance Notation Bureau, September 24, 1988, DNB; and Anna Sokolow to Kathleen Berman, 4 October 1988, DNB.

6. I thank John Giffin for this term.

7. Anna Sokolow, quoted in Murphy and Rhodes, *They Are their Own Gifts* outtakes, quoted in Warren, *Rebellious Spirit*, 125.

8. Hall, "The Solo Recital," 4, (see Chap. 1, n40); and Graff, *Stepping Left*, 29–31 (see Preface, n2).

9. Sokolow, interview by Newman, 58 (see Chap. 1, n106). See also Dal Negro, "Return from Moscow," 27 (see Chap. 2, n5).

10. Sokolow, interview by Wolfe (see Chap. 3, n126).

spectatorship came from the way she engaged her audience members with the injustices she presented instead of plainly telling them what to think.

The revisionist narrative Sokolow offered in the 1975 interview suggested to later audiences that, because she never ended a dance with a fist in the air, she was not active in leftist politics when it was popular to incorporate communist imagery. Once the Second Red Scare subsided, Sokolow acknowledged her political stance to varying degrees, depending on the situation. In her 1961 grant proposal to the America–Israel Cultural Foundation for funds to build what became her Lyric Theatre in Israel, Sokolow identified herself as an American socialist, likely to show that her beliefs aligned with the young socialist Israeli state.[11] In 1975, Sokolow was unapologetic about her 1930s work: "We were all very Left at that time and it was no sin; it was before McCarthy. . . .We all had deep ideals about the principles of life."[12] In 1987, Sokolow reframed her works' politics to be humanist and universal, stating in an interview that her 1930s dances contained "Not political themes. . . but themes of humanity."[13] This shift to a generalized view of her social statements resounded with the New Left's broad liberalism.

As Sokolow's work circulates through new generations of dancers' bodies after the initial thirty-year period in which it produced communist ideology, the question remains how residue in corporeal markers implicates practitioners in the values of the choreography. Highlighting the raced, gendered, and commodified stakes of choreography's circulating nature, Anthea Kraut argued that dances "carry strong ties to the bodies that generate them; dance-makers' bodies are deeply implicated in the circulation of their choreography."[14] Can choreographers and movement practitioners change the meanings or cultural values inherent in choreographic residue, and if so, what are the ethics of this action? Sokolow broke Graham's technique down to its component parts and recontextualized elements like torso contractions and back spirals into firing mechanisms for her own revolutionary ends. Sokolow's dances like *Rooms* and *Steps of Silence* (1968), another of her Holocaust works, are often staged from Labanotation score. Performing these dances during contemporary humanitarian crises can help present the situation anew through historical resonances, and stepping into them can change the way performers understand their corporeality in relation to that from another time. Embodying the postures and kinetic sequences from these dances does not always signal their discourse to dancers who do not know the historical context, but the performers nevertheless become part of the dances' circulation. The kinesthetic trail that Sokolow left

11. Sokolow, "Suggestions," (see Chap. 5, n53).

12. Anna Sokolow, quoted in Kisselgoff, "In Anna Sokolow's Dance, Her Beliefs," 46 (see Introduction, n36).

13. Anna Sokolow, quoted in David Shifren, "Anna Sokolow: An Interview," *New American—Émigré Voices: Ex-Soviets Speak Out*, December–January 1987, 15, SDF.

14. Anthea Kraut, *Choreographing Copyright: Race, Gender, and Intellectual Property Rights in American Dance* (New York: Oxford University Press, 2016), xiv.

through the United States, Mexico, Israel, and other locales where she taught technique classes and staged her work contributes to a transnational conversation on how her technical and choreographic values disseminated meaning, political affect, and movement characteristics across decades, and how their revolutionary residue informs contemporary contexts.

SELECTED BIBLIOGRAPHY

Adams, Michael C. C. *The Best War Ever: America and World War II.* Baltimore, MD: Johns Hopkins University Press, 1994.

Albright, Ann Cooper. *Traces of Light: Absence and Presence in the Work of Loïe Fuller.* Middletown, CT: Wesleyan University Press, 2007.

Albright, Ann Cooper. "Tracing the Past: Writing History Through the Body." In *The Routledge Dance Studies Reader.* 2nd ed., edited by Alexandra Carter and Janet O'Shea, 101–110. London: Routledge, 2010.

Aldor, Gaby. "The Borders of Contemporary Israeli Dance: 'Invisible Unless in Final Pain.'" *Dance Research Journal* 35, no. 1 (2003): 81–97. http://www.jstor.org/stable/1478480.

Anderson, Benedict. *Imagined Communities: Reflections on the Origin and Spread of Nationalism.* 1983. Revised edition, London and New York: Verso, 2006.

Antler, Joyce. *The Journey Home: Jewish Women and the American Century.* New York: Free Press, 1997.

Antler, Joyce, ed. *Talking Back: Images of Jewish Women in American Popular Culture.* Hanover, NH: Brandeis University Press/University Press of New England, 1998.

Baigell, Matthew. *Jewish-American Artists and the Holocaust.* New Brunswick, NJ: Rutgers University Press, 1997.

Bales, Melanie and Karen Eliot, eds. *Dance on Its Own Terms: Histories and Methodologies.* New York: Oxford University Press, 2013.

Banes, Sally and Noël Carroll. "Cunningham, Balanchine, and Postmodern Dance." *Dance Chronicle* 29 (2006): 49–68. doi:10.1080/01472520500538057.

Barthes, Roland. "The Death of the Author." In *Image, Music, Text,* translated by Stephen Heath, 142–148. New York: Hill and Wang, 1977.

Beller, Jonathan L. "The Spectatorship of the Proletariat." *boundary 2* 22, no. 3 (1995): 171–228.

Berghaus, Günter. *Futurism and Politics: Between Anarchist Rebellion and Fascist Reaction, 1909–1944.* Providence, RI: Berghahn Books, 1996.

Bird, Dorothy and Joyce Greenberg. *Bird's Eye View: Dancing with Martha Graham and on Broadway.* Pittsburgh, PA: University of Pittsburgh Press, 1997.

Blanco Borelli, Melissa. "'¿Y ahora qué vas a hacer, mulata?': Hip Choreographies in the Mexican *Cabaretera* Film *Mulata* (1954)." *Women & Performance: A Journal of Feminist Theory* 18, no. 3 (2008): 215–233. doi: 10.1080/07407700802495951.

Boyarin, Daniel, Daniel Itzkovitz, and Ann Pellegrini, eds. *Queer Theory and the Jewish Question.* New York: Columbia University Press, 2003.

Boyd, Nan Alamilla. *Wide Open Town: A History of Queer San Francisco to 1965.* Berkeley: University of California Press, 2003.

Briginshaw, Valerie A. *Dance, Space and Subjectivity.* Hampshire and New York: Palgrave, 2001.

Brodkin, Karen. *How Jews Became White Folks and What That Says about Race in America*. New Brunswick, NJ: Rutgers University Press, 2000.

Buck, Sarah A. "The Meaning of the Women's Vote in Mexico, 1917–1953." In *The Women's Revolution in Mexico, 1910–1953*, edited by Stephanie Mitchell and Patience Schell, 73–98. Lanham, MD: Rowman & Littlefield, 2007.

Burt, Ramsay. *Alien Bodies: Representations of Modernity, "Race" and Nation in Early Modern Dance*. London: Routledge, 1998.

Butler, Judith. *Bodies That Matter: On the Discursive Limits of "Sex."* New York: Routledge, 1993.

Butler, Judith. *Gender Trouble: Feminism and the Subversion of Identity*. 1990. New York and London: Routledge, 2006.

Calinescu, Matei. *Five Faces of Modernity*. Durham, NC: Duke University Press, 1987.

Carr, Barry. *Marxism and Communism in Twentieth-Century Mexico*. Lincoln: University of Nebraska Press, 1992.

Carter, Julian B. *The Heart of Whiteness: Normal Sexuality and Race in America, 1880–1940*. Durham, NC: Duke University Press, 2007.

Chauncey, George. *Gay New York: Gender, Urban Culture, and the Making of the Gay Male World 1890–1940*. New York: BasicBooks, 1994.

Chazin-Bennahum, Judith. *René Blum & The Ballets Russes: In Search of a Lost Life*. New York: Oxford University Press, 2011.

Cimet, Adina. *Ashkenazi Jews in Mexico: Ideologies in the Structuring of a Community*. Albany: State University of New York Press, 1997.

Conner, Lynne. "'What the Modern Dance Should Be': Socialist Agendas in the Modern Dance, 1931–38." In *Crucibles of Crisis: Performing Social Change*, edited by Janelle Reinelt, 231–248. Ann Arbor: University of Michigan Press, 1996.

Craven, David. *Art and Revolution in Latin America, 1910–1990*. New Haven, CT: Yale University Press, 2002.

Croft, Clare. *Dancers as Diplomats: American Choreography in Cultural Exchange*. New York: Oxford University Press, 2015.

Croft, Clare. "Feminist Dance Criticism and Ballet." *Dance Chronicle* 37, no. 2 (2014): 195–217.

Dallal, Alberto. *La Danza en México en el Siglo XX*. Xoco, CP, México, DF: Dirección General de Publicaciones, 1997.

D'Emilio, John. *Sexual Politics, Sexual Communities: The Making of a Homosexual Minority in the United States, 1940–1970*. 2nd ed. 1983. Reprint, Chicago: University of Chicago Press, 1998.

de Lauretis, Teresa. "Queer Theory: Lesbian and Gay Sexualities—An Introduction." *differences: A Journal of Feminist Cultural Studies* 3, no. 2 (1991): iii–xviii.

Denning, Michael. *The Cultural Front: The Laboring of American Culture in the Twentieth Century*. London and New York: Verso, 1996.

Desmond, Jane C., ed. *Dancing Desires: Choreographing Sexualities On & Off the Stage*. Madison: University of Wisonsin Press, 2001.

Dixon Gottschild, Brenda. *Digging the Africanist Presence in American Performance: Dance and Other Contexts*. Westport, CT, and London: Praeger, 1998.

Dolan, Jill. *Utopia in Performance: Finding Hope at the Theater*. Ann Arbor: University of Michigan Press, 2005.

Duggan, Lisa. *Sapphic Slashers: Sex, Violence, and American Modernity*. Durham, NC: Duke University Press, 2000.

Earle, Rebecca. *The Return of the Native: Indians and Myth-Making in Spanish America, 1810–1930*. Durham, NC: Duke University Press, 2007.

Eilberg-Schwartz, Howard, ed. *People of the Body: Jews and Judaism from an Embodied Perspective*. Albany: State University of New York Press, 1992.

Elswit, Kate. *Watching Weimar Dance*. New York: Oxford University Press, 2014.

Erdman, Harley. *Staging the Jew: The Performance of American Ethnicity, 1860–1920*. New Brunswick, NJ: Rutgers University Press, 1997.

Finaldi, Giuseppe. *Mussolini and Italian Fascism*. Harlow, England: Pearson Longman, 2008.

Foner, Eric. *The Story of American Freedom*. New York and London: Norton, 1998.

Foster, Hal. "Prosthetic Gods." *Modernism/Modernity* 4, no. 2 (1997): 5–38. doi:10.1353/mod.1997.0030

Foster, Susan Leigh. "Choreographies of Gender." *Signs* 24, no. 1 (1998): 1–33.

Foster, Susan Leigh. "Choreographies of Protest." *Theatre Journal* 55, no. 3 (2003): 395–412.

Foster, Susan Leigh. *Choreographing Empathy: Kinesthesia in Performance*. London: Routledge, 2011.

Foster, Susan Leigh. *Reading Dancing: Bodies and Subjects in Contemporary Dance*. Berkeley: University of California Press, 1986.

Foster, Susan Leigh. "Simply(?) the Doing of It, Like Two Arms Going Round and Round." In *Continuous Replay: The Photographs of Arnie Zane*, edited by Jonathan Green, 109–117. Cambridge, MA: MIT Press, 1999.

Foucault, Michel. "What Is an Author?" In *Language, Counter-Memory, Practice: Selected Essays and Interviews by Michel Foucault*, edited by Donald F. Bouchard, 113–138. Ithaca, NY: Cornell University Press, 1977.

Foulkes, Julia L. "Angels 'Rewolt!': Jewish Women in Modern Dance in the 1930s." *American Jewish History* 88, no. 2 (2000): 233–252. Accessed August 15, 2014. doi:10.1353/ajh.2000.0029.

Franco, Susanne and Marina Nordera, eds. *Dance Discourses: Keywords in Dance Research*. London: Routledge, 2007.

Frankel, Jonathan, ed. *Dark Times, Dire Decisions: Jews and Communism*. New York: Oxford University Press, 2004.

Franko, Mark. "Dance and the Political: States of Exception." In *Dance Discourses: Keywords in Dance Research*, edited by Susanne Franco and Marina Nordera, 11–28. London: Routledge, 2007.

Franko, Mark. *Dancing Modernism/Performing Politics*. Bloomington and Indianapolis: Indiana University Press, 1995.

Franko, Mark. *Martha Graham in Love and War: The Life in the Work*. New York: Oxford University Press, 2012.

Franko, Mark. *The Work of Dance: Labor, Movement, and Identity in the 1930s*. Middletown, CT: Wesleyan University Press, 2002.

Garafola, Lynn, ed. *Of, By, and For the People: Dancing on the Left in the 1930s*. Studies in Dance History: The Journal of the Society of Dance History Scholars 5, no. 1 (1994): 1–113.

Garafola, Lynn. "Writing on the Left: The Remarkable Career of Edna Ocko." *Dance Research Journal* 34, 1 (2002): 53–61. http://www.jstor.org/stable/1478133.

García-Márquez, Vicente. *The Ballets Russes: Colonel de Basil's Ballets Russes de Monte Carlo 1932–1952*. New York: Knopf, 1990.

George-Graves, Nadine. "Diasporic Spidering: Constructing Contemporary Black Identities." In *Black Performance Theory*, edited by Thomas F. DeFrantz and Anita Gonzalez, 33–44. Durham, NC: Duke University Press, 2014.

George-Graves, Nadine. *Urban Bush Women: Twenty Years of African American Dance Theater, Community Engagement, and Working It Out*. Madison: University of Wisconsin Press, 2010.

Gleizer, Daniela. *Unwelcome Exiles: Mexico and the Jewish Refugees from Nazism, 1933–1945*. Translated by Susan Thomae. Leiden, The Netherlands, and Boston: Brill, 2013.

Golan, Galia. "Militarization and Gender: The Israeli Experience." *Women's Studies International Forum* 20, nos. 5/6 (1997): 581–586. doi:10.1016/S0277-5395(97)00063-0.

Graff, Ellen. *Stepping Left: Dance and Politics in New York City, 1928–1942.* Durham, NC: Duke University Press, 1997.

Gonzalez, Anita. *Jarocho's Soul: Cultural Identity and Afro-American Dance.* Lanham, MD: University Press of America, 2004.

Guilbaut, Serge. "The New Adventures of the Avant-Garde in America: Greenberg, Pollock, or From Trotskyism to the New Liberalism of the 'Vital Center.'" Trans. Thomas Repensek. *October* 15 (1980): 61–78. http://www.jstor.org/stable/778453.

Halberstam, David. *The Fifties.* New York: Fawcett Columbine, 1993.

Halpern, Ben and Jehuda Reinharz. *Zionism and the Creation of a New Society.* New York: Oxford University Press, 1998.

Hedrick, Tace. *Mestizo Modernism: Race, Nation, and Identity in Latin American Culture, 1900–1940.* New Brunswick, NJ: Rutgers University Press, 2003.

Hellier-Tinoco, Ruth. *Embodying Mexico: Tourism, Nationalism & Performance.* New York: Oxford University Press, 2011.

Henderson, Sanya Shoilevska. *Alex North, Film Composer.* Jefferson, NC: McFarland & Company, 2003.

Herzog, Hanna. "Homefront and Battlefront: The Status of Jewish and Palestinian Women in Israel." In *Israeli Women's Studies: A Reader,* edited by Esther Fuchs, 208–228. New Brunswick, NJ: Rutgers University Press, 2005.

Hobsbawm, Eric. "Introduction: Inventing Traditions." In *The Invention of Tradition,* edited by Eric Hobsbawm and Terence Ranger, 1–14. Cambridge: Cambridge, University Press, 1983.

Hubbs, Nadine. *The Queer Composition of America's Sound: Gay Modernists, American Music, and National Identity.* Berkeley: University of California Press, 2004.

Hyman, Paula E. *Gender and Assimilation in Modern Jewish History: The Roles and Representation of Women.* Seattle and London: University of Washington Press, 1995.

Ingber, Judith Brin, ed. *Seeing Israeli and Jewish Dance.* Detroit, MI: Wayne State University Press, 2011.

Isserman, Maurice. *If I Had a Hammer: The Death of the Old Left and the Birth of the New Left.* 1987. Reprint, Urbana: University of Illinois Press, 1993.

Jackson, Naomi. *Converging Movements: Dance and Jewish Culture at the 92nd Street Y.* Hanover, CT, and London: Wesleyan University Press, 2000.

Jackson, Naomi. "Jewishness and Modern Dance in Sophie Maslow's *The Village I Knew.*" In *Dancing Texts: Intertextuality in Interpretation,* edited by Janet Adshead-Lansdale, 83–103. London: Dance Books, 1999.

Jacobson, Matthew Frye. *Whiteness of a Different Color: European Immigrants and the Alchemy of Race.* Cambridge, MA: Harvard University Press, 1998.

Jennison, Ruth. "Combining Uneven Developments: Louis Zukofsky and the Political Economy of Revolutionary Modernism." *Cultural Critique* 77 (2011): 146–179. doi:10.5749/culturalcritique.77.2011.0146

Johnson, David K. *The Lavender Scare: The Cold War Persecution of Gays and Lesbians in the Federal Government.* Chicago: University of Chicago Press, 2004.

Johnson, Haynes. *The Age of Anxiety: McCarthyism to Terrorism.* Orlando, FL: Harcourt, 2006.

Jones, Amelia. "Material Traces: Performativity, Artistic 'Work,' and New Concepts of Agency." *TDR: The Drama Review* 59, no. 4 (2015): 18–35.

Jowitt, Deborah. *Time and the Dancing Image.* Berkeley: University of California Press, 1988.

Juhasz, Suzanne. "Queer Swans: Those Fabulous Avians in the *Swan Lakes* of Les Ballets Trockadero and Matthew Bourne." *Dance Chronicle* 31, no. 1 (2008): 54–83.

Kant, Marion. "German Dance and Modernity: Don't Mention the Nazis." In *Rethinking Dance History: A Reader,* edited by Alexandra Carter, 107–118. London: Routledge, 2004.

Kant, Marion. "Joseph Lewitan and the Nazification of Dance in Germany." In *The Art of Being Jewish in Modern Times,* edited by Barbara Kirshenblatt-Gimblett and Jonathan Karp, 335–352. Philadelphia: University of Pennsylvania Press, 2008.

Karina, Lillian and Kant, Marion. *Hitler's Dancers: German Modern Dance and the Third Reich.* Translated by Jonathan Steinberg. New York and Oxford: Berghahn Books, 2003.

Katz, Emily Alice. *Bringing Zion Home: Israel in American Jewish Culture, 1948–1967.* Albany: State University of New York Press, 2015.

Katz, Friedrich. *The Secret War in Mexico: Europe, the United States, and the Mexican Revolution.* Chicago: University of Chicago Press, 1981.

Kaye, Lynn. "Fixity and Time in Talmudic Law and Legal Language." *Journal of Jewish Thought and Philosophy* 23, no. 2 (2015): 127–160.

Kennedy, David M. *The American People in the Great Depression: Freedom from Fear: Part I.* Oxford: Oxford University Press, 1999.

Kirshenblatt-Gimblett, Barbara. "The Corporeal Turn." *Jewish Quarterly Review* 95, no. 3 (2005): 447–461. doi:10.1353/jqr.2005.0058.

Kosstrin, Hannah. "Notation Score as Embodied Documentary Presence: A Response to Amelia Jones' 'Presence in Absentia.'" *The International Journal of Screendance* 2 (2012): 44–47.

Kowal, Rebekah J. "Being Motion: Alwin Nikolais' Queer Objectivity." In *The Returns of Alwin Nikolais: Bodies, Boundaries, and the Dance Canon,* edited by Claudia Gitelman and Randy Martin, 82–106. Middletown, CT: Wesleyan University Press, 2007.

Kowal, Rebekah J. "Choreographing Interculturalism: International Dance Performance at the American Museum of Natural History, 1943–1952." In *The Oxford Handbook of Dance and Ethnicity,* edited by Anthony Shay and Barbara Sellers-Young, 454–479. New York: Oxford University Press, 2016.

Kowal, Rebekah J. *How To Do Things with Dance: Performing Change in Postwar America.* Middletown, CT: Wesleyan University Press, 2010.

Kraut, Anthea. *Choreographing the Folk: The Dance Stagings of Zora Neale Hurston.* Minneapolis: University of Minnesota Press, 2008.

Kraut, Anthea. *Choreographing Copyright: Race, Gender, and Intellectual Property Rights in American Dance.* New York: Oxford University Press, 2016.

Lansdale, Janet. "A Tapestry of Intertexts: Dance Analysis for the Twenty-First Century." In *The Routledge Dance Studies Reader.* 2nd ed., edited by Alexandra Carter and Janet O'Shea, 158–167. London: Routledge, 2010.

Lynton Snyder, Anadel. *Anna Sokolow.* Cuadernos 20. Ciudad de México: INBA, Dirección de Investigación y Documentación de las Artes, CENIDI-DANZA, 1988.

Madrid, Alejandro L. "Transnational Musical Encounters at the U.S.–Mexico Border: An Introduction." In *Transnational Encounters: Music and Performance at the U.S.–Mexico Border,* edited by Alejandro L. Madrid, 1–16. New York: Oxford University Press, 2011.

Manning, Susan. *Ecstasy and the Demon: The Dances of Mary Wigman.* Berkeley: University of California Press, 1993. 2nd ed., Minneapolis: University of Minnesota Press, 2006.

Manning, Susan. *Modern Dance, Negro Dance: Race in Motion.* Minneapolis: University of Minnesota Press, 2004.

Martin, Randy. *Critical Moves: Dance Studies in Theory and Politics.* Durham, NC: Duke University Press, 1998.

Meir, Natan. *Kiev: Jewish Metropolis, A History, 1859–1914.* Bloomington: Indiana University Press, 2010.

Moore, Deborah Dash. *At Home in America: Second Generation New York Jews.* New York: Columbia University Press, 1981.

Moore, Deborah Dash. *GI Jews: How World War II Changed a Generation*. Cambridge, MA: Harvard University Press, 2004.

Moore, Deborah Dash and S. Ilan Troen, eds. *Divergent Jewish Cultures: Israel and America*. New Haven, CT: Yale University Press, 2001.

Morris, Gay. *A Game for Dancers: Performing Modernism in the Postwar Years 1945–1960*. Middletown, CT: Wesleyan University Press, 2006.

Nadell, Pamela S. ed. *American Jewish Women's History: A Reader*. New York and London: New York University Press, 2003.

Nadell, Pamela and Jonathan Sarna, eds. *Women and American Judaism: Historical Perspectives*. Hanover, NH: Brandeis University Press, 2001.

Nájera-Ramírez, Olga, Norma E. Cantú, and Brenda M. Romero, eds. *Dancing Across Borders: Danzas y Bailes Mexicanos*. Urbana and Chicago: University of Illinois Press, 2009.

Ofer, Dalia. "The Holocaust, the Creation of Israel, and the Shaping of Israeli Society." In *Shared Histories: A Palestinian-Israeli Dialogue*, edited by Paul Scham, Walid Salem, and Benjamin Pogrund, 135–147. Walnut Creek, CA: Left Coast Press, 2005.

Oja, Carol J. "Composer with a Conscience: Elie Siegmeister in Profile." *American Music* 6, no. 2 (1988): 158–180.

Olcott, Jocelyn. *Revolutionary Women in Postrevolutionary Mexico*. Durham, NC: Duke University Press, 2005.

Olcott, Jocelyn, Mary Kay Vaughan, and Gabriela Cano, eds. *Sex in Revolution: Gender, Politics, and Power in Modern Mexico*. Durham, NC: Duke University Press, 2006.

Perelman, Josh. "Choreographing Identity: Modern Dance and American Jewish Life, 1924–1954." PhD diss., New York University, 2008. ProQuest (3330351).

Peskowitz, Miriam and Levitt, Laura, eds. *Judaism Since Gender*. New York and London: Routledge, 1997.

Phillips Geduld, Victoria. "Performing Communism in the American Dance: Culture, Politics and the New Dance Group." *American Communist History* 7, no. 1 (2008): 39–65. doi:10.1080/14743890802121886.

Pianko, Noam. *Jewish Peoplehood: An American Innovation*. New Brunswick, NJ: Rutgers University Press, 2015.

Prell, Riv-Ellen. *Fighting to Become Americans: Jews, Gender, and the Anxiety of Assimilation*. Boston: Beacon, 1999.

Preston, Carrie J. *Modernism's Mythic Pose: Gender, Genre, Solo Performance*. New York: Oxford University Press, 2011.

Prevots, Naima. *Dance for Export: Cultural Diplomacy and the Cold War*. Middletown, CT: Wesleyan University Press, 1998.

Prickett, Stacey. "Dance and the Workers' Struggle." *Dance Research: The Journal of the Society for Dance Research* 8, no. 1 (1990): 47–61.

Prickett, Stacey. "From Workers' Dance to New Dance." *Dance Research: The Journal for the Society for Dance Research* 7, no. 1 (1989): 47–64.

Revivi, Menachem and Ezra Kopelowitz, eds. *Jewish Peoplehood: Change and Challenge*. Boston: Academic Studies, 2009

Reynoso, José Luis. "Choreographing Politics, Dancing Modernity: Ballet and Modern Dance in the Construction of Modern Mexico (1919–1940)." PhD diss., University of California, Los Angeles, 2012. ProQuest (3516285).

Roby, Bryan K. *The Mizrahi Era of Rebellion: Israel's Forgotten Civil Rights Struggle, 1948–1966*. Syracuse, NY: Syracuse University Press, 2015.

Roginsky, Dina. "Orientalism, the Body, and Cultural Politics in Israel: Sara Levi Tanai and the Inbal Dance Theater." *Nashim: A Journal of Jewish Women's Studies and Gender Issues* 11 (2006): 164–197. doi: 10.1353/nsh.2006.0012.

Ross, Janice. *Like a Bomb Going Off: Leonid Jakobson and Ballet as Resistance in Soviet Russia.* New Haven, CT: Yale University Press, 2015.

Rossen, Rebecca. *Dancing Jewish: Jewish Identity in American Modern and Postmodern Dance.* New York: Oxford University Press, 2014.

Rossen, Rebecca. "Dancing Jews and Jewesses: Jewishness, Ethnicity, and Exoticism in American Dance." In *The Oxford Handbook of Dance and Ethnicity*, edited by Anthony Shay and Barbara Sellers-Young, 66–90. New York: Oxford University Press, 2016.

Rossen, Rebecca. "Hasidic Drag: Jewishness and Transvestism in the Modern Dances of Pauline Koner and Hadassah." *Feminist Studies* 37, no. 2 (2011): 334–364.

Rottenberg, Henia. "Anna Sokolow: A Seminal Force in the Development of Theatrical Dance in Israel." *Dance Chronicle* 36 (2013): 36–58.

Samuel, Yael. "Meredith Monk: Between Time and Timelessness in *Book of Days*." *NASHIM: A Journal of Jewish Women's Studies and Gender Issues* 14 (2007): 9–29. doi: 10.2979/nas.2007.-.14.9

Schneider, Rebecca. *Performing Remains: Art and War in Times of Theatrical Reenactment.* Abingdon, England: Routledge, 2011.

Schrecker, Ellen. *The Age of McCarthyism: A Brief History with Documents.* 2nd ed. New York: Palgrave, 2002.

Schrecker, Ellen. *Many Are the Crimes: McCarthyism in America.* Princeton, NJ: Princeton University Press, 1998.

Schwadron, Hannah. "White Nose, (Post) Bawdy Bodies, and the Un/dancing Sexy Jewess." PhD diss., University of California, Riverside, 2013. ProQuest (3590062).

Shavit, Ari. *My Promised Land: The Triumph and Tragedy of Israel.* New York: Spiegel and Grau, 2015.

Shea Murphy, Jacqueline. *The People Have Never Stopped Dancing: Native American Modern Dance Histories.* Minneapolis: University of Minnesota Press, 2007.

Sheramy, Rona. "'Resistance and War': The Holocaust in American Jewish Education, 1945–1960." *American Jewish History* 91, no. 2 (2003): 287–313. doi:10.1353/ajh.2004.0058

Solomon, Alisa. "Balancing Act: *Fiddler*'s Bottle Dance and the Transformation of 'Tradition.'" *TDR: The Drama Review* 55, no. 3 (2011): 21–30. https://muse.jhu.edu/article/448647.

Spenser, Daniela. *The Impossible Triangle: Mexico, Soviet Russia, and the United States in the 1920s.* Durham, NC: Duke University Press, 1999.

Spenser, Daniela. *Los Primeros Tropiezos de la Internacional Comunista en México.* México, DF: Centro de Investicaciones y Estudios Superiores en Antroplogiá Social, 2009.

Spenser, Daniela. "Standing Conventional Cold War History on Its Head." In *In From the Cold: Latin America's New Encounter With the Cold War*, edited by Gilbert M. Joseph and Daniela Spenser, 381–396. Durham, NC: Duke University Press, 2008.

Spiegel, Nina. *Embodying Hebrew Culture: Aesthetics, Athletics, and Dance in the Jewish Community of Mandate Palestine.* Detroit, MI: Wayne State University Press, 2013.

Srinivasan, Priya. *Sweating Saris: Indian Dance as Transnational Labor.* Philadelphia: Temple University Press, 2012.

Stepan, Nancy Leys. *"The Hour of Eugenics": Race, Gender, and Nation in Latin America.* Ithaca, NY: Cornell University Press, 1991.

Taylor, Diana. *The Archive and the Repertoire: Performing Cultural Memory in the Americas.* Durham, NC: Duke University Press, 2003.

Tibol, Raquel. *Pasos en la Danza Mexicana*. Ciudad Universitaria, México, DF: Universidad Nacional Autónoma de México, 1982.

Tomko, Linda. *Dancing Class: Gender, Ethnicity, and Social Divides in American Dance, 1890–1920*. Bloomington and Indianapolis: Indiana University Press, 1999.

Tortajada Quiroz, Margarita. *Frutos de Mujer: La Mujeres en la Danza Escénia*. México: Teoría y Práctica de Arte, 2001.

Trapp, Erin. "Arendt, Preference, and the Revolutionary Spectator." *Cultural Critique* 86 (2014): 31–64.

Vaughan, Mary Kay and Stephen E. Lewis, eds. *The Eagle and the Virgin: Nation and Cultural Revolution in Mexico, 1920–1940*. Durham, NC: Duke University Press, 2006.

von Eschen, Penny M. *Satchmo Blows Up the World: Jazz Ambassadors Play the Cold War*. Cambridge, MA, and London: Harvard University Press, 2004.

Warren, Larry. *Anna Sokolow: The Rebellious Spirit*. Princeton, NJ: Princeton Book Company, 1991.

Welter, Barbara. "The Cult of True Womanhood: 1820–1860." *American Quarterly* 18, no. 2 (1966): 151–174.

Wenger, Beth S. *New York Jews and the Great Depression: Uncertain Promise*. New Haven, CT: Yale University Press, 1996.

Wolf, Stacy. "'Never Gonna Be a Man/Catch Me if You Can/I Won't Grow Up': A Lesbian Account of Mary Martin's Peter Pan." *Theatre Journal* 49, no. 4 (1997): 493–509.

Yerushalmi, Yosef Hayim. *Zakhor: Jewish History and Jewish Memory*. Seattle: University of Washington Press, 1982.

INDEX

International Workers Order (IWO), 42, 76,
152, 159
Isaacson, Charles, 146
Israel, 3–6, 13, 101, 164–65, 190–217, 221,
226–27, 232
and Anna Sokolow's influence, 9, 27
and bonds, 161–64; 192, 204
and critics, 207, 210–11, 213, 215, 217,
219, 221, 224
and dancers, 28, 208–10, 214, 216
establishment of state, 163, 193, 197
and Holocaust, 214–15, 222–25
and influence of Martha Graham, 192,
207, 216
and *Opus* series, 187, 189, 206
and Russian community in, 208
and Six-Day War/1967 Arab-Israeli
War, 24–25
and socialist Zionism, 17, 164, 196,
198, 208
See also America-Israel Cultural
Foundation (AICF); Inbal Dance
Theater; Lyric Theatre; sabra
physicality; socialist Zionism
Israeli Bond Corporation, 162
Israeli Philharmonic Orchestra, 205
Isserman, Maurice, 229, 231
Italy, 54–58, 61–62, 64–66, 99

Jackson, Larry, 77
Jackson, Naomi, 18, 132
Jackson, Thurman, 78–79
Jacobson, Matthew Frye, 169
Japan, 77, 190
jazz, 206, 210–12
and Alex North, 63–64
and American modernism, 158–59
and *Opus* series, 186–88
and Popular Front, 63, 159
and *Rooms*, 170, 172, 178, 188
and uses by Anna Sokolow, 27, 42, 51,
159–60, 190, 230
Jerusalem, 24, 101, 164, 193,
215, 226
Jews
and alliances with African Americans, 25,
42, 51, 159, 213
and American proletarianism, 31,
115, 167

and anti-Semitism, 8
and assimilation in America, 3, 20, 22, 42,
156, 167, 215
and Catholicism, 122, 15
and dance, 18, 20–22, 163
and Diaspora, 2, 5, 165, 215
and *Don Lindo de Almería*, 109–11
and gender, 22–23, 25, 150
and Israel, 5, 193, 195, 200, 214
and Jerome Robbins, 164
and Jewish peoplehood, 14, 195
and Jewishness in Sokolow's
dancers, 13–14
and *Kaddish*, 128–41
and Kurt Jooss, 61
and *Lyric Suite*, 165
and *Mexican Retablo*, 141–42, 144
and Mexico, 85–89, 91, 96, 100, 102–3,
105, 113
and "muscular Judaism," 198
and "New Jew," 165, 194, 196–98, 203–4,
207, 213, 216, 221–22, 225
in New York, 14, 52, 123, 162
and persecution in Europe, 26, 57, 60,
97–99, 103–4, 150
and revolutionary modernism, 17, 23
and revolutionary spectatorship, 4
and *Rooms*, 5, 27, 170–72
and satire, 37–38
and scapegoating alongside gay people,
176, 185
and socialism, 15, 227
and Sokolow's identity, 29
and Spain, 107
and transnational Left, 25
See also Ashkenazi (Jews); Mizrahi
(Jews); Sephardi (Jews); Yiddish
Joffrey Ballet, 24, 190
Johnson, David K., 176–77
Joint Anti-Fascist Refugee Committee, 186
Jones, Bill T., 7–8
Jooss, Kurt, 53, 58–61, 65, 81. See also *The
Green Table*
Jowitt, Deborah, 190
Juhasz, Suzanne, 175, 185
Juilliard Dance Ensemble, 152,
168, 190
The Juilliard School, 64, 226
Junger, Esther, 53